Cushman Genealogy and General History

Including the Descendants of the Fayette County, Pennsylvania, and Monongalia County, Virginia, Families

Alvah Walford Burt

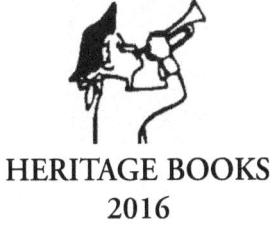

HERITAGE BOOKS
2016

HERITAGE BOOKS
AN IMPRINT OF HERITAGE BOOKS, INC.

Books, CDs, and more—Worldwide

For our listing of thousands of titles see our website
at
www.HeritageBooks.com

A Facsimile Reprint
Published 2016 by
HERITAGE BOOKS, INC.
Publishing Division
5810 Ruatan Street
Berwyn Heights, Md. 20740

Originally published
Press of
Wm. Mitchell Printing Company
Greenfield, Indiana
1942

— Publisher's Notice —
In reprints such as this, it is often not possible to remove blemishes from the original. We feel the contents of this book warrant its reissue despite these blemishes and hope you will agree and read it with pleasure.

International Standard Book Numbers
Paperbound: 978-0-7884-4708-2
Clothbound: 978-0-7884-6457-7

ALVAH WALFORD BURT

Dedicated to the memory of my beloved mother
EMILY FRANCES CUSHMAN BURT

"O ye, who proudly boast,
 In your free veins, the blood of Sires like these,
 Look to their lineaments. Dread lest ye loose
 Their likeness in your sons.
 Turn ye to Plymouth Rock, and where they knelt,
 Kneel and renew the vow they breathed to God."
—SIGOURNEY.

APPRECIATION

The publication of this volume has been possible only through the assistance and cooperation of many, and to whom I owe a debt of gratitude, for without their assistance I feel I would have failed.

I, therefore, desire to express a pre-word of appreciation and sincere thanks to all those who have so kindly in person, in conference, correspondence, contribution, and permission to use and to quote:

First—To my beloved wife, Ida Keaten Burt, then to:
Little, Brown & Co., Boston, Mass.
Lewis Historical Publishing Co., New York City, N. Y.
New England Historical & Genealogical Society (Register), Boston, Mass.
Messrs. Houghton-Mifflin Company, Boston, Mass.
John Grant, Booksellers, Ltd., Edinburgh, Scotland.
Mrs. Estella M. Shroyer (sister of the author), Lake Park, Iowa.
Mr. Theodore Parker Adams, Plymouth, Mass.
Miss Jessica Ferguson, Genealogical Librarian, State Library and Museum, Harrisburg, Pa.
Prof. Oren E. Frazee, LaCrosse, Wis.
Mrs. Dicie F. Donley, Carmichaels, Pa.
Mrs. Mary Bolander & Family, Fortville, Ind.
Mr. Ernst Wynn, R. F. D., Danville, Ill.
Miss Dea Carter, Danville, Ill.
Miss Carmine Collier, Murfreesboro, Tenn.
Mrs. Mary Cushman Donnell, R. F. D., Greensburg, Ind.
Mr. William W. Garlow, Maidsville, W. Va.
Miss Cora L. Garlow, Maidsville, W. Va.
Mrs. Frances Dixon Ball Goggin, Germantown, Ky.
Mrs. Annie M. Hiday, Inglewood, Calif.
Mrs. Dayse Whitecotton Proctor, Kansas City, Mo.
Mrs. Rosa E. Pence, Rossville, Ill.
Miss Anna Rose Pence, Rossville, Ill.
Mr. Jouett M. Hoffman, Mt. Sterling, Ky.
Mrs. Clara Lane.
Mrs. Henry Lloyd, Lexington, Ky.

Clara Jane Lane, Ottumwa, Iowa.
Mrs. Lenore Chumlea Jones, West Lafayette, Ind.
Mr. Ralph Burdsal Woodmansee, Cincinnati, Ohio.
Mrs. Ivanilla Dunham Ball, Clinton, Ill.
Mrs. Michael J. Gibbons, Dayton, Ohio.
Mrs. Emza H. Godsey, Anderson, Ind.

I also wish to express a kindly and appreciative thought for the many library attendants who have extended me service and courtesy; also to the various state house, county court house and town record clerks, in the different localities of the United States, who so cheerfully assisted me in my search for material needed.

The following abbreviations at times are used: B. born, M. married, D. death, @ at, C. child or children, Abt. about.

INTRODUCTION

To My Readers:

A much better understanding of the purpose and intent of this work will be had by taking time to carefully read this foreword.

On page one of Henry Wyles Cushman's "Historical and Biographical Genealogy of the Cushmans" he starts with: "Robert Cushman, the ancestor of all the Cushmans in the United States, was born in England" etc.; and further, on page 85 in footnote No. 3 he writes: "From Thomas Cushman and his wife, Mary, and their descendants have come all the Cushmans in the United States; they are therefore of full blood Puritan stock, both their paternal and maternal ancestors having been among the Pilgrims who settled at Plymouth."

Throughout the generations our descent from Robert Cushman has been regarded and esteemed a family heritage, and in my own family it has been taught with studious and diligent care, almost religious care. In my early childhood I recall the devotion of my mother to instill into my young mind and that of my brother and sisters, the value of the Cushman birthright and heritage that was ours.

At an early date in life I recognized the neglect of our branch of the family to have in print and record these facts concerning us from the sixth generation on, as there seemed to be no publication of Cushman general history after the year 1855.

The clear and broad knowledge with the unusual ability to tell of our history, possessed by the brother of our beloved mother, Melandez Woodmansee Cushman, found in me a ready listener with an eager ear, which in after years, when I found myself in retirement from active business pursuits, caused me to feel that in this knowledge of family history there was excellent worth and value for the generations from the Sixth on down to the present (which in some instances is the fourteenth generation) I began to feel it a duty slowly developing into a determination, to try to compile the old and accepted historical facts relating to the Cushmans, and as nearly as possible to obtain the names and other vital statistics necessary for a genealogical record, together with such biographical features of interest as available for me, for the purpose of making a printed record of Cushman history and genealogy; adding to this such photography as possible for me to secure which I felt would assist in completing my work in book form in the belief that it would strengthen morale, build character, and be of more than usual worth and value to the Cushmans of the present and the future.

Therefore, with intrepid spirit and a seeming uncontrollable and unconquerable desire to correct in some manner the neglect of the past by others in not having made and put in printed and proper record form, our lineal descent from Robert Cushman, I have devoted myself seriously to investigation, photographing features of Cushman interest, traveling to confirm the things I had heard, and slowly and surely compiling for print that which I considered a reasonably dependable record of our branch of the Cushman family.

In recording and making of copy I have endeavored to make my record and copy as free of error as possible; also, I have hoped that the spelling of given names as furnished me might be free from error and that birth dates, marriages and death dates were free as well. In copying family records from old-family-records and books where there were several children in a family, a slight mistake is not only possible but very easy to make in the day of the month and even in the correct spelling of a given name; however, I have given special care whenever doubt arose concerning either, to seek and secure satisfying evidence concerning the doubt and to establish the facts. With all this care it is likely that in some instance a name may have been mis-spelled or the exact day of a month not absolutely correct.

In view of my radical departure from the form or style and abbreviations usually employed by writers, authors and publishers of genealogical work, I may have invited severe criticism from the professional. Here in this work I have made record up to the fourteenth generation in some families, and have found so many Roberts, Thomases and Isaacs and have further noticed in some families the use of the same given-first-name through three successive generations, that should the name happen to have been George, there would have been quite a few Georges and confusing as to which George was meant when the name was pronounced or written; therefore, I felt the necessity of giving to each a definite expression of relationship to parentage, so that in tracing back there could be no mistake made as to just which George and to which family some certain George belonged. If in doing so I transgress your ethical sense of custom and propriety, I trust my attempt to clarify and eliminate doubt will compensate and assuage your irritation.

In my desire to establish our line of descent from Robert Cushman, I discovered the effort made by others to correct the error printed in the Historical and Biographical Genealogy of the Cushmans, by Henry Wyles Cushman, which effort established the existence of Thomas Cushman, the grandson of Elder Thomas Cushman, which resulted through research of James Thomas Cushman and Theodore Parker Adams. Through correspondence with Mr. Theodore P. Adams, A. B., of Plymouth, Mass., I found that Thomas Cushman, son of Elder Thomas Cushman, who first married Ruth Howland, and secondly Abigail Fuller, did have a son named Thomas, which fact was confirmed from existing records, and in further correspondence with Mr. Adams he suggested to me that most likely we belonged to the Lebanon, Conn., branch. After reflecting upon the fact that my great-grandfather, Isaac Cushman, with his elder brother Thomas, did come down to Monongalia County, Va., and Fayette County, Penn., from Essex County, New Jersey, it was easy to trace back through to Lebanon, New London County, verifying the suggestion of Mr. Adams.

Then making contact with the descendants of Thomas Cushman, the elder brother of my great-grandfather, a few families, the descendants of Thomas, now living in eastern Kentucky, in Mason County and Fleming County, and these descendants having established their descent from the Lebanon branch, and they having been admitted to membership in both the Society of the Mayflower and also in the Daughters

FREDERIC ALONZO TURNER
PRESIDENT

DAVENPORT BROWN
VICE PRESIDENT

JAMES MELVILLE HUNNEWELL
TREASURER

EVERETT JEFTS BEEDE
RECORDING SECRETARY

MRS. FRANKLIN EARL SCOTTY
LIBRARIAN

MISS MARGERY A. LEAVITT
ASSISTANT LIBRARIAN

WILLIAM PRESCOTT GREENLAW
LIBRARIAN EMERITUS AND
ASSISTANT TREASURER

MRS. JOSEPH CURTIS HOWES
CURATOR

HAROLD CLARKE DURRELL
EDITOR, HISTORIAN, AND
CORRESPONDING SECRETARY

MISS ELSIE MCCORMACK
ASSISTANT EDITOR AND
ASSISTANT SECRETARY

HENRY EDWARDS SCOTT
EDITOR EMERITUS

New England Historic Genealogical Society
9 ASHBURTON PLACE, BOSTON, MASS.

March 5, 1942.

Dear Mr. Burt:

Your letter about your compilation of the descendants of your great-grandfather, Isaac Cushman, and his elder brother, Thomas Cushman, is most interesting.

Your courteous request to use certain material (relating to the Cushman family) which appeared in the REGISTER is, of course, granted with great pleasure.

The REGISTER is not copyrighted, hence any one can use material appearing in it, but we do desire that proper acknowledgment be given where any of the printed matter is used. Your desire to do this is deeply appreciated.

For a few years this Society offered to edit and print genealogies for anyone who desired it, the price charged allowing the Society to make a small profit; but this plan did not work out as successfully as hoped and the project was soon abandoned.

The average genealogy, with pages about the size of the REGISTER, can be printed for $5 a page. This will cover cost of printing, author's corrections, paper, and binding.

In recent years the new processes of printing by the plantograph method has made a marked reduction in the cost as compared with the printing from type; and a definite saving can be made by adopting this method.

The result is a facsimilie of the typewritten page, reduced to whatever size one desires.

If we have failed to answer your questions, please do not hesitate to let us know. It is a pleasure to help you in any way we can.

      Cordially yours,

      (Harold Clarke Durrell)
        Editor

Mr. Alvah W. Burt
3031 Temple Ave., Cincinnati, Ohio

of the American Revolution, I then felt sure of my ground.
In further correspondence with Mr. Adams he referred to
his co-authorship with Mr. James Thomas Cushman of Seattle,
Wash., and their joint contribution of an article establishing
beyond doubt the fact that Elder Thomas Cushman did have
a grandson whose name was Thomas Cushman and who married Sarah Strong, daughter of Jedediah Strong, and that
this Thomas moved from Duxbury, Mass., down to Lebanon,
Conn. This article appeared in the New England Historical
and Genealogical Register, and the following is copied there-
from, Volume 72, Pages 10 to 15:

A GRANDSON OF ELDER THOMAS CUSHMAN
AND SOME OF HIS DESCENDANTS:
Compiled by James Thomas Cushman of Seattle, Wash-
ington, and communicated by Theodore Parker
Adams, A. B. of Plymouth, Mass.

In Henry Wyles Cushman's "Genealogy of The Cushmans"
of New England, Thomas Cushman, eldest child of Elder
Thomas Cushman of Plymouth in New England, is said to
have had five children, viz. by Ruth Howland, afterwards his
first wife, a son named Robert, who was born 4th of Oct. 1664,
and by his second wife, Abigail Fuller, four sons, Job, born
probably about 1680, Bartholomew, baptized 13 March 1684/5,
Samuel, born 16 July 1687 and Benjamin, baptized 1. Mar.
1690/91. Neither to this Thomas, however, nor to any one
of his three brothers, Rev. Isaac, Deacon Elkanah, and Eleazer,
has a son named Thomas been assigned in printed accounts of
the family, and therefore it has been believed that no son of
Elder Thomas Cushman had a son named Thomas.

It is the purpose of this article to show that Thomas Cushman the eldest child of Elder Thomas, *had* a son named
Thomas and to trace to the present day one line of descendants of this last named Thomas. In a deed dated 3 Feb. 1702
(1702/3) Thomas Cushman of Plymouth undoubtedly the
son of the Elder Thomas, conveyed land in Duxbury to Thomas
Loring of Plymouth, "being the spot upon which my son,
Thomas Cushman, hath built." The deed is acknowledged,
5 Feb. 1702/3, by Thomas Cushman and his wife Abigail,

and proves that Thomas Cushman, son of the Elder, had a son who bore his father's name. (Plymouth Deeds Book 4, Page 167.)

In a deed dated 4 Feb. 1702/3 Thomas Loring of Plymouth and Thomas Cushman of Duxbury (probably the son Thomas mentioned in the deed the previous day) conveyed land in Duxbury to Maj. John Bradford of Plymouth, Sarah, wife of Thomas, joining, 5 Feb. 1702/3 in acknowledging the deed. (1b, Book 10, Part 1, P. 221.)

This Thomas Cushman of Duxbury removed to Lebanon, Conn., a deed recorded at Lebanon showing that on 1—April 1703—Thomas Cushman of Duxbury, in the province of Massachusetts Bay, bought land in Lebanon of Henry Woodward of Lebanon. (Lebanon Land Records, Vol. 1, P. 281.)

This Thomas Cushman was born, therefore, about 1670, and must have been the son of Thomas Cushman by the latter's first wife, Ruth Howland, a daughter of John and Elizabeth (Tilley) Howland, both of whom were passengers in the Mayflower in 1620. Sarah, wife of Thomas Cushman of Duxbury and Lebanon, was daughter of Jedediah Strong of Coventry, Conn., as is proved by a receipt (dated Coventry, 25 Sept. 1733) from William Cushman (son of Thomas and Sarah) to "Preserved Strong, Executor of Ye last Will and Testament of his Father Jedediah Strong, late of Coventry, deceased," for 9S, 9D, "in full of what was will'd to me by my honored Grandfather Jedediah Strong." (Windham, Conn., Probate Records, Vol. 2, P. 260.)

The following brief genealogy shows some of the descendants of Elder Thomas Cushman in the line of his grandson, Thomas of Duxbury and Lebanon; and it will be observed that the name Thomas has descended in this branch of the family from Father to Son from Elder Thomas of Plymouth almost to the present day.

Robert Cutchman or Cushman, baptized at Rolvenden, Co. Kent, England, 9 Feb. 1577/8, died in England, probably in the summer of 1625. He married first in the Parish of St. Alphege, Canterbury, England 1. July 1606, Sarah Reder—who dwelt in the precincts of the Cathedral at Canterbury and whose parentage has not been discovered; and secondly, Leyden, Holland, 5. June, 1617, Mary (Clarke) Shingleton, widow of Thomas of Sandwich, Co. Kent, shoemaker, the license for her marriage to her first husband which was to be celebrated at St. Mary Bedman's, Canterbury; being dated 28. Jan. 1610/11. Robert Cushman is well known as the agent of the Leyden Pilgrims in England, and arrived at Plymouth in New England, with his son Thomas, in the Fortune, in November 1621. He sailed for England on the same ship about a month later, on business for the Colony, leaving his son Thomas in the care of Governor Bradford.

Child by his first wife: Thomas (2) baptized in the parish of St. Andrew, Canterbury, Co. Kent, Eng., 8. Feb. 1607/8.

Elder Thomas (2) Cushman, of Plymouth in New England, baptized in the Parish of St. Andrew, Canterbury, Co. Kent, England, 8. Feb. 1607/8. Came to New England with his father in the Fortune, arriving at Plymouth in Nov. 1621, and died at Plymouth, 10 or 11th, Dec. 1691, "neere the end of the 84th yeare of his life." He married at Plymouth, probably about 1636, Mary Allerton, born at Leyden, Holland, about 1610, died at Plymouth 28. Nov. 1699, daughter of Isaac and Mary (Norris) Allerton and the last female survivor of those who came in the Mayflower in 1620.

Children born:
1. Thomas, (3) B. at Plymouth, 16 Sept., 1637.
2. Sarah, M. 11 Apr. 1661, as his second wife, John Hawkes of Lynn, Mass. 8 children.
3. Lydia, M. William Harlow, Jr.
4. Rev. Isaac, B. at Plymouth 8 Feb. 1648/9. D. at Plympton, Mass. 21. Oct. 1732—M. about 1675 Rebecca Rickard B. about 1654. D. at Plympton 3. Sept. 1727. For many years he was pastor of the Church at Plympton. 6 Children.
5. Dea. Elkanah of Plympton, Mass. B. at Plymouth 1. June, 1651, D. at Plympton, 4 Sept. 1727. M. (1) at Plymouth 10. Feb. 1677/8 Elizabeth Cole who died there 4. Jan. 1681/2. Daughter of James, Jr. M.(2) at Plymouth 2 Mar. 1683/4 Martha Cooke, B. at Plymouth, 16. Mar. 1659/60. D. at Plympton 17. Sept. 1722—Daughter of Jacob of Plymouth. 3 Children by 1st wife and 5 by second wife.

His was the first appeal for the ears of a king for the "Liberty of Conscience" embodying both the Liberty of the Mind and the Liberty of the Spirit. His two trips from Leyden, Holland, to England with John Carver to obtain a grant or Charter for the establishment of a colony in America although without result, laid the foundation for the third trip made for that purpose by himself and William Brewster, they succeeding in obtaining the Grant or Charter and although their appeal for "Liberty of Conscience" was not explicitly obtained they did obtain its equivalent or almost so in other words, to wit: "If they behaved themselves quietly and were faithful subjects of his Majesty King James 1, they were not to be molested although their creed and form of worship were essentially unsound and heretical."

He, together with John Carver were instrumental in effecting the emigration of the Pilgrims to Holland where he latterly joined them and he and John Carver chartered the Mayflower and bought the Speedwell preparatory to their emigrating to America.

Robert Cushman, as Assistant Governor, embarked on the Speedwell August 5th, 1620 with his family when the two ships began their first voyage toward America; but later when the Mayflower sailed alone on September 6th with but a part of the company, Mr. Cushman was left to act as Governor for those left behind and agent for the Pilgrims in New England.

During the last of August of 1621 he sailed for New England on the Fortune together with his son Thomas Cushman and thirty-four others, arriving at Cape Cod on Friday, November 9th.

On the 9th day of December, 1621 Robert Cushman preached his memorable, *First Sermon in America to go into Print*, "on the Sin and danger of self-love and the sweetness of true friendship."

He returned to England leaving Plymouth, December 13th, 1621 to act as the agent of the Colony, leaving his son Thomas in the family of Governor William Bradford.

On January 1st, 1623 he, Robert Cushman, together with Edward Winslow obtained a Charter or Grant of land on Cape Ann, Mass., which they turned over to the Colonists for a Fishing and Hunting settlement and which proved to be of great value to them.

Thomas Cushman was, in his manhood, always the confidential adviser and friend of Governor Bradford; about 1635 he married Mary Allerton, daughter of Isaac Allerton.

In April, 1649, following the death of Elder Brewster, Thomas Cushman was chosen Ruling Elder of the first Church of Plymouth and so continued until his death, December 11th, 1691, being almost 84 years of age.

There were eight children born to Thomas and Mary Allerton Cushman and in the years following, connections by marriage were made into the following families:

One of the Cushmans married into a family claiming Governor Bradford an ancestor; Sarah, the daughter of Thomas and Mary, married John Hawkes; one daughter born to them married James Smith of Fair Haven, Mass.; Benjamin Cushman, a grandson of Thomas and Mary married Sarah Eaton in 1712; Elizabeth Cushman, daughter of James Cushman of the 5th generation, married Captain Ephraim Delano.

Believing that quite a number of our line would enjoy reading the following book the author suggests that you call at your City-Public-Library and peruse the pages of: "Franklin D. Roosevelt's Colonial Ancestors" by Alvin Paige Johnson, published and copyrighted in 1933 by Lothrop, Lee and Shepard Company of Boston, Mass.

While there also ask to see "The Compendium of American Genealogy" edited by Frederick Adams Virkus; F. I. A. G. and copyrighted in 1937 by The Institute of American Genealogy, Volume 6, and upon page 19 you will find other Cushman Lineage of interest. From the above it is obvious President Franklin Delano Roosevelt is a Cushman Descendant through Eleazar Cushman, son of Elder Thomas Cushman and his wife, Mary Allerton Cushman. President Roosevelt is the 9th generation from Robert Cushman (1st generation).

CHARLOTTE SAUNDERS CUSHMAN

Inasmuch as I have been asked several times about Charlotte Saunders Cushman and since I have not carried the descendancy of Deacon Elkannah Cushman through, and since she was considered by many to be the greatest actress of her day, and her father Deacon Elkannah Cushman, one of the noted of his day, the following is taken from pages 497 to 510 of Henry Wyles Cushman's Genealogy of the Cushmans:

"Charlotte Cushman was born in Boston, July 23rd, 1816; Among those who reflected honor and credit upon the Cushman name, no one has done more for it, in her department of the great world of letters and art, than Charlotte Saunders Cushman, and no one has marked it more with the unmistakable efforts of talent, or clothed it in brightness with the ray of reflected genius than she.

In adopting the profession of the stage Miss Cushman followed the dictates of a strong natural taste. With her it has never been the servile task for livlihood but the love and adoration of enobled art which urged her onward, and supported her drooping spirits when others would have fainted in their toils. It is because we recognize in Miss Cushman an approach to our ideal of the greatly pure in art, that we regard her as one of its noblest representatives.

There is a natural breadth and grandeur in her mind which enables her to take large views, and hence her impersonation of character is strongly drawn in clear, broad outline, with a fullness of finish that gives to it that extraordinary completeness for which it is remarkable.

Besides this, there is in her own character great truth and earnestness. She is possessed of sober judgement and calm, good sense, combined with wonderful enthusiasm and force of expression, which enables her fully to feel and faithfully to delineate every character she assumes. She is great, not only because she is nobly gifted by nature, but because she takes a noble view of her art and is not satisfied without doing her best at all times.

In her case nature and art are one, with this difference, that *art* is the representative and interpreter of *nature*. She died in Boston Feb. 17, 1876, and was the most powerful actress America has produced.

She also had a sister, Susan Webb Cushman, an actress who gained some prominence, who was born March 17th, 1822 and died May 10th, 1859.''

Deacon Elkannah Cushman is distinguished in having been one of the seven founders of the Old Colony Club in 1769. It was the first organization formed to commemorate the landing of the Pilgrims. From it has come the present Pilgrim Society, founded about 1820. Elkannah an officer and its stewart had charge of the first dinner given by the Club; the first toast given at that dinner was "to the memory of Robert Cushman." (For a more complete record and history of Deacon Elkannah Cushman and his family you are referred to pages 497 to 510 of H. W. C.—publication mentioned above.)

The record of the first celebration of the landing of the Pilgrims at Plymouth, Mass., held by The Old Colony Club at Boston, January 22nd, 1770 and published by Samuel Blake in 1850 is quite interesting:

The following toasts were drunk by the company; viz:

No. 1 "To the Memory of John Carver and all the other Worthy Governors of the Old Colony."

No. 2 "To the Memory of That Brave Man and Good Officer Captain Miles Standish."

No. 3 "To the Memory of That Pious Man and Faithful Historian Mr. Secretary Morton."

No. 4 "To the Memory of Sachem Massasoit our First and Best Friend and Ally."

No. 5 "To the Memory of Robert Cushman who preached the first sermon in New England."

No. 6 May every person be possessed of the same noble sentiments against arbitrary power that our worthy ancestors were endowed with. May every enemy of Civil or Religious Liberty meet the same or a worse fate than Archbishop Laud. May the Colonies be speedily relieved from all the burthens and oppressions they now labor under.

When the conflict with the Mother Country arose, the Cushmans proved loyal to their new home land.

Captain Jonathan of New Bedford; Joshua at Valley Forge, the first advocate of pensions for soldiers of the Revolution who also delivered one of the first Fourth of July Orations at Augusta, Maine; Thomas of Elizabeth, N. J. and Monongalia County of Virginia and Isaac of Fayette County, Wharton Township, Penn. Jeremiah Cushman was an officer in the War of 1812.

Two or three have asked the question: "Will your book make me eligible to membership in the Society of the Mayflower?" And since this has been placed directly to me I feel that I owe this statement in relation thereto. This work was not the outgrowth of a social desire, as I have written before; I have devoted several years to it, absolutely free of hope of personal gain, as at the time of this writing I am in my 73rd year and childless; the urge and motivation therefore free from selfish end was on the contrary inspired first to right the wrong of neglect in the past, that, some one of our descent had not put into print our relation to that greatest, grandest and noblest of all human inspirations, Spiritual Freedom; and then its growing and broadening into that final American freedom and our Glorious American Liberty—America, the forerunner of National freedom and Liberty, inspiring the Nations of the earth to dream of that end, the Conquestors and Invaders notwithstanding.

Second, with the presentation of the fact that our forebear Mr. Robert Cushman was first, so far as I know to make a plea for the ears of a King, for "The Liberty of Conscience," embodying both the freedom of the mind and of the spirit; and that he was of sufficient courage to state that the preachment of the clergy of his Church did not edify, and that "he could prove it by the word of God," for which statement he was excommunicated. We next find him exiled to Leyden, Holland because he joined the Pilgrim and Puritan band, devoted to the principle of religious freedom, and next we find him foremost, selected with John Carver, to go to London to negotiate for the right to settle in America. This enterprise ending in failure, they returned. Later, Mr. Robert Cushman and John Carver were again sent on the same errand and after long and tedious effort they again returned to Leyden with such unsatisfactory conditions as they had been able to obtain. Being resolute in determination, the unyielding Mr. Cushman with William Brewster, again was sent when they with perseverance and zeal finally after long and tedious negotiation, obtained a patent or grant to settle in America. And again repeating for your reconsideration, "And although 'Religious Liberty', in terms was not granted them, yet if they behaved themselves quietly and were faithful subjects of his Majesty King James, they were not to be molested, although their creed and form of worship were essentially unsound and heretical."

Therefore the unwavering, unyielding Cushman finally accomplished in words equivalent to his first appeal "Liberty of Conscience."

Therefore, *my appeal to you*, Young Cushmans of today and tomorrow, FORGET NOT the lessons taught in this early history of your blood, that your forebear Robert Cushman was nearly always referred to as *Mr. Cushman*; that he strove for human rights. LIFT YOURSELF above the more common things of life and you too see if you can not do something in life to the credit of your Honorable Name and to leave this Mortality when you do go, with the full sense and satisfaction that this world has not suffered from your presence; and it is my hope that it will be left a bit better for your having been here. Therefore, whether this publication be accepted here or there is of little consequence, as against its author's hope of value in the sustaining and vitalizing influence upon the present and future Cushman descent.

The writer presents no claim as author but rather a compiler of such facts relating to our family as he has by diligence and devotion succeeded in gathering together. He has not a large family to whom he might leave this work, but on the contrary, although married, is childless; his brother's son, Robert Cushman Burt, and his sister's granddaughters, however, are of much interest, and too, he also feels an interest in each and every young person of Cushman descent; and since he has undertaken this work his interest in them has grown because of the feeling that there is for each of them a value in the knowledge that they have a fine heritage and family history back of them.

It is a pleasure to say, that in all the great number of Cushmans I have personally met in the search of Cushman history and genealogical descent, that I have never contacted one of the inebriate, or one of the oft-referred-to "rough neck" or "red neck" type. Some have been very prosperous and some very poor, but to me all appeared to be self-respecting and gentle folk; a great many speaking with pride of their church connection and affiliation and many of their own church activities and church work.

Before disembarking, the Mayflower weighed anchor in the Bay of Cape Cod and the following Compact was signed in the Cabin of the Mayflower:

THE COMPACT
Signed Nov. 11th, Old Style
or Nov. 21st, New Style, 1620

"In the name of God, amen, we whose names are under written, the loyal subjects of our dread soveraigne Lord, King James, by the grace of God, of Great Britain, Franc and Ireland King, defender of the faith, etc., having undertaken, for the glorie of God, and advancements of the Christian faith, and honor of our king and countrie, a voyage to plant the first colonie in the Northerne parts of Virginia, doe by these presents solemnly and mutually in the presence of God, and one of another, covenant and combine ourselves together into a civill body politick, for our better ordering and preservation and furtherence of the ends aforesaid: and by virtue hereof to enacte, constitute and frame such just and equall laws, ordenances, acts, constitutions and offices, from time to time, as shall be thought most meete and convenient for the general good of the colonie, unto which we promise all due submission and obedience. In witness whereof we have hereunto subscribed our names at Cap-Codd, the 11 of November, in the year of the raigne of our soveraigne lord, King James of England, Franc and Ireland, the eighteenth, and of Scotland the fifty-fourth. ANO DOM 1620."

THE FAMOUS PLYMOUTH ROCK ON WHICH THE PILGRIMS FROM
THE MAYFLOWER LANDED AT PLYMOUTH, NEW ENGLAND.

The Above Canopy or Portico is Constructed Over the Famous "Plymouth Rock," the Floor Being Probably 8 or 10 Feet Above the Reposing Place of the Rock.

The Rock is exposed to the view of the visitor through a rectangular opening in the floor, surrounded by an iron fencing and protected by guards, who from period to period give a lecture detailing the history of the landing at the Rock and the establishment of Plymouth, New England.

CABLE ADDRESS
MULIER BOSTON

THE RIVERSIDE PRESS
Cambridge, Massachusetts

HOUGHTON MIFFLIN COMPANY
2 PARK STREET · BOSTON

July
twenty-second
1942

Mr. Alvah W. Burt
3031 Temple Avenue
Cincinnati, Ohio

Dear Mr. Burt:

   Your letter of July 18th addressed to our New York Office has been referred to this, the home office, for reply.

   STORY OF THE PILGRIM FATHERS was imported from Ward and Downey, Ltd. (now John Grant, 31 George IV Bridge, Edinburgh) so therefore was not copyrighted in this country. However, as we dropped the title from our list some years ago, we do not know whether the publishers ever contracted with another American publisher to bring out a popular edition, perhaps setting here. If so, of course, the work would be copyrighted.

   Therefore we think that in order not to infringe on the copyright you had better contact John Grant at the address given stating your request, since they would have all records dealing with this title.

           Very truly yours,

           P C. Smith

          HOUGHTON MIFFLIN COMPANY
           Copyright Department

PCS/ps

TELEPHONE: EDINBURGH 20836.   TELEGRAMS: "BOOKS, EDINBURGH."   DIRECTORS: ROBERT GRANT.   JOHN GRANT.   IAN R. GRANT.

JOHN GRANT BOOKSELLERS LTD.
31 GEORGE IV BRIDGE
EDINBURGH, I

31st August
1942

Alvah W. Burt Esq.
   3031 Temple Avenue
      Westwood
          Cincinnati
              Ohio
                 U. S. A.

Dear Sir:

                  Arber - Story of the Pilgrim Fathers

        In reply to your letter of 25th inst. the publishing firm of Ward & Downey has been out of existence now for many years. I took over the stocks of several of their publications but it is doubtful if the copyright of this book was transferred to me. However, should that have been done I am quite pleased that it should be re-issued in the United States of America.

        In the event of publication it will be a favour if you forward a copy to me for file purposes.

        The last paragraph of your letter is most interesting and I hope you will succeed in bringing together all the historical matter relative to your ancestors, more especially to the original Robert Cushman. Original research work such as this is invaluable these days.

        The two letters you enclosed are returned.

        With compliments and thanks

                  Yours faithfully
               John Grant: Booksellers: Ltd.

                      Robert Grant

encs:

Reflecting upon the whole and digressing to some extent, the writer feels that the bitterness of the Pilgrim toward the English rules and regulations of life, which made life and living under English Law and Form so hard at that period, encouraging disaffection and spiritual disagreement was really far more responsible for the formation of the Pilgrim Church and the final determination to obtain a greater spiritual freedom, and eventually the embarkation to America, than was the English Church itself; with the constant political tyranny of the Scottish rule and law working through it at that time.

The writer being a communicant of the American Protestant Episcopal Church may be bent to a spiritual easement concerning these events but opines, that, if the Church of England existed then as it does today, there would have been no Pilgrim Movement; and there is little or no doubt in his mind, that the separation from the old Church was made with a hesitant determination, tempered, to an extent with regret that conditions at that time made the separation necessary; and no doubt later on reflected upon by some, more as a misfortune than as an inspirational blessing.

To understand what wild and perilous days the early Pilgrims lived through is to reflect upon early English history concerning individual rights: That in the 1600s the King was of Divine right by either blood or inheritance and that it was the duty of the subject to obey, and up to almost the 1700s the Sovereign was the LAW and the people his subjects. The first king to accept the Crown upon the condition that the Law was above the King was the one following the revolution of 1688, when the Whig doctrine placed the Law above the King.

Since such recognition of the rights of the people came many years after the embarkation to America, it is not hard to partially picture in one's mind, the conflict of thought and temper that possessed the people of the early sixteen and seventeen-hundreds.

During this early period mental and spiritual acceptances were conveyed by word of mouth; there was NO liberty of the press; Printing was possible only in a few of the larger cities, (only four or five) and then only by a Licensed Printer or a Freeman of the Company of Stationers.

It was a felony for a man to buy or to own a hand printing press or types, for which offence he would at once be sent to prison. Searchers appointed by the Stationers Company went from house to house of the Master-Printers from week to week to see that no unlicensed books were printed; and therefore few books were printed which did not conform to the will and pleasure of the King and the Bishops of the Church.

THE STUARTS, had an instinctive hatred for the press and its power, and all work printed was inspected and licensed by two persons beforehand: FIRST by two wardens of the Company of Stationers and Second by a Chaplain of the Archbishop of Canterbury or the Bishop of London; and so the early struggles against the STUART KINGS were ceaseless and strenuous.

The Puritans found themselves abused, hunted, hounded, imprisoned, their houses and homes watched by day and by night, and finally all felt inclined to go someplace where life possessed more hope and freedom; and since they had heard that in Holland there was Freedom of Religion for all, they in 1607 and 1608 migrated toward Amsterdam, and from there later into Leyden. At the first, under distressful going and great difficulties and hindrances, and lastly to escape the guards, they were forced to steal over in a small group or in small parties, as best they could.

They temporarily, at first, joined up with the exiled English Church at Amsterdam, but after a short period found their beliefs and conduct did not harmonize with that of the new Association. The conduct of the Amsterdam Church was described by one writer as "Wrongheadedness and violence; of hypocricy, wrangling and immorality." The Pilgrims for principle's sake then migrated to Leyden, striving to do what they thought to be right in the most peaceable way.

William Brewster, The Ruling Elder of the Church, guilty of printing, was a hunted man for more than a year before leaving in 1620. During the preceding year, 1619 the types belonging to Thomas Brewer were seized by the University of Leyden and he was sent to prison. He was a partner of William Brewster in the operation of the Pilgrim Press, producing only Pilgrim Books and for this cause the Pilgrim-Press was suppressed. They owned the types only and arranged with a Dutch Master Printer to do the printing.

The foregoing is given to refresh you concerning your early English History, and to make for a clearer understanding as to why America was looked upon as the HOPE for Religious Liberty.

In making their final preparation for their embarkation the reason for their selection of the place they did for their departure, was that if they had gone to London to embark, many if not all, would have been sent to prison, especially William Brewster, and by so doing they were by good fortune able to leave England without hindrance from the Government or from the Church Bishops.

Owing to the confusing statements that have been printed relating to the turning back of the Speedwell, twice for repairs and finally being rejected and latterly sold, that she was leaky and un-seaworthy and dangerous, I give you first a letter written by Robert Cushman who was very much deceived or else the Boat was in a very bad condition; this agreeing with the generally accepted and printed story of her having been rejected because of her un-seaworthy state. The next, that there was a conspiracy to break the agreement to service and man the boat.

The Cushman Letter follows:

TO HIS LOVING FRIEND ED(WARD) S(OUTHWORTH) AT HENIGE HOUSE, IN THE DUKE PLACE, (LONDON)

DARTMOUTH; (THURSDAY,) AUGUST 17, ANNO 1620.

Loving Friend:

My most kind remembrance to you, and your wife, with loving E. M. etc.; whom in this world I never look to see again. For, besides the eminent (imminent) dangers of this Voyage which are no less than deadly, an infirmity of body hath seized me which will not, in liklihood, leave me till death. What to call it, I know not. But it is a bundle of lead as if it were crushing my heart more and more these fourteen days

(3-17 August), as that, although I do the actions of a living man, yet I am but as dead. But the will of GOD be done!

Our pinnance, (the Speedwell), will not cease leaking; else, I think, we had been half way at Virginia. Our Voyage hither hath been as full of crosses as ourselves have been of crookedness. We put in here to trim her; and I think, as others also, if we had stayed at sea but three or four hours more, she would have sunk right down. And though she was twice trimmed at (South)hampton; yet now she is as open and (as) leaky as a seive: and there was a board, two feet long, a man might have pulled off with his fingers; where the water came in as at a mole hole.

We lay at (South)hampton seven days (30 July-5 Aug. 1620), in fair weather, waiting for her: and now we lie here waiting for her in as fair a wind as can blow, and so have done these four days (13-17 August); and are like(ly) to lie four more; (they actually left on 23 August), and by that time the wind will happily (Haply) turn, as it did at (Sout)hampton. Our victuals will be half eaten up, I think, before we go from the coast of England; and, if the voyage last long, we shall not have a month's victuals when we come in the country.

Near(ly) £700 hath been bestowed (spent) at (Sout)hampton, upon what I know not. Master (Christopher) Martin[1] saith, He neither can, nor will, give any account of it. And if he be called upon for accounts; he crieth out of unthankfulness for his pains and care, that we are suspicious of him: and flings away, and will end nothing. Also he so insulteth over our poor people (the Leyden Pilgrims), with such scorn and contempt, as if they were not good enough to wipe his shoes. It would break your heart to see his dealing, and the mourning of our people. They complain to me; and, alas, I can do nothing for them. If I speak to him, he flies in my face, as (if I were) mutinous; and saith, No complaints shall be heard or received but by himself: and saith, They are a froward and waspish discontented people, and I do ill to hear them. There are others that would loose all that they have put in, or make

---

[1] He was Governor in the bigger ship; and Master-Cushman, Assistant. (W. B.)

satisfaction for what they have had, that they might depart: but he will not hear them; not suffer them to go ashore, lest they should run away. The sailors also are so offended at his ignorant boldness in medling and controling in things he knows not what belongs to (them), as that some threaten to mischief him. Others say, They will leave the ship, and go their way, but at the best, this cometh of it, that he makes himself a scorn and (a) laughing stock unto them.

As for Master WESTON, except grace due greatly sway with him, he will hate us ten times more than he ever loved us, for not confirming the *Conditions*. But now since some pinches have taken them, they begin to reveal the truth, and say, Master Robinson was in the fault,[1] who charged them never to consent to those *Conditions* nor choose me into Office; but indeed appointed them to choose them they did choose. But he and they will rue too late. They may now see, and all be ashamed when it is too late, that they were so ignorant, yea, and so inordinate in their courses. I am sure as they were not resolved to seal those *Conditions*, I was not so resolute (? as resolute) at (South)hampton to have left the whole business, except they would seal them; and better the Voyage to have broken off then, than to have brought such misery to ourselves, dishonour to GOD, and detriment to our loving friends, as now it is lik(ly) to do. Four or five of the Chief of them which came from Leyden, came resolved never to go on those *Conditions*.

And Master (CHRISTOPHER) MARTIN, he said, He never received no money on those *Conditions*! He was not beholden to the Merchants for a pin! They were blood suckers! and I know not what. Simple man! He indeed never made any *Conditions* with the Merchants, nor ever spake with them: but did (made) all that money (the £700) fly to (at) (Sout) hampton, or was it his own? Who will go and lay out money so rashly and lavishly as he did; and never know how he comes by it, or on what conditions?

Secondly, I told him of the alterations long ago, and he was

---

[1] I think he was deceived in these things. (W. B.)

content: but now he domineers, and said, I had betrayed them into the hands of slaves! He is not beholden to them! He can set out two ships himself to a voyage! when good man! he hath but £50 in (the venture); and if he should give up his accounts, he would not have a penny left him (i. e. of his own),[1] as I am persuaded & etc.

Friend, if ever we make a Plantation, GOD works a miracle! especially considering how scant we shall be of victuals; and, most of all, ununited amongst ourselves, and devoid of good tutors and regiment (leaders and organisation). Violence will break all. Where is the meek and humble spirit of Moses? and of Nehemiah, who re-edified the walls of Jerusalem, and the State of Israel? Is not the sound of Rehoboam's brags daily heard amongst us? Have not the philosophers and all wise men observed that, even in settled Common Wealths, violent Governors bring, either themselves, or (the) people, or both, to ruin? How much more in the raising of Common Wealths, when the mortar is yet scarce tempered that should bind the walls?

If I should write to you of all things which promiscuously forerun our ruin, I should overcharge my weak head, and grieve your tender heart: only this I pray you, Prepare for evil tidings of us every day! But pray for us instantly (without ceasing)! It may be the Lord will be yet intreated, one way or other, to make for us. I see not, in reason, how we shall escape, even the gasping of hunger-starved persons: but GOD can do much; and his will be done!

It is better for me to die, than for me to bear it: which I do daily, and expect it hourly; having received these sentence of death both within me and without me. Poor WILLIAM KING and myself do strive who meat first for the fishes; but we look for a glorious resurrection, knowing CHRIST JESUS after the flesh no more: but looking unto the joy that is before us, we will endure all these things, and account them light in comparison of that joy we hope for.

Remember me in all love to our friends, as if I named them: whose prayers I desire earnestly, and wish again to see (them); but not till I can, with more comfort, look them in the

---

[1]This was found true afterward. (W. B.)

face. The Lord give us that true comfort which none can take from! I had a desire to make a brief Relation of our estate to some friend. I doubt not but your wisdom will teach you seasonably to utter things, as hereafter you shall be callled to it. That which I have written is true; and many things more, which I have foreborne. I write it, as upon my life and last confession in England. What is of use to be spoken of presently (at once), you may speak of it; and what is fit to conceal, conceal! Pass by my weak manner! for my head is weak, and my body feeble. The Lord make me strong in him, and keep both you and yours!

Your loving friend,

Dartmouth, August 17, 1620.   ROBERT CUSHMAN

Then follows the opposite as related in "THE STORY OF THE PILGRIM FATHERS, by Edward Arber, F. S. A.: "But here, by the way, let me show, how afterwards it was found that the leakiness of this ship was partly by her being overmasted, and too much pressed with sails. For after she was sold[1] and put to her old trim, she made many voyages and performed her service very sufficiently, to the great profit of her owners."

But more especially, by the cunning and deceit of the Master and his (ships) company; who were hired to stay a whole year in the country; And now fancying dislike, and fearing want of victuals, they plotted this strategem to free themselves, as was afterwards known, and by some of them confessed, for they apprehended (thought) that the greater ship, being of force (better manned and armed) and in which most of the provisions were stowed; she would retain enough for herself, whatsoever became of them or the passengers."

After perusing the foregoing you may decide for yourself as to the sea-worthiness of the Speedwell; I, the writer, have always felt that blame should attach more to the ship's officers than to the condition of the boat.

Finally after deciding that the Speedwell should not make

---

[1]The Speedwell had been bot with Leyden money, the proceeds of her sale, after her return to London, would, of course, go to the credit of the common Joint Stock there. (E. A.)

the voyage and as to just who were to go in the Mayflower, they to go were instructed to get aboard the Mayflower. They departed September 6th. 1620; and on the 9th of November they sighted land; The Mayflower then anchored in the Bay of Cape Cod the 11th of November, 1620.

On their way over they encountered, many times, cross winds and also many times heavy storms terribly shaking the ship, making her quite leaky; One of the main beams amidships bowed and cracked causing much fear but the carpenter and workmen put a post under the cracked beam and bound it feeling that it would be safe to continue the voyage.

In some of these storms the winds were so fierce and the seas so high that they could not have out any sails but forced to drift about without sail. In one of these storms as they thus lay at hull, in a mighty storm, a lusty young man, called John Howland, coming upon some occasion above gratings, was with the rollings or pitching of the ship, thrown into the sea. He catching hold of the topsail hallyards, which hung overboard and by hanging on, though several feet under water, was hauled up by rope and with a boat-hook got onto the ship again and his life saved.

On November 11th after dropping anchor in the bay of Cape Cod they at once prepared to do some exploring.

On Wednesday the 15th of November, the weather permitting, they again tried exploring, and seeing some Indians with a dog in the distance tried to approach them, but the Indians being fearful ran away with all their might; they followed them until nightfall when they camped until the morning.

On the 16th they continued further inland on Cape-Cod and found some corn buried, they also found a large kettle which had been made in Europe. They also found some good drinking water, which they were very much in need of. On the 17th. it having rained all the night before, they found their guns so damp in the morning that they had to re-load them so that they would go-off. They found that day a deer trap set by the Indians to catch deer; also more good drinking water and more corn; all the corn found was saved to be used for seeding purposes.

For a period of several days following they having to contend with bad weather and having by then about six inches of snow, some of them were taking heavy colds.

During the 28th and 29th they found more corn and now having altogether about ten bushels saved up for spring seeding. On the 30th they found a place of habitation of recent use and seemingly deserted as no people were about.

By now all had colds and coughs and it was debated as to whether they should make Cape-Cod a permanent home place or not.

Wednesday the 6th of December it being very cold and disagreeable weather, two of the party became very sick that day. The water froze on their clothes and made them like coats of iron.

Seeing some Indians very busy at something near the shore, the Indians upon seeing the explorers, ran to and fro as though carrying something away. The explorers then landed about two leagues, (six miles) from where the Indians were.

The next morning the 7th of Dec. they went to the place where they saw the Indians and there found a great fish dead, called a Grampus; they also found two other fish; the fish had been cast up by the high waters and storms and they had been unable to get back into the water from off the frost and ice. The fish were from 12 to 15 feet long, having about two inches of fat and fleshed somewhat like swine, they would have yielded a great deal of oil if there had been time and means to have taken it.

A little further back on land they found where corn had been planted during some former year; also a burying place but not so pretentious as some they had looked at near Corn-Hill. They then found five Indian houses and a little further on two baskets of parched corn but still saw no people.

They then went to the shore and signaled to the shallop to come and then they began to arrange for a camp for the night. After the shallop came they ate what victuals they had, and prepared for a nights rest, but about midnight they heard a hideous cry causing them to scramble to arms and then firing off a couple of their muskets after which the noise ceased. The next morning, after prayer, they prepared for breakfast and then a journey, and owing to approaching daylight they thought best to carry the things down to the shallop. Those who took their things down to the shore in coming back up to breakfast, laid their arms down and came on up, when all of a sudden they heard that same cry that they had heard in the night time before, and one of the company came running in and cried! "They are Indians!" And almost by that time the arrows from the Indians came flying among them; the men who had left their arms down on the shore rushed after and luckily recovered them. There were thirty or forty of the Indians and after a short demonstration and the belief that their leader or captain had been shot or somewhat wounded, the Indians ran away after which the explorers picked up several of their arrows, eighteen in all, to take back to the big boat as souvenirs.

On December the eleventh they sounded the harbor thereabout and then returned to the Mayflower the next day to comfort those on board with the news they had gained.

December the 14th the ship Mayflower, weighed anchor to go to the place they had discovered, (Clark's Island) and coming within two leagues of the place, were prevented by heavy winds from landing.

On December the 16th they again put out to sea and came safely into a mainland harbor. The harbor being a bay greater in size than that of Cape Cod, there being much wild fowl and good fishing; also great mussels, crabs and lobsters. On the Sabbath Day they again rested.

The next day, Monday, going ashore they went toward where Kingston later became located, finding good rich land, an abundance of good timber, good drinking water, also vines, cherry trees, plum trees, many kinds of herbs, strawberries, liverwort, water cress, leek and onions.

On Tuesday, December the 19th some went on land at the same place and others took the small boat to go further up. Those on land found Jones River and went up about three miles, but the location being so far from fishing, their principal hope for profit, and too on account of heavy woods about, therefore with greater danger from Indian annoyance, they concluded that it was better to try that location later on when they could feel safer.

On the morning of the 20th. of December they realizing that victuals were becoming more scarce and they reviewing what they had so far observed on the mainland and at Clark's Island, they concluded, and that by the most voices or vote, to select the mainland on the high ground where there was a great deal of cleared land and where corn had been planted three or four years before, and on one field, a great hill, afterward called "Fort Hill" and now "Old Burial Hill" upon which they planned to make a platform or fort, from which they could see far out into the bay and the ocean.

The 21st was a bad wet day and those who remained on shore could not see to make shelter and were themselves wet and the night came on with high winds and much rain, and they on shore without victuals. About eleven o'clock the next day the shallop went ashore with provisions but could not return to the ship, Mayflower—the wind blew so strong. The storm continued all through the day, Friday, and so strong and heavy that they could not get either way, from the boat toward land or from the land to the boat; and on this day December 22nd Mary Allerton, wife of Isaac Allerton was delivered of a son, but born dead.

On Saturday the 23rd as many as could went ashore to fell timber, and to carry, with which to make a building. Sunday was a day of rest and prayer.

Monday, December 25th. Christmas Day, they went to work again in the timber, some sawing, some riving, some carrying. They all drank water until evening and that night those on boat were given some beer, but they on shore had none.

Tuesday, the weather was bad but Wednesday with better weather they went to work again on the Fort or Platform upon which to place their Ordinance. In the afternoon they went out to measure the ground for the two rows of houses, single men to go with a family of their choice so as to need but nineteen houses to be located closely on Leyden Street.

There having been so much stormy, wet and bad weather, so much of the time, the people became troubled and discouraged as many were having heavy colds and others sick, besides being anxious to land, as the Mayflower lay about one and one-half miles from shore, being 180 tons and drew so much water.

Seeing much smoke in the distance which they believed surely caused by Indians clearing ground for corn, Captain Miles Standish with others went out to see if they could meet some of the savages; on their way home they shot an eagle which made some excellent meat. Work and labor progressed as the weather permitted. The "Common House" or Fort was to be 20 feet square.

In chasing a deer two of the explorers, with dogs, got lost but finally found their way back. On Sunday the 14th of January the new Common House caught fire but was saved from being destroyed or before great damage was caused.

On the 19th they started building a shed for their provisions and by Saturday the 20th the shed was completed as a store house, and on Monday the 22nd the long boat and the shallop brought their common goods for storage.

On Friday the 9th of February the weather was cold and little work could be done. Captain Jones went ashore and killed five geese which were distributed among the sick families. That afternoon the little house caught fire from a spark but it was soon put out. Captain Jones also found a deer that had been killed by the Indians, they having only taken the horns.

Captain Miles Standish and Francis Cooke being at work in the woods, on coming home left their tools behind, but before they returned their tools were taken away by the savages.

Saturday the 17th of February while holding a consultation, two Indians presented themselves on the hilltop a short distance and signaled to come to them; they were then signaled to come on, not doing so, the Pilgrims then arming themselves, sent Captain Miles Standish and Stephen Brooke to go over the brook and up to them but the Indians being fearful would not meet them and fled.

This experience made necessary their placing their ordinance in position and the Minion, a cannon of 1200 lbs. with a $3\frac{1}{4}$ inch bore and firing 340 yards, and a Sacre, a cannon of 1500 lbs. with a bore of $3\frac{1}{2}$ inchs firing 360 yards, together with two Bases, small cannon of about 200 lbs. with a bore of $1\frac{1}{4}$ inches, being advantageously placed made for a feeling of greater safety.

Saturday March 3rd was spring-like, the birds singing and sun shining and then about 1. P. M. came a clap of heavy thunder which was the first heard since coming over.

Friday the 16th of March, being a warm promising day, they by now having been able to plant some seeds, were busy with their work when they heard some Indians about, but did not see them; however, a little later on one presented himself, coming boldly and alone, he saluted in English and bade them welcome. He said his name was Samoset and of Pemaqued; he discoursed freely of the surrounding country, knowing the Sagamores or Chiefs. He was given some biscuit and butter, cheese, pudding and a piece of Mallard, with something to drink.

He told them that the place where they were, was called Patuxet and also told of the plague that killed the people off, who formerly lived there, which occurred about four years before.

Being presented with a knife, a bracelet and a ring, he went his way but promised to return with some of the tribe of the Massasoyt, their closest neighbors and who were about 60 strong. He told them that the Nausites were their next near neighbors after the Massasoyts and that they were about 100 strong, and were much incensed against the English, because Captain Hunt, had on pretext of trade, coaxed 20 of the Pautuxet tribe together with seven of the tribe of the Nausites, carrying them off to Spain where he sold them into slavery at £20 or $100 per man.

On Sunday March 18th Samoset returned bringing five other men and each had a deer skin and one had a wild cat skin; all had loose leggings up to the groin and from there up to their waist, another leather.

They had left their bows and arrows about one quarter mile back as instructed through agreement with Samoset. They liked the English victuals. They left their skins behind; upon leaving the Pilgrims, they returned homeward for more, and on returning, they brought back the tools which they had taken from the woods. From this on, the acquaintance grew.

On Wednesday, March 21st, 1621 the carpenter of the Mayflower getting the shallop in condition, all the remaining

Pilgrim Fathers and families on the Mayflower were brought to shore.

On the 22nd of March came Samoset again and with him Tisquanto (or Squanto for short) WHO HAD LIVED IN England with Master John Slanie, they telling that their great Sagamore Massasoyt and his brother Quadequina were near by, and so the lifelong friendship between the Pilgrims and the Indians was begun.

A treaty of peace was established, as follows:

TREATY OF PEACE WITH MASSOYT

1. That neither he, nor any of his, should injure, or do hurt, to any of our people.
2. And if any of his did hurt to any of ours; he should send the offender (to us), that we might punish him.
3. That if any of our tools were taken away, when our people were at work; he should cause them to be restored; and if ours did any harm to any of his, we would do the like to them.
4. If any did unjustly war against him; we would aid him. If any did war against us, he should aid us.
5. He should send to his neighbouring confederates, to certify them of this, that they might not wrong us; but might be likewise comprised in the "Conditions of Peace."
6. That when their men came to us, they should leave their bows and arrows behind them; as we should do our pieces, when we came to them.
7. Lastly, that doing thus, King James would esteem of him as his friend and ally.

All the above which their King seemed to like well, and it was applauded of by his followers.

FROM this point, a clear description of the prayerful preparation made, preceding the embarkation, will be found in the work of Henry Wyle Cushman a little further on.

I give you here the definition of "A Pilgrim Father" as described and published by Edward Arber, F. S. A. in his "The Story of the PILGRIM Fathers."

All those members of the Separatist Church at Leyden, who

voted for the migration to America; whether they were actually able to go or not: together with such others as joined their Church from England.

Membership in the Pilgrim Church was the first qualification; intended, or actual, emigration to New England, was the second one.

This general definition will include Rev. John Robinson and his family, who were unable to leave Leyden. It also includes the thirty-five members of the Leyden Church who arrived at Plymouth in New England in the Fortune, in November 1621; the sixty who arrived in the boats Ann and Little James in August 1623; the thirty-five with their families, who arrived in the Mayflower in 1629; and the sixty who arrived in the Handmaid, in May, 1630.

It likewise includes Christopher Martin and his wife, who joined from Billercak in Essex, and Richard Warren and John Billington Sr. and his family who came from London. It also embraces William King. It further includes hired men such as John Howland, a man servant in Governor Carver's family and John Alden, "The Cooper" both who came in the Mayflower and eventually embraced the Pilgrim Cause and became honoured men among the Pilgrim Fathers.

IT EXCLUDES: All those members of the Pilgrim Church who did not wish to go to America and all hired men who went in the Mayflower and did not become members of the church; AND SO all the Mayflower passengers were not Pilgrim Fathers. IT ALSO EXCLUDES: Thomas Weston, and all the seventy Adventurers as such; for having shares in the "Joint Stock" did not make them "Pilgrim Fathers". Governor Bradford in 1650 refers to the passengers in the Mayflower as "The Old Stock."

Here ends the items and features borrowed from: "The Story Of The Pilgrim Fathers" and its present owner, The John Grant Publishing Company of Edinburgh, Scotland.

On Coles Hill overlooking the Granite Canopy or Portico protecting Plymouth Rock at Plymouth, Mass. stands this Sarcophagus, upon the first burying ground of the passengers of the Mayflower.

In tiresome and painful watching, often in hunger and

cold, they laid the foundations of a State wherein all Men in future ages should enjoy the freedom and liberty to worship God according to conscience and free-will: may each new generation re-dedicate itself to do their part in perpetuating American Freedom and Democracy. They were two months and five days crossing the great Atlantic Ocean in the Mayflower, and before leaving the ship a constitution was drawn up; the Pilgrims at first to possess everything in common. John Carver was selected to be the first Governor and in the following April, 1621, William Bradford was elected Governor; and held the office thereafter for thirty-one years. They arrived at Cape Cod, November 11, 1620, and at Plymouth Rock early in December, 1620, with housing to construct and a hard winter and winter's exposure to be faced, and on Mar. 21st. 1621 all remaining on the Mayflower of the Pilgrim Fathers and families, were brought to shore.

Of the 104 passengers of the Mayflower, 46 died the first winter no doubt from exposure, poor food and malnutrition; they dying so rapidly and fearing the Indians might have a way of accounting and a massacre occur, they therefore held their funerals in the darkness of night with the grave leveled flat with the ground and no identification placed to mark the spot of burial. Years afterwards the descendants of the Mayflower and the 46 thus buried had a large granite Memorial or Sarcophagus placed on the brow of the hill overlooking Plymouth Rock, and in size about as near as the writer can guess, without having made actual measurements, 3-1/2 feet wide 12 to 15 feet long, and about 8 or 10 feet high, hewn out, box form, and all the bones of the 46 placed therein conglomerate, the great lid was sealed thereon, and the names affixed alphabetically, in bronze letters placed thereon. The name of the mother of our Mary Allerton Cushman wife of Elder Thomas Cushman, appearing second thereon.

Old Plymouth is a spot of interest to all lovers of History, and intensely so to those of us whose forebears first landed there; the name of the Rock, the town and all seem to relate to them somehow in a semi-sacred way, consecrated by the sufferings and hopes of the Pilgrims and dedicated by them

This Beautiful Barre Granite Memorial or Sarcophagus Marks the First Burying Ground in Plymouth of the Passengers of the Mayflower.

to spiritual freedom; we approach the spot with reverent step and a feeling of deep respect and veneration.

The Sarcophagus is on the first natural terrace above the famous Rock, and then Old Burial Hill on the second, rising almost back of the business section of Plymouth, probably about 150 or 200 feet in elevation above the famous Rock. On a clear day one can see to the north the Myles Standish Monument and Duxbury, the town from which our progenitor, Thomas Cushman, came on down to Lebanon, Conn. to locate.

A few years before the landing of the passengers from the Mayflower on the Famous Rock, a strange ship approached the American shore and coaxed some young Indians aboard, making prisoners of them, carrying them on down to Spain and selling them as slaves. One of them, named Tisquanto, called Squanto for brief, escaped and went up to England, and in London a merchant named John Slanie showed kindness and sympathy to Squanto. Many a sailor touching the American shore thereafter was shown no mercy, suffering for the act of the captain who kidnapped Squanto and his friends, never knowing he was suffering because of an act of another white man some years before.

A few years after the kidnapping of Squanto his tribe was stricken with a plague so severe that within a short period of time the few who had not suffered or died feared to stay and left, leaving behind their stores of buried corn and other provisions. Knowing nothing of this, Squanto in London was living with the hope of seeing his people again, for Mr. Slanie had promised to help him back to America again, and the year before the Mayflower sailed, he, Squanto, did get back to America, but he found only the empty forests; his people, all of them, gone. He went to live with a tribe some forty or more miles away.

The next year the Mayflower sailed late in the year reaching Plymouth in early December; with no houses, a northern severe winter ahead of them, they landed on the edge of deep forests, strange and silent. They wondered about Indians and when they were to be attacked, expecting most anything to happen at any time. They slowly gathered courage as silence prevailed, they found the heaps of corn and kept an

Entrance from the Main Thoroughfare or Street About One Square Back to the Second Terrace Upon Which You Find Old Burial Hill at Plymouth, Mass.

account of what they took expecting to pay back for what they used. Bitter winter came upon them and with food about gone, almost half of them dead, hope and courage almost exhausted, yet with faith and trust they continued on. Then springtime came, renewing hope and anticipation in those yet alive, and to them with it came Squanto, able to speak English, coming not with hate and as a warrior, but as a friend speaking English. An English merchant had been his friend, and his coming was a blessing of love and kindness never to be forgotten by them.

Squanto taught them how to plant and care for the crops, how to fish and provide food, saving them from starvation. He further taught them how to trade with the Indian tribes. Squanto lived with them, true and dependable until his death.

The following taken from the "New England Historical and Genealogical Register," Vol. 68, under the Heading: Genealogical Research in England, is to show the serious relation of the Godfather to his Godchild in baptism, and his feeling and devotion to this obligation throughout his life:

The Will of John Crocheman of Rolvenden, Co. of Kent, 2, March 1523 (1523/4) to be buried in the Churchyard of Rolvenden.—To the Reparation of the Church of Rolvenden, 6 S. 8D.; Toward the buying of a Cope for said Church 5 Marks; To an honest priest to sing in said Church for one year, 10 Marks; To the highway between the house of John Asten, the elder, and the Church, 3S—4D; to Johane Crocheman, my sister, 13S—4—D: To Ewens Widow, Vinkels Widow, John Blacke, Elyne Wederly and to Gabryell 12D each; To Symon Harkwod all debts due me from him at this date; and to Goddeley Harkwod his wife, a barn adjoining the house he dwelleth in, with the ground around it, with reversion at her death to her son John and his issue and for default of such to her other children or else to my brother *Thomas Crocheman and his heirs forever.*

THE WILL OF Thomas Couchman of the Parish of Rolvenden, Co. of Kent, Husbandman, 10 February 1585 (1585/6) to be buried in the Churchyard of Rolvenden; To the Poormens Box of Rolvenden, 2 S; To my son Rychard Couchman, 10£ at the age of one and twenty years; *To my younger son,*

Robarte Couchman 10L at the age of one and twenty year; To my daughter Sylvester Couchman, 6£ 13S 4D. at the age of twenty years or day of marriage; If any of my children die under age, reversion to the survivors; *To my Godchild Thomas Bredman 12D—To my Godchildren, Thomas Coyle, Thomas Gabriell, Marion Hasleman and Jane Couchman, a sheep each.*

FIRST OF THE FAMILY NAMED: Croucheman, Crocheman, Couchman, Cuchman, Cushman,

THOMAS, Died June 14th. 1567
Joan or Johne,
John Died, March 1523/4 Will proved May 10th. 1524

THOMAS, (Above) had six (6) children:
1. Thomas, Born 1538, Married July 1568 Elynor Hubbarde, Maydn.
2. Elizabeth, Died Sept. 30th. 1576, Married John Sennersell.
3. Richarde, Died Sept. 15th. 1575 Married Frances Bahlwinner.
4. John, Died Mar. 4th. 1568, Married Mary Sheaffe.
5. Anne, Died, Dec. 2nd. 1562.
6. Jan (or) Johne, Married Richard Haxman.

THOMAS COUCHMAN (Cushman) Born 1538 Died and Buried Feb. 14th. 1585, Married 1568 Elynor Hubbarde, Maydn. He was Arch-Deacon of the Church of Canterbury. Children Born,
1. Alys, Baptized, April 20th. 1572, Died May 9th. 1572.
2. Syluister, Baptized Oct. 30th. 1574.
3. Robert, Baptized Feb. 9th. 1577/8 Married Sarah Reder Died 1625.
4. Margaret, Baptized Mar. 25th. 1582 Buried Feb. 5th. 1583..
5. Henry, Baptized July 26th. 1584, Buried April 11th. 1585.

THE FOLLOWING TAKEN FROM CUSHMAN ENTRIES IN THE ARCHDEACONS' TRANSCRIPTS OF THE Parish Registers of Rolvenden, Co. of Kent, 1560/1612.

1568, July, The same day agaiyn (xvllJ) was marryid Thomas Couchman and Elynour Hubbarde, Maydn.
1572, Alys, daughter of Thomas Cutchman, baptized 20" April
1572, Alys, daughter of Thomas Cutchman, Buried, 9" May
1574, Syluister, daughter of Thomas Cutchman, Baptized, 30" October
1575, John, Son of Christopher Croochman, Baptized, 8" May
1577, The IX daye of the same month of February was baptized Robert Cutchman, Sone of Thomas Cutchman, (1577/8)
1582, Margaret, daughter of Thomas Cuchman, Baptized, 25" March
1583, Margaret, daughter of Thomas Cuchman, Buried 5" February.
1584, Henry, Son of Thomas Cuchman, Baptized 26" July.
1585, Henry, Son of Thomas Cuchman, Buried, 11" April.
1585, Thomas Couchman, Householder, Buried 14" Feb.
1587, Emanuel Evernden & Ellyn Couchman, Widow, married 17" Oct.
1589, Emanuel Evernden Householder, Buried 3" Dec.
1593, Stephen Evernden of Tetterden, broadweaver, and Sylvester Coucheman were marryed, 7" Nov.

THIS FROM THE REGISTERS OF PARISH OF ST. ALPHEGE, Canterbury, 1606, Robert Cushman unto Sara Reder dwelling within the precincts of Christ Churche, ("The Cathedral") married 31" July.

THIS FROM THE REGISTERS of the PARISH of St. Andrew, Canterbury: 1608, Thomas Cushman, sone of Robert baptized, 8" Feb. (1607/8).

TAKEN FROM the Visitation books of the Archdeacon of Canterbury: 1603, 14" November, The Churchwardens of St. Andrew's Canterbury, present Robert Cushman, servant to George Maisters, for the like as the common fame goeth (Ie., "for that he doth say he will not come to his Parish Church because he cannot be edified and saith he can and will defend it by the word of God"). When he appeared 15 October 1604 in the Court of the Archdeacon he was warned that he would have to acknowledge his offense in the Parish Church of St. Anthony, Canterbury, on some Sunday in the time of service according to the schedule (not given) and there to certify the Court afterwards. Not doing this he was ex-communicated 12" November 1604. On June 28" 1605 he appeared and asked to be absolved and on 7" July 1605 his request was granted. VOLUME for 1598-1608 Part 2 for 31.

TAKEN FROM Canterbury Marriage Licenses:
1610, Thomas Shingleton of Sandwich, shoemaker, and Mary Clarke of the same Parish, Virgin, at St. Mary Bredman's Canterbury, 28" January, 1610/11.

TRANSLATION FROM The Dutch Records at Leyden:
Robert Cushman, Woolcomber from Canterbury, England, Widower of Sara Cushman, dwelling in a little alley of the Nunsgate, accompanied by John Keble, his friend *with Mary Shingleton from Sandwich in England,* widow of Thomas Shingleton, accompanied by Catharine Carver, her friend, *were married before Andries Jasperson VanVesanevelt* and Jacob Peadts, Sheriffs, this fifth of June 1617. (*The entries show the bans were published three times, on 20" and 27" May and 3" June 1617.*)

FROM the foregoing data the pedigree has been prepared:
Thomas Couchman of Rolvenden, Husbandman, the testator, of 1585/6 who was born about 1538 and *buried at Rolvenden 14" February 1585/6,* married there *18" July 1586 Elynor Hubbarde whose ancestry has not been found; She married secondly 17th October 1587 Emanuel Everden of Rolvenden,* the testator of 1589 who was buried at Rolvenden, 3" December 1589.

The Howland House is the Oldest House in Plymouth, Mass., and was Built in 1667.

JOHN HOWLAND

John Howland, Born 1592, D. 2/23/1673. Married Elizabeth Tilley (B. 1607 in Holland, D. 12/21/1687 in Plymouth, Mass.) a daughter of John Tilley.

John Howland, John Tilley and his wife Bridget Van Der Velde Tilley and their daughter Elizabeth Tilley all came over in the Mayflower together in 1620. John Tilley and his wife both died the first winter after their arrival at Plymouth, Mass. as did 44 others out of the 104 that came over in the Mayflower.

Inasmuch as our line is descended from Thomas Cushman, the son of Elder Thomas Cushman and Mary Allerton Cushman, who married Ruth Howland, and the second child born to Thomas Cushman and Ruth Howland was named Thomas Cushman, who married Sarah Strong, the daughter of Jedediah Strong:

I devote this space to the memory of John Howland; I also present a picture of the Howland House on a preceding page.

John Howland was a sturdy Pilgrim and on Old Burial Hill at Plymouth, Mass. is a monument or stone erected to his memory, of a brown or a reddish-brown color, bearing the following inscription:

> Here ended the Pilgrimage of
> JOHN HOWLAND
> Died February 23rd, 1672/3
> Aged above 80 years
> He married Elizabeth, daughter
> of John Tilley
> who came with him in the
> Mayflower, 1620.

From them are descended a numerous posterity.

In the old Burial Ground east of the village of Lebanon, New London County, Connecticut, on State Highway Number 207, I have made pictures of the grave stones at the graves of Thomas Cushman of the fourth generation, heretofore referred to, and of his wife Sarah Strong Cushman, and also made

The Gravestone at the Left to the Memory of Thomas Cushman, Fourth Generation, and the One to Its Right to the Memory of His Wife, Sarah (Strong) Cushman.

record of the epitaph or inscription on each of the headstones:
The inscription at the bottom of the Stone at the grave of Thomas Cushman, reads:

Here lies the body of Mr. Thomas Cushman late husband of Mrs. Sarah Cushman—Died January 9—1727 age 57 years.

Here lies our honored father dear who was our helpful guide here, also lies our mother dear entombed by his side.

AND UPON HER STONE:

Here lies the body of Mrs. Sarah Cushman who died December 25th 1726 aged 52 years.

Here lies ye womb within this tomb from whence we took our nature. We hope they both are now at rest in God their great Creator.

At the entrance to this cemetery or burial ground is a bronze memorial upon which one reads:

"OLD CEMETERY contains the tomb of Brother Jonathan Trumbull, Revolutionary War Governor of Connecticut; The friend and advisor of George Washington; William Williams, signer of the Declaration of Independence."

This cemetery also contains the graves of other early settlers and patriots including Rev. James Fitch, Rev. John Robinson, and several of the Hale family.

The will of Thomas Cushman (4th Generation) is on record in the Court-House of Wyndham County, Williamantic, Connecticut, entered in book number 1, dated January 9. 1726/27, pages 167/169, approved February 28th 1726/1727 and probated March 7th 1726/1727.

There also is record of the administration of the estate of William Cushman, 5th generation, son of Thomas Cushman, 4th Generation, by his son Peter; The original papers relating to this administration are on file with the Secretary of State at Hartford, Conn.

The Cushman Monument erected to the memory of Robert Cushman in the Cemetery on Old Burial Hill at Plymouth, Mass. standing above Old Plymouth-Rock, is the largest and most conspicuous monument in the Cemetery; it is a fine

THE CUSHMAN MEMORIAL AND THE TWO SMALLER CUSHMAN MONUMENTS IN THE FOREGROUND DEDICATED TO ELDER THOMAS CUSHMAN ON OLD BURIAL HILL, PLYMOUTH, MASS.

granite column about twenty-five or more feet in height, with a bronze tablet inset on each of the four sides. Directly in front of the North face of this monument there stands, probably twelve feet or fifteen feet away, two stones erected to the memory of his son, Elder Thomas Cushman. This picture I have taken depicts both the Memorial and also the two smaller stones to Elder Thomas.

I have been informed that the larger monument or Memorial is now on the spot where the smaller ones formerly stood and that they were moved a little distance forward to make room for the larger Memorial, and that the remains of Elder Thomas and his wife Mary Allerton Cushman most likely repose beneath the larger one.

The following inscription is on the smaller stone:

"Here lyeth buried ye body of that precious servant of God, Mr. Thomas Cushman, who after he had served his generation according to the will of God, and particularly the church of Plymouth for many years in the office of a Ruling Elder, fell asleep in Jesus, Decmr. Ye 10, 1691 & ye 84 year of his age."

The Tablet on the larger of the two can be easily read with a glass.

ROBERT CUSHMAN,
Fellow-Exile with the Pilgrims in Holland,
Afterwards their chief agent in England,
Arrived here IX—November, MDCXXI,
With Thomas Cushman his son:
Preached—IX—December
His memorable sermon on "The Danger of Self-love
And the Sweetness of True Friendship:"
Returned to England XIII—December,
To vindicate the enterprise of Christian emigration;
And there remained in the service of the Colony
Till MDCXXV,
When, having prepared to make Plymouth
His permanent home,

The above made from a photograph of the Bronze Tablet on the North side of the Memorial, reading:

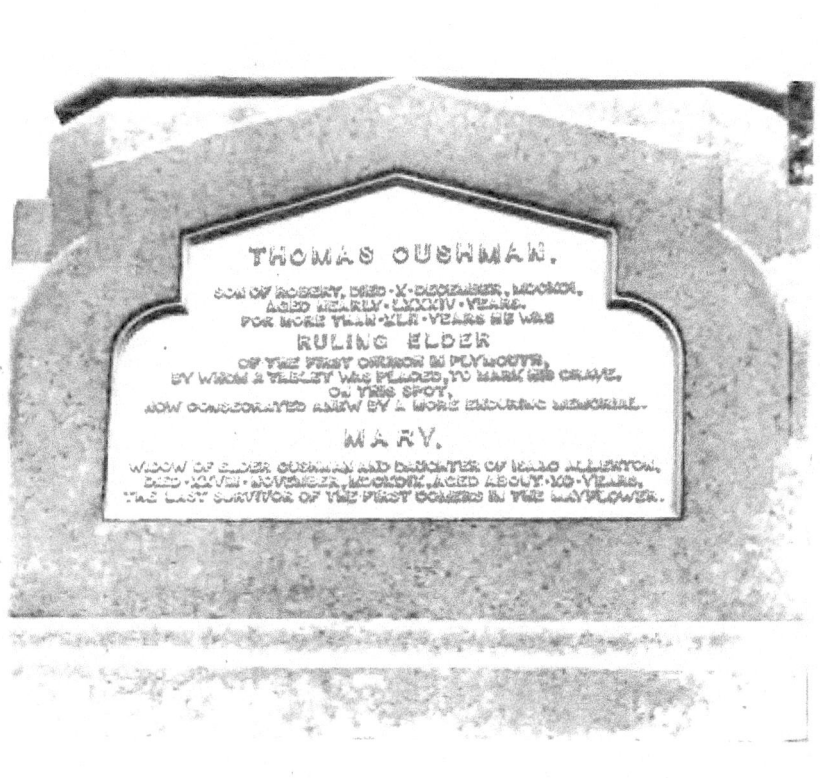

On the South side of the Memorial a Bronze Tablet reads:
THOMAS CUSHMAN,
Son of Robert, died—X— December, MDCXCI,
Aged nearly LXXXIV years.
For more than XLII—Years he was
RULING ELDER
Of the First Church in Plymouth,
By whom a tablet was placed, to mark his grave
on this spot,
Now consecrated anew by a more enduring memorial.
MARY
Widow of Elder Cushman and daughter of Isaac Allerton
Died XXVIII—November, MDCXCIX, aged about XC years
The last survivor of the first comers in the Mayflower.

On the West side of the Memorial a Bronze Tablet reads:
He died, lamented by the forefathers
as "their ancient friend,—who was as
their right hand with their friends
the adventurers, and for divers years
had done and agitated all their business
with them to their great advantage."
"And you my loving friends, the adventurers
to this plantation, as your care has been first
to settle religion here before either profit
or popularity, so, I pray you, go on.—
I rejoice——that you thus honor God
with your riches, and I trust you shall be repaid;
again double and treble in this world, yea,
and the memory of this action shall never die."
DEDICATION OF THE SERMON.

On the East side of the Memorial a Bronze Tablet reads:
Erected by
The descendants of
Robert Cushman
In memory of their Pilgrim Ancestors,
XVI—September, MDCCCLVIII

The accompanying two photographs will give the reader an idea of the bronze tablets inserted one on each of the four sides.

LEWIS HISTORICAL *Publishing Company*
INCORPORATED
Largest Publishers of
HISTORY, GENEALOGY, BIOGRAPHY, HERALDRY

TELEPHONE
WATKINS 9-7750
CABLE ADDRESS
LEWHOSO-NEWYORK

COUNTY TRUST BUILDING
8TH AVENUE AT 14TH STREET
NEW YORK, N.Y.

February 6th, 1942

Mr. Alvah W. Burt,
3031 Temple Avenue,
Cincinnati, Ohio

Dear Mr; Burt:

     In reply to your letter of January 27th, we wish to say that we are very happy indeed to grant you permission to quote from page 426 of our "GENEALOGY OF NEW ENGLAND FAMILIES" but we ask that you be so kind as to give us recognition for this service.

     Thanking you and wishing you success with your book, we are,

                  Yours very truly,
            LEWIS HISTORICAL PUBLISHING COMPANY, Inc.

                  M.M. Lewis
        Director of Research and Statistics

FROM GENEALOGY OF NEW ENGLAND FAMILIES

Published by Lewis Historical Publishing Co. of New York City and used with their permission:

Robert Cushman born in 1580 in England. He early became interested in the movement for greater freedom of religious opinion and joined the little church at Scroby, with Rev. John Robinson (afterward its pastor) Elder Brewster, Governor Carver, Governor Bradford, Isaac Allerton and others, in 1602.

Subsequently they removed to Holland, but were not satisfied with the conditions at Leyden and resolved to make application to the Virginia Company, whose authority extended over a considerable portion of the North American continent, for liberty to settle in the company's territory in America. For that purpose Robert Cushman and Deacon John Carver were selected to go to London in 1617 and open negotiations. The mission was not successful. Later they arranged with Thomas Weston and the Merchant Adventurers of London to go to America.

The "Speedwell" was purchased in Holland, but not being large enough to take all who wished to go, Robert Cushman hired the "Mayflower," a much larger vessel. The "Speedwell" proved unseaworthy and its passengers were left behind, there not being room for them on the "Mayflower." One of them was Robert Cushman, who went with them to London to look after their interests and arrange for passage later.

In 1621 the "Fortune" was chartered, and carried thirty-six passengers, including Robert Cushman and his son, Thomas. He had arranged to return to London when the vessel went back, so he had only about a month to learn the sad news of the death of half of his friends of the "Mayflower" during the first winter. The day before he sailed he preached a sermon to his old friends, designed to give them hope and courage.

Though he was not a clergyman or teaching elder, it was a remarkable discourse and the first one delivered in New England that was printed.

He was most active and influential in securing a Charter for the Plymouth Colony and also for the first settlement of the Massachusetts Bay Colony at Cape Ann. He continued to perform his duties as agent of the Colony in London, and did his best to promote its interests.

He died somewhat suddenly in 1625 before he could return to America as he had planned. Governor Bradford said of him: "He was our right hand with the Adventurers, who for divers years has managed all our business with them to our great advantage."

His son, Thomas, who came with him, is the only child known, and through him the line continued.

Thomas, son of Robert Cushman, was born in England, February, 1608. He came to New England with his father in 1621, and remained in the family of Governor Bradford when his father returned to England.

In a letter his father entreated the Governor "to have a care for my boy as your own." He settled in that part of Plymouth now Kingston, and in 1635 was on the Jury. He was appointed successor to Elder Brewster in 1649, continuing in the office until his death, Dec. 11th, 1691. More than 43 years, the Church records say: "He has been a rich blessing to this church scores of years. He was grave, sober, holy and temperate, very studious for the peace and prosperity of the Church and to prevent and heal all breaches."

He married in 1636, Mary, daughter of Isaac Allerton, of the "Mayflower." He for several years was assistant to the Governor, and went to London five times in the interest of the Colony. He spent the latter part of his life in New Haven, where he died December 11th, 1691. She died at the age of ninety, surviving her husband, and was the last survivor of those who came over in the "Mayflower."

Their children, born in Plymouth, Thomas, Sarah, Lydia, Rev. Isaac, born Feb. 8th, 1647, a prominent minister, Deacon Elkanah June 1st, 1651, Feare, June 20, 1653, Eleazar, Feb. 20, 1656, and Mary.

3rd Gen.

Rev. Isaac Cushman, second son of Thomas and Mary (Allerton) Cushman, was born Feb. 8th 1638, at Plymouth, and died Oct. 22, 1732 at Plympton, Mass. He was a member of the Church at Plymouth, and obtained a better education than most men of that day. In 1685 he was one of the selectmen of Plymouth, and in June, 1690 he was elected a deputy to the general court, being associated in the same office with John Broadforce. The same men were selected deputies to another session held in August, same year. In June following they were again elected and attended the last session previous to the union, of the Plymouth and Massachusetts Colonies in 1692.

At the death of his father in 1691 he was chosen Ruling Elder. He was called to the pastorate of the Church in Middleboro, and of the new church established in Plympton. He accepted the latter and continued minister there from 1695 to 1732. His settlement there followed an extended controversy. He was more liberal in religious matters than his contemporaries, and secured the adoption of new articles of faith, which have remained to the present day, with little change as the creed of the Congregational Church.

At the time of his settlement in Plymouth he was in the prime of life and was evidently a very able man. Little is known of his talent as a preacher, none of his sermons having been printed, but he was among the most useful members of his profession. During his ministry of thirty-seven years, two hundred and forty-seven persons became members of the Church and he solemnized one hundred and forty-seven marriages.

The history of the church written by Louis Bradford says: He was a pious and godly man. He had not a college education. He used to preach without notes, but studied his sermons beforehand and committed to memory. Instead of a wig, he used to wear a black velvet cap. His salary in 1701 was thirty-five pounds, and it was increased from time to time till in 1728 was 85 pounds a year. He married, about 1675, Mary Rickard, born in 1654, died Sept. 27th, 1727 at Plympton. Children: Isaac, Rebeckah, Mary, Sarah, Ichabod, and Fear.

The following is used by the permission of Messrs. Little, Brown & Co. of Boston, Mass., published by them in 1855,

LITTLE, BROWN & COMPANY
PUBLISHERS
34 BEACON STREET, BOSTON

EDITORIAL DEPARTMENT

November 24, 1939

Mr. Alvah W. Burt
3031 Temple Avenue
Cincinnati, Ohio

Dear Mr. Burt:

In reply to your letter of November 21, any book published by us in 1855 is long out of copyright and as far as we are concerned you may use any of the material from it. We would not be interested in such a book as you describe but we are grateful to you for writing us.

Very truly yours,
LITTLE, BROWN & COMPANY

CBB:GH

entitled "HISTORICAL & BIOGRAPHICAL GENEALOGY OF THE CUSHMANS From 1617 to 1855" by Henry Wyles Cushman:

PREFACE

"To attend to the neglected and remember the forgotten" has ever been considered by the wise and good an object of great importance.

"Enquire, I pray thee, of the former age, and prepare thyself to the search of their fathers" is an injunction as well of patriotism and filial affection as of sacred writ.

Influenced by such sentiments, and desirous of saving from oblivion and of placing in an enduring form the character, principles and history, of my ancestors, I have now the satisfaction, after many years of labor, to present to the descendants of Robert Cushman, the Puritan, a complete Historical and Biographical Genealogy of the Cushman race and of those connected with them, for a period of two hundred and thirty-eight years.

That it has been a work of great labor, how much, no one but myself can ever know, must be obvious to all. But the old maxim, "Nil Magnum sine labore", and an anxious desire in this way to erect a monument to our name, more lasting than marble or granite, has carried me on through many trials, perplexities and discouragements, to the end.

It is now ten years since this work was commenced, and it has constantly grown on my hands to this day. At first I designed to publish the Cushman Genealogy in a pamphlet form, and now it makes a volume of over six hundred pages. It contains an account of more than doubly the number of Cushmans and others than I estimated, after I had made considerable progress in the work.

I am sensible that this volume is rather too large for convenience. It is twice as large as I supposed it would be. And even now I have left out, probably, a hundred printed pages of matter that I had prepared, much of which was valuable and interesting. Necessity compelled me to reduce many articles one half, and to leave out entirely, after the Seventh Generation, the children of Cushman Mothers, and also other names. This is my apology, I hope it may be satisfactory for omitting much that has been communicated to me.

In preparing this volume, my correspondence has necessarily extended to all parts of the United States, to the Canadas, England and France. I have written with my own hand and received over fourteen hundred letters.

Feeling that this was a work for the future more than the present, and that hereafter it will be used as authority for the facts here stated, I have aimed at great accuracy, and have entirely omitted what was apocryphal in its character—preferring to omit rather than misstate an event. Nevertheless, errors will doubtless be found; some, perhaps of the pen or the type, but more from the wrong information communicated to me, or from the impossibility of decyphering the chirography of many. While all have been cautioned "to give accurate dates and to write names so plain that they will not be mistaken," it has not always been done. How could I ascertain the date of a birth if it was given "1864" or "Feb. 31st" which has been done.

I have found that when persons relied on their memory for dates of births, marriages, etc. they have, frequently, been wrong. The memory is not sufficiently certain for such statements. Errors arising, from that cause, will, no doubt, be found, for I have in some cases corrected the memory by record evidence.

The latter has always been chosen, when practicable, as being most certain. I have taken unwearied pains and great labor to be right in names and dates, but I am sensible, for the reasons I have given above, that there will be found some that are incorrect. In the language of the Historian, Dr. Thatcher, I would say: "Should errors be detected in this work, the Author would only observe that perfect works come only from perfect Wisdom but if assiduity and care can bring any work to a respectable standard of correctness, he may in this instance have some ground to hope for public approbation."

It may appear that I have related too many minute circumstances and events. My answer is, that in my judgment minuteness and accuracy are the great and fundamental principles of a genealogical work. "Minuteness of detail", says an eminent historian, "is indispensable in the delineation of character or a faithful relation of transactions under the most trying circumstances." It is such a course that renders a genealogy to the historian and the antiquarian; and without them it would loose much of its value. As the ocean is composed of drops, so the history of a country is made up of the acts of each individual person. And those acts, in the aggregate, give the character of the people as well as an indication of the policy and administration of the government. Hence the importance of genealogies.

In compiling this work, I have, as far as practicable, used the language of others, including records, obituaries and autobiographies, believing that such a course would be more valuable and more acceptible than any language of my own. I owe an apology for using the auto-biography of several persons, without their consent. I trust I shall be forgiven.

The orthography of proper names being entirely arbitrary, and every person having the undoubted right to spell the names of their children as they please, I have made it a rule to follow the copy that has been furnished me, although that has led to different ways of spelling the same name. If I have, therefore, spelled any name wrong, the blame must be laid to those who furnished such spelling. Time has worked great changes with names, as with other things. For example, the name which is now spelled Zurviah, was formerly spelled Zuruiah, which made a different name of it. By custom of society, Sally has been changed to Sarah; Molly to Mary; Susannah to Susan, etc., and other changes are now in progress, such as William to Willie, James to Jamie, Caroline to Carrie, Elizabeth to Lizzie, etc.

In some cases I have found one name in the early record of a birth or baptism, changed by the person, as Sally, written Sarah. This may lead to some confusion. I have always given the name that has been communicated to me, whether right or wrong, for I have had no means of making the correction.

Residences are always given when known, as they serve to distinguish those of the same Christian name. When the person has lived in several towns, he is called of that town where he lived the longest, or where he died.

In regard to the Origin of the Cushman race we are in great doubt. It is quite certain we are not from Cush, the son of Ham (Vide 10th Chap. Genesis) for, by the common translation, the descendants of Ham were of the African or Negro races. And we find in our family no traces, either phrenological or ethnological of that race. But if the theory of Mr. Gliddon in his work on "The Types of Mankind" is correct, that the common translation of Genesis is incorrect, and that the descendants of Cush were Arabian, then we may possibly have come from that race. But all such speculations are, necessarily, crude and uncertain.

Some have supposed we are of German origin, from the name of "Kaughman" which is found in Germany, and are, therefore of Anglo-German blood. But there is no doubt but that, at a later period we were of English descent.

In regard to the formation of the name, it probably originated in this way; at first it was the Man of Cush—a place,—and in time, by a very natural change, it became Cush-man.

It has been supposed by some that Cush-ing and Cush-man were from the same origin. But there is no evidence of that fact, and we are of the opinion that the names were never synonymous, but were of entirely different races.

The race whose history I have here portrayed is not one that has been remarkably celebrated. "I am not preserving from oblivion the names of heroes whose chief merit was the overthrow of cities, provinces and empires, but the names of the founders of a flourishing town and colony, if not of the whole American Republic." I have found but few who have been very remarkable for their genius or their talents, and few who, according to the common remark of the old world, have been or are very wealthy. On the other hand I have never found among the descendants of Robert Cushman, the Puritan, a single pauper, or person of adult age, that could not read and write. Out of nearly thirty-four hundred, whose history I have here given, I have found only two who have been sentenced to a penitentiary, and only three who have been convicted of any felonious violations of the law. And I have enquired for the bad deeds as well as the good.

A very large proportion of Cushmans have been and now

are, farmers and mechanics. Hence they have been persons of good morals and reputation. Benevolence and veneration seem to be prominent in the physical organization of the family. Hence we find the religious sentiment extensively prevailing among them. The first three generations were persons of deep, ardent and practical piety, and their organization and example have extended to their descendants. These facts may well excite a laudable pride in the heart of every descendant of our Puritan ancestor.

I feel it my duty to acknowledge my obligation to many persons who have cheerfully and perseveringly aided me in my genealogical labors. I should be glad to name them all if I had space. I have in several cases mentioned them in the body of this work. But I am particularly indebted to Bezaleel Cushman of Portland, Maine, for very great assistance. The Genealogy of a very large number of families in Maine was collected and arranged by him in the very best manner. I am also greatly indebted to Don Alonzo Cushman of New York City.; Thomas Cushman of Bridgewater who has been a great searcher of the early records; Capt. A. C. Cushman of New Bedford; Mrs. Maria J. Cushman of Troy, N. Y.; Charles U. Cushman of Newburgh, N. Y.; Robert S. and William M. C. Cushman of Albany, N. Y.; Rev. Robert W. Cushman, Dr. N. B. Shurtleff and Samuel A. Eaton of Boston and Charles Ketcham of Penn Yan, N. Y. for their valuable correspondence and services. I wish also, to express my thanks to S. Y. Drake, Esq. of Boston, Editor of Genealogical Register; to Wm. S. Russell, Esq. of Plymouth; J. W. Thornton, Esq. of Boston and H. G. Somerby, Esq., now resident in England, as well as other gentlemen not connected with the family, for valuable assistance and advice in preparing this work.

My letters have generally, been promptly answered. A few have made me extra labor and trouble by their procrastination in replying to my enquiries. If any such should read these lines, let them be admonished to be more punctual hereafter. I must say however, that among my female correspondents (and I have had quite a number) they have all been prompt in their replies, and have been the most intelligent and valuable auxiliaries in my extended researches.

In hundreds of cases I have received the most encouraging sympathy and approval of my work. Scarcely a letter has come to hand that did not contain a "God Speed" to my labors. One single exception has occurred. One Cushman desired *not* to have his name mentioned in this book. For the honor of our name I rejoice there is but one. His request has been complied with.

Old and New Style

Previous to the year 1752 the dates of births are usually given in O. S. To change Old Style to New Style add ten (10) days to all dates previous to the year 1700. Eleven days to all dates from 1700 to 1800 and 12 days from 1800 to 1900.

The practice of double dating, as it was called, of all dates previous to the year 1752 the legal or ecclesiastical years commenced on the 25th day of March. While the historical year commenced Jan. 1st. In 1751 it was changed by an act of Parliament, and the year was to commence the 1st of January, beginning with 1752.

As the dates from Jan. 1st to March 24th inclusive, previous to 1752, were usually written thus,—1673-4 or 1673/4.

HISTORICAL AND BIOGRAPHICAL GENEALOGY OF THE CUSHMANS

The Descendants of Robert Cushman, the Puritan, from the Year of 1617 to 1855

By Henry Wyles Cushman

Robert Cushman the ancestor of all the Cushmans in the United States was born in England probably between the years 1580 and 1585. In his opinions he was a non-conformist or Puritan, and was of that band of pilgrims who left their native country for the sake of worshiping God according to the dictates of their own consciences.

In order to understand correctly the principles, character and acts of the men who made the first settlement in New England, at Plymouth, which subsequently have had such a predominating and controlling influence in the civilization of the whole world, it is necessary to glance at the political and theological position of England for one or two centuries previous to this event.

About the year 1534, the reformation of the Roman Catholic religion by Calvin, Luther and their colleagues, having extensively prevailed in England separated the protestants gradually into two classes; one of these united with the English Government, contended for hereditary prerogative and monarchial rights, claimed the civil government, per-se was the head of the church; that the church, of right, owed obedience and subservency to the Crown and thus Church and State were united, constituting the established Church of England, which has continued to this day.

On the other hand, another body of men, strong in intellect and of a deep religious feeling, advocated the entire separation of the Church and State. They had seen and felt the corruption and tyranny of Papacy, and they were deeply grieved to see the Church which they had venerated and loved, taking any of the forms or symbols of "the old dragon of Rome."

Protestants in religion, they were also deeply tinctured with republican views of government, and thus while opposing the established Church they imbibed hatred to the Crown which sustained the Church. Such was the state of things generally during the reign of Elizabeth, one of the ablest and wisest of the English sovereigns.

In the early part of the sixteenth century, the dread of a common enemy, the Papal Church, kept these two parties of Protestants from an open rupture, but during the latter part of that century, the breach between them was widened, there was no external force to keep them together. A separation, very natural and inevitable, was the consequence[1], and persecution on the part of the civil government and the hierarchy confirmed them more fully in their opinions, and made them more determined in their acts. Says Macaulay, "It found them a Sect, it made them a Faction."

As the controversy increased, the persecutions became more

---

[1]The settlement of New England was a result of the Reformation; not of the contest between the new opinions and the authority of Rome but of implacable differences between Protestant dissenters and the established Anglican Church.—Bancroft's History of the United States.

violent. Stripes, fines, imprisonment, death even, were often suffered by these men for the faith that was in them. At first they were called seceders, non-conformists, dissenters, and afterwards Brownists and Puritans. And it is a singular and quite a suggestive fact that the name of Puritan, which in the latter periods became so popular and renowned, was first given them as a term of reproach and disrespect.[1]

In the year 1564 their lordships began to show their authority by urging the Clergy of their several dioceses to subscribe the liturgy, ceremonies and discipline of the church, when those that refused were first called Puritans, a name of reproach, derived from the Cathari or Puritan of the third century after Christ. "A Puritan was therefore, a man of severe morals, a Calvinist in doctrine and a non-conformist to the doctrines and ceremonies of the Church though they did not totally separate from it."—Neals History of the Puritans.

Towards the close of the sixteenth and the early part of the seventeenth centuries, the persecution of those who dissented from the established Church of England was carried to the greatest extent.

They were treated as criminals, and were subjected to all sorts of indignities and punishment. "I will have one doctrine and one discipline, one religion in substance and ceremony" said King James in 1604.[2]

In order to show the manifest injustice of the course pursued by the English Government and the Anglican Church towards the Puritans, we insert here a concise statement of

---

"The era of the English Puritans, properly begins in 1550, when Hooper for a time refused to be consecrated in the ecclesiastical habits. An old writer quoted by Prince, says: "They are called Puritans who would have the Church radically reformed: that is purged from all those inventions which have been brought into it since the age of the Apostles, and reduced entirely to the scripture purity."—Young's Chronicles.

[1] "And to cast contempt the more on the sincere servants of God, they opprobriously and injuriously gave unto and imposed upon them that name of Puritans."—Bradford.

[2] For some were taken and clapped up in prisons, others had their houses watched by night and day, and hardly escaped their hands; and the most were fain to fly and leave their houses and habitations and the means of their livelihood.—Bradford in Young.

the doctrine maintained and the principles held by these men. The Puritan doctrines were:

1st. That Private judgment ought to be formed upon examination, and that religion is a free and unforced thing.

2nd. They hold and maintain the absolute perfection of the Holy Scriptures, both as to faith and worship.

3rd. That every congregation or assembly of men ordinarily joining together in the worship of God, is a true, visible worship of Christ.

4th. That all such churches are equal and independent.[1] "But the severities against the Puritans, instead of reconciling them to the Church, drove them further from it; for men do not come to be beat from their principles by the artillery of cannons, injunctions and penal laws, nor can they be in love with a Church that uses such methods of conversion."

As a natural result, therefore, of the persecutions of the Crown, Church and Government of England, these men became more thoroughly convinced of the errors of the established Church and of the truth, soundness and importance of their own religious views and worship.

They were men such as have been found in all ages of the world, of radical minds and deep religious feelings, who place the will as they understand it, before every thing else in the world, and who will sacrifice office, property and the dearest relations of life, and will even suffer death in the most cruel forms, rather than disobey the "Higher Law" of conscience and of God. Such men are seldom found among courtiers, officers of government or men of great wealth or power, but in the midling walks of life. The main body of them came from the small freeholders in the country and the shopkeepers and mechanics in the towns.[2]

In the north of England, in the rural districts, and particularly in the counties of Nottinghamshire, Lincolnshire and Yorkshire, men of such organizations were more generally found. A common sympathy made them acquaintances and associates, and suffering in a common cause, united their hearts

---

[1] Neal's History of the Puritans.
[2] Macauley's History of England.

and hands in a common organization for the purpose of religious worship. They manfully resolved, "whatever it should cost them, to enjoy liberty of conscience."

Two churches were therefore formed in the northeastern part of England, composed of members, we may suppose, widely separated, uniting at some central point for religious worship in such a manner as they thought right. Of one of these churches Mr. John Smith, "a man of able gifts, and a good preacher," became pastor. The members of this church emigrated to Holland; but "adopting some errors in the low countries" they finally disbanded and it became extinct.

Of the other church, the Rev. Richard Clifton "a man of grave deportment and a successful preacher" had the pastoral care. To this church belonged the Rev. John Robinson, afterwards its pastor, Elder Brewster, Gov. Carver, Gov. Bradford, Mr. Robert Cushman, Isaac Allerton and others, who made the first settlement at Plymouth. This church commenced holding its meetings at the house of Elder Brewster, in the town of Scroiby, about the year 1602; and as a consequence the power of the hierarchy, that controlled the government, was brought more directly and severely upon them.

At this day of perfect religious freedom, it seems most astonishing that men should have been fined, imprisoned, whipped, almost starved, and even burned at the stake, merely for their religious belief, and that but a little more than two centuries ago. In truth it may be said of the church, as well as of civil government, that

"Man's inhumanity to Man
Makes countless thousands mourn."

The men who formed Mr. Robinson's church, were many of them persons of good education and of superior minds and judgments. It is a source of much regret that the early history of these men is, comparatively, unknown. Recent investigations have brought to light something in that particular; and it is most ardently hoped that further examinations will give us more knowledge of the origin of these men, who with great truth it may be said, were "founders of our Republic."

To such an extent were the persecutions of the Puritans

carried, increasing with every passing year, that during the years 1607 and 1608, they resolved "with joint consent, to remove to Holland, where they heard was freedom of religion for all men."

"Hard was their lot to leave their dwellings, their lands and relations, to go, they knew not where, to obtain a living, they knew not how." But though persecuted, they were not dismayed; though distressed, their courage did not forsake them. Resolved to go, they were not even allowed to depart in peace.

The strong arm of the law barred every harbor and vessel against them. Yet with perseverance that would overcome all obstacles, they finally succeeded, and left forever their native land, actuated by the highest human motives, "the right to worship God according to the dictates of their own consciences."

"1609. This spring more of Mr. Robinson's church, through great difficulties from the pursuers, got over to Holland, and afterwards the rest, with Mr. Robinson and Mr. Brewster, who are of the last, having tarried to help the weakest over before them."[1] They first settled at Amsterdam, but seeing the evils and contentions of Rev. Smith's church, after remaining there about a year, they removed to Leyden, and there made a permanent settlement. "There they grew in gifts and grace; they lived in peace and love and holiness. Numbers came to them from England; they had a great congregation, at one time numbering three hundred communicants."

"1610. This year comes out a justification of separation from the Church of England, by John Robinson, 476 pages in quarto—and about this time and the following year, many came to this church at Leyden, from divers parts of England, so as they grew a great congregation."[2]

Having remained at Leyden eight or nine years, they began to examine their situation and to think of emigrating to America. They foresaw the obvious fact, that in course of time they must become merged with the Dutch, by whom they were surrounded. With the most lofty notions of religious liberty, with a deep conviction of the value and importance

---

[1]Bradford, in Prince's New England Chronology.
[2]Prince.

of religion to the souls of men, and its influence in moulding the character as well as the institutions of the age, and with an anxious desire "to spread the Gospel among the Heathen" they began to think of emigrating in a body to this, then uncultivated and uncivilized land. But how could it be done? was the great question.[1]

A company had been formed in England under the Royal sanction called the Virginia Company, whose authority extended over a considerable portion of the North American Continent.

After a long consultation and much consideration, "after their humble prayers unto God for his direction and assistance," it was finally resolved to make an application to that company at London for liberty to settle in the Company's territory in North America, and "to see if the King would give them Liberty of conscience there." For that purpose Mr. Robert Cushman and Deacon John Carver[2] two of the most active, reliable and judicious members of their community, were selected to go to London in the year 1617 and open negotiations for that purpose.

And this is the first mention that is made, in the history, of that period, of Mr. Robert Cushman[3] and it should be here noticed that Governor Bradford, Mortons Memorial, and other contemporaneous writers, are all scrupulously particular in adding to his name the honourable prefix of "Mr." an undoubted indication, at that time, of a conventional superiority

---

[1] "After the Puritans at Leyden had resolved on their 'terminus quo,' the next and not less difficult question was the 'terminus ad quere'."

[2] "Mr. Cushman, one of the members of the church, and Mr. Carver, one of the Deacons, were dispatched to England as agents of the exiled company, to seek permission of the King to settle in some parts of Virginia."—Ashton's Memoir of Rev. John Robinson.

[3] It is deeply regretted that the early history of Robert Cushman and his colleagues, in the great work of establishing religious liberty and of founding a nation is so little known. Not a single circumstance of himself or his family or ancestors is known, up to the time when he and Governor Carver were appointed on the mission to England, as above stated. The birthplace, genealogy, and early history of Governor Bradford, having been recently brought to light, it is hoped that like success will crown the efforts that are now in progress to give the same information of Robert Cushman.

and a comparatively high degree of education, talents, and of the Christian profession and virtues.

Messrs. Cushman and Carver went to England, probably in the spring or summer of 1617. But they soon found their mission a difficult one. The Virginia Company were willing and desirous to have them go to their colony on the James River in Virginia. They would grant them a patent to the soil, "With as ample privileges as they had granted or could grant to any," and some of the "chief of the Company" were of the opinion that the King would grant "their suit for liberty in religion."[1] The Virginia Company, thinking to make a profit by it urged the King, through one of his principal secretaries, (Sir Robert Naunton) to grant their request. He would give them liberty to settle in America; for, in truth, he was anxious to get rid of them. But it was a "Sina qua non" with the Puritans, to have freedom of religious worship, or not to move. Hence they contended stoutly for that point. "But it proved all in vain. He would connive at them and not molest them. But to allow or tolerate them by his public authority, under his seal, they found it would not be granted."[2]

After a long and tedious negotiation, Messrs. Cushman and Carver returned to their friends at Leyden, with the best terms they could make, and "to what issue things had come." But the result was entirely unsatisfactory. They had no confidence either in the honesty or toleration of King James.

The Envoys of the Leyden Church probably returned in November, 1617, for they carried with them a letter from Sir Edwin Sandys, directed to Mr. John Robinson and Mr. William Brewster, dated November 12th, 1617, in which he says,—"After my hearty salutation,—the agents of your congregation, Robert Cushman and John Carver, have been in communication with divers select gentlemen of His Majesty's

---

[1]Sir Ferdinando Gorges, one of the leaders of the second or Plymouth Company, says, "It was necessary that means might be used to draw into those enterprises some of those families that had retired themselves into Holland for scruples of conscience, giving them such liberty and freedom as might stand to their likings," and that advice was harkened to, etc.—Mass. Hist. Coll., XXVI, 73.

[2]Bradford's Journal.

Council for Virginia; and by writing of several articles, subscribed with your names, have given them that good degree of satisfaction which hath carried them on with a resolution to set forward your desire in the best sort that may be for your own and the public good; divers particulars whereof we leave to their faithful report, having carried themselves here with that good discretion, as is both to their own and their credit from whom they came. And whenever, being to treat for a multitude of people, they have requested further time to confer with them that are to be interested in this action about the several particulars which in the prosecution thereof will fall out considerable, it hath been very willingly assented to; and so they do now return to you.[1] If therefore, it may please God so to direct your desires, as that on your parts there fall out no just impediments, I trust by the same direction it shall likewise appear that on our parts all forwardness to set you forward shall be found in the best sort, which with reason may be expected. And so I betake you with this design, (which I hope verily is the work of God) to the gracious protection and blessing of the Highest. Your very loving friend. London, Nov. 12th, 1617.—Edwin Sandys."[2]

After a full, deliberate and prayerful consideration of the terms offered by the Virginia Company and the King, the Leyden Church sent again the same agents, Messrs. Cushman and Carver, to urge upon the King the great point with them "Freedom to worship God." This fact is evident from the reply of Messrs. Robinson and Brewster to the foregoing letter of Sir Edwin Sandys. Their answer was as follows:

"Right Worshipful,—Our humble duties remembered, in our own, our messengers and our churches name, with all thankful acknowledgment of your singular love, expressing itself as otherwise so more especially in your great care and earnest

---

[1] From the expression "They do *now* return to you" it is evident the Agents must have returned to Leyden soon after the letter was written, of which they were undoubtedly the bearers,—that is between Nov. 12th, the date of the letter, and Dec. 15th, the date of Robinson's and Brewster's answer to it.—Young's Chronicles.

[2] Sir Edwin Sandys was one of the principal members of the Virginia Company. He was a member of Parliament, and was ever a sincere, devoted and active friend of Mr. Robinson's Church. He died in 1629.

endeavor of our good in the weighty business about Virginia, which the less able we are to requite, we shall think ourselves the more bound to commend in our prayers unto God for recompense.

We have with the best speed and consideration with all that we could, set down our requests in writing, subscribed as you willed, with the hands of the greatest part of our congregation, and have sent the same unto the council, by an agent, a deacon of our church, John Carver, unto whom we have also requested a gentleman of our company to adjoin himself; to the care and discretion of which two we do refer the prosecuting of the business.

Now we persuade ourselves, right worshipful, that we need not to provoke our godly loving mind to any further or more tender care of us, since you have pleased so far to interest us in yourself, that, under God, above all persons and things in the world, we rely upon you, expecting the care of your love, the counsel of your wisdom and the help and countenance of your authority."

This interesting letter, the largest part of which we omit, was dated "Leyden, Dec. 15th, 1617" and was, undoubtedly, carried to England by Messrs. Cushman and Carver.[1] But they had no better success than before. For, says Governor Bradford's Journal, "The Virginia Council was now so disturbed by factions and quarrels amongst themselves, as no business could well go forward."

But these men were not to be dismayed with disappoint-

---

[1]There is a general impression that Cushman and Carver went to England but once in the early part of these negotiations. But from an examination of Governor Bradford's Journal and the correspondence between Robinson and Brewster and Sir Edwin Sandys and others in England it is evident that the agents, Messrs. Cushman and Carver, went over to England from Holland on that mission first in the summer of 1617, and afterwards the bearer of Robinson's and Brewster's letter, which we have given above, in December, 1617. Says Governor Bradford's Journal, "These things being long in agitation, and messengers passing to and again about them, after all their hopes they were long delayed by many obstacles that fell in the way. For at the return of these messengers into England, they found things far otherwise than they expected."

ments or discouraged by the want of present success. For, says Bradford's and Brewster's letter, "We verily believe, and trust the Lord is with us, unto whom and whose service we have given ourselves in many trials, and that he will graciously prosper our endeavors according to the simplicity of our hearts therein.

And it is not with us as with other men, whom small things can discourage, or small discontentments cause to wish themselves home again.

Persevering in this matter, therefore, the Leyden Church after a considerable delay, appointed two other agents to go to England and urge their requests. Those Agents were Robert Cushman and William Brewster.[1] They probably went over in the early part of 1619, and pursued the great object of their desires with a zeal, perseverance and ability worthy of the cause.

To accomplish an object to the Puritans so important, to carry on a negotiation with a weak, dishonest and pusilanimous administration, and to procure a grant of what was then so universally denied by nerely all governments, was indeed, a great task, and required a skill at diplomacy which but few men possessed. Yet notwithstanding "the great discouragements the agents met with, from the King and Bishop's refusing to allow them liberty of conscience," they persevered. "Trusting in God and in themselves" they were not dismayed.

On the 8th of May, 1619, Robert Cushman wrote the following letter to Rev. Mr. Robinson and the Leyden Church:

To His Loving Friends

I had thought long since to have writ unto you; but could not effect that which I aimed at neither can yet set things as I wished. Yet, notwithstanding, I doubt not but Mr. Brewster has written to Mr. Robinson; but I think myself bound also to do something, lest I be thought to neglect you.

The main hindrance of our proceedings in the Virginia business is the dissentions and factions, as they term it, amongst the Council of the Company of Virginia, which are such that ever since we came up no business could by them be despatched.

The occasion of this trouble amongst them, is that a while since Sir Thomas Smith, repining at his many offices and troubles, wished the Company of Virginia to ease him of his office in being treasurer, and governor of the Virginia Company. Whereupon the Company took occasion to dismiss him, and chose Sir Edwin Sandys treasurer and governor of the Company, he having sixty voices, Sir John Wolstenholme, sixteen voices, and alderman Johnson twenty-four. But Sir Thomas Smith, when he saw some part of his honor lost, was very angry, and raised a faction to cavil and contend about the election, and sought to tax Sir Edwin with many things that might both disgrace him and also put him by his office of Governor. In which contentions they yet stick, and are not fit nor ready to intermeddle in any business; and what issue things will come to, I know not, nor are we yet certain. It is most like Sir Edwin will carry it away; and if he do, things will go well in Virginia; if otherwise, they will go ill enough always. We hope in two or three Court days things will settle. Mean space I think to go down into Kent, and come up again about fourteen days or three weeks hence; except either by their aforesaid contentions, or by the ill tidings from Virginia, we be wholly discouraged, of which tidings as followeth.

Capt. Argall is come home this week. He, upon notice of the intent of the Council, came away before Sir George Yeardley came there, and so there was no small dissention. But his tidings is ill, although his person be welcome. He saith Mr. Blackwell's ship came not there until March; but going towards winter they had still northwest winds, which carried them to the Southward beyond their course; and the master of the ship and some six of mariners dying, it seemed they could not find the Bay, till after long seeking and beating about.

Mr. Blackwell is dead, and Mr. Maggner, the Captain, Yea there are dead, he saith, a hundred and thirty persons, one and other, in the ship.

It is said there was in all a hundred and eighty persons in the ship, so as they were packed together like herrings. They had amongst them a flux, and also a want of fresh water; so as it is here rather wondered that so many are alive, than that so many are dead. The merchants here say it was Mr. Blackwell's fault to pack so many in the ship; Yea, and there was a great murmuring and repining amongst them, and upbraiding of Mr. Blackwell for his dealing and disposing of them, when they saw how he had disposed of them and how he insulted over them. Yea, the streets at Gravesand rang of their extreme quarreling, crying out one of another, "Thou hast brought me to this, I may thank thee for this." Heavy news it is, and I would be glad to hear how far it will discourage. I see none here discouraged much, but rather desire to learn to beware by other men's harms, and to amend that wherein they have failed; as we desire to serve one another in love, so take heed of being enthralled by other imperious persons, especially if they be discerned to have an eye to themselves.

It doth often trouble me to think that in this business we are to learn and none to teach, but better so than to depend upon such teachers as Mr. Blackwell was.

Such a stratagem he made for Mr. Johnson and his people at Emden; much was their subversion. But though he then cleanlily yet unhonestly plucked his neck out of the collar, yet at last his foot is caught.

Here are no letters come. The ship Captain Argall came in, is yet in the west parts. All that we hear is but his report. It seemeth he came away secretly. The ship Mr. Blackwell went in will be here shortly. It is as Mr. Robinson once said, he thought we should hear no good of them. Mr. Brewster is not well at this time. Whether he will go back to you or go into the north, I yet know not. For myself, I hope to see an end of this business ere I come, though I am sorry to be thus from you. If things had gone roundly forward, I should have been with you within this fourteen days. I pray God direct us, and give us that spirit which is fitting such a business.

Thus having summarily pointed at things which Mr. Brewster, I think, hath more largely writ of to Mr. Robinson, I leave you to the Lord's protection. Yours in all readiness at London, May 8th, 1619. Robert Cushman.

On Sept. 4th, 1619, a Mr. Sabin Starsmore "a Puritan," writing from prison to Deacon Carver, dated "from my chamber in Wood Street counter,"[1] says respecting his imprisonment, "Somewhat I have written to Mr. Cushman how the matter still continues," etc.

After great procrastination and long tedious negotiations, the prospects of the Leyden Church brighten, and success seems to crown the labors and trials of their agents. A patent is finally obtained, under the grant seal of the Virginia Company, and "connived at" by the King and his ministers, by which they were allowed to settle in America. And although religious liberty, in terms, was not granted them, yet, if they behaved themselves quietly and were faithful subjects of his Majesty, King James I. they were not to be molested although their creed and form of worship were essentially unsound and heretical.

The patent was not taken out in the names of any of Mr. Robinson's Church—probably on account of their living out of the realm—but in the name of John Wincob,[1] a religious gentleman (belonging to the Countess of Lincoln) who intended to emigrate with the Puritans.

"But Providence so ordered it" as Governor Bradford's Journal says "He never went and the patent,[2] in his name, was never used, although it had cost them so much labor and charge."

But a determination to emigrate had so completely filled the minds of the Leyden Puritans that they were not to be daunted by misfortunes or rebuffs. They felt that their cause was *right*, and that God would finally, in his own good time, aid and prosper them.

"Up in each girded breast
There sprang a rooted and mysterious strength,—
A loftiness,—to face a world in arms,—
To strip the pomp from Scepters,—and to lay
upon the Sacred Alter the warm blood

---

[1]Nothing is known of John Wincob, except that he was the protege of the Countess of Lincoln, and was probably her Steward, or private secretary, as we now say.

[2]Nothing further of this patent is known. Hubbard's History says, "Where it is or how it came to be lost, is not known to any that belong to the Colony." It was probably dated the latter part of 1619.

of slain affections, where they rise between
the Soul and God."
—The Pilgrims, by Mrs. Sigourney.

Thus situated, they looked for other ways to accomplish their objects. The projects of settling in the New World began to be somewhat popular; it gains friends and friendly opinions. "Mr. Thomas Weston, merchant of London, and other friends and merchants make proposals for their transmigration, and they were requested to prepare to go."[1]

On the receipt of these things by one of the messengers, they had a solemn meeting, and a day of humiliation to seek the Lord for his direction. Their pastor, Rev. Mr. Robinson, took for his text "First Samuel, 23:3 and 4. 'And David's men said unto him, See we be afraid here in Judah. How much more if we come to Kilah, against the host of the Philistines. Then David asked counsel of the Lord again.' From that text he taught many things very aptly and befitting to their present occasion and condition, to strengthen them against their fears, and encourage them in their resolution."[2]

Having determined to emigrate to America, the question arose, who should go first; for so large a number could not all go at once. Winslow's brief Narrative says, "The youngest and strongest part go,—and they that went should offer themselves freely."

As the largest number could not go, it was arranged that their Pastor, Rev. Mr. Robinson, should remain, and their Ruling Elder, William Brewster, should go; and that those who go first were to constitute an absolute Church of themselves. The Church at Plymouth thus became the "First Independent or Congregational Church in America."[3]

The great object that was ever uppermost in the minds of the Puritans, undoubtedly was, "freedom of religious belief and worship"—Yet their secular wants and their new home, as well as means for the purpose of getting there, must be provided for. To accomplish the latter, a kind of stock com-

---

[1] Prince's Chronology.
[2] Bradford's Journal.
[3] Young's Chronicle, No. 3. Smith's History of Virginia.

pany was formed, composed of those who were to emigrate, on the one hand, and those who were to furnish the capital, on the other. The latter were called "The Merchant Adventurers", of whom little is known. Capt. John Smith, writing in 1624, says, "The adventurers who raised the stock to begin and supply this plantation, were about 70,—some gentlemen, some merchants, some handicraftsmen; some adventuring great sums, some small, as their estate and affections served."

"These dwell mostly about London. They are not a corporation, but knit together by a voluntary combination, in a society without constraint or penalty, aiming to do good and plant religion."[3]

"The conditions on which those of Leyden engaged with the merchants, the adventurers, were hard enough at first for the poor people who were to adventure their persons as well as their estates."

"Yet were their agents forced to change two of them, although it was very unsatisfactory and distasteful to them. The altering of these two conditions was very afflicting to them who were concerned in the voyage. But Mr. Cushman, their principal agent, answered their complaints peremptorily, that unless they had so ordered the conditions, the whole design would have fallen to the ground."

"The Puritans submitted, therefore, from necessity; but the sequel of the transaction shows that while the adventurers made but little profit from the investment, "Yet those that adventured their lives in carrying on the business of the plantation, were much the greatest sufferers."[1]

The contract between the adventurers and those who were to emigrate, is contained in ten articles of agreement. They provide generally, that "Their joint stock and partnership shall continue for seven years; that every person that goeth, over sixteen years of age, shall be rated at £10; and that £10 shall be accounted a single share.

---

[1]Bradford's Journal.

At the end of seven years the entire property of the association is to be equally divided among the adventurers."[1]

Hard as were these two terms, they were the best that could be obtained, and it is fortunate for the cause of civil and religious liberty in after ages, that they knew little how hard they would prove to those who consented to accept them.

We have given a more particular account of the preliminary contract and arrangements of the Puritans, because the subject of this article—Robert Cushman—was the principal agent and manager in that affair. And from what he did we may form a tolerably accurate opinion of his abilities and character, and his standing with his associates.

The Agents of the Leyden Company, Messrs. Cushman and Brewster, having formed the Association or Joint Stock Company in England which was to furnish the money, went back to Leyden with the Articles of agreement, ten in number, Mr. Weston,[2] a wealthy merchant of Leyden with them, "and the people agree with him on articles, both for shipping and money, to assist in their transportation."

The preliminaries being then all arranged, and the persons selected who were to commence this hazardous and uncertain enterprise, they send Mr. Cushman and Mr. Carver to England to receive the money and provide for the voyage; Mr. Cushman at London and Mr. Carver at Southampton. Those who are to go first, prepare with speed, sell their estates, put their money in the common stock, to be disposed of by their managers for making general provisions. There was also one

---

[1]The two conditions the alteration of which was so afflictive to those who were to form the settlement, related to a division of their houses, improved lands and gardens; and second that the planters should have two days in the week for their own private employment. These two provisions were in the original agreement; but were stricken out, as Robert Cushman told them, from absolute necessity.

We can easily see that it must have been a severe trial to submit to such hard terms. But necessity, they said, having no law, they were constrained to be silent.

[2]Thomas Weston, one of the most active of the Merchant Adventurers. He advanced £500 to promote the interest of the Plymouth Colony, but afterward became inimical to his former friends.

Mr. Martin[1] chosen in England to join unto Mr. Carver and Cushman. He came from Billerica, in Essex, from which county came several others, as also from London and other places to go with them.[2] But in this great and difficult work, like most others, delays and disappointments often occurred; they are among the incidents of humanity, designed, undoubtedly, for our benefit; and the Pilgrims could not expect to be exempt from the ordinary laws of creation. But to them, doubtless, it was as troublesome as those who live 230 years later.

"June 4th, 1620 Mr. Robinson writes to Mr. Carver, and complains of Mr. Weston's neglect in getting shipping in England; for want of which they are in a piteous case at Leyden. And Samuel Fuller, Edward Winslow, William Bradford and Isaac Allerton write from Leyden to Mr. Carver and Mr. Cushman June 10 that the coming of Mr. Nash and their pilot is a great encouragement to them."

The shipping that Mr. Robinson so much desired, was undoubtedly a vessel to carry the Emigrants from Leyden to Southampton. The "Speedwell" was finally obtained in Holland for that purpose. She was commanded by an English captain by the name of Reynolds, and it was their design to keep her in their new settlement for the purpose of trade and commerce.

"June 10th, 1620 Mr. Cushman in a letter from London to Mr. Carver at Southampton[3] says that Mr. Crabe, a minister, has promised to go, but is much oppressed, and is like to fail, and in a letter to the people at Leyden, that he had hired an-

---

[1]Christopher Martin, who with his wife and two children, came over in the Mayflower, his name stands the ninth in the subscription to the compact, signed at Cape Cod, November 11th, 1620, O. S., and he died January 8th, 1621.—Young's Chronicles.

[2]Bradford's Journal.

[3]It is a singular fact that the truth of history is falsified with great painting of the Embarkation of the Pilgrims, at Delf Haven, Holland, now in the Rotunda at Washington, by Weir, where Mr. Carver is represented as one of the most conspicuous characters in the painting; when in fact he was at that time at Southampton, actively engaged in making arrangements for their final departure. (See Bradford's Journal.)

other pilot, one Mr. Clark,[1] who went last year to Virginia; that he is getting a ship; hopes he shall make all ready at London in fourteen days, and would have Mr. Reynolds tarry in Holland and bring the ship thence to Southampton."[2]

But the time for their departure was at hand. "After much travail and turmoils and debates which they went through, things were gotten ready for their departure from Leyden." The little ship, "The Speedwell", had been purchased, and was lying at Delft Haven, a commodious port on the Maas, twenty-four miles south of Leyden, all ready to transport those who were to go from the Leyden Church to meet others and a larger ship at Southampton. The Speedwell was a ship of only sixty (or as Smith and Purchase say of Seventy) tuns Burthen, smaller than the average size of the fishing smacks that go to the Grand Bank for Cod fish,—too small, it would seem, to cross an almost unknown ocean. Yet it was of the ordinary size of vessels of that day for such purposes.

In the meantime Cushman had been actively engaged in the part assigned to him. He had hired at London a larger vessel, the Mayflower,[3] "of burden about nine score" and had sent her round to Southampton, there to meet his comrades from Holland.

The Speedwell being ready, they had a day of Solemn humiliation, their pastor taking for his text Ezra, 8th Chapter, 21st verse: "And there, at the river, by Ahava, I proclaimed a fast, that we might humble ourselves before our God and seek of him a right way for us, and for our children, and for all our substance." Upon which, he spent a good part of the day very profitably and suitably to their present occasion. The rest of the time was spent in pouring out prayers to the Lord with great fervency, mixed with an abundance of tears.

The Rev. Mr. Robinson's farewell discourse, a portion of

---

[1]Clark was Master's mate on board of the Mayflower—Clark's Island in Plymouth Harbor was named after him.

[2]Bradford in Prince.

[3]The Mayflower has become a ship of world renown. Besides carrying the Pilgrims safely to their destination, she was one of the five vessels, which in 1629, conveyed Higginson's Company to Salem, and also one of the fleet which in 1630 brought over Governor Winthrop and his Colony to Massachusetts Bay.—(Savage's Winthrop.)

which is included in "Winslow's Brief Narrative" contains certain sentiments far in advance of the age in which he lived, and which show him to have been a man of an enlarged, noble and truly Christian mind. As the ages advance, and men approximate nearer to a practice of the pure principles of Christ, such views as Mr. Robinson expressed to his little band of Puritan hearers, will be more and more appreciated, and will render his name "a Burning and shining light" among the distinguished divines of the Christian Church. We give a single extract from that remarkable discourse:

"We are now, ere long to part assunder, and the Lord knoweth whether ever I shall live to see your faces again. But whether the Lord hath appointed it or not, I charge you before God and his blessed Angels to follow me no further than I follow Christ; and if God should reveal anything to you, by any other instrument of his, to be ready to receive it as ever you were to receive any truth from my ministry; for I am very confident the Lord hath more truth and light yet to break forth out of his holy word."

Blessed words! prophetic language! progressive thoughts! most Christian precepts! Soon may the day arrive when such sentiments shall universally prevail. Then the millenium will be near at hand.

"Such noble words and faith sublime
Are themes that through all coming time
Should our admiring plaudits raise
And be embalmed in grateful praise."
—RUSSELL

But the sad hour which was to separate these long tried and true friends, was at hand. "Farewell is a sad word, but it must be said," was the remark of the eloquent Kossuth. To them it was desolate indeed for it had but a slight hope of any future re-union.

"They little thought how pure the light
With years, should gather round that day;
How love should keep their memories bright,
How wide a realm their sons should sway."
—BRYANT

On leaving Leyden, where they had resided, they were accompanied to Delf Haven by their friends "to see them shipped and to take leave of them. So they left that goodly and pleasant city, which had been their resting place of near twelve years. But they knew they were Pilgrims[1] and looked not much on those things, but lifted up their eyes to Heaven, their dearest country, and quieted their spirits."

It is probable that nerely the whole company accompanied those who were to depart, as far as Delf Haven, twenty-four miles and there took a final farewell. "The night before they went was spent in little sleep" says Bradford, but with friendly entertainment and Christian discourse and other real expressions of true Christian love."

The next day, July 22nd, 1620, O. S. every thing being ready and the wind fair, they went on board, "when doleful was the sight of that sad and mournful parting."

Hoisting sail and with a prosperous wind, they soon arrived at Southampton[2] where they found the larger ship, the Mayflower, lying ready with all the rest of their company.

Mr. Cushman and Mr. Jones[3] the mate of the Mayflower, with others who were to accompany them from England, had been waiting at Southampton for them seven days.[4] "After a joyful welcome and mutual congratulations, with other friendly entertainments, they fell to parley about their proceedings. Seven Hundred pounds sterling are laid out at Southampton, and they carry about seventeen hundred pounds venture with them; and Mr. Weston comes hither from London to see them dispatched.

At length the hour of their departure draws nigh. The

---

[1]The term Pilgrims, belongs exclusively to the Plymouth Colonists. (Young.)

[2]Southampton is a seaport town in the southwesterly part of England, about seventy-three miles from London by land, and about two hundred miles by water, and it is about three hundred miles from Delf Haven in Holland. It was the Rendezvous of Seven of Winthrop's fleet in 1630, and is now the stopping place of the mail steamers from Bremen to the United States.

[3]Jones' River, in Kingston, Mass., hereafter spoken of in this work, was called after the mate of the Mayflower.

[4]Bradford in Prince.

whole company were called together, and a farewell letter from their late pastor, Rev. Mr. Robinson, is read to them. It contained the most affectionate and godly counsel, couched in language singularly appropriate and proper; and, says Bradford "it had good acceptation with all and after-fruit with many."

"Then they ordered and distributed their company for either ship, and chose a Governor and two or three Assistants for each ship, to order the people by the way and see to the disposing of the provisions."

Every thing being in readiness, on Saturday, the 5th day of August, O. S., 1620, the two vessels, the Mayflower and the Speedwell, set sail, having on board 120 persons besides the officers and sailors.

Robert Cushman and his family were among that number. How many his family consisted of at that time we have no knowledge. In the Spring of 1621, when he went over to Plymouth, we have reason to suppose he had no wife and but one son, a boy then fourteen years of age. "But alas," says Bradford, "The best enterprises oftentimes meet with many discouragements." They had been at sea but a short time before Captain Reynolds, the master of the Speedwell, complained that he found his vessel so leaky that he durst not go further to sea. Both vessels, therefore, put back, and on the 13th of August went into Dartmouth[1] one of the nearest English ports.

After remaining there eight days and thoroughly repairing the lesser ship, she was judged sufficient for the voyage by the workmen that mended her and both vessels again unfurled their sails and proceeded on their voyage, on Monday the 21st day of August.

But difficulties are yet in their way. The Puritans are not to be exempt from the ordinary laws of humanity. They are to be made strong and powerful by trials, disappointments, vicissitudes. They had not sailed more than two or three days, a distance of some three hundred miles, when Captain Rey-

---

[1]Dartmouth is a small port in the southwestern part of England, on the British Channel.

nolds again became alarmed, and pronounced his ship unseaworthy and in danger.

Thereupon both ships bore up again and went into Plymouth.[1]

These things thus falling out, it was finally resolved by the whole to dismiss the lesser ship (The Speedwell) and part of the company with her, and that the other part of the company should proceed in the bigger ship (The Mayflower).

And here a difficult task arose, to determine who should go and who should remain; for a part must be left behind, as the Mayflower could not carry the whole. Prince says, "they agree to dismiss her (The Speedwell) and those who were willing to return to London though this was very grevious and discouraging; Mr. Cushman and family returning with them."

The probabilities are that in determining who should go, the strong, resolute and healthy were selected, and the others of an opposite health and temperament remained. Robert Cushman, having been one of the chief managers of the enterprise, was undoubtedly selected to return to London with those who were in the Speedwell, for the purpose of taking care of them and of facilitating their trans-shipment at a future time. His deep interest in the plan of emigration, his zeal and self-sacrificing spirit, and his strong attachment to the Puritan cause, all show most conclusively that it was not from any wavering mind or pusilanimous spirit, or from any discouragement whatever, that caused him to return; but on the other hand, the success and best interests of his associates required it. Those who went back undoubtedly needed a leader and head. For such a station he was admirably qualified. However "grevious and discouraging" it was to him, as Bradford remarks, duty was his ruling principle. If he could do more good and prosper the enterprise by remaining in England for the present, managing the affairs of the company there, and providing for those who could not go in the Speedwell, he was

---

[1]Plymouth a small town on British channel. Bradford says "That it was after ascertained that it was not so much the leaky and unsound condition of the Speedwell, that caused her master to report her unsafe, as it was his treachery and cowardice; for on searching her again no great matter appeared."

ready to do it. A review of his life, so far as we have any knowledge of it, satisfactorily shows us that such was the temper, spirit and action of the man.

Some historical writers have committed an error in imputing unworthy motives and feelings to those who returned to London in the Speedwell, which Dr. Young, in his valuable work, —"Chronicles of the Pilgrims" has fully refuted. As Robert Cushman was one of the number, we quote Dr. Young's remarks in the extenso:

Neal, in his History of New England, says:

Mr. Cushman and his family and some others that were more fearful, went ashore and did not proceed on the voyage. Baylies, in his "History of Plymouth,"[1] also says "about twenty of the passengers were discouraged and would not re-embark." There is no ground for such an imputation on the courage and perseverance of any of the emigrants; and it is a matter of regret that Mr. Bancroft (in his History of the United States) should have lent to it the sanction of his authority. He says, "the timid and hesitating were all freely allowed to abandon the expedition. Having thus winnowed their numbers of the cowardly and the disaffected, etc." Yet, Robert Cushman one of the most energetic and resolute of the Pilgrims, "who was as their right hand," as Governor Bradford said, and who came over in the next ship, The Fortune, in November, 1621, was among those thus "winnowed."

The dismissal of a part was a matter of necessity, as the Mayflower could not carry the whole. Bradford, as quoted by Prince, says "They agree to dismiss her (The Speedwell) and those who were willing to return to London, though this was very grevious and discouraging—" And he further says "it was resolved by the whole to dismiss the lesser ship and part of the company with her." "It was the captain and crew of the Speedwell, not his passengers, that were unwilling to go."—Young's Chronicles.

The reputation and character of Robert Cushman is thus fully vindicated and placed in its true light.

"Having thus determined who should go in the Mayflower,"

---

[1] Plymouth is a small town on the British Channel, not far from Land's End, about 215 miles from London.

another sad parting took place. "The Speedwell goes back to London and the Mayflower proceeds on her voyage."

On Wednesday the 6th of September, O. S. 1620, their troubles being blown over, and now all being compact in one ship, they put to sea again with a prosperous wind.

The subject of this article having returned to London, we now leave this little pilgrim band of one hundred[1] persons, (twenty having returned in the Speedwell) and the ship in which they had taken passage and which in after years became so famous, to meet them again in fifteen months, at their new home at Plymouth, in New England.

For some months we hear nothing of Mr. Cushman, either from Bradford's Journal or by contemporaneous correspondence. He was we may reasonably suppose, actively engaged as he was wont to be, in having the care of his Pilgrim associates and in promoting the interests of the Puritan cause. But early in the year 1621 the subject of immigration to America received considerable public attention. The hope of great profits from the fur trade and the fisheries excited the ambition of some, while a desire to extend the benefits of Christianity and civilization among the aborigines of North America, induced others to turn their attention westward, across the Atlantic, and to encourage emigration to the unknown land. Mr. Cushman being the devoted friend and agent of the Pilgrims who had gone before him to their new residence, and being desirous to persuade others to "go and do likewise" wrote and published in England an article on the subject of settling in America, which is here given entire in order to show the state of the issue before the public of England, as well as something of his ability and industry.

---

[1]Not 101, as is generally said. One hundred sailed, one died on the passage, and one child was born—so that exactly one hundred arrived at Cape Cod. This is conclusively shown by referring to the list of those who signed the compact at Cape Cod, and the number of persons in the family of each, taken from Governor Bradford's Manuscript. See Dr. N. B. Shurtleff's Historical Tract, "The Passengers of the Mayflower."

"REASONS AND Considerations touching
the lawfulness of removing out of
England into the PARTS OF AMERICA"

Forasmuch as many exceptions are daily made against the going into and inhabiting of foreign desert-places, to the hindrances of plantations abroad, and the increase of distractions at home; it is not amiss that some which have been ear-witnesses of the exception made, and are either agents or abettors of such removals and plantations, do seek to give content to the world in all things that they possibly can. And although the most of the opposites are such as either dream of raising their fortunes here to that than to which there is nothing more unlike, or such as affecting their home-born country so vehemently, as that they had rather with all their friends beg, yea, starve in it, than undergo a little difficulty in seeking abroad; yet are there some who, out of doubt and tenderness of conscience, and fear to offend God by running before they be called, are straightened and do straighten others from going to foreign plantations.

For whose cause especially I have been drawn, out of my good affection to them, to publish some reasons that might give them content and satisfaction, and also stay and stop the wilful and witty caviller; and herein I trust I shall not be blamed of any godly wise, though in my slender judgment I should miss the mark, and not strike the nail on the head, considering it is the first attempt that hath been made (that I know of) to defend these enterprises. Reason would, therefore, that if any man of deeper reach and better judgment see further or otherwise, that he rather instruct me than deride me. And being studious for brevity, we must first consider, that whereas God of old did call and summon our Fathers by predictions, dreams, visions, and certain illuminations, to go from their countries, places and habitations, to reside and dwell here or there, and to wander up and down from city to city, and land to land according to his will and pleasure; now there is no such calling to be expected for any matter whatsoever, neither must any so much as imagine that there will now be any such thing. God did once so train up his people, but now he doth not, but speaks in another manner, and so we must apply ourselves to God's present dealing, and not to his wonted dealing; and as the miracle of giving manna ceased, when the fruits of the land became plenty, so God having such a plentiful storehouse of directions in his holy word, there must not now be any extraordinary revelations be expected. But now the ordinary examples and precepts of the scriptures, reasonably and rightly understood and applied, must be the voice and the word, that must call us, press us and direct us in every action.

Neither is there any land or possession now, like unto the possession which the Jews had in Canaan, being legally holy and appropriated unto a holy people, the seed of Abraham, in which they dwelt securely, and had their days prolonged, it being by an immediate voice said, that he (The Lord) gave it them as a land of rest after their weary travels, and a type of eternal rest in heaven. But now there is no land of that sanctimony, no land so appropriated, none typical; much less any that can be said to be given of God to any nation, as was Canaan, which they and their seed must dwell in, till God sendeth upon them sword or captivity. But now we are all, in all places, strangers and pilgrims, travelers and sojourners, most properly, having no dwelling but in this earthern tabernacle; our dwelling is but a wandering, and our abiding but as fleeting, and in a word our home is but nowhere but in the heavens, in that house not made with hands, whose maker and builder is God, and to which all ascend, that love the coming of our Lord Jesus.

Though then there may be reasons to persuade a man to live in this or that land, yet there cannot be the same reasons which the Jews had; but now, as natural, civil and religious bands tie men, so they are bound, and as good reasons for things terrene and heavenly appear, so they must be led.

And so here falleth our question, how a man that is here born and bred, and hath lived some years, may remove himself into another country.

I answer, a man must not respect to live, and do good to himself, but he should see where he can live to do most good to others; for as one saith: "He whose living is but for himself, it is time he were dead." Some men there are who of necessity must here live, as being tied to duties either to church, commonwealth, household, kindred, etc.; but others, and that many, who do no good in none of these, nor can do none, as being not able, or not in favor, or as wanting opportunity, and live as outcasts,—nobodies, eye-sores, eating but for themselves, teaching but themselves, and doing good to none, either in soul or body, and so pass over days, years and months, yea, so live and die. Now such should lift up their eyes and see whether there be not some other place or country to which they may go to do good, and have use toward others of that knowledge, wisdom, humanity, reason, strength, skill, faculty, etc. which God hath given them for the service of others and his own glory.

But not to pass the bounds of modesty so far as to name any, though I confess I know many, who sit here still with their talent in a napkin, having notable endowments both of body and mind, and might do great good if they were in some places, which here do none, nor can do none, and yet through fleshly fear, niceness, straitness of heart, etc. sit still and look on, and will not hazard a drachm of health, nor a day of pleasure, nor an hour of rest to further the knowledge of the sons of Adam in that new world, where a drop of the knowledge of Christ is most precious, which is here not set by. Now what shall we say to such a profession of Christ, to which is joined no more denial of a man's self?

But some will say, What right have I to go, live in the heathens' country?

Letting pass the ancient discoveries, contracts and agreements which our Englishmen have long since made in those parts, together with the acknowledgment of the histories and chronicles of other nations, who profess the land of America from the Cape de Florida to the bay of Canada (which is south and north three hundred leagues and upwards, and east and west further than has yet been discovered) is proper to the King of England, yet letting that pass, lest I be thought to meddle further than it concerns me, or further than I have discerning, I will mention such things as are within my reach, knowledge, sight and practice, since I have traveled in these affairs. And first, seeing we daily pray for the conversion of the heathens, we must consider whether there be not some ordinary means and course for us to take to convert them, or whether prayer for them be only referred to God's extraordinary work from heaven. Now it seemeth unto me that we ought also to endeavor and use the means to convert them; and the means can not be used unless we go to them, or they come to us. To us they cannot come, our land is full; to them we may go, their land is empty.

This then is a sufficient reason to prove our going thither to live, lawful. Their land is spacious and void, and there are few, and do but run over the grass, as do also foxes and wild beasts. They are not industrious, neither have art, science, skill or faculty to use either the land or the commodities of it; but all spoils, rots, and is marred for want of manuring, gather, ordering, etc. As the ancient patriarchs, therefore, removed from straiter places into more roomy, where the land lay idle and waste, and none used it, though there dwelt inhabitants by them, as Gen. XIII; 6, 11, 12 and XXXIV; 21, and XII, 20, so is it lawful now to take a land which none useth, and make use of it; and as it is common land, or unused and undressed country; so we have it by common consent, composition and agreement; which agreement is double. First the imperial governor, Massasoit, whose circuits, in likelihood, are larger than England and Scotland, hath acknowledged the King's Majesty of England to be his master and commander, and that once in my hearing, yea, and in writing under his hand, to Captain Standish, both he and many other kings which are under him, as Pamet, Nauset, Cummaquid, Narrowhiggonset, Namsachet, etc. with divers others that dwell about the bays of Patuxet and Massachusett. Neither hath this been accomplished by threats and blows, or shaking of sword and sound of trumpet; for as our faculty that way is small, and our strength less, so our warring with them is after another manner, namely, by friendly usage, love, peace, honest and just carriages, good counsel that so we and they may not only live in peace in that land, and they yield to subjection to an earthly prince, but as voluntaries they may be persuaded at length to embrace the Prince of Peace, Christ Jesus, and rest in peace with him forever.

Secondly, this composition is also more particular and applicatory, as touching ourselves there inhabiting. The Emperor, by a joint consent, hath promised and appointed us to live at peace where we will in all his dominions, taking what place we will, and as much land as we will, and bringing as many people as we will; and that for these two causes. First because we are the servants of James, King of England, whose the land (as he confesseth) is. Secondly, because he hath found us just, honest, kind and peaceable and so loves our company. Yea, and that in these things there is no dissimulation on his part, nor fear of breach (except our security engender in them some unthought of treachery, or our incivility provoke them to anger) is most plain in other relations, which show that the things they did were more out of love than out of fear.

It being there, first, a vast and empty chaos; secondly, acknowledged the right of our sovereign King; thirdly, by a peaceable composition in part possessed of divers of his loving subjects, I see not who can doubt or call in question the lawfulness of inhabiting or dwelling there; but that it may be as lawful for such as are not tied upon some special occasion here, to live there as well as here. Yea, and as the enterprise is weighty and difficult, so the honor is more worthy, to plant a rude wilderness, to enlarge the honor and fame of our dread sovereign, but chiefly to display the efficacy and power of the Gospel, both in zealous preaching, professing, and wise walking under it, before the faces of these poor blind infidels.

As for such as object the tediousness of the voyage thither, the danger of pirates' robbery, of savages' treachery, etc., these are but lions in the way; and it were well for such men if they were in heaven. For who can show them a place in this world where iniquity shall not compass them at the heels, and where they shall have a day without grief, or a lease of life for a moment? And who can tell, but God, what danger may lie at our doors, even in our native country, or what plots may be abroad, or when God will cause the sun to go down at noon-day, and, in the midst of our security, lay upon us some lasting scourge for our so long neglect and contempt of his most glorious Gospel?

But we have here great peace, plenty of Gospel, and many sweet delights, and variety of comforts.

True, indeed; and far be it from us to deny and diminish the least of these mercies. But have we rendered unto God thankful obedience for this long peace, whilst other peoples have been at wars. Have we not rather murmured, repined and fallen at jars among ourselves, whilst our peace hath lasted with foreign power?

Was there ever more suits in law, more envy, contempt, and reproach than nowadays? Abraham and Lot departed assunder when there fell a breach betwixt them, which was occasioned by the straitness of the land; and surely I am persuaded, that howsoever the frailties of men are principal in all contentions, yet the straitness of the place is such, as each man is fain to pluck his means, as it were, out of his neighbor's throat, there is such pressing and oppressing in town and country, about farms, trades, traffick, etc., so as a man can hardly any where set up a trade but he shall pull down two of his neighbors.

The towns abound with young tradesmen, and the hospitals are full of the ancient; the country is replenished with new farmers, and the almhouses are filled with old laborers. Many there are who get their living with bearing burdens; but more are fain to burden the land with their whole bodies.

Multitudes get their means of life by prating, and so do numbers more by begging. Neither come these straits upon men always through intemperance, ill husbandry, indiscretion, etc., as some think; but even the most wise, sober, and discreet men go often to the wall, when they have done their best; wherein, as God's providence swayeth all, so it is easy to see that the straitness of the place, having it in so many strait hearts, cannot but produce such affects more and more; so as every indifferent minded man should be ready to say with father Abraham, "Take thou the right hand, and I will take the left:" let us not thus oppress, straiten, and afflict one another; but seeing there is a spacious land, the way to which is through the sea, we will end this difference in a day.

That I speak nothing about the bitter contention that hath been about religion, by writing, disputing and inveighing earnestly one against another, the heat of which zeal, if it were turned against the rude barbarism of the heathens, it might do more good in a day than it hath done here in many years. Neither of the little love to the Gospel, and profit which is made by the preachers in most places, which might easily drive the zealous to the heathens; who, no doubt, if they had but a drop of knowledge which here flyeth about the streets, would be filled with exceeding great joy and gladness, as that they would even pluck the kingdom of heaven by violence, and take it as it were, by force.

The greatest let that is yet behind is the sweet fellowship of friends, and the satiety of bodily delights.

But can there be two nearer friends almost than Abraham and Lot, or than Paul and Barnabus? And yet, upon as little occasion as we have here, they parted asunder, two of them being patriarchs of the Church of old, the other the apostles of the Church which is new; and their covenants were such as it seemeth might bind as much as any covenant between men at this day; and yet to avoid greater inconveniences, they departed asunder.

Neither must men take so much thought for the flesh, as not to be pleased except they can pamper their bodies with variety of dainties.

Nature is content with little, and health is much endangered by mixtures upon the stomach. The delights of the palate do often inflame the vital parts; as the tongue setteth a-fire the whole body. Secondly, varieties here are not common to all, but many good men are glad to snap at a crust. The rent-taker lives on sweet morsels, but the rent-payer eats a dry crust often with watery eyes; and it is nothing to say what some one of a hundred hath, but what the bulk, body and commonalty hath; which I warrent you is short enough.

And they also which live so sweetly, hardly will their children attain to that privilege; but some circumventor or other will outstrip them, and make them sit in the dust, to which men are brought in one age, but cannot get out of it again in seven generations.

To conclude without all partiality, the present consumption which groweth upon us here, whilst the land groaneth under so many close-fisted and unmerciful men, being compared with the easiness, plainness and plentifulness in living in those remote places, may quickly persuade any man to a liking of this course, and to practice a removal; which being done by honest, godly and industrious men, they shall there be right heartily welcome; but for other of dissolute and profane life, their rooms are better than their companies. For if here, where the Gospel hath been so long and plentifully taught, they are yet frequent in such vices as the heathen would shame to speak of, what will they be when there is less restraint in word and deed? My only suit to all men is, that whether they live there or here, they would learn to use this world as they used it not, keeping faith and a good conscience, both with God and men, that when the day of account shall come, they may come forth as good and faithful servants, and freely be received, and enter into the joy of their master.

ROBERT CUSHMAN.

On the 6th of May, 1621, the good ship, the Mayflower, arrived home at England, from her voyage to America, and brought the first intelligence from Bradford, Brewster, Allerton and their associates to their Puritan friends in England, and to the "Merchant Adventurers" who had furnished the vessel and outfit for the voyage.

The first success of the settlement at "New Plymouth" in New England[1] having thus been satisfactorily ascertained, Robert Cushman made early arrangements to transport himself and family, and others who had been left behind, the year before, to the New World.

The Fortune, a small vessel of fifty-five tons burthen, less in size than our small fishing vessels which go to Grand Banks for Cod fish was chartered for a voyage to New England. She sailed from London early in July but owing to bad weather she could not clear the British-Channel till the end

---

[1]Plymouth in England was the last place left by the Pilgrims; they, therefore, called their new settlement the same name, or for many years, New Plymouth, in order to distinguish it from Plymouth in England.

of August. She carried out thirty-six passengers, including Robert Cushman and his son Thomas.[1]

On Friday the 9th day of November, O. S. 1621, the Fortune arrived at Cape Cod, some eight or ten leagues from Plymouth. Some friendly Indians, discrying the vessel coming up Plymouth Bay, communicated the intelligence to the colony, who supposed "it to be a Frenchman, for we expected not a friend so soon. The Governor, thereupon, commanded a great piece to be shot off to call home such as were abroad at work. Whereupon every man, yea, boy, that could handle a gun, were ready with full resolution, that if she were an enemy we would stand by our just defence, not fearing them. But God provided better for us than we expected."[2]

"These (the passengers in the Fortune) came all in health, not any being sick by the way, otherwise than by sea-sickness, and so continue to this time, by the blessing of God."

"Good wife Foord was delivered of a son the first night she landed, and both of them are very well."[3]

The meeting of Robert Cushman and his thirty-five associates, with those from whom they had separated fifteen months before, must have been one of great joy, mingled with much that was painful and sad. At their last parting at Plymouth in old England, the one hundred who sailed in the Mayflower were in good health; now one-half of that number had been laid in the grave. Such scenes must have been a very severe trial of their faith, their patience, and their unfailing trust in God.

But the little vessel, the Fortune, must soon return. Before Mr. Cushman left London, he probably had made arrangement to return with her and report to the adventurers the condition and prospects of the Colony; and it was undoubtedly the wish of Governor Bradford to have him do so and to continue the Agent of the Pilgrims. It would seem, from the

---

[1] Fortunately, an accurate list of the adult passengers of the "Fortune" has been preserved. See Young's Chronicles; Farmer's Genealogical Register, etc.

[2] The Fortune had a long passage of over 10 weeks after she left the British Channel.

[3] Bradford's Journal.

fact that he brought his only son (probably all of his family) with him, and from his subsequent correspondence, that he designed to settle permanently in this country as soon as the interests of the Colony would allow it. During his stay at "New Plymouth" he had observed some uneasiness of feeling; some dissatisfaction with the arrangements made in England for their transportation and support:—some abatement of that noble flow of public spirit which was necessary for their preservation and safety.

Although not a clergyman or even a "Teaching Elder" he prepared and delivered on Wednesday the 12th day of December, the day before he sailed for England, a sermon suitable to the occasion. This sermon, together with its prefatory dedication, "To his loving friends, The Adventurers for New England" has become quite noted, from its ability and from the fact that it was the *First Sermon Delivered In New England That Was Printed.*

It was delivered in the "Common House of the Colony" a framed building, 20 ft. square, which stood on the south side of Leyden Street in Plymouth just where the steep descent of the hill commences, on the ground covered by the present residence of Capt. Samuel D. Holmes.

Let us for a moment picture in our minds the condition of Plymouth at the time, of the delivery of that discourse, and imagine the audience that assembled to hear it, just as the speaker was about to leave on his return to England. It was then just about one year since they first landed. But fifty of the whole number who came in the Mayflower were then living. Thirty-six had arrived in the Fortune. So that his audience could not have exceeded 60 to seventy persons of all ages and both sexes.

The "Common House" was the place where they held their religious meetings and their municipal gatherings. We may suppose that it was rude in its construction and unfinished in many parts. Its roof was "thatched" and to us it must have presented an unique appearance and indicated a semi-civilized community.

There, in that little building, were gathered together the hopes of the Puritan; the germ of a mighty Republic; the beginnings of a civilization of which the mind, in its farthest reach, cannot conceive the end.

Their friend, their coadjutor for many years, their companion through many trials, was about to depart and as it proved, it was a last farewell. He desired to speak to them words of consolation, of hope, of advice, before he left.

On the 12th of December, therefore, that little community assembled to hear the parting words of one, on whom they had oftentimes relied. On his right, in the "Common House", we may suppose, was seated with great dignity and decorum, the Governor, William Bradford, whose wisdom was their support in many dark and doleful days. Near him was his "Assistant" in the government, Isaac Allerton, who with Bradford, then constituted the whole administration of the civil power of the Colony. On his left sat Elder Brewster, the perfect personification of religious devotion and trust in God. Nerely in front, was probably, the place of Captain Standish, who then exercised the military command of the colony; and who, in every move and look, indicated that he felt the importance and the dignity and the honor of his office. Edward Winslow, a pillar of the little community, must have been in a conspicuous place. Ranged around them were others, their brethren of a common faith, their wives and children, forming a group such as the world has seldom seen.

Under such circumstances and to such an audience was the sermon of Robert Cushman, "on the sin and danger of self-love" delivered. And it seems to us quite singular, that to a body of men so self-sacrificing, so zealously devoted to the common cause, such a subject was selected and deemed necessary. But they were the best judges of what was fit and proper and best for themselves.

This sermon was first published in London, in the year after its delivery, 1622; afterwards reprinted in Boston in 1724. "And though his name is not prefixed to either edition, yet unquestioned tradition renders it certain that he was the author, and even transmits to us a knowledge of the spot where it was delivered."¹ Subsequently it was printed at Plymouth, Mass. by Nathaniel Coverly, in 1780; another edition at Boston, in 1815; and another at Stockbridge, Mass. in 1822, and again at Boston, by Charles Ewer, in 1846, and a portion of it in Dr. Young's Chronicles of the Pilgrims, in 1841.² As the Sermon illustrates not merely one aspect of the condition of the Plymouth Colony, but also something of the style, manner of thought and literary composition of the times as well as the ability and character of its Author, we give it entire, together with the prefatory address. We copy from one of the oldest editions.

To His Loving Friends and Adventurers and
Well-Wishers Thereunto,
Grace and Peace, etc.

New England, so called, not only (to avoid novelties) because of the resemblance that is in it, of England, the native soil of Englishmen; it being much what the same, for heat and cold in summer and winter, it being Champaign ground, but no high mountains, somewhat like the soil in Kent and Essex; full of dales and meadow ground, full of rivers and sweet springs, as England is. But principally, so far as we can yet find, it is an island, and near about the quantity of England, being cut out from the main land in America, as England is from the main of Europe, by a great arm of the Sea, which entereth in forty degrees and runneth up North West and by West, and goeth out either into the South-Sea or else into the Bay of Canada. The certainty whereof, and secrets of which, we have not yet so found as that as eye-witnesses we can make narration thereof, but if God give time and means, we shall, ere long, discover both the extent of that river, together with the secrets thereof; and so try what territories, habitations or commodities, may be found, either in it, or about it.

---

¹Judge Davis' Biographical Sketch of Robert Cushman, printed in the Plymouth edition of his Sermon.

²Dr. Young does not print the entire sermon. He says he publishes "all that is of any general or historical value in the discourse." It is a source of regret that one who is usually so full and complete as Dr. Young is, should have omitted, in his valuable work, an interesting portion of that sermon.

It pertaineth not to my purpose to speak anything either in praise, or dispraise of the country; so it is by God's Providence, that a few of us are there planted to our consent, and have with great charge and difficulty attained quiet and competent dwellings there. And thus much I will say for the satisfaction of such as have any thought of going hither to inhabit? That for men which have a large heart, and look after great riches, ease, pleasures, dainties, and jolity in this world (except they will live by other men's sweat, or have great riches) I would not advise them to come there, for as yet the country will afford no such matters; but if there be any who are content to lay out their estates, spend their time, labors, and endeavors, for the benefit of them that shall come after, and in desire to further the Gospel among those poor heathens, quietly contenting themselves with such hardship and difficulties, as by God's Providence shall fall upon them, being yet young and in their strength, such men I would advise and encourage to go, for their ends cannot fail them.

And if it should please God to punish his people in the Christian countries of Europe, (for their coldness, carnality, wonton abuse of the gospel, contention, etc.) either by Turkish slavery, or by popish tyranny, which God forbid, yet, if the time come, or shall come, (as who knoweth) when Satan shall be let loose to cast out his floods against them, (Rev. 12. 14, 15.) here is a way opened for such as have wings to fly into this wilderness; and as by the dispersion of the Jewish Church through persecution, the Lord brought in the fullness of the Gentiles, (Act 11. 20, 31) so who knoweth, whether now by tyranny and affliction, he suffereth to come upon them, he will not by little and little chase them even amongst the heathens, that so a light may rise up in the dark, (Luke 2. 32.) and the Kingdom of Heaven be taken from them which now have it, and given to a prophet that shall bring forth the fruit of it. (Mat. 21. 43) This I leave to the Godly-wise being neither prophet nor son of a prophet (Amos 7. 14.) but considering God's dealing of old, (2 Kings. 17. 23.) and seeing the name of Christian to be very great, but the true thereof almost quite lost in all degrees and sects, I cannot think but that there is some judgment not far off, and that God will shortly, even of stones, raise up children unto Abraham (Mat. 3-5.)

And who so rightly considereth what manner of entrance, abiding and proceedings we have had among these poor heathens since we come hither, will easily think that God has some great work to do towards them.

They were wont to be the most cruel and treacherous people in all these parts, even like lions, but to us they have been like lambs, so kind, so submissive, and trusty as a man may truly say, many Christians are not so kind, nor sincere.

They were very much wasted of late, by reason of a great mortality that fell amongst them three years since, which together with their own civil dissentions and bloody wars, hath so wasted them, as I think the twentieth person is scarcely left alive, and those that are left, have their courage much abated and their countenance is dejected, and they seem as a people affrighted. And though when we came first into the country, we were few, and many of us were sick, and many died by reason of the cold and wet, it being the depth of winter, and we having no houses nor shelter, yet when there were not six able persons among us and that they came daily to us, by the hundreds, with their Sachems and Kings, and might in one hour have made a dispatch of us, yet such a fear was upon them, as that they never offered us the least injury in word or deed.

And by reason of one Tisquanto, that lives amongst us, that can speak English, we have daily commerce with their kings, and can know what is done or intended toward us among the savages; also we can acquaint them with our courses and purposes, both human and religious. And the greatest commander of the country called Massasoit, cometh often to visit us, though he lives fifty miles away from us, often sends us presents, he having with many other of their governors, promised, yea, subscribed obedience to our sovereign Lord, King James, and for his cause to spend both strength and life. And we for our parts; through God's Grace, have with that equity, justice and compassion, carried ourselves toward them, as that they have received much favor, help and aid from us, but never the least injury or wrong by us.[1] We found the place where we live empty, the people being all dead and gone away, and none living near by eight or ten miles; and though in the time of some hardship we found (traveling abroad) near eight bushels of corn hid up in a cave, and knew no owners of it, yet afterwards hearing of the owners of it, we gave them (in their estimation) double the value of it.

Our care hath been to maintain peace amongst them and have always set ourselves against such of them as used any rebellion, or treachery against their governors, and not only threatened such, but in some sort paid them their due deserts; and when any of them are in want, as often they are in the winter, when their corn is done, we supply them to our power, and have them in our houses eating and drinking, and warming themselves, which thing (though it be something of a trouble to us) yet because they should see and take knowledge of our labors, order and diligence, both for this life and a better, we are content to bear it, and we find in many of them, especially the younger sort, such a tractable disposition, both to religion and humanity, as that if we had the means to apparel them, and wholly retain them with us (as their desire is) they would doubtless in time prove servicable to God and man, and if God ever sends us means we will bring up hundreds of their children, both to labor and learning.

But *leaving to speak of them till a further occasion be offered;* if any shall marvel at the publishing of this treatise in England, seeing there is no want of good books, but, rather men to use good books, let them know that the special end is, that we, may keep their motives in memory for ourselves, and those that shall come after, to be a remedy against self-love, the bane of all societies. And that we might also testify to our Christian countrymen, who judge diversely of us, that though we be in a heathen country, yet the grace of Christ is not quenched in us, but we still hold and teach the same points of faith, mortification, and sanctification, which we have heard and learned, in a most ample and large manner in our own country. If any shall think it too rude and unlearned for this

---

[1] "They offer us to dwell where we will."

curious age, let them know, that to paint out the Gospel in plain and flat English, among a company of plain Englishmen (as we are) is the best and most profitable teaching; and we will study plainness, not curiosity, neither in things human, nor heavenly. If any error or unsoundness be in it, (as who knoweth) impute it to that frail man which endited it, which professeth to know nothing, as he ought to know it. I have not set down my name, partly because I seek no name, and principally, because I would have nothing esteemed by names, for I see a number of evils to arise through names, when the persons are either famous, or infamous, and God and man is often injured. If any good or profit arise to thee in the receiving of it, give God the praise and esteem me as a son of Adam, subject to all such frailties as other men are.

And you my loving friends, the Adventurers of this plantation; as your care has been, first to settle religion here, before either profit or popularity, so I pray you, go on, to do it much more, and to be careful to send godly men, though they want some of the worldly policy which this world hath in her own generation, and so though you lose, the Lord shall gain.

I rejoice greatly in your free and ready minds to your powers, yea, and beyond your powers to further this work, that you thus honor God with your riches, and I trust you shall be paid again double and treble in this world, yea, and the memory of this action shall never die, but above all adding unto this, (as I trust you do) like freeness in all other God's services both at home and abroad, you shall find reward with God ten thousand fold surpassing all that you can do or think; be not, therefore discouraged, for no labor is lost nor money spent which is bestowed for God, your ends were good, your success is good, and your profit is coming, even in this life, and in the life to come much more: and what shall I say now a word to men of understanding, sufficeth, pardon I pray you my boldness, read over the ensuing treatise, and judge wisely of the poor weakling of the Lord, the God of land and sea, stretch out his arm of protection over you and us, and over all our lawful and good enterprises, either this, or any other way.

Plymouth in New England, December 12. 1621.

"THE SERMON"

The Sin and Danger of Self-Love

Preached at Plymouth, In New England, 1621

By ROBERT CUSHMAN

1. Corinthians, 10, 24.

Let no Man Seek His Own: But Every Man Another's Wealth.

The occasion of these words by the Apostle Paul, was because of the abuses which were in the Church of Corinth. Which abuses arose chiefly through swelling pride, self-love and concretedness, for although this church was planted by Paul and watered by Apollos, and much increased by the Lord; yet the sower of tares was not wanting to stir up evil workers and fleshly minded hypocrites, under a show of godliness, and with angel-like holiness in appearance, to creep in amongst them to disturb their peace, try their soundness and prove their constancy. And this the Apostle complains of very often: as first, in their carnal divisions, Chapter 1. then in their extolling their eloquent teachers and despising Paul, Chapter 4. Then in their offensive going to Law, before the heathen judges, Chapter 6. Then in eating those things offered to idols, to the destroying of the tender consciences of their brethren, Chapter 8. Then in their insatiable love feasts, in the time and place of their Church meetings, the rich which could together feed to fullness, despising and contemning the poor, that had not to lay it on as they had, Chapter 11. Finally in both the Epistles, he very often nippeth them in their pride, and self-love, straitness and censoriousness, so that in the last chapter he willeth them again and again to prove, try and examine themselves, to see whether Christ were in them or not, for howsoever many of them seemeth, as thousands of them do at this day to soar aloft, and go with full sail to Heaven; yet as men that row in boats, set their faces one way, when yet their whole body goeth apace another way; so there are many which set such a face upon religion, and have their mouth full of great swelling words, as if they would even blow open the doors of heaven, despising all humble-minded and broken-hearted people, as weak, simple, sottish, etc., when yet notwithstanding, these blusterers, which seem to go so fast, and leave all others behind them, if like these glosing Corinthians, they carry affectly their own glory with them, and seem thus to stand for the glory of God. What do they else but join flesh to spirit, serving not God for naught, but for wages, and so serving their bellies, whose end will be damnation, except a speedy and sound remedy be thought of, which remedy is even that which our Saviour teacheth the rich young gallant, and which Paul here prescribeth, in willing them not to seek their own, but every man another's wealth, which physic is as terrible to carnal professors, as abstinence from drink is to a man that hath the dropsy; and it is a sure note, that a man is sick of this disease of self-love, if this be grievous to him, as appeareth in the man whom Christ bid sell that he had, and he went away very sorrowful, yet surely this vein must be pricked, and this humor let out, else it will spoil all, it will infect both soul and body, yea, and the contagion of it is such (as we shall see anon) as will even hazard the welfare of that society where self seekers and self lovers are.

As God then did direct this Apostle to lay down this brief direction as a remedy for that evil in Corinth, so you may think it is by God's special providence that I am now to speak unto you from this text; and say in your hearts, surely something is amiss this way: let us know it and amend it.

The parts of this text are two, 1. a Dehortation. 2. An Exhortation. The Dehortation, Let no man seek his own. The Exhortation; but every man another's wealth. In handling of which I will first, open the words. Secondly, gather the doctrine. Thirdly, illustrate the doctrine by Scriptures, experience and reasons. Fourthly, apply the same, to every one his portion.

The proper drift of the Apostles here is not to tax the Corinthians, for seeking their own evil ends in evil actions, but for aiming at themselves, and their own benefits in actions lawful, and that appeareth in the former verse, where he saith, "All are Lawful," etc. Viz: All such things as we now speak of, to eat any of God's creatures, offered to idols or not, to feast and be merry together, to show love and kindness to this or that persons, etc., but when by such means we seek ourselves, and have not a charitable loving and reverent regard of others, then they are unexpedient, unprofitable, yea, unlawful, and must be forbourne, and he that hath not learned to deny himself even the very use of lawful things, when it tendeth to the contempt, reproach, grief, offence and shame of his other brethren and associates, hath learned nothing aright, but is, apparently, a man that seeks himself, and against whom the Apostle here dealeth most properly.

The manner of the speech, may seem as counsel left at Liberty; as Mat. 27. 29. And in our ordinary speech, we think they be but weak charges, which are thus delivered, let a man do this, or let him do that. But we must learn the apostle's modesty, and know that whatsoever the terms seem to imply, yet even this and other the like in this epistle, are most absolute charges: as, *Let a man esteem of us, as the ministers of Christ, Chapter 41.* That is, a man ought so to esteem of us. *Let a man examine himself,* 1 Cor. 11. 28. That is, as if he said, a man must examine himself. *Let your women keep silence in the Churches, 1 Cor. 14, 34.* that is, they ought so to do.

The meaning then summarily is, as if the said, the bane of all these mischiefs which arise among you is, that men are too cleaving to themselves and their own matters, and disregard and contemn all others: and therefore I charge you, let this self seeking be left off, and turn the stream another way, namely, seek the good of your brethren, please them, honor them, reverence them, for otherwise it will never go well amongst you.

Objection: But doth not the Apostle elsewhere say? *That he, which careth not for his own, is worse than an infidel.* 1 Tim. 5. 8.

Answer. True, but by (own) there, he meaneth properly, a man's kindred, and here by (own) he meaneth properly a man's self.

Secondly, he there especially taxeth such as were negligent in their labors and callings, and so made themselves unable to give relief and entertainment to such poor widows and orphans as were of their own flesh and blood.

Thirdly, be it so, that some man should even neglect his own self, his own wife, children, friends, and etc. And give that he had to strangers, that were but some rare vice, in some one unnatural man, and if this vice slay a thousand, self-love slayeth ten thousands.

And this the wisdom of God did well foresee, and hath set no caveats in the scriptures either to tax man or forewarn them from loving others, neither saith God anywhere, let no man seek out the good of another, but let no man seek his own, and every where in the scriptures he hath set watch words against self-good, self-profit, self-seeking, etc. And thus the sense being cleared, I come to the doctrine.

Doct. 1. *All men are too apt and ready to seek themselves too much, and to prefer their own matters and causes beyond the* due and lawful measure, even to excess and offense against God, yea, danger of their own souls.

And this is true not only in wicked men which are given over to God of vile lusts, as *Absalom* in getting favor in his father's court: *Jereboam,* in settling his kingdom fast in *Samaria; Ahab* in vehement seeking Naboth's vineyard, but men otherwise godly, have through frailty been foiled herein, and many thousands which have a show of godliness, are lovers of themselves: *David* was about to seek himself when he was going to kill *Naball*: *Asa* in putting *Hanani* in prison: *Josiah* when he would go to war with *Necho,* against the counsel of God, and reason; *Peter* when he dissembled about the ceremonies of the law, yea, and *Paul* complains of all his followers (Timothy excepted) that they sought their own too inordinately.

And why else are these caveats in the scriptures, but to warn the godly that they be not tainted herewith? as, *Look not every man on his own things, but on the things of another: Love seeketh not her own things. Be not desirous of vain glory,* etc. Philip. 2. 4. 1 Cor. 13. 6. Gal. 5. 26.

Yea and doth not experience teach, that even amongst professors of religion, almost all the love and favor that is shewed unto others is with a secret aim at themselves, they will take pains to do a man good, provided that he will take twice so much for them, they will give a penny so as it may advantage them a pound, labor hard so as all the profit may come to themselves, else they are heartless and feeble. The vain and corrupt heart of man cannot better be resembled than by a belly-god, host, or innkeeper which welcometh his guests with smilings, and salutations, and a thousand welcomes, and rejoiceth greatly to have their company to dice, cards, eat, drink, and be merry, but should not the box be paid, the pot be filling, and the money telling, all this while, the epicure's joy would soon be turned into sorrow, and his smiles turned into frowns, and the door set open, and their absence craved: even so men blow the bellows hard, when they have an iron of their own a heating, work hard whilst their own house is in building, dig hard whilst their own garden is in planting, but is it so as the profit must go wholly or partly to others; their hands wax feeble, their hearts wax faint, they grow churlish, and give cross answers, like *Naball*, they are sour, discontent, and nothing will please them. And where is that man to be found, that will disperse abroad, and cast his bread upon the waters, that will lend, looking for nothing again, that will do all duties to others freely and cheerfully in conscience to God, and love unto men, without his close and secret ends or aiming at himself; such a man, out of doubt, is a black swan, a white crow almost, and yet such shall stand before God with boldness at the last day, when others which have sought themselves, though for love of themselves they have sought heaven, yea, and through self-love persuaded themselves they should find it, yet wanting love unto others, they will be found as sounding brass, and as a tinkling cimbal, and whilst they have neglected others, and not cared how others live, so as themselves may fare well, they will be found amongst them, that the Lord will say unto, *I know you not, depart ye cursed into everlasting fire.* Mat. 25. 41. 42.

But that I may not talk in generalities, the particular ways by which men seek their own are these: First, such as are covetous, seek their own by seeking riches, wealth, money, as *Felix* pretending unto *Paul*, sent for him often, but it was in hope of money. Many there are who say, *who will shew us any good*, Psal. 4. 7. And pretend religion, as some of the Jews did the keeping of the Sabbath, which yet cried out, when will the Sabbath be done, that we may sell corn, and get gain; if a man can tell how to get gold out of a flint, and silver out of the adamant, no pains shall be spared, no time shall be neglected, for gold is their hope, and the wedge of gold is their confidence, their hearts are set upon the pelf of this world, and for love of it, all things are let slip, even all duties to God or men, they care not how basely they serve, how wretchedly they neglect all others, so as they may get wealth: pinch who will, and wring who will; all times are alike with them, and they run for the bribe and Gehazie; and this is the first way that men seek their own.

Now the contrary is seen in *Nehemiah*, who when the people were hard put to it, and the land raw, he took not the duties which were due to him being a magistrate, he bought no land, nor grew rich, for it was no time; but he maintained at his table many of his brethren the Jews, and so spent even his own proper goods. And *Paul* sought no man's gold nor silver but though he had authority, yet he took not bread of the churches, but labored with his hands: and why? It was no time to take, some churches were poor and stood in want, as *Thessalonica*, others were in danger to be preyed upon by covetous bellygods, as *Corinth*: and therefore he saw it no fit time now to take any thing of them.

And indeed here is the difference between a covetous worldling, and an honest, thrifty Christian, it is lawful sometimes for men to gather wealth, and grow rich, even as there was a time for *Joseph* to store up corn, but a godly and sincere Christian will see when this time is, and will not hoard up when he sees others of his brethren and associates to want, but then is a time, if he have anything, to fetch it out and disperse it, but the covetous gathers goods, he like *Achan* covets all that he seeth; and neglects no time, but gathers still and holds all fast, and if it were to save the life of his brother, his bags must not be diminished, nor his chests lighted, nor his field set to sale, gather as much as he can, but it's death to diminish the least part of it.

2. The second way by which men seek their own, is when they seek ease, or pleasure, as the *Scribes* and *Pharisees*, who would not touch the burden with one of their fingers; for there

is a generation, which think to have more in this world than *Adam's* felicity in innocency, being born (as they think) to take their pleasures, and their ease, let the roof of the house drop through, they stir not; let the field be overgrown with weeds, they care not; they must not foul their hands nor wet their foot, it's enough for them to say, Go you, not let us go, though never so much need; such idle drones, are intolerable in a settled commonwealth, much more in a commonwealth which is but as it were in the bud; of what earth I pray thee art thou made, of any better than the other of the sons of *Adam?* And canst thou see other of thy brethren toil their hearts out, and thou sit idle at home, or takest thy pleasure abroad? Remember the example of *Uriah*, who would not take his ease nor his pleasure, though the King required him, and why? Because his brethren, his associates, better men than himself (as he esteemed them) were under hard labors and conditions, lay in the field in tents, caves, etc.

3. The third way is when men seek their own bellies, as some did in the Apostles' times, which went about with new doctrines and devices, knowing that the people had itching ears, and would easily entertain and willingly feed such novelists, which brought in dissensions, schisms, and contentions, and such were rocks or pillars in their love-feasts, as *Jude* speaketh. ver. 12.

They were shadows in God's service, but when feasting came, then they were substances, then they were in their element. And certainly there are some men which shape even their religion, human state, and all, even as the belly cheer is best, and that they must have, else all heart and life is gone; let all conscience, care of others go, let *Lazarus* starve at the gate, let *Joseph's* affliction be increased, they must have their dishes, their dainties, or no content. The contrary was seen in *Nehemiah* who would not take his large portion allotted to the governor, because he knew it went short with others of his brethren; and *Uriah* would not receive the King's present, and go banquet with his wife, because he knew the whole host, his brethren, were fain to snap short in the fields.

And the difference between a temperate good man, and a belly-god is this: a good man will not eat his morsels alone, especially, if he have better than others, but if by God's providence, he have gotten some meat which is better than ordinary, and better than his other brethren, he can have no rest in himself, except he make others partake with him. But a belly-god will slop all in his own throat, yea, though his neighbor come in and behold him eat, yet his gripple-gut shameth not to swallow all. And this may be done sometimes, as well in mean fare as in greater dainties, for all countries afford not alike.

4. The fourth way by which men seek their own, is by seeking outward honor, fame and respect with men; as King *Saul* when he had lost all respect and favor with God, then thought to give content to his heart by being honored before the Elders of the people; and it is wonderful to see how some men are *desirous of vain glory*, Gal. 5. 26. And how earnestly they seek praise, favor, and respect with men, and can have no quiet longer than their worldly favor lasteth, and that they will have what dishonor soever come to God, or disgrace unto men, yea, they will disgrace, reproach, and disdain others, to gain honor and advancement to themselves, yea, they will make bold with the Scriptures and Word of God, to wrest and wring, and slight it over for their credit's sake. And let a man mark some men's talk, stories, discourses, etc. and he shall see their whole drift is to extol and set out themselves, and get praise and commendation of men.

Now the contrary was seen in *Paul*, he saith, *He needed no letters of commendations*, 2 Cor. 3. 2. And again, *He is not affected with men's praise*, 1 Cor. 10, 12. And here is indeed the difference between an humble-minded Christian, and a proud self-lover; an humble man often hath praise, as *David, Hezekiah*, and *Josiah*, but he seeks it not, he desires it not, he is content to go without it, he loves not the praise of men, for he knows it but froth and vanity: but a proud self-lover, he seeks it still, get it or not get it, and if he get it he is fully satisfied, if he get it not he hangs his head like a bull-rush, and hath no comfort.

5. The fifth way by which men seek their own, is *by seeking to have their wills;* as the wrong doers in *Corinth*, who thought it not enough to do wrong and harm to their brethren,

but to have their wills enough of them, drew them before the Heathen magistrates.

And truly some men are so prince-like, or rather Papal, that their very will and word is become a law, and if they have said it, it must be so, else there is no rest or quietness to be had, let never so many reasons be brought to the contrary, it is but fighting with the wind. They are like the obstinate Jews, who when against God's law, and reason, they asked a King, though *Samuel* shewed them that it would turn in the end to their own smart, yet still held the conclusion, and said, nay, *But we will have a King*, 1 Sam. 8. 19. Thus men are caught by their own words, and insnared by the straitness of their own hearts, and it is death to them not to have their wills, and howsoever sometimes (like Jezebel) they are cut short of their purposes, yet self-willed men will strut and swell like *Absalom*, saying neither good nor bad, 2. Sam. 13. 22. but hope for the day, and threaten like prophane *Esau*, Gen. 27. 41. Now the contrary is seen in *David*, though a prince, a captain, a warrior, who having said, yea sworn, that he would kill *Naball* and all his family that day, yet upon reasonable counsel given, and that by a weak woman, he changed his mind, altered his purpose, and returned, without striking one stroke, an example rare, and worthy imitation; and when men are sick of will, let them think of *David*, it was his grace and honor to go back from his word and practice, when reason came. So was it Herod's disgrace and shame to hold his word and will against reason and conscience. Math. 14. 8. 9.

Question: But some men happily will say unto me, It is true, that men seek their own by all these ways, *But what should be the reason and cause of this? that men seek so earnestly themselves in seeking riches, honor, ease, belly-cheer, will, and something there is that carrieth them.*

Answer. True, and the reasons and causes are specially these three: First, pride and high conceitedness, when men overvalue themselves: and this made *Absalom* to seek his father's kingdom because he thought himself worthy of it. 2 Sam. 15. 4. This made *Haman* so sore vexed, because *Mordecai* bowed not to him, because he highly valued himself. Esther, 3. 5.

And surely that which a man valueth much, he giveth much respect to, and so it is a sure sign that a man loves himself most when he giveth most to himself; and some intolerable proud persons even think all the world is for them and all their purposes and endeavors shew what a large conceit they have for themselves.

Secondly, want of due consideration and valuation of other men's endowments, abilities and deserts; when men pass those things by, though they have both seen, heard, and felt them; as Pharaoh's butler forgot Joseph's eminency when he was restored to his place, Gen. 40. 23. So men used to write their own good actions in brass, but other men's in ashes, never remembering or considering the pains, labor, good properties, etc., which others have, and so they have no love to them, but only to themselves; as if God had made all other men unreasonable beasts, and them only reasonable men.

Thirdly, want of heavenly conversation, and spiritual eye to behold the glory, greatness, and majesty, and goodness of God; as the Queen of *Sheba,* thought highly of her own glory, wisdom and happiness, till she saw *Solomon's* wisdom and glory, and then she cried out, not of the happiness of her own servants, but of his servants that stood before him, 1 Kings 10. 7. 8. And verily, if men were conversant courtiers in Heaven, they would cry out with *Paul,* Rom. 11. 33., *Oh the depth of the riches, wisdom and knowledge of God,* etc., and would be ashamed of their own sinfulness, nakedness and misery; for, as countrymen which never saw the state of cities, nor the glory of courts, admire even their own country Orders: and as the savages here which are clad in skins, and creep in woods and holes, think their own brutish and inhuman life the best, which if they saw and did rightly apprehend the benefit of comely humanity, the sweetness of religion and the service of God, they would even shamefully hide themselves from the eye of all noble Christians. Even so, if men in serious contemplation, by the eye of faith, would behold the glory of God, and what great riches, beauty, fulness, perfection, power, dignity and greatness is in God, they would leave admiring of themselves, and seeking of themselves, and would say with *David, What am I? And what is my father's house?*

that thou shouldst thus bless me? 2 Sam. 7. 18. *Yea, What is man? or the son of man that thou so regardest him?* Psal. 8. 3. But it is time to come to apply these things more particularly to ourselves, and see what Use is to be made of them.

Use 1. Is it so, that God seeth a proneness in all the sons of *Adam*, to seek themselves too much, and hath given them warnings and watch-words thereof, as we have heard, and doth experience confirm him? Then hence are reproved a number of men, who think they can never shew love enough to themselves, nor seek their own enough, but think all cost, charges, cherishing, praise, honor, etc., too little for them, and no man needeth to say to them, as *Peter* did to Christ, *favor thyself;* but if they do a little for another man, they account it a great matter, though it be but a morsel of bread, or a single penny; but no varieties of dainties is too good for them, no silk, purple, cloth, or stuff is too good to clothe them, the poor man's idleness and ill husbandry is oft thrown in his dish, but their own carnal delights and fleshy wantonness is never thought upon; and why? Because they think even God and man owes all to them, but they owe nothing to none. Why, thou foolish and besotted man, hath not the Holy Ghost read it in the very face of every son of *Adam*, that he is too apt to seek his own, and art thou wiser than God, to think thou never seekest thine own enough? or dreamest thou that thou art made of other, and better mettle, than other men are? Surely, I know no way to escape, having of corruption to thy father, and the worm to thy sister and brother. And if God had anywhere in all the Scriptures said, love thyself, make much of thyself, provide for one, etc., there were some reason for thee to take up the niggard's proverbs, *Every man for himself, and God for us all; Charity beginneth at home,* etc. But God never taught thee these things; no, they are Satan's positions. Doth God ever commend a man for carnal love of himself? Nay he brand it, and disgraceth it, as *self-love taking thought for the flesh; loving of pleasure,* etc. Rom. 13. 14. 2 Tim. 34.

Objection. *It is a point of good natural policy, for a man to care and provide for himself.*

Answer. Then the most fools have most natural policy, for you see not the greatest drones and novices, either in church, or commonwealth, to be the greatest scratchers and scrapers, and gatherers of riches? Are they not also for the most part, best fed and clad? And live they not most easily? What shall I say? Even hogs, dogs, and brute beasts know their own ease, and can seek that which is good for themselves; and what doth this shifting, progging, and fat feeding which some use, more resemble anything than the fashion of hogs? And so let it be what natural policy it will.

Use 2. If God see this disease of self-love so dangerous in us, then it standeth us all in hand to suspect ourselves, and so to seek out the root of this disease, that it may be cured. If a learned physician shall see by our countenance and eye, that we have some dangerous disease growing on us, our hearts will smite us, and we will bethink ourselves where the most grief lieth, and how it should come, whether with cold, heat, surfeit, overflowing of blood, or through grief, melancholy, or any such way, and every man will bestir himself to get rid of it, and will prevent always that which feeds the disease, and cherish all courses that would destroy it.

Now, how much ought we to bestir ourselves, for this matter of self-love, since God himself hath cast all our waters, and felt all our pulses, and pronounceth us all dangerously sick of this disease? Believe it, God cannot lie, nor be deceived; He that made the heart, doth not he know it? Let every man's heart smite him, and let him fall to the examination of himself and see first, whether he love not riches and worldly wealth too much, whether his heart be not too jocund at the coming of it in, and too heavy at the going of it out, for if you find it so there is great danger, if thou canst not buy as if thou possessed not, and use this world as though thou used it not, (1 Cor. 7. 30, 31.) thou art sick, and had need to look to it. So, if thou lovest thine ease and pleasure, see whether thou can be content to receive at God's hands evil as well as good, (Job. 2. 10.) whether thou have learned as well to abound as to want, (Phil. 4. 10.) as well to endure hard labor, as to live at ease; and art as willing to go to the house of mourning as to the house of mirth, (Eccl. 7. 6.) for, else, out of doubt, thou lovest thy carnal pleasure and ease too much.

Again, see whether thy heart cannot be as merry, and thy

mind as joyful, and thy countenance as cheerful, with coarse fare, with pulse, with bread and water, (if God offer thee no better, nor the times afford other) as if thou had the greatest dainties: (Dan. 1. 5.) So also whether thou can be content as well with scorns of men, when thou hast done well, as with their praises, so if thou can with comfort and good conscience say, I pass little for man's judgment; whether, thou can do thy duty that God requireth, and despise the shame, referring thyself unto God, for if thou be disheartened, discouraged, and weakened in any duty because of men's dispraises, it's a sign thou lovest thyself too much.

So for the will, if thou can be content to give way even from that which thou hast said shall be, yea, vowed shall be, when better reason cometh, and hast that reverence of other men, as that when it standeth but upon a matter of will, thou art as willing their wills should stand as thine, and art not sad, churlish, or discontented, (1 Kings 21. 24.) but cheerful in thine heart, though thy will be crossed, it is a good sign, but if not, thou art sick of a self-will, and must purge it out.

I the rather press these things, because I see many men both wise and religious, which yet are so tainted with the pestilent self-love, as that it is in them even as a dead fly to the apothecaries' ointment, spoiling the efficacy of all their graces, making their lives uncomfortable to themselves, and unprofitable to others, being neither fit for church nor commonwealth, but have even their very souls in hazard thereby, and therefore who can say too much against it.

It is reported, that there are many men gone to that other plantation in *Virginia,* which, whilst they lived in *England,* seemed very religious, zealous, and conscionable; and have now lost even the sap of grace, and edge to all goodness; and are become mere worldlings. This testimony I believe to be partly true, and amongst many causes of it, this self-love is not the least. It is indeed a matter of some commendation for a man to remove himself out of a thronged place into a wide wilderness; to take in hand so long and dangerous a journey, to be an instrument to carry the Gospel and humanity among the brutish heathen; but there may be many goodly shews and glosses and yet a pad in the straw, men may make a great appearance of respect unto God, and yet but dissemble with him, having their own lusts carrying them; and, out of doubt, men that have taken in hand hither to come, out of discontentment in regard of their estates in England; and aiming at great matters here, affecting it to be gentlemen, landed men, or hoping for office, place, dignity, or fleshly liberty; let the shew be what it will, the substance is naught, and that bird of self-love which was hatched at home, if it be not looked to, will eat out the life of all grace and goodness: and though men have escaped the danger of the sea, and that cruel mortality, which swept away so many of our loving friends and brethren; yet except they purge out this self-love, a worse mischief is prepared for them: And who knoweth whether God in mercy has delivered those just men which here departed, from the evils to come; and from unreasonable men, in whom there neither was, nor is, any comfort, but grief, sorrow, affliction, and misery, till they cast out this spawn of self-love.

But I have dwelt too long upon this first part; I come now to the second, which concerns an Exhortation, as I have shewed you, in the Division.

But every man another's wealth. In direct opposition, he should say, *Let every man seek another's,* but the first part being compared with the latter, and (*seek*) being taken out of the former and put to the latter, and (*wealth*) taken out or rather implied, in the former, the whole sentence is thus resolved, *Let no man seek his own wealth, but let every man seek another's wealth.*

And the word here translated *wealth,* is the same with that in Rom. 13. 4. and may not be taken only for riches, as Englishmen commonly understand it, but for all kinds of benefits, favors, comforts, either for soul or body; and so here again, as before you must understand an Affirmative Commandment as the Negative was before: and lest any should say, If I may not seek my own good, I may do nothing; Yes saith *Paul,* I'll tell thee, thou shalt seek the good of another, whereas now all thy seeking helps but one, by this means thou shalt help many: and this is further enforced by these two circumstances, (no man) may seek his own be he rich, learned, wise, etc. *But everyman must seek the good of another.*

The point of instruction is taken from the very letter and phrase, viz:

Doctrine 2. *A man must seek the good, the wealth, the profit of others.*

I say he *must* seek it, he must seek the comfort, profit and benefit of his neighbor, brother, associate, etc. His own good he need not seek, it will offer itself to him every hour; but the good of others must be sought, a man must not stay from doing good to others till he is sought unto, pulled and hauled, (as it were,) like the unjust judge, for every benefit that is first craved, cometh too late. And thus the ancient patriarchs did practice, when the traveller and wayfaring men came by, they did not tarry till they came and asked relief and refreshment, but sat at the gates to watch for such, (Judges 19. 20, 21.) and looked in the streets to find them, yea, set open their doors that they might freely and boldly enter in. And howsoever, some may think this too large a practice, since now the world is so full of people, yet I see not but the more people there is, the larger charity ought to be.

But be it so, as a man may neglect in some sort the general world, yet those to whom he is bound, either in natural, civil or religious bands, them he must seek how to do them good. A notable example you have in *David*, who, because there was twixt him and *Jonathan* a bond and covenant, therefore he enquired, *Whether there was any left of the house of Saul, to whom he might show mercy for Jonathan's sake*, 2 Sam. 9. 1. So this people of *Corinth*, to whom *Paul* writeth, they were in a spiritual league and covenant in the *Gospel*, and so were a body. Now for one member in the body to seek himself, and neglect all others were, as if a man should clothe one arm or one leg of his body with gold and purple, and let all the rest of the members go naked. 1 Cor. 12. 27.

Now brethren, I pray you, remember yourselves, and know, that you are not in a retired monastical course, but have given your names and promises one to another and covenanted here to cleave together in the service of God, and the King; What then must you do? May you live as retired hermits? And look after nobody? Nay, you must seek still the wealth of one another; and enquire as *David*, how liveth such a man? How is he clad? How is he fed? He is my brother, my associate; we ventured our lives together here, and had a hard brunt of it and we are in league together. Is his labor harder than mine? surely I will ease him; hath he no bed to lie on? Why, I have two, I'll lend him one; hath he no apparel? Why, I have two suits, I'll give him one of them; eats he coarse fare, bread and water, and I have better, why, surely we will part stakes. He is as good a man as I, and we are bound each to other, so that his wants must be my wants, his sorrows my sorrows, his sickness my sickness, and his welfare my welfare, for I am as he is. And such a sweet sympathy were excellent, comfortable, yea, heavenly, and is the only maker and conserver of churches and commonwealths, and where this is wanting, ruin comes on quickly, as it did here in *Corinth*. But besides these motives, there are other reasons to provoke us not only to do good one to another; but even to seek and search how to do it.

1. As first, to maintain modesty in all our associates, that of hungry wanters, they become not bold beggars and impudent cravers; for as one saith of women, that, when they have lost their shamefacedness, they have lost half their honesty, so may it be truly said of a man that when he hath lost his modesty, and puts on a begging face, he hath lost his majesty, and the image of that noble creature; and man should not beg and crave of man, but only of God. True it is, that as Christ was fain to crave water of the Samaritan woman, (John 4. 5.) so men are forced to ask sometimes rather than starve, but indeed in all societies it should be offered them. Men often complain of men's boldness in asking, but how cometh this to pass, but because the world have been so full of self-lovers as no man would offer their money, meat, garments, though they saw men hungry, harborless, poor, and naked in the streets; and what is it that makes men brazen-faced, bold, brutish, tumultuous, but because they are pinched with want, and see others of their companions (which it may be have less deserved) to live in prosperity and pleasure?

2. It wonderfully encourageth men in their duties, when they see the burthen equally borne; but when some withdraw themselves and retire to their own particular ease, pleasure, or profit; what heart can men have to go on in their business?

When men are come together to lift some weighty piece of
timber or vessel; if one stand still and do not lift, shall not
the rest be weakened and disheartened? Will not a few idle
drones spoil the whole stock of laborious bees? So one idle-
belly, one murmurer, one complainer, one self-lover will
weaken and dishearten a whole colony. Great matters have
been brought to pass where men have cheerfully, as with one
heart, hand, and shoulder, gone about it, both in wars, building, and plantations, but where every man seeks himself, all
cometh to nothing.

3. The present necessity requireth it, as it did in the days
of the *Jews*, returning from captivity, and as it was here in
Corinth. The country is yet raw, the land untilled, the cities
not builded, the cattle not settled, we are compassed about
with a helpless and idle people, the natives of the country,
which cannot in any comely or comfortable manner help themselves, much less us. We also have been very chargeable to
many of our loving friends, which helped us hither, and now
again supplied us, so that before we think of gathering riches,
we must even in conscience think of requiting their charge,
love and labor, and cursed be that profit and gain which
aimeth not at this. Besides, how many of our dear friends did
here die at our first entrance, many of them, no doubt for
want of good lodging, shelter, and comfortable things, and
many more may go after them quickly, if care be not taken. Is
this then a time for men to begin to seek themselves? *Paul*
saith, that men in the last days shall be lovers of themselves,
(2 Tim. 3. 2.) but it is here yet but the first days, and (as it
were) the dawning of the new world, it is now therefore no
time for men to look to get riches, brave clothes, dainty fare,
but to look to present necessities; it is now no time to pamper
the flesh, live at ease, snatch, catch, scrape, and pill, and hoard
up, but rather to open the doors, the chests, and vessels, and
say, brother, neighbor, friend, what want ye, anything that
I have? Make bold with it, it is yours to command, to do you
good, to comfort and cherish you, and glad I am that I have
it for you.

4. And even the example of God Himself, who we should
follow in all things within our power and capacity, may teach

us this lesson, for (with reverence to his Majesty be it spoken) He might have kept all grace, goodness, and glory to Himself, but He hath communicated it to us, even as far as we are capable of it in this life, and will communicate His glory in all fullness with his elect in that life to come; even so His son Jesus Christ left His glory eclipsed for a time, and abased himself to a poor and distressed life in this world that He might, by it, bring us to happiness in the world to come. If God then have delighted in thus doing good and relieving frail and miserable man, so far inferior to Himself, what delight ought man to have to relieve and comfort man, which is equal to himself.

5. Even as we deal with others, ourselves and others shall be dealt withal. Carest thou not how others fare, how they toil, are grieved, sick, pinched, cold, harborless, so as thou be in health, livest at ease, warm in thy nest, farest well? The days will come when thou shalt labor and none shall pity thee, be poor and none relieve thee, be sick, and lie and die and none visit thee, yea, and thy children shall lie and starve in the streets, and none shall relieve them, *for it is the merciful that shall obtain mercy;* Mat. 5. 7. and *the memory of the just shall be blessed even in his seed;* (Prov. 10.) and a merciful and loving man when he dies, though he leaves his children small and desolate, yet every one is mercifully stirred up for the father's sake to shew compassion, but the unkindness, currishness and self-love of a father, is through God's just judgment recompensed upon the children with neglect and cruelty.

6. Lastly, That we may draw to an end; A merciless man, and a man without natural affection or love, is reckoned among such as are given over of God to a reprobate mind, (Rom. 1. 30.) and (as it were) transformed into a beast-like humor; for, what is man if he be not sociable, kind, affable, free-hearted, liberal; he is a beast in the shape of a man; or rather an infernal spirit, walking amongst men, which makes the world a hell what in him lieth; for, it is even a hell to live where there are such men; such the Scriptures calleth *Nabals,* which signifieth *fools,* (Psal. 14. 1.) and decayed men, which have lost both the sap of grace and nature; and such merciless men are called *goats,* and shall be set at Christ's left hand

at the last day, (Math. 25. 33.) *Oh therefore seek the wealth one of another.*

Objection: But some will say, *It is true, and it were well if men would so do, but we see every man is so for himself, as that if I should not do so, I should do full ill, for if I have it not of my own, I may snap short sometimes, for I see no body showeth me any kindness, nor giveth me anything; if I have gold or silver, that goeth for payment, and if I want it I may lie in the street, therefore, I had best keep that I have, and not be so liberal as you would have me, except I saw others would be so towards me.*

Answer. This objection seemeth but equal and reasonable, as did the answer of *Nabal* to David's men, but it is most foolish and carnal, as his also was; for, if we should measure our courses by most men's practices, a man should never do any godly duty; for, do not the most, yea, almost all, go the broad way that leadeth to death and damnation, (Luke. 13. 23, 24.) Who then will follow a multitude? It is the word of God, and the examples of the best men that we must follow. And what if others will do nothing for thee, but are unkind and unmerciful to thee? Knowest thou not that they which will be the children of God must be kind to the unkind, loving to their enemies, and bless those that curse them? (Mat. 5. 44, 47.) If all men were kind to thee, it were put *publicans'* righteousness to be kind to them? If all men be evil, wilt thou be so too? When *David* cried out, *Help Lord, for not a godly man is left,* (Psal. 12. 1.) did he himself turn ungodly also? Nay, he was rather the more strict. So, if love and charity be departed out this world, be thou one of them that shall first bring it in again.

And let this be the first rule, which I will with two others conclude for this time.

1. Never measure the course by the most, but by the best, yea, and principally by God's word: Look not what others do to thee, but consider what thou art to do to them, seek to please God, not thyself. Did they in Mat. 25. 44. plead, that others did nothing for them? No such matter, no such plea will stand before God, his word is plain to the contrary, therefore, though all the world should neglect thee, disregard thee,

and contemn thee, yet remember thou hast not to do with men, but with the highest God, and so thou must do thy duty to them notwithstanding.

2. And let there be no prodigal person to come forth and say, "Give me the portion of lands and goods that appertaineth to me, and let me shift for myself;" (*Luke* 15. 12.) It is yet too soon to put men to their shifts; *Israel* was seven years in *Canaan*, before the land was divided unto tribes, much longer before it was divided unto families: and why wouldst thou have thy particular portion, but because thou thinkest to live better than thy neighbor, and scornest to live so meanly as he? But of who, I pray thee, brought this particularizing first into the world? Did not Satan, who was not content to keep that equal state with his fellows, but would set his throne above the stars? Did not he also entice man to despise his general felicity and happiness, and go try particular knowledge of good and evil; and nothing in this world doth more resemble heavenly happiness, than for men to live as one, being of one heart, and one soul; neither anything more resembles hellish horror, than for every man to shift for himself; for if it be a good mind and practise, thus to affect particulars; *mine* and *thine*, then it should be best also for God to provide one heaven for thee, and another for thy neighbor.

Objection. But some will say, *If all men will do their endeavors as I do, I could be content with this generality—but many are idle and slothful, and eat up other's labors, and therefore it is best to part, and then every man may do his pleasure.*

First, this, indeed, is the common plea of such as will endure no inconveniences, and so for the hardness of men's hearts, God and man doth often give way to that which is not best, nor perpetual, but indeed if we take this course to change ordinances and practices because of inconveniences, we shall have every day new laws.

Secondly, if others be idle and thou diligent, thy fellowship, provocation, and example, may well help to cure that malady in them, being together, but being asunder, shall they not be more idle, and shall not gentry and beggary be quickly the glorious ensigns of your commonwealth?

Thirdly, construe things in the best part, be not too hasty to say, men are idle and slothful, all men have not strength, skill, faculty, spirit, and courage to work alike; it is thy glory and credit, that thou canst do so well, and his shame and reproach, that can do no better; and are not these sufficient rewards to you both.

Fourthly, if any be idle apparently, you have a law and governors to execute the same, and to follow that rule of the Apostle, to keep back their bread, and let them not eat, go not therefore whispering, to charge men with idleness; but go to the governor and prove them idle; and thou shall see them have their deserts. (Acts. 19. 38. 2 Thes. 3. 10. Deut. 19. 15.)

And as you are a body together, so hang not together by skins and gymocks, but labor to be jointed together and knit by flesh and sinews; away with envy at the good of others, and rejoice in his good, and sorrow for his evil. Let his joy be thy joy, and his sorrow thy sorrow: Let his sickness be thy sickness: his hunger thy hunger, his poverty thy poverty; and if you profess friendship, be friends in adversity; for then a friend is known and tried, and not before.

3. Lay away all thought of former things and forget them, and think upon the things that are; look not gapingly one upon other, pleading your goodness, your birth, your life you lived, your means you had and might have had; here you are by God's providence under difficulties; be thankful to God, it is no worse, and take it in good part that which is, and lift not up yourself because of former privileges; when *Job* was brought to the dunghill, he sat down upon it, (Job. 2. 8.) and when the Almighty had been bitter to *Naomi*, she would be called *Marah;* consider therefore what you are now, and whose you are; say not I could have lived thus and thus; but say thus and thus I must live; for God and natural necessity requireth, if your difficulties be great, you had need to cleave the faster together, and comfort and cheer up one another, laboring to make each other's burden lighter; there is no grief so tedious as a churlish companion and nothing makes sorrows easy more than cheerful associates; bear ye therefore one another's burthen, and be not a burthen one to another; avoid all factions, forwardness, singularity and withdrawings, and

cleave fast to the Lord, and one to another continually; so
shall you be a notable precedent to these poor heathens, whose
eyes are upon you, and who very brutishly and cruelly do
daily eat and consume one another, through their emulations,
ways and contentions; be you therefore ashamed of it, and win
them to peace both with yourselves, and one another, by your
peaceable examples, which will preach louder to them, than
if you could cry in their barbarous language; so also shall you
be an encouragement to many of your Christian friends in
your native country, to come to you when they hear of your
peace, love, and kindness that is amongst you; but above all,
it shall go well with your souls, when that God of peace and
unity shall come to visit you with death as He hath done many
of your associates, you being found of Him, not in murmur-
ings, discontent and jars, but in brotherly love, and peace, may
be translated from this wandering wilderness unto that joyful
and heavenly Canaan. Amen.

On Thursday, the 13th of December, (O. S.,) 1621, the day
after the delivery of the foregoing sermon, the Fortune sailed
for England, and Robert Cushman in her "as the Adventurers
had appointed;" and it was the last time he was ever to see
those friends with whom he had suffered and endured so much,
and for whom he had toiled most assiduously for so many
years.

His only son Thomas, then fourteen years of age, had accompanied him in the Fortune; his wife had undoubtedly died
some time previous; but the date of her death as well as her
name are unknown. As he was to leave his minor son among
strangers, he placed him in the care and in the family of his
intimate friend "and brother in the Lord," Governor Bradford, where he remained till he arrived at the age of manhood.
The history of his *protege* who in after years became a pillar
of the Church as well as of the Colony, will show how faithfully Governor Bradford executed the trust reposed in him by
his friend and coadjutor, Robert Cushman. In a subsequent
letter to Governor Bradford, speaking of his son, Mr. Cushman
remarks, "I must entreat you still to have a care of my son
as your own, and I shall rest bound unto you."

The Fortune carried out on her return voyage, "two hhds.

of bear and other skins and good clap-boards, as full as she could hold; the freight estimated at near £500."

Governor Winslow in a letter written to a friend in England and sent by the Fortune says, "that we have gotten we send by this ship; and though it be not much it will witness for us that we have not been idle."

But *mis*-fortunes attended the return voyage of the *Fortune*, "As she neared the English coast she was taken by the French, carried into France,—the Isle Deu,—kept there fourteen or fifteen days,—robbed of all she had worth taking, and then the ship and the people are released, and they arrive at London on Monday, February 17th, 1622."[1]

In July, 1622, Mr. Weston, a member of the Virginia Company, and formerly a firm friend of the Pilgrims, "sent over fifty or sixty men, at his own charge, to plant for him."[2] They came upon no religious design, as did the planters of Plymouth; so they were far from being Puritans.

Mr. Cushman writes to the Plymouth Colony respecting these men, "They are no men for us, and I fear they will hardly deal so well with the savages as they should. I pray you, therefore, signify to Squanto, that they are a distinct body from us, and we have nothing to do with them, nor must be blamed for their faults, much less can warrant their fidelity."

In the spring of 1623, there was for the first time, a division and assignment of land among those who had settled at Plymouth; but this was for one year only.

In 1624 "the people requested the Governor to have some land for continuance and not by yearly lot as before, and he gives every person an acre of land."

In the first volume of the Old Colony Records we find the following entry:

"1623
Robert Cochman
one acre
These lye on the south side of the
Brook to the Baywards."

---

[1]Bradford in Prince.
[2]They settled in Weymouth.

This was unquestionably the same as Robert Cushman,—the error being in the spelling of his name. Although he was not at Plymouth, personally, (being then in London, supervising the affairs of the Colony,) yet land was, nevertheless, assigned him, the same as though he was there to occupy it. This shows the important position that he occupied, in the opinion of the Governor and the Colony.

July, 1623, says Bradford, as quoted by Prince, "The ship Anne arrives. By this ship, Mr. C., their Agent, writes—some few of your old friends are come, they come dropping to you and by degrees. I hope ere long you shall enjoy them all," etc.

March, 1624. "Mr. Winslow, our Agent, comes over in the ship Charity, and brings a bull and three heifers, the first cattle of the kind in the land; but therewith a sad account of a strong faction among the Adventurers against us." Mr. Winslow brings a letter from Robert Cushman to Governor Bradford, dated at London, January 24, 1623-4,—wherein he writes, "They send a carpenter to build two ketches, etc., a salt man to make salt, and a preacher,[1] though not the most eminent, for whose going Mr. Winslow and I gave way to give content to some at London,—the ship to be laden and sent back; we have taken a Patent for Cape Ann."

In the year 1623, Robert Cushman, in connection with Edward Winslow, who had been sent to England as an Agent of the Plymouth Colony, negotiated with Lord Sheffield[2] for a tract of land lying on Cape Ann, (in the present town of Gloucester,) for the purpose of establishing a Colony there,—thus benefiting the Pilgrim colonists at Plymouth as well as extending the settlement of the country. And it is an interesting fact that the Colony which was commenced under the Charter

[1] John Lyford. He was opposed to the emigration of Rev. John Robinson, and did what he could to prevent it. He was expelled from the Plymouth Colony for misconduct, and afterwards died in Virginia.

[2] "Among those whose interest was gained by Cushman and Winslow, the first Colonial Agents from New England to old England, was Edward, Lord Sheffield, then one of the leading statesmen of England, and a prominent member of the Council for New England. It was in the exercise of authority from that Company that he granted this charter." *Thornton's Cape Anne Charter.*

obtained by Cushman and Winslow, and under the auspices of the Plymouth Colony, was the first permanent settlement on the territory of the Massachusetts Colony. As this Charter[1] is another evidence of the industry and ability of Robert Cushman, as well as an interesting portion of the history of the times, we give it entire, retaining the abbreviations and orthography of the original as far as modern type will allow.

THE CHARTER

This Indenture: made the first day of January Anno Dni 1623[2] And in the Years of the Raigne of or Soveraigne Lord James by the grace of God King of England, France and Ireland, defender of the faith & the One and Twentieth And of Scotland the seaven and fyftyth between the right honourable Edmond Lord Sheffield, knight of the most noble order of the garter on throne part And Robert Cushman and Edward Winslowe for themselves, and their Associates and Planters at Plymouth in New England in America on thother part, WITNESSETH: That the said Lord Sheffield, (As well in consideracon) that the said Robert and Edward in divers of theire Associates have already adventured themselves in person, and have likewise at theire owne proper Costs and Charges transported dyvers persons into New England aforsaid And for that the said Robert and Edward And their Associates also intend as well to transport more persons as also further plant at Plymouth aforsaid, and in other places in New England aforsaid As for the better Advancement and furtherance of the said Planters, and encouragement of the said Vndertakers Hath Gyven, graunted, assigned, allotted,

---

[1]The public are indebted to J. Wingate Thornton, Esq., of Boston, for the discovery and publication of this Charter, which for more than two hundred years has been unknown or forgotten. Thus Roger Conant is found to be Governor of the first Massachusetts Colony, and another interesting page is added to the history of the old Bay State. (See Thornton's late work, ''The Landing at Cape Anne; or the Charter of the first permanent Colony on the territory of Massachusetts Company, now discovered and published from the original manuscript.''—(Boston, October, 1854, p. 84.)

[2]It should be 1623-4.

and appointed And by these pnts doth Gyve, graunt, assigne, allot, and appoint unto and for the said Robert and Edward and their Associates As well a certaine Tract of Ground in New England aforsaid lying in Fortythree Degrees or thereabout of Northerly latitude and in a knowne place there comonly called Cape Ann, Together with the free use and benefit as well of the Bay of Cape Anne, as also of the Islands within the said Bay And free liberty, to fish, fowle, hawke, and hunt, truck, and trade in the Lands thereabout, and in all other places in New England aforsaid; Whereof the said Lord Sheffield is, or hath byn possessed, or which have been allotted to him the said Lord Sheffield, or within his Jurisdiccon (not nowe being inhabited, or hereafter to be inhabited by any English) Together also with five hundred Acres of Free Land adjoining to the said Bay to be ymployed for publig uses, as for the building of a Towne, Scholes, Churches, Hospitals[1] and for mayntenance of such Ministers, Officers, and Magistrats, as by the said undertakers, and their Associates are there already appointed, or which hereafter shall, with their good liking, reside, and inhabit there And also Thirty Acres of Land, over and besyde the fyve hundred acres of land before mentioned to be allotted, and appointed for every perticuler person, young or olde, being the Associates, or servants of the said undertakers or their scucessor's that shall come and dwell at the aforsaid Cape Anne with Seaven years, next after the Date hereof, which Thirty Acres of Land soe appointed to every person as aforsaid, shall be taken as the same doth lye together upon the said Bay in one entire place, and not stragling, in dyvers, or remote parcells not exceeding an English Mile, and a halfe in length on the Waters side of the said Bay—YIELDING AND PAYING for ever yearely unto the said Lord Sheffield, his heires, successors, Rent gatherer, or assignes for every Thirty Acres soe to be obtayned, and pos-

---

[1] No where is the embryo of New England more visible than in this Charter. Schools, Churches and Hospitals are provided for; laws and elections to be only with their good liking, and every man to be landholder. There we see the germ of Republican institutions we now enjoy. Says Thornton, "It (the Charter) displays a political wisdom superior to Locke, or any theorist, probably the wisdom of Winslow and Cushman."

sessed by the said Robert and Edward theire heires, successors or Associats Twelve Pence of lawful English money At the feast of St. Michael Tharchaungell only (if it be lawfully demaunded) The first payment thereof To begynne ymediately from and after thend and expiracon of the first seaven years next after the date hereof AND THE SAID Lord Sheffield for himself his heires, successors, and assignes doth covenant, promise, and graunt to and with the said Robert Cushman and Edward Winslow their heires, associats, and assignes That they the said Robert, and Edward, and such other persons as shall plant, and contract with them, shall freely and quyetly, have, hold, possesse, and enjoy All such profitts, rights, previlidges, benefits, Comodities, advantages, and preheminces, as shall hereafter by the labor, search, and diligence of the said Vndertakers their Associats, servants, or Assignes be obtayned, found out, or made within the said Tract of Ground soe graunted unto them as aforesaid; Reserving unto the said Lord Sheffield His heires, successors and assignes the one Moyety of all such Mynes as shall be discovered, or found out at any tyme by the said Vndertakers, or any their heires, successors, or assignes upon the Grounds aforsaid AND further That it shall and may be lawful to, and for the said Robert Cushman and Edward Winslow their heires, associats, and Assignes from tyme to tyme and at all tymes hereafter soe soon as they or their assignes have taken possession, or entered into any of the said Lands To forbyd, repell, repulse and resist by force of Armes All and every such person as shall build, plant, or inhabit, or which shall offer, or make shew to build, plant, or inhabit, within the Lands soe as aforesaid graunted, without the leave, and license of the said Robert, and Edward or theire assignes AND THE SAID Lord Sheffield doth further Covenant, and graunt that upon a lawful survey hadd, and taken of the aforesaid Lands, and good informacion gyven to the said Lord Sheffield, his heirs, or assigns of the Meats, Bounds and quantity of Lands which the said Robert, and Edward their heirs, associates, or assigns shall take in and be by them their Associates, Servants, or Assigns inhabited as aforsaid; he the said Lord Sheffield his heires, or assignes, at and upon the reasonable request of the

said Vndertakers or theire Associates, shall and will by good
and sufficient Assurance in the Lawe Graunt, enfeoffe, confirm and allot unto the said Robert Cushman and Edward
Winslowe their Associates, and Assigns All and every the said
Lands soe to be taken in within the space of Seaven yeares
next after the Date hereof in as larg, ample, and beneficiall
manner, as the said Lord Sheffield his heires, or assignes nowe
have, or hereafter shall have the same Lands, or any of them
graunted unto him, or them; for such rent, and under such
Covenants, Provisos as herene are conteyned (Mutatis Mutandis) AND shall and will also at all tymes hereafter upon
reasonable request made to him the said Lord Sheffield his
heires, or assignes by the said Edward and Robert their heires,
associates, or assignes, or any of them graunt, procure, and
make good, lawful, and sufficient Letters, or other Graunts
of Incorporacon whereby the said Vndertakers, and their Associates shall have liberty and lawful authority from tyme to
tyme to make and establish Lawes, Ordynnces, and Constitucons for the ruling, ordering, and governing of such persons
as now are resident, or which hereafter shall be planted, and
inhabett there And in the mean tyme until such Graunt be
made It shall be lawful for the said Robert and Edward, their
heires, associates and Assignes by consent of the greater part
of them to Establish such Laws, Provisions and Ordynnces as
are or shall be by them thought most fit and convenient for the
government of the said plantacon which shall be from tyme to
tyme executed and administered by such Officer or Officers,
as the Vndertakers or their Associates or the most part of them
shall elect, and make choice of PROVYDED alwaies That the
said Lawes, Provisions, and Ordynnces which are, or shall be
agreed upon, be not repugnant to the Lawes of England or to
the Orders, and Constitucons of the President and Councell
of New England, PROVYDED further That the said Vndertakers their heires, and successors shall fore acknowledge the
Said Lord Sheffield his heires and successors, to be theire
Chief Lord, answeare and doe service unto his Lord or his
Successors, at his, or theire Court when upon his, or theire own
Plantacon The same shall be established, and kept IN
WYTNES whereof the said parties to these present Indentures

Interchangeably have putt their Hands and Seals The day and yeares first above written.

SHEFFEYLD
Seal Pendent

The strip of parchment at the foot of the instrument, to which the seal was pendant, yet remains as represented in the fac-simile. By the law and usage of that day, the Original instrument was executed by the Grantor only, which accounts for the omission on this parchment of the names of the Guaranters whose signatures would be affixed to the counterpart remaining in the hands of Sheffield. Hence the Autograph of Robert Cushman is on the Original document in England, if it could be found. It will be noticed that the name of Robert Cushman is, all through that Charter, placed first, or before that of Winslow; an undoubted indication of his conventional position.

To Robert Cushman, therefore, belongs (in part) the reputation of procuring a Charter for the Plymouth Colony—and a Charter for the first permanent settlement on the territory of the Massachusetts Colony at Cape Ann. The two first settlements in Massachusetts were, therefore, the result, to a considerable extent of his zeal or perseverance in the Puritan Cause, and his labors extend to the area of civil and religious liberty.

In performance of his duties as Agent of the Colony, Mr. Cushman wrote the following letter, dated December 18th, 1624:

To our beloved friends, Mr. Wm. Bradford, Mr. Isaac Allerton, Mr. Wm. Brewster, and the rest of the general society at Plymouth in New England,—Salutation,

Though the thing we feared be come upon us, and the evils we strove against have overtaken us: yet cannot we forget you, nor our friendship nor fellowship, which together we have some years; wherein, though our expressions have been small, yet our hearty affection towards you (unknown by face) have been no less than to our nearest friends, yea even to our own selves. And though you and our friend Mr. Winslow, can tell you the estate of things here, and what hath befallen us; yet lest we should seem to neglect you, to whom, by a wonderful providence of God, we are so nearly united; we have thought good once more to write you, and the arguments of our letter must consist of these three points: First, to shew you what is here befallen; 2dly, the reason and cause of that which is fallen; 3dly, our purpose and desires towards you hereafter. * * *

As there hath been a faction and siding amongst us now more than two years: so now there is an utter breach and sequestration amongst us and in two parts of us, a full desertion and forsaking of you, without any intent or purpose of meddling more with you. * * *

And if in nothing else, you can be approved, yet let your honesty and conscience be still approved and lose not one jot of your innocense amidst your many crosses and afflictions. * * *

And surely, if you upon this alteration behave yourselves wisely and go on fairly, as men whose hope is not in this life, you shall need no other weapon to wound your adversaries; for when your righteousness is revealed as the light, they shall cover their faces with shame, that causelessly have sought your overthrow.

And although (we hope) you need not our counsel in these things, having learned of God how to behave yourselves, in all estates in this world: yet a word for your advice and direction, to spur those forward which we hope run already.

At first seeing our generality here is dissolved, let yours be the more firm: and do not you, like carnal people (which run into inconveniences and evils by examples) but rather be warned by your harmes, to cleave faster together hereafter; take heed of long and sharp disputes, and oppositions, give no passage to the waters, no, not a tittle; let not hatred or heart-burning be harbored in the breast of any of you one moment, but forget and forgive all former failings and abuses and renew your love and friendship together daily. There is often more sound friendship and sweeter fellowship in afflictions and crosses than in prosperity and favours; and there is reason for it, because envy flyeth away, when there is nothing but necessities to be looked on; but it is always a *bold* guest when prosperity shows itself. * * *

We have a trade and custom of talebearing, whispering, and changing of old friends for new, and these things with us are incurable; but you which do as it were, *begin a new world* and lay a foundation of sound piety and humanity for others to follow, must suffer no such weeds in your garden, but nip them in the head and cast them out forever; and must follow peace and study quietness, having fervent love among yourselves as a perfect and entire bond to uphold you when all else fails you.

* * *

And if any amongst you, for all that, have still a withdrawing heart, and will be all to himself and nothing to his neighbour, let him think of these things: 1st, The providence of God in bringing you there together. 2d, His marvelous preserving you from so many dangers, the particulars whereof you know and must never forget. 3d, The hopes that yet are of effecting somewhat for yourselves, and more for your posterity, if hand join in hand. 4th, The woful estate of him which is alone, especially in a wilderness. 5th, The succor and comfort which the generality can daily afford, having built houses, planted corn, framed boats, erected salt works, obtained cattle, swine, and pulling together with the divers varieties of trades and faculties, employed by sea and land, the gains of every one stretching itself into all, whilst they are in the general; but such as withdraw themselves, tempting God and despising their neighbours, must look for no share nor part in any of these things; but as they will be in a commonwealth alone, so alone they must work, and alone they must eat, and alone they must be sick and die, or else languishing under the frustration of their vain hopes, alone return to England and there to help all cry out of the country and the people; * * * 6th, The conscience of making restitution and paying those debts and charges which hath fallen to bring you them and send those things to you, which you have had, must hold you together; and for him that withdraws himself from the general, we look upon him as upon a man, who, having served his turn and fulfilled his desires, cares not what becomes of others, neither making conscience of any debt or duty at all, but thinketh to slide away under secret colors to abuse and deceive his friends; and against whom we need say little, seeing the Lord will never cease to curse his course.

* * *

In a word, since it thus still falleth out, that all things between us, are as you see, let us all endeavour to keep a fair and honest course, and see what time will bring forth and how God, in his providence, will work for us.

We still are persuaded you are the people, that must make a plantation, and erect a city in these remote places, when all others fail and return; and your experience of God's providence, and preservation of you is such, that we hope your hearts will not now fail you, though your friends should forsake you (which we ourselves shall not do, whilst we live, so long as your honesty so well appeareth) yet surely help would arise from some other place, whilst you wait on God with uprightness, though we should leave you also.

To conclude, as you are especially now to renew your love to one another: so we advise you, as your friends, to these particulars. First let all sharpness, reprehension and convictions of opposite persons, be still used sparingly, and take no advantage against any, for any for respects; but rather wait for their mending amongst you, than to mend them yourselves by thrusting them away, of whom there is any hope of any good to be had. 2. *Make your corporation* as *formal* as *you can, under the name* of the *Society* of *Plymouth* in *New England,* allowing some peculiar privileges, to all the members thereof, according to the tenure of the patents.

3d, Let your *practices and course in religion,* in the Church be made complete and full; let all that fear God amongst you, join themselves thereunto, without delay: and let all the ordinances of God be used completely in the Church without longer waiting upon uncertainties, or keeping the gap open for opposites. *4thly, Let the worship and service of God, be strictly kept on the Sabbath,* and both together and asunder, let the day be sanctified; and let your care be seen on the working days, every where and upon all occasions, to set forward the service of God. And lastly be you all entreated, to walk so circumspectly and carry yourselves so uprightly in all your ways, as that no man can make exceptions against you; and more especially that the favor and countenance of God, may be so towards you, as that you may find abundant joy and peace even amidst tribulations.

We have sent you some cattle, cloth, hose, shoes, leather, etc., but in another nature than formerly, as it stood us in hand to do; we have committed them to the custody and charge of, as our factors, Mr. Allerton and Mr. Winslow, at whose direction they are to be sold, and commodities taken for them, as is fitting. Good friends, as you buy them, keep a decorum in distributing them, and let none have varieties, and things for delight, when others want for their mere necessities, and have an eye rather on your ill deservings, at God's hand, than upon the failings of your friends towards you; rather admiring His mercies, than repining at His crosses, with the assurance of faith, that what is wanting here, shall be made up in glory a thousand fold. Go on, good friends, comfortably, pluck up your hearts cheerfully, and *quit yourselves like men in all your difficulties,* that notwithstanding all the displeasure and threats of men, yet the work may go on, which you are about, and not be neglected, which is so much for the glory of God, and the furtherance of our countrymen, as that a man may, with more comfort, spend his life in it, than live the life of Methuselah in wasting the plenty of a tilled land or eating the fruit of a green tree.

Thus, having not time to write further unto you, leaving other things to the relation of our friends; with all hearty salutations to you all and hearty prayers for you all, we lovingly take our leave this 18th of December, 1624.

Your assured friends to our power,

James Sherley, (sick)   Thomas Fletcher,
William Collier,   Robert Holland.

("This letter was wrote with Mr. Cushman's hand; and it is likely was penned by him at the other request"). From Governor Bradford's Letter Book.

—Massachusetts Hist. Coll. 1st Series, V. 3, pp. 29 to 34.

The following letter from Mr. Cushman, is probably the last that he ever wrote to his friends in America.

Mr. Robert Cushman to Governor Bradford.

December 22, 1624

Sir: My hearty love remembered unto you, and unto your wife, with trust of your health and contentment, amidst so many difficulties. I am now to write unto you, from my friend, and from myself, my friend and your friend. Mr. Sherley, who lieth even at the point of death, entreated me, even with tears, to write to excuse him, and signify how it was with him; he remembers his hearty, and as he thinks, his last, salutations to you, and all the rest, who love our common cause. And If God does again raise him up, he will be more for you (I am persuaded) than ever he was. His unfeigned love towards us has been such, as I cannot indeed express; and though he be a man not swayed by passion, or led by uninferred affections, yet hath he cloven to us still amidst all persuasions of the opposites, and could not be moved to have an evil thought of us, for all their clamors. His patience and contentment in being oppressed, hath been much; he hath sometimes lent £800 at one time, for other men to adventure in this business, all to draw them on; and hath indeed, by his free heartedness, been the only glue of the company. And if God should take him now away, I scarce think much more would be done, save as to inquire at the dividend what is to be had.

He saith he hath received the tokens you sent, and thanks you for them; he hath sent you a cheese, etc. Also he hath sent an heifer to the plantation, to begin a stock for the poor. There is also a bull and three or four jades to be sold unto you with many other things, for apparel and other uses; which are committed to Mr. Allerton and Mr. Winslow, who as factors, are to sell them to you; and it was fitter, for many reasons, to make them factors than yourself, as I hope you will easily conceive.

And I hope, though the first project cease, yet it shall be never the worse for you, neither will any man be discouraged, but wait on God, using the good means you can. I have no time to write many things unto you; I doubt not, but upon the hearing of this alteration, some discontent may arise, but the Lord I hope will teach you the way which you shall choose.

For myself, as I have labored by all means to hold things here together, so I have patiently suffered this alteration; and do yet hope it shall be good for you all, if you be not too rash and hasty; which if any be, let them take heed, that they reap not the fruit of their own vanities.

But for you, good sir, I hope you will do nothing rashly, neither will you be swayed by misreports, beside your ordinary course, but will persuade who may be, to patience and peace, and to the bearing of labours and crosses in love together.

I hope the failings of your friends, here, will make you the more friendly one to another, that so all our hopes may not be dashed. Labour to settle things both in your civil and religious courses, as firm and as full as you can. Lastly, I must entreat you still, to have a care of my son as your own; and I shall rest bound unto you; I pray you let him sometimes practice writing. I hope the next ships to come to you; in the mean space and ever, the Lord be all your direction and turn all our crosses and troubles, to his own glory, and our comforts, and give you to walk so wisely, and holily, as none may justly say, but they have always found you honestly minded, though never so poor. Salute our friends, and supply, I pray you, what is failing in my letters.

From London, December 22, A. D. 1624.

The following note was by Governor Bradford:

"These were his last letters. And now we lost the help of a wise and faithful friend; he wrote of the sickness and probability of the death of another; but knew not that his own was so near; what cause have we therefore ever to be ready! He proposed to be with us the next ships, but the Lord did otherwise dispose; and had appointed him a greater journey to a better place. He was now taken from these troubles, into which (by this division) we were so deeply plunged. And here I must leave him to rest with the Lord. And will proceed with other letters, which will further show our proceedings and how things went on." (Hist. Coll. 1st Series, Vol. 3, pp. 34 and 35.)

In June 1625, Governor Bradford wrote to Mr. Cushman

the following letter. We omit portions of it as being unimportant.

Governor Bradford to Robert Cushman.

"Loving and kind Friend:

I would most heartily thank you; and would be right glad to see you here and many others of our old and dear friends, that we might strengthen and comfort one another, after our many troubles, travails and hardships. I long greatly for friends of Leyden, but I fear I shall not now, scarce ever see them, save in Heaven; but the will of the Lord be done. We have rid ourselves of the company of many of those who have been troublesome to us; though I fear we are not rid of the troubles themselves. * * *

We have sent by this first ship a good parcel of commodities, to wit: as much beaver and other furs as will amount to upwards of £277 sterling at the rates they were sold the last year, in part of payment of those goods they and you sent to be sold to us. But except we may have things, both new, serviceable, and at better rates, we shall never be able to rub through; therefore, if we could have some ready money disbursed to buy things at the best hand, it would be greatly in our way. * * * Our people will never agree any way again to unite with the company who have cut them off with such reproach and contempt, and also returned their bills and all debts in their hands. But as for those, our loving friends, who have and do stick to us, and are deeply engaged for us, and are most careful of our goods, for our parts we will ever be ready to do any thing, that should be thought equal and mete.

But I think it will be best to press a clearance with the company; either by coming to a dividend or some other indifferent course or composition; for the longer we hang and continue in this confused and lingering condition, the worse it will be, for it takes away all heart and courage, from men to do anything. For notwithstanding our persuasion to the contrary, many protest they will never build houses, fence grounds or plant fruits for those, who not only forsake them, but use them as enemies, lading them with reproach and contumely. Nay, they will rather ruin that which is done, than they should possess it. Whereas if they knew what they should trust to, the place would quickly grow and flourish with plenty; for they never felt the sweetness of the country till this year; and not only we, but all planters in the land begin to do it. * * *

Your son and all of us are in good health (blessed be God); he received the things you sent him. I hope God will *make him a good man.* My wife remembers her love unto you and thanks you for her spice. Billington still rails against you and threatens to arrest you. I know not wherefore; he is a knave and so will live and die.[1]

The Lord hath so graciously disposed, that when our opposites thought they may would have followed their faction, they so distracted their palpable dishonest dealings, that they stuck more firmly unto us and joined themselves to the Church. But time cuts me off; for other things I refer you to my other more general and longer letters; and so with my renewed salutations, and best love remembered unto you, I commend you and all our affairs to the guidance of the Most High, and so rest your assured loving friend, William Bradford. New Plymouth, June 9, 1625.

(Mr. Cushman died before this letter arrived.)[2]

"April, 1626. Captain Standish arrives from England, bringing intelligence of the death of Mr. John Robinson, who died Tuesday, March 1st, (O. S.,) 1625."[3]

"Our Captain also brings us notice of the death of our ancient friend Mr. Cushman, *who was as our right hand with the Adventurers and who for divers years had managed all our business with them to our great advantage.* He had wrote to the Governor a few months before (see his last letter page —) of the severe sickness of Mr. James Sherley, who was a chief friend of the Plantation."[4]

The exact date of Robert Cushman's death is not known.

---

[1]The prophecy was fulfilled, for he was hung (the first execution in the Colony) October, 1630, for waylaying and shooting a young man by the name of Newcomen.

[2]Bradford's Letter Book in Mass. Hist. Coll., V. 3.

[3]See Roger White's letter to Governor Bradford in Young's Chronicles.

[4]Governor Bradford's Journal.

As his last letter bore date, 22nd December, 1624, and as he died a few weeks before Mr. Robinson, who deceased March 1st, we may therefore reasonably conclude that he died in January or February, 1625.[1]

For the purpose of showing the high estimation in which Mr. Robert Cushman has been held, we shall give extracts from the writings of his contemporaries and from more recent historical works.

Says Governor Bradford, in 1625, speaking of his death: "And now we lost a wise and faithful friend. He proposed to be with us the next ship, but the Lord did otherwise dispose, and had appointed him a greater journey to a better place. * * * He was our right hand with the Adventurers; who for divers years has managed all our business with them to our great advantage."

Honorable John Davis, a Judge of the United States District Court of Massachusetts in a "Biographical Sketch" of Robert Cushman, published with an edition of his sermon in 1785, remarks,—"Robert Cushman was one of the most distinguished characters among the collection of worthies, who quitted England on account of their religious difficulties and settled with Mr. John Robinson, their Pastor, in the city of Leyden, in 1609."

"The news of his death and Mr. Robinson's, arrived at the same time at Plymouth, by Captain Standish, and seem to have been *equally lamented* by their bereaved and suffering friends here. He was zealously engaged in the success of the plantation; a man of activity and enterprise; well versed in business; respectable in point of intellectual abilities; well accomplished in scriptural knowledge; an unaffected professor and a steady, sincere practicer of religion."

And in a note to the foregoing at the time of the publication of another edition of that sermon, in 1846, Dr. N. B. Shurtleff of Boston, who seldom errs in any matters relating to the Plymouth Pilgrims, remarks,—"It seems to be a mistaken idea that Mr. Cushman started in the smaller vessel,

---

[1] In regard to his *age* at the time of his death, we think, from a variety of circumstances, that he was somewhere between 40 and 50 years. In 1621, he had a son 14 years of age.

which put back on account of its proving leaky. This mistake has arisen from the fact that Mr. Cushman was left in England in 1620 and did not come over in the Mayflower with the first emigrants. The fact is that Mr. Cushman procured "the larger vessel," the Mayflower, and its pilot at London and left in that vessel; but in consequence of the unsoundness of "the smaller vessel," the Speedwell, it became necessary that a part of the Pilgrims should be left behind, and consequently Mr. Cushman was selected as one who would be best able to keep together that portion of the flock left behind. Although Mr. Cushman did not come over in the Mayflower, yet such was the respect for him among those who did come, that his name is placed at the head of those who came in that ship, in the allotment of land (in 1623) at a time when he was not in New England."

And at a later period (1846) Judge Davis remarked in a letter to Charles Ewer, Esq., the publisher of a new edition of Mr. Cushman's sermon,—"That discourse is a precious relic of ancient times; the sound good sense, good advice and pious spirit which it manifests, will, it may be hoped, now and in all future time, meet with approval and beneficial acceptance in our community."

Says the venerable Dr. Dwight, formerly President of Yale College, in a volume of his travels in the United States, published in 1800, "By me the names of Carver, Bradford, *Cushman* and Standish, will never be forgotten until I lose the power of recollection."

Allen's Biographical Dictionary, under the head of Robert Cushman, has the following: "He was distinguished in the history of Plymouth Colony; was one of those worthies who quitted England on account of *liberty of conscience.* * * * He was a man of activity and enterprise; respectable for his talents and virtues; well acquainted with the scriptures and a professed disciple of Jesus Christ."

Russell's "Recollections of Plymouth," published in 1846, speaking of Robert Cushman, says,—"Perhaps no individual of the Rev. Mr. Robinson's Church, possessed in a higher degree the qualifications required for discharging the important duties incident to the trust assigned him."

Hubbard's History of New England, says, "Robert Cushman, was an active and faithful instrument for the public good."

From the Ecclesiastical History of Massachusetts, published in Mass. Hist. Coll., V. 7: "Robert Cushman, * * * one of the most important and worthy characters among those who formed the first settlement (at Plymouth). His sermon, preached to our venerable fathers, in 1621, contains the best advice, and may be read by their posterity for other reasons besides this, that it is a curiosity worth preserving among the ancient things of this country."

Baylies' History of New Plymouth, says of Robert Cushman, "He was a learned, acute, sagacious and enterprising person. He had great knowledge of human nature, and was a sincere and pious Christian. While at Plymouth he delivered a discourse, which is a performance of uncommon merit."

At the second celebration of the landing of the Pilgrims, by the Old Colony Club, December 22, 1770, after their dinner, several appropriate toasts were delivered by Dr. Lazarus Le Baron of Plymouth. The sixth was as follows:

"6. To the memory of Mr. Robert Cushman, who preached the first Sermon in New England."

From an "Account of the Church of Christ in Plymouth," by John Cotton, Esq., published in 1760:

"That servant of Christ, Mr. Robert Cushman, who had been their chief agent in transacting all their affairs in England, both before and after their leaving for Holland, till the year 1625."[1]

The question, then, may properly be asked,—if Robert Cushman was such a leading mind among the Puritans at Leyden, and subsequently was so active and influential in their emigration to, and first in settlement at Plymouth,—why he has never been as noted in history as his colleagues, Carver, Bradford, Brewster and others?

The following letter, written by one of the most distinguished of the name,[2] to a kinsman, will explain that apparent

---

[1] Mass. Hist. Coll., V. 4.
[2] Rev. Robert W. Cushman, D. D., late of the Bowdoin Street Baptist Church, at Boston.

anomaly as far as it can be done after a lapse of nearly two and a half centuries.

Boston, Feb. 24th, 1846.

To Joseph Cushman, Esq. :

My Dear Namesake—I rejoice that you have undertaken to call the attention of the descendants of our common ancestor to the debt which as citizens of this country, they owe to his memory; and that you propose to erect, by means of a contribution from them all, so far as they can be reached, a monument on the spot near the Plymouth Rock, where he delivered his memorable discourse to his brother Pilgrims before his departure.

We sometimes speak of "the caprices of fortune:" I have often thought how strange and how *unjust*, sometimes, are the accidents of fame. How strange, how passing strange that the man who was the chief instrument in the first settlement of New England—as is clear from his being the uniformly appointed agent of the Pilgrims to the Virginia Company and to the King, whoever else was associated with him in the different missions;—the man whom Governor Bradford himself, his colleague in the second mission, calls, "our right hand;" the man who first vindicated the enterprise to the world through the Press, and made the first public appeal that was ever made to the Protestant Christians of England, in behalf of the religious interests of the Aborigines of America; the man who, to save the Colony from the perils to which he saw it exposed, wrote and delivered, though neither Minister nor Elder, the first Sermon ever published from a New England man, and the first ever written on New England soil; the man whose devotion to his "loving friends the Adventurers" led him, after securing with great difficulty the Mayflower and a skillful pilot for her, who had been on the American coast, to take his own passage in the rickety Speedwell; and, after her third failure, to disembark, look after and share the fate of those who must be left behind; and, after he had crossed the ocean, to return and live and die not only "separate from his brethren," but separate from his only son, that he might watch over their interests near a jealous and intolerant throne:—that this man, I say, should have been overlooked by seven generations, while scarcely a fourth-rate politician has risen to bluster about "liberty" and "glory of America," whose name has not been honored and perpetuated as the appellation of some portion of its territory, is, I confess, a painful comment on the "gratitude of Republics," and the justice of posterity. While Carver and Brewster—successively his associates in negotiation, together with Standish, and Winslow, and Hopkins, and I know not how many others of the first Pilgrims in humble life, have been remembered and honored in the names of towns; while the very pilot, the benefit of whose skill he surrendered, has been immortalized in one of our island; while even the loafer Billington, who "slipped in" among the Pilgrims of Southampton and "was of no benefit to the colony," has been saved from merited oblivion by "Billington Sea;" and while geography and history have been vieing with each other, and painting has violated the truth (I allude to the National Picture at Washington, which places Carver among its figures of the Pilgrims at the embarkation in Holland, when, in fact, he was waiting their arrival at Southampton) in her eagerness to render homage to the fathers of the nation; the name of *Cushman*—a name to which New England and the country owe more, if we speak of generative influence, than almost any other of the page on American history—is still unborne by any county, town, island, mountain, lake, river, or rill in America.

All this is to be attributed to what I have called one of the accidents of fame; the injustice of which, however, is the more grievous, inasmuch as the very acts—the staying behind to take care of those who had been left, and his return to and continuance in England as the Argus of the Colony—which enhanced his title to grateful remembrance, were the cause of his being thus forgotten by posterity. But he, no doubt, if cognizant of earth's affairs, is better satisfied that it should be so than you and I are. "*I seek no name,*" said he, "*though the memory of this action shall never die.*"

I hope it may suffice, however, that past generations have shown such tender regard to his modesty, and that, by a union of all who know his blood to be flowing in their veins, a monument at least, standing where the ashes of his fellow pilgrims slumber, may tell to the generations following the part he bore in giving civilization, christianity and freedom to the western world.

Yours most truly,
ROBERT W. CUSHMAN.

Such was the life of Robert Cushman during the eight years in which we have any account of him. Enough during that period has transpired to give us a good idea of the character of the man,—his education, religious principles and habits, and his labors and sacrifices in behalf of the Puritan cause.

From the fact that he was the first Agent of the Pilgrims to negotiate with the Virginia Company, the King and the hierarchy of England, in connection with Mr. Carver, who was the first Governor of the Colony, and was a man of great wisdom and discretion,—and was continued in that agency the next year, in connection with Elder Brewster, who was the very head and pillar of the Puritan movement; that by his diplomatic skill and sagacity he finally obtained a Patent and afterwards made an agreement with the Merchant Adventurers, by which the Puritans were enabled to emigrate to America; that he was left, very reluctantly and much against his will, to take charge of the passengers of the Speedwell, as being the one best able to provide for, and keep together that portion of the flock, that were, from necessity, left behind; that he went to New England in the second ship that carried over emigrants, and left his only son there in the family of Governor Bradford; that he continued the faithful and unwearied friend and Agent of the Colony, and was in frequent correspondence with the Governor and other prominent members of that community; and that at the time of his decease, in the very prime and meridian of life, he was in expectation of coming here to settle and here to end his days;—from all these circumstances, we may reasonably infer that *he was one in the first movers and main instruments of the Puritan dissent of England, their pilgrimage to Holland, and their final settlement in America*. And when we consider the *immense consequences* of that movement in effecting the highest interests of man, in every department of life, how much the political, religious and civil rights of the *whole world,* even, have depended on the success of that enterprise, impartial justice as historians and biographers requires us to place *high up* in the *Temple of Fame* the *leaders* of the *Pilgrim Fathers* of *New England.*

> "And never may they rest unsung,
> While Liberty can find a tongue.
> Twine, Gratitude, a wreath for them,
> More deathless than the diadem,
> Who to life's noblest end,
> Gave up life's noblest powers;
> And bade the legacy descend,
> Down, down to us and ours."

Second Generation.

Thomas, familiarly known by the name of Elder Thomas Cushman, was born in England in February, 1608. He was probably in the Mayflower when his father with the other Pilgrims sailed for America, in August, 1620; for "Robert Cushman and his family" were among that famous band of Puritan brethren,—and with his father went back to London in the Speedwell.

In July, 1621, the ship Fortune sailed for New England, having on board thirty-five passengers, among whom were Robert Cushman and his family,—consisting of an only son, Thomas, then fourteen years of age.

Thomas arrived at Plymouth, in good health, in November, 1621. In a few days his father returned to England, leaving his only son in the family of his particular friend, Governor Bradford. And in a subsequent letter, he entreats the Governor "to have a care of my son, as your own, and I shall be bound unto you."

If it is true, that, "As the twig is bent the tree's inclined," then we have the very best evidence that Governor Bradford was faithful to the trust imposed in him by his absent friend. In a letter from Governor Bradford to Robert Cushman, dated June, 1625, he says, "Your son is in good health (blessed be

God). He received the things you sent him. I hope God will make him a *good man.*" And such proved to be the case as his history will show.

"1627. At a public Court held on the 22d of May, it is considered by the whole company, that the cattle which were the company's, to wit,—the cows and the goats should be equally divided by lot to all persons of the same company." The cattle and goats were, therefore, divided into twelve lots, and thirteen persons appointed to each lot.

The *eleventh* lot fell to Governor Bradford and those with him, among whom was Thomas Cushman, then in the 20th year of his age. "To this lot fell an heifer of the last year, which was of the great white back cow that was brought over in the Ann,[1] and two she goats."

Jan. 1, 1633. "These following were admitted into the freedom of the society, viz: Mr. William Collins, Thomas Willett, John Cooke and Thomas Cushman." He was then twenty-five or twenty-six years of age.

July 1, 1634. "At a generall Court holden before Governor and Councill, Thomas Cushman plantife agaynst John Combe, Gent. defendant, being cast and adiudged to pay the sayd summe of ten pounds to the plaintife or his Assigns at or before the first of Aug. or else to deliver to him a sufficient cow-cafe weaned or weanable."[2]

1635. Thomas Cushman first served as a Juryman.

About the year 1635 or 1636 he married Mary Allerton, the third child of Isaac Allerton, who came over in the Mayflower in 1620.[3]

In that matrimonial relation they lived together the long period of fifty-five years: she surviving him nearly ten years.

In 1637 there was granted "to Thomas Cushman the remaynder of the marsh before the house he liveth in wch Mrs.

---

[1] The first cattle imported from England were "a bull and three heifers," by Edward Winslow, in 1624.

[2] Plymouth Colony Records; Court Order 3, Vol. 1.

[3] From Thomas and his wife Mary and their descendants, have come all the Cushmans in the United States, except those mentioned in Appendix E. They are, therefore, of *full blood* Puritan stock; both their paternal and maternal ancestors having been among the Pilgrims who settled at Plymouth.

Fuller doth not vse and the little pcell at the wading place on the other side Joanes River." It is supposed that he removed to Jones River (now Kingston) about this time, which was not long after he was married, and that there he lived and died.

1645, he purchased "Prence's farm" at Jones River (now "Rocky Nook" in Kingston,) by exchanging land at Sowams (on Naragansett Bay in Rhode Island) for it, for £75. It was first owned by his father-in-law, Isaac Allerton.

The exact locality of his house is now pointed out, and a spring of water near it has for many years, received the cognomen of "the Elder's Spring," from Elder Thomas Cushman, whose house stood near it. It is located in that part of Kingston now called "Rocky Nook," about fifty rods northerly from the present traveled highway, on the border of the marsh. A description and the boundaries of the land as given in the early Colony Records, show, beyond a doubt, that the tradition respecting that spring and the location of the Elder's House, must be correct. Men and things have changed in the course of two hundred years: yet the topography of that vicinity remains the same.

The "Elder's Spring" is often visited by antiquarians, and by those who have sprung from the stock of the Pilgrims, and who venerate their deeds. The writer of this has drank from that pure spring, where his venerable ancestor allayed his thirst in days of yore; and he hopes he has thus become inspired with something of the Pilgrim's faith, and a fearless determination, "to worship God according to the dictates of his own conscience and judgment;" and in the strong and emphatic language of another,[1] "has sworn upon the altar of God, eternal hostility against every form of tyranny over the mind of man."

In 1649, the office of Ruling Elder of the Church at Plymouth, having become vacant by the death of the venerable Elder Brewster, Thomas Cushman was appointed to that office and continued in it to his death,—a period of over forty-three years. He was ordained to that office by appropriate

---

[1]Thomas Jefferson's letter to Dr. Rush, dated at Monticello, Virginia, September 23, 1800.

ceremonies and religious services, on Friday the 6th of April, 1649.

In order to show the importance of the office of Ruling Elder, that was held for so long a period by our worthy ancestor, we give, from Prince's Chronology, the following summary of the religious tenets of the Plyothean Fathers, so far as they relate to Church government:

"They maintained that every Christian congregation ought to be governed by its own laws, without depending on the jurisdiction of Bishops, or being subject to the authority of Synods, Presbyteries, or *any ecclesiastical assembly whatever.* They maintained that the inspired scriptures only contain the true religion, and that every man has the right of judging for himself and worshipping according to his apprehension of the meaning of them.

"Their officers were *Pastors* or teaching Elders, who have the power of overseeing and teaching, and of administering the sacraments, etc.

"2d, *Ruling Elders* who are to help the Pastor in ruling and overseeing.

"3d, *Deacons* who are to take care of the treasury of the Church; distribute to the needy and minister at the Lord's Table."

We thus see that Thomas Cushman held a highly responsible and important office in the hierarchy of the Plymouth Colony.

April 4, 1654. Mrs. Sarah Jenny[1] of Plymouth, by her Will, gave "To Elder Cushman the Bible which was my daughter Susannah's."

From an "Account of the Church of Christ in Plymouth, by John Cotton, Esq., a member, published in 1760," we take the following statement of the duties and character of Elder Thomas Cushman:

"About four or five years after Mr. Brewster's death, (he died Tuesday, 16 April, 1644,) the Church chose Mr. Thomas Cushman as his successor in the office of Ruling Elder, son of that servant of Christ, Mr. Robert Cushman, who had been their chief agent in transacting all their affairs in England,

---

[1]The wife of John Jenny, who came over in the ship Ann, in 1623. He was a member of Rev. Mr. Robinson's Church, at Leyden.

both before and after their leaving of Holland, till the year 1625. And this his son, inheriting the same spirit and being completely qualified, with gifts and graces, proved a great blessing to the Church; assisting Mr. Rayner (Pastor of the Church at Plymouth) not only in ruling, catechising and visiting, but also in public teaching, as Mr. Brewster had done before him: it being the professed principle of this Church in their first formation "to choose none for governing Elders, but such as are able to teach;" which abilities (as Mr. Robinson observes in one of his letters) other reformed Churches did not require of their Ruling Elders."

Extract from a Deed of land:

"Two acres of marsh meadow bee it more or lesse lying before the house and land of the Elder Cushman at Joaneses Rieuer next vnto a pcell of meadow which was Phineas Prats."

March 29, 1653. Ousamequin (Massasoit) and his oldest son Wamsitto convey by deed a tract of land in Rehoboth to Thomas Prence, Thomas Cushman and others, for which they pay the sum of thirty-five pounds sterling. This is another evidence of the *justice* of our fathers. They showed their *faith* by their *works*.

"About the year 1650 to 1660 the Quakers proved very troublesome to the Church and subverted many. The Lord was pleased to bless the endeavors of their faithful Elder, Mr. Cushman, in concurrence with several of the abler brethren, to prevent the efficacy of error and delusion; and (though destitute of a Pastor) the body of the Church were upheld in their integrity and in a constant opposition to their pernicious tenets. And we desire, say the records, that the good providence of God herein may never be forgotten, but that the Lord may have all the praise and glory thereof; for how easily might these wolves in sheep's clothing have ruined this poor flock of Christ, if the Lord had not interposed by his almighty power and goodness; improving *this our good elder* as a special instrument in this worthy work, both by teaching the will of God every Lord's day, for a considerable time, plainly, powerfully, and profitably; and seconding the same by a blameless life and conversation."

"After Rev. Mr. Rayner left, the worship of God was carried on by their Elder, Mr. Cushman, assisted by some of the brethren: insomuch that not one Sabbath passed without two public meetings."

Elder Cushman, having been raised and educated in the family of Governor Bradford, was ever his intimate and confidential friend. He was, therefore, the principal witness to his Will, which was proved at Plymouth, June 3, 1657. The Governor's estate was also inventoried by Thomas Cushman.

June 30, 1669. Mr. John Cotton, Jr., son of the famous Rev. John Cotton, Pastor of the first Church in Boston, was ordained as Pastor of the first Church in Plymouth. "Elder Thomas Cushman gave the charge and the aged Mr. John Howland (whose daughter had married his son, Thomas Cushman, Jr.,) was appointed by the Church to join in imposition of hands."[1]

"The Ruling Elder (Cushman) with the new Pastor, made it their first special work to pass through the whole town, from family to family, to enquire into the state of souls."

The following is a fac-simile of the signatures of Elder Cushman and of his minister, Rev. Mr. Cotton, written in the year 1682.

March 16 81
—
Plimouth 82
—

John Cotton Pastor
Thomas Cushman Elder

(In the edition "Genealogy of the Cushmans, the Descendants of Robert Cushman, the Puritan." Compiled and edited by Henry Wyles Cushman, published by Little, Brown and

---

[1] It was for a time the practice in Congregational ordinations for laymen to bear a part in the solemnities, by laying on of hands. Dr. Elliott in his Biographical Dictionary, gives us the following anecdote: When Israel Chauncy, son of the President, was ordained minister of Stratford, Conn., in 1665, one of the lay brothers, in laying on hands, forgot to take off his *mitten*, and this was ridiculed by the Episcopalians by styling it the *leather mitten* ordination.—*Dr. Thacher's History of Plymouth.*

Company, Boston, in 1855. On page 89 will be found this fac-simile referred to above.)

The first volume of the records of the first Church at Plymouth, contains the following notice of Elder Cushman's death:

"1691. It pleased God to seize upon our good Elder, Mr. Thomas Cushman, by sickness, and in this year to take him from us. He was chosen and ordained Elder of this Church, April 6, 1649; he was neere 43 yeares in his office, his sicknesse lasted about eleven weeks; he had bin a rich blessing to this church scores of yeares, he was grave, sober, holy and temperate, very studious, and solicitous for the peace and prosperity of the church and to prevent and heale all breaches: He dyed, December 11, near the end of the 84th yeare of his life; December 16 was kept as a day of humiliation for his death,—the Pastor prayed and preached. Mr. Arnold and the Pastor's 2 sons assisted in prayer; much of God's presence went away from this church when this blessed Pillar was removed."

"A liberal contribution was made that fast day for the Elder's widow, as an acknowledgment of his great services to the church whilst living."

In another place we find the following in the Plymouth Church Records:

"1691. Elder Thomas Cushman dyed December 11: having within two months finished the 84th year of his life."

And at a later period, we find on those records the following:

"August 7, 1715. A contribution was moved and made, both by the church and congregation to defray the expense of Grave Stones sett upon the grave of that worthy and useful servant of God, Elder Thomas Cushman; the whole congregation were very forward in it."

He died on Friday the 11th day of Dec., 1691, and we may, therefore, reasonably conclude that his funeral was attended on the following Sunday.

He was buried on the southerly brow of "Burying Hill," in a very beautiful locality, commanding a full view of Plymouth harbor, of the town, of the green hills in the distance, and of the "Meeting House" in which for more than seventy years he had prayed and worshiped.

The grave stone, erected by the Plymouth Church, twenty-four years after his death is a plain slab of mica slate, about 3½ feet in height, and was probably imported from England. It is now in a good state of preservation, and although it has stood nearly one hundred and forty years, the inscription is yet distinct and legible. Such a tribute as that to his memory, by the Church of which he was a member, speaks volumes in his praise.

The inscription is as follows:

> Here lyeth buried ye body
> of that precious servant of
> God: Mr. Thomas Cushman who
> after he had served his
> generation according to
> the will of God and
> particularly the Church of
> Plymouth for many years in
> the office of a Ruling Elder
> fell asleep in Jesus Decmr
> ye 10 1691 and in ye
> 84 year of his age.

The foregoing is nearly a fac-simile, except that the letters are about three-fourths of an inch in size.

At his grave stands a board with this inscription, of recent origin, undoubtedly, designed to direct the stranger to the graves of one of the most noted of the old Pilgrims:

> The Grave of
> Eld. Thomas Cushman
> Died Dec. 10, 1691.
> 334.

It will be noticed that the day of his death by the Church Records, is Dec. 11th,—but by his grave stone it is Dec. 10th; which is correct is unknown.

About a year before his death, Elder Cushman made his Will. As a part of his history, we give it entire.

From the quantity of real estate devised to his children, and the amount of the inventory of his personal property,—a copy of which is subjoined,—we must infer that the Elder was prosperous in temporal things, as well as in spiritual. His personal estate amounted to £50, of which £4 was in books. Considering the value of money at that time,—much greater than now,—he must have been quite wealthy.

Elder Cushman's Will.

Copy of Probate Records for the County of Plymouth—Book 1, Commencing with page 129.

"To all People to whom these presents shall come, etc.—

Know ye that I Thomas Cushman, Sen'r, of the town of Plymouth in New England, being through God's mercy and goodness unto me at this present in some measure of good health of body and of sound understanding and strength of memory, yet considering my frailty and uncertainty of my abiding in this vale of tears, do make this to be my last will and testament. And by these presents I do make this to be my last will and testament to remain firm and invincible forever as followeth:

Imprimis—I give and bequeath my soul to God that gave it, and my body to ye dust and to be decently buried in hopes of ye grace of God through Jesus Christ to enter into a joyful resurrection. And for my outward estate I dispose of as followeth, viz: I will and bequeath unto my dear and loving wife Mary Cushman all my house and housing, together with all my uplands and meadow lands I am now possessed of in the township of New Plimouth, to be for her use and support during ye time of her natural life, excepting such parcels as I do in this my will give to my children.

Item,—I give unto my son Thomas Cushman two twenty acre lots lying upon ye southerly side of Mr. Joseph Bradford's land, as also ye enlargements of ye head of these lots; and also twenty acres of upland, more or less, lying upon ye easterly side of Jones River by the bridge, with a skirt of meadow lying by said river; and also one-third of my meadow at Winnatuxet, (now in Plympton) and also a parcel of salt marsh meadow from our spring unto a cross westerly of a salt hole and so down to ye river, which said parcel of meadow is to be his after our decease. All ye above said parcels of upland and meadow I do by these presents give and bequeath unto my son Thomas Cushman, to him and his heirs forever.

Item,—I give unto my son Isaac Cushman, one twenty acre lot, with ye addition of ye head lying on the northerly side of Samuel Flanders land in ye Township of Plimouth, and also the one half of my land lying at Nemasket Pond in ye Township of Middleborough as also ye one half of my right in the sixteen shilling purchase, so called, in Township above sa'd, and also one third part of my meadow at Winnatuxet in Plimouth, all which parcels of upland and meadow last above expressed, I do by these presents give and bequeath unto my son Isaac Cushman, and to him and his heirs forever, together with all the privileges thereunto belonging.

Item,—I do give unto my son Elkanah Cushman one twenty acre lot with the addition of the head lying on the northerly side of ye land I now improve, but in case my son Thomas's new dwelling house be upon part of this lot, my will is my son Thomas enjoy ye land his house now standeth on without molestation. As also I give to my son Elkanah Cushman the one half of my land lying at Nemasket Pond, as also ye one half of the sixteen shilling purchase above expressed, as also one third of my meadow at Winnatuxet. All the above said parcels of land and meadows last above expressed, with all the privileges thereunto belonging I do by these presents give unto my son Elkanah Cushman, and to his heirs forever.

Item,—I do give unto my son Eleazer Cushman the rest of my lands both upland and meadow lands not above deposed of in Plimouth and Duxborough, as also my new dwelling house and out housing, which house and lands I do by these presents give and bequeath unto my son Eleazer Cushman, to him and his heirs forever to enjoy after I and my wife are deceased.

And my will is that my four sons Thomas, Isaac, Elkanah and Eleazer shall each of them allow twenty to their sisters, that is to say Sarah Hauks and Lidiah Harlow. As also my will is that if any of my sons se cause to make sale of their land I have given them in Plimouth, that they do let their brothers that do reside in Plimouth have the said lands as they shall be valued by five different men as also my will is, and I do by these presents give and bequeath unto my three grandchildren in Line the children of my daughter Mary Hutchinson deceased, to each of them twenty shillings to be paid unto them out of my estate soon after my decease.

And I do constitute and appoint my dear and loving wife Mary Cushman to be the sole executrix of this my last Will and Testament, my debts, legacies and funeral charges being first paid my will is that whatever other estate is found of mine in goods, chattels or debts either in Plimouth or elsewhere shall be for ye support of my wife during her natural life; and my will is that what remains of my estate at my wife's decease the one half I do give to my son Eleazur Cushman and the other half unto my two daughters, to Sarah Hauks and Lidiah Harlow to be equally divided between them. And my will is, and I do by these presents appoint my two sons Thomas Cushman and Isaac Cushman and Thomas Faunce to be ye supervisors of this my last will and testament, much confiding in their love and faithfulness to be helpful to my s'd executrix in the acting and disposing of particulars according to the tenore thereof, thus hoping that this my last will and testament will be performed and kept, revoking all other wills, written or verball. I have in witness thereof set my hand and seal on the 22d of October, 1690.

Signed, sealed and declared to be his last will and testament in presence of us witnesses.

James Warner,   Thomas Cushman
Thomas Faunce.   And a (L.S.)

James Warner and Thomas Faunce, the witnesses here named, made oath before the County Court of Plymouth, March ye 16th 1691/2,—that they were present and saw the above named Mr. Thomas Cushman sign and seal, and heard him declare the above written to be his last Will and Testament, and that to ye best of their judgement he was of sound mind and memory when he so did.

Attest,   Samuel Sprague, Clerk.

An addition to ye last Will of Thomas Cushman, Sen'r, which is as followeth:

Whereas in my last Will, which was in sixteen hundred and ninety that I then left out a certain piece of land undisposed of which was one hundred acres of land lying in the Township of Plimouth upon a brook commonly called Colchester Brook, (in Plympton) on both sides of ye said brook, which I reserved to sell for my support, or my wife's after my decease. My will is therefore that my son Thomas Cushman and my son Isaac Cushman shall have the above hundred acres of land to be divided equally between them to them and their heirs and assigns forever, provided that they equally shall pay or cause to be paid ten pounds in current silver money to me above said Thomas Cushman, Sen'r, or my two daughters, Sarah Hauks and Lidia Harlow. Also I the above said Thomas Cushman do will and bequeath to my four sons, Thomas Cushman and Isaac Cushman and Elkanah Cushman and Eleazer Cushman, all of my books, equally to be divided among them, only two small books to my daughter, Lidia Harlow, and my best bible to my loving wife Mary Cushman, likewise also I do give and bequeath unto my son Elkanah Cushman one acre of meadow which was granted unto me, lying at Doties meadows. This addition is to the last will of me Elder Thomas Cushman of Plimouth being now in perfect understanding, April 1, 1691.

THOMAS CUSHMAN, SEN. (L.S.)

Signed, sealed and declared in presence of us witnesses.
Jonathan Shaw, Sen.,
Persis Shaw, Her P mark.

Jonathan Shaw one of ye witnesses here named made oath before ye County Court of Plimouth March 16th, 1691/2, that he was present and saw Elder Thomas Cushman above named sign, seal and heard him declare the above written codicil to be his will, an addition to his former will, and that he ye said Shaw subscribed to it as a witness, and that he saw Persis, his wife subscribe with him as a witness also.

Attest,   Sam'l Sprague, Clerk.

March 16th, 1691/2. Mrs. Mary Cushman relict widow of Elder Thomas Cushman, late of Plimouth deceased coming personally before ye County Court then held at Plimouth, did freely acknowledge she had received fifty-two shillings and six pence of Isaac Cushman her son in part of ye five pounds which ye said Isaac is to pay for his part of ye hundred acres of land at Colchester above said.

Attest,   Sam'l Sprague, Clerk.

Memorandum that Persis Shaw ye other witness made oath before Wm. Bradford, Esq., Judge of Probate, that she also was present and saw and heard ye within named Elder Cushman sign, seal and declare this within written codicill as an addition to his will, and that he was of sound mind and memory when he did ye same to ye best of her judgment.

Attest,   Sam'l Sprague, Register.
Sept. 25th, 1701.

An inventory of the estate of Mr. Thomas Cushman, Sen'r, of Plymouth, deceased, taken and appraised by us, whose names hereunto subscribed, on ye 17th day of December, 1691:

Imprimis, his wearing apparel,

both linen and woolen,	£04	sh 02	d 00
Item—his books,	04	00	00
Item—in cash,	01	02	00
Item—in 2 beds and bedding to them	£10	sh 00	d 00
Item—in pewter and brass,	£02	sh 15	d 00
Item—in iron pots and kettles and other iron vessels[1]	£01	sh 12	d 00
Item—in tables and chests and chairs	£01	sh 16	d 00
Item—in cotton and sheep's wool and linen yarn and flax,	£01	sh 03	d 00
Item—in saddle, bridle and pillion,	£01	sh 05	d 00

---

[1] A *spoon* is now in the Museum of the Pilgrim Society at Plymouth, which belonged to Elder Cushman, and is kept as a memento of him.

Item—in linen wheel and old lumber	£00	sh 15	d 00
Item—in iron wedges and glass bottles	£00	sh 05	d 00
Item—in cart tacklin	£00	sh 10	d 00
Item—in Indian and English corn,	£04	sh 01	d 00
Item—in neat cattle,	£13	sh 10	d 00
Item—in sheep,	£01	sh 00	d 00
Item—in swine,	£00	sh 18	d 00
Item in a Loom,	£01	sh 05	d 00
Item—in debts due from ye estate,	£00	sh 08	d 00

Thomas Cushman,
Isaac Cushman,
Thomas Faunce.

Mrs. Mary Cushman relict widdow of Elder Thomas Cushman late of Plimouth deceased made oath before ye County Court at Plimouth March 16th, 1691/2 that ye above written is a true inventory of the goods and chattels of her said late husband, so far as she yet knoweth, and that if more shall be discovered to her she will make it known.

Attest, Sam'l Sprague, Clericus.

Such was the life and such the death of Elder Thomas Cushman. But few men, comparatively, live so long and still fewer live so *well* as he did.

In early life, having had the training and example of Governor Bradford,—than whom few men's history stands as high and as pure,—we may reasonably conclude that he was taught "the law and the prophets," and constantly "walked in wisdom's ways."

At the mature age of about twenty-eight, he married Mary Allerton, who had sat under the teachings of Rev. John Robinson, a leader of the Puritans, and had joined the Church under the instructions of the pious Elder Brewster.

Thus trained in the school of Puritan theology, and practising daily the most rigid morals, formed after the model of Christ himself; and with an organization in which benevolence and veneration largely predominated, we can judge something of the character of the man and of his works. His antecedents had well prepared him for the high duties of Ruling Elder of a Puritan Church. In that office, the records of the Church he served so long and so faithfully, as well as all other contemporaneous evidence, give him the highest commendation. For upwards of forty-three years he "ruled and governed" the Church of Plymouth, and ever proved himself to be the worthy successor of the discreet and devoted Brewster. For a portion of that time he was the only preacher. After the dismissal of Rev. Mr. Rayner, in 1654, and before the settlement of Rev. Mr. Cotton, in 1657, he continued the religious services of the Sabbath, so that no Sunday passed without having two meetings as usual. To a poorly educated layman, this must have been a task of no small magnitude. But having the "gifts and graces" of a true, zealous and devoted christian, he taught as well as governed, in the absence of the minister.

It was during that period that the Quakers, possessing something of a fanatical spirit, and pushed on by opposition and persecution, were a source of much trouble to the Plymouth Church. The oppressions of the Anglican Church, in their native land, had not learned the Puritans the somewhat difficult lesson of charity and toleration to others of a different faith. Like most other professing christians, the Puritans had their defects,—their short comings, their errors. But we may fairly and truly say they were the defects of the age; the errors of the head, not of the heart.

When will men learn that the fullest toleration is essentially consistent with the soundest faith, the purest walk, the highest devotion, the nearest approach to God and to Heaven?

That Elder Cushman partook of the characteristics of the age and of his brethren in the Lord, we cannot doubt. Still we have no evidence that he ever violated that highest of moral principles, "Do unto others as ye would that others should do unto you," in his government of the Plymouth Church and in his treatment of heretics and heresy. The uniform meekness and humility of his life would lead us to an opposite conclusion.

He continued in his office till death; he died with his armor on; and so deeply was he lamented that the church records say, somewhat figuratively, we may suppose, that "much of God's presence went away from the Church when that blessed Pillar was removed."

Mary Allerton, wife of Elder Cushman, came over in the Mayflower in 1620. She was then about eleven years of age. With her husband she was a member of the Church at Plymouth, and as we may well suppose, she was a worthy companion of her excellent, pious and useful husband, during his long ministry as Ruling Elder of the Church. She survived him seven or eight years, and died at the advance age of ninety. Her name has become quite famous from the fact that she was the last survivor of the one hundred persons who came over in the Mayflower. She was probably buried by the side of her husband, in the Burying Hill Cemetery at Plymouth, though no monument has ever been erected to her memory.[1]

In contemplating the long life of Elder Thomas Cushman, which extended through a period of more than four score years, two circumstances are most observable,

1st, The peculiarly interesting period during which he lived;—for a large part of the seventeenth century, which was crowded with great events,—he was on the stage of active life. When he landed at Plymouth, the entire Colony consisted of only fifty persons; and seventy years afterwards, the time of his decease, there were more than that number of thousands of the Anglo-Saxon race in New England. He lived to see the sister Colonies of Rhode Island, Massachusetts, Connecticut and New Hampshire, spring up,—establish their governments, and extending far and wide the area of civilization and christianity. He was a participator of the first treaty with Massasoit and Samoset, which continued unviolated by both parties for more than fifty years; and afterwards was a spectator of the bloody and exterminating war of King Phillip and the Indian tribes of New England.

He had seen, also, during his protracted life, in his native

---

[1] We trust her numerous descendants will not allow this to continue so much longer. Let the marble or granite perpetuate her memory and commemorate her virtues.

country, old England, a weak and dishonest King brought to the block and executed as a malefactor; and the government passing into the hands of Cromwell, established on the basis of a Commonwealth. Almost as transient as the morning dew, he saw that pass away with the death of its great progenitor; another King in power and another fleeing for his life, and finally monarchy again firmly established under the dynasty of William and Mary in 1688.

In his own community and Church he had experienced equally great changes. The wise and discreet Bradford, the zealous and devout Brewster, the chivalrous and fearless Standish, the active and enterprising Allerton, and the shrewd and intelligent Winslow, had all passed away and gone to their rest. But few of his contemporaries were then living. The Church that he had loved, and for which he had labored and prayed, had been blessed by the labors of a Rayner and a Cotton, and had spread out its branches all around.

In his social relations, too, great changes had occurred. He had raised up a family of seven children, all of whom had married and settled around him; and grandchildren were rejoicing in his arms. His father-in-law (Isaac Allerton), being more liberal and wiser than the age, had refused to take part against the Quakers, and thus lost the confidence of the Colony and the Church. He had left for a home in the then, far-off Dutch settlement at New Netherland, now New York City, and years before had

> "Gone to that bourne from
> which no traveller returns."

Such are some of the incidents that had been enacted and had passed away during the long pilgrimage of the subject of this memoir.

The 2d noticeable point in the career of Elder Cushman, was *the perfect consistency of his character,* and his entire and unchanging devotion to the Church, of which he was for more than forty years the Ruling Elder. During all the mutations of that period,—the changes of Pastors, the colonization of other Churches, the coming on of a new generation,—less intelligent, we may suppose, and less devout than their fathers;

the controversy with the Quakers, which seemed to stir up the community to its lowest depths; and in his own family, the conviction, by the judicial tribunals of the Colony, of his eldest son, of the sin of unchastity,—all of these must have been most severe trials of his christian principles.

But we find him ever the same prayerful, practical, true-hearted christian. The Plymouth Church was his first love, his beacon-light, his undying hope. And, but for him, we may safely conclude, at some trying periods of its existence, it must have languished,—perhaps died.

The last act of that Church, so far as he was concerned, was the crowning event of all. A quarter of a century after his death, the Plymouth Church erected a monument to his memory, now standing conspicuous on the southern brow of the old Burying Ground in Plymouth, on which they inscribed his character as "that precious Servant of God."

In the beautiful language of Montgomery, we may conclude this memoir of Elder Cushman:

"Servant of God, well done!
Rest from they loved employ,—
And while eternal ages run,
Be in thy Saviour's joy."

NOTE.—Sara Cushman married William Hodgekin, 2 November, 1636, say the Old Colony Records. Who she was, we know not. From her age (being marriageable sixteen years after the first landing at Plymouth) she must have emigrated from England. But her name is nowhere mentioned in the lists of passengers. She might have been a sister of Elder Thomas, though there is no evidence to that effect. From the fact that her husband, William Hodgekin, married the second time to Ann Haynes, 21 Dec. 1638, it is evident that she must have died before that time, or in about two years after her marriage; and so far as we know left no issue.

THIRD GENERATION

Thomas, Elder (2) of Plymouth had Children.

3. 1. Thomas[3] (II) born 16th September, 1637, married first Ruth Howland, daughter of John Howland, "one of the

old comers," 17th November, 1664. She was living when her father's Will was made, 29th May, 1672 and as he was married the second time in 1679, his first wife must have died between those dates. He married second Abigail Fuller, of Rehoboth, 16th October, 1679. He and his second wife were members of the church at Plympton. He lived on the west side of the highway that leads from Plympton meeting house to the north part of the town, and "Colchester Brook" ran through his farm, which contained a large quantity of land.

He was, during a long life, a worthy member of the Congregational Church at Plympton, of which his brother was the Pastor. He died 23rd August, 1726, ae. 89 and was interred in the Centre Burying Ground at Plympton, thirty-three feet north-easterly from the gate, on the west side.

> Here lyes ye
> body of mr. Thomas
> Cushman who dec'd
> Augst Ye 23d
> 1726 in
> Ye 89th year
> of his age

4. II Sarah[3] born ——, married John Hawks of Lynn, 11 April, 1661. (His name is sometimes erroneously written Hooks). She was his second wife and had chil. viz:
1. Susanna, born 29th November, 1662;
2. Adam, born 12th May, 1664;
3. Anna, born 3rd May, 1666;
4. John, born 25th April, 1668;
5. Rebecca, born 18th October, 1670;
6. Thomas, born 18th May, 1673;
7. Mary, born 14th November, 1675;

Susanna, Anna and Rebecca died November, 1675.

5. III Lydia,[3] born ——, married William Harlow, Jr.

6. IV Isaac, Rev. (16) born at Plymouth 8th February 1647-8. Married Mary Rickard, probably about the year 1675, as their first child was born November, 1676. She was born 1654, and died at Plympton 27th September, 1727, ae. 73. He

was a member of the church at Plymouth, and obtained a better education than most of that day.

In 1685 he was one of the Selectmen of Plymouth, and in June, 1690 he and John Bradford were the Deputies from Plymouth to the General Court of the Plymouth Colony, and in August the same year another General Court was held and the same Deputies were re-elected.

In June, 1691, John Bradford and Isaac Cushman were again elected Deputies to the General Court, from Plymouth, and it was the last one previous to the union of the Plymouth and Massachusetts Colonies, which took place in 1692. The first General Court of the new Province was held 8th June, 1692.

His venerable father, Elder Thomas Cushman, having died in 1691, the church at Plymouth was without a "Ruling Elder," then an office of great importance and responsibility. We may reasonably suppose that the early attention and thoughts of the church were directed to the consideration of a successor; but we find no evidence of any church sanction till 1694. We copy from the first volume of the Plymouth church Records, page 22:

"1694, March 7, was a church meeting which the Sabbath before the church had notice and were then desired to prepare their thoughts to nominate some brethren to serve in the office of Elders and Deacons. The church spoke man by man, and all but two or three of the brethren nominated Deacon Faunce and Bro. Isaac Cushman for Elders."

"1695, June 16: the matter of Elders being named and then nominated, desired to give their answers; Bro. Faunce declined a present acceptance of the call from sense of his own unfitness. Bro. Isaac Cushman desired further time of consideration; in which time our brethren engaged in promoting a new society in our western precincts, gave Bro. Cushman an earnest call to teach the word of God to them, and desired our church to consent thereto. Also in this time Mr. Samuel Fuller, the Teacher of the church at Middlebury, a sincere Godly man whom we had the last yeare dismissed to that service, died August 29th: being about 66 years old, a great loss to that place, immediately upon which that church and

Towne sent letters to our church to desire our consent that Bro. Isaac Cushman might be their Teacher, upon all which accounts the church was called to meet on September 1 : which they did, and the Pastor acquainted them with those two calls our brother had. The church manifested generally their good respect to him and desires not to part with him, but that he should be an Elder here in his blessed Father's room, and desired him now to give his answer to that call, which accordingly he did: That the Providence of God was mysterious but he apprehended he should rather accept the call of this church to be Elder here, because it was first given before the other two calls; the church acted no further in that matter at that time, only voted that it would be noe offence but acceptable to them if Bro. Cushman did improve his gifts in teaching at Middlebury or any other place where the orderly providence of God should call him. God soe disposed that he hearkened to the call of our Brethren and neighbours of the new society where he now lives and constantly attends the work of Preaching amongst them and is well accepted and acknowledged by them."

Such is the record of his election as Elder of the Plymouth church, his call to the ministry of the church in Middleboro, and also as Pastor of the new church then established in Plympton, the western Precinct of Plymouth. Which should be accepted, was, indeed, a difficult question to decide. A controversy ensued of more or less warmth, which, as the sequel will show was amicably settled.

We give a fac-simile of his autograph, written in 1694-5, at the age of 47.

Isaac Cushman

(In the edition "Genealogy of the Cushmans, the Descendants of Robert Cushman, the Puritan." Compiled and edited by Henry Wyles Cushman, published by Little, Brown, and Company. Boston, in 1855. On page 103 will be found this fac-simile referred to above.)

Isaac, having attained the age of about forty-five years, and under the direction and example of his venerable father, Elder Cushman, having been taught the dogmas and the precepts of the Pilgrims, and having "walked in all the ways of his fathers," and withal being a man of strong intellectual powers and devotional feelings, with benevolence and veneration fully developed in his organization, he resolved to enter the ministry, for which he undoubtedly had peculiar "gifts and graces." As a member of the church and as a Deacon, which office he had held several years, he had, undoubtedly, led in their prayers, had exhorted in their conference meetings, and was thus well prepared to become a Pastor.

But here a difficulty occurred. The Pilgrims were particular in the smaller matters of the law as well as the more important. He had not served as a Ruling Elder; and the question arose among the Rabbis of the Colony,—Can a man, according to the rules of the Church and the precepts of the Savior, be ordained as Pastor, who has not been ordained and served as Ruling Elder? That was a knotty question, indeed,—especially so at that time, when the Pilgrims who had argued with the hierarchy in England and against Arminianism in Holland, had now all passed away.

The Rev. Mr. Cotton, Pastor of the Plymouth church, and a minority of that church took the negative side of that question; while Isaac Cushman and a majority of the church took an opposite view of it. Meeting after meeting was held to discuss that *great* question. The excitement increased. Mr. Cotton felt that the power and influence, as well as the usefulness of the clergy, were at stake, Even the ministers of the Pilgrim church were not entirely destitute of a love of denomination,—especially when they felt that they were right. On the other hand, Mr. Cushman and a major part of the church argued that the majority should rule, and that it was a long settled principle of the Congregational body of believers, that each church was entirely independent in its organization from all others.

The question waxed hotter,—each side claiming that they were following in the footsteps of their predecessors, the English Puritans.

In the mean time Mr. Cushman commenced preaching at

Plympton to a branch of the Plymouth church, without being ordained. That increased the flame, and contention was, for a time, the order of the day in the Plymouth church.

Says Dr. Thatcher, "the controversy continued about three years, with considerable warmth and occasioned the withdrawal of some of the members of the church. Many ill reports were propagated, injurious to the reputation and feelings of Mr. Cotton."

At length it became apparent that Mr. Cushman, his friends and his side of the question must prevail; for he *would* preach and the people at Plympton *would* hear him,—ordained or not. And on every principle of the Congregational Church were they not right? Thereupon Mr. Cotton asked for a dismissal, which was granted him; and with his departure, the minority abandoned all opposition to Mr. Cushman's ordination; and peace and harmony were again restored to the Plymouth Church.

We may smile at the apparent *smallness* of that controversy; but in our day have not even more diminutive and less important questions divided and distracted the church, the advent of which proclaimed "peace on earth and good will to men?"

The following from the Plymouth Church Records, vol. 1, page 26, is the record evidence of the full settlement of the whole matter, by the interested parties:

1696 July 16. It was there signified to the church that our brethren of the new Society were ready to attend the church whenever they pleased to appoint a meeting for that end; the Pastor appointd the church to meet on August 19, at his house, which they did in the morning, it being the lecture day; before the lecture the Pastor and three of the brethren spent the time in prayer. After lecture, there was a particular agitation of matters, and the issue was satisfying and comfortable. The brethren of the new Society professed their judgments to be, that brethren should have the advise and approbation of the church whereto they belonged, in setting up distinct worship by themselves and that they apprehended that the church had by some former act of theirs consented they should soe do; the church hereupon declared themselves satisfyed with these brethren, as to their carrying on the worship of God themselves, their habitations being soe remote from us, and that Bro. Cushman might, without any offence to us, continue to dispense the word to them, and that nothing heretofore passed betwixt us in word or action of any kinde, should hinder our communion together in sealing ordinances as heretofore. The whole church our brethren concurred (for ought appeared,) did every one of us express our consent hereunto by an universal lifting up of our hands, and this way declared to be a final issue of this matter and all differences that had thereby bin occasioned amongst us; and that the church voted that Deacon Faunce, D. Wood and D. Clark should joyne with the Pastor in subscribing their hands to this conclusion, written and voted, which they did, and a copy thereof soe subscribed, was delivered to Bro. Isaac Cushman before they departed from the Pastor's house; and as a testimony of our reconciliation one with another and mutual forgiveness of all past offences, Bro. Cushman himself and all our members of that Society, both brethren and sisters, (that were capable,) came together and sat down with us at the Lord's Table on August 30 following. This church meeting, August 19th, was concluded with prayer and thankfulness to God for that issue with our brethren.

We continue, the history of Isaac Cushman's connection with the church at Plympton, in the language of the Plympton Church Records,—a small quarto volume, bound with parchment, now lying before us. It was written by himself, or by his son Isaac, whose writing it somewhat resembles, and who was for many years Town Clerk of Plympton.

The title-page of that volume, in the hand writing of Mr. Cushman, is as follows:

"The Records of ye Church of Plympton
    1714/5 March ye 9th
transcribed from loose papers."

The Records commence with the following "Confession of Faith," which was adopted at the formation of the church, and was undoubtedly drawn up by its first Pastor, Rev. Isaac

Cushman. We give it *verbatim et literatim*, from the original Record:

"Whereas the Inhabitance of the western part of Plimouth in ye year 1695 obtained liberty of being a distinct Society by themselves from the generall Court, having before sought to God for help and direction, did, on the first daye of Janewary in said year set apart a daye for thanksgivin—after which upon their desire Mr. Isaac Cushman preached the Gospell there untill the 27th daye of October, in ye year 1698, upon which daye after a confession of faith and a church covenant was made, he was chosen and ordained to the pastorell office amongst them by the Elders and messengers of thre of the neighbouring churches, viz: Plimouth, Duxborough and Marsfeeld being those present and assisting."

THE CONFESSION

Was as followeth:

"We do believe with our heart and confess with our mouths that the holy scriptures of the old and new Testaments are the word of God and given by the divine inspiration of God to be the rule of faith and life.

2ly. That there is but one only true God and that in the unity of ye Godhead three persons of one substance, power and eternity—God the father—God the Son and God the Holy Ghost.

3ly. That the one God, father, Son and Holy Ghost made the whole world and all things therein in ye space of six days, very good.

4ly. And that God mad man after his own image in knowledg, righteousness and true holiness.

5ly. And that our first parents being seduced by the subtilty of Satan, eating the forbidden fruit Sinned against God and fell from ye esteat wherein they were created and that all mankind descending from them by ordinary Generation sinned and fell with them in the first transgression and so were brought into an esteat of sin and misery loosing communion with God and falling under his curse and wrath.

6ly. That God in his eternal purpose Chose and ordained

the Lord Jesus his only begotten sone To be the one only Mediator between God and Man, the Prophet, Priest and King,— The Souvrain of the Church.

7ly. That Jesus Christ, the second person in the Trinity is the very God eternal of one substance and Equal with the father and that when the fullness of time was come, the Sone of God, the second person in ye Trinity took upon him Man's nature, being conceived by the power of the Holy Ghost in the womb of the Virgin Mary of her substance so that the Godhead was joined together in one person, which person is very God and very man, yet one Christ, the only mediator between Man and God.

8ly. The Lord Jesus Christ by his perfect obedience and sacrifices of himself upon the Cross, hath fully satisfied the Justice of his Father and purchased not only reconcilliation with God but an Everlasting inheritance in ye Kingdom of Heaven for all those that the Father hath given to him.

9ly—That the elect of God are made partakers of the redemption purchased by Jesus Christ by the effectual application of it to their souls by his word and spirit.

10ly—That justification is an act of God's free Grace unto sinners in which he pardoneth all their sins and excepteth their persons in his sight not for any thing wrought in them or don by them but only for the perfect obedience of Christ imputed unto him by God and received by faith-alone.

11ly—Sanctification is an act of God's Grace unto sinners whereby the Elect renewed in the whole man after the Image of God and are enabled more and more to dye unto sinn and to live unto righteousness.

12ly—That whosoever God hath accepted in Jesus Christ effectually called and sanctified by his spirit, can neither totally nor finally fall awaye from the state of Grace, but shall certainly persevere unto ye end and eternaly saved.

13ly—That the Grace of Faith whereby the Elect are enabled to believe to the saving of their souls is ye work of the spirit of Christ in their hearts and is ordinarily wrought by the ministry of the word by which also and by the Administration of the Sacraments and prayer it is increased and strengthened.

14ly—That the visible church under the Gospel is not confined to one Nation as it was under the Law, but consisteth of all those throughout the world that profess the True Religion according to Gospel order and in the kingdom of our Lord Jesus Christ and the house and family of God, and that to the Church of Christ hath given the ministry of grace and ordinances of God for ye gathering and perfecting of the saints unto the end of the world, and doth by his own prents and spirit, according to his promises, make them effectuall.

15ly—That the singing of psalms, Reading the Scriptures, the sound preaching and conscionable hearing of the word, as also the due Administration and worthy Receiving of the Sacrament instituted by Christ, family Baptism and the Lord Super and all partes of the ordinary Religious worship besides sollem Fastings and Thanks Givings upon special occasions in there severall times and seasons are to be used in a holy religious manner.

16ly—That the Lord Jesus who is the alone head of his Church hath appointed officers in his hous for ye regular carrying on of the affairs of his Kingdom and each particular Church hath power from Christ regularly to administer cencers to offending members and to carry on the affairs of his visible kingdom according to his word.

17ly—That the bodyes of men after Death turn to ye dust and see corruption, but their souls which neither dye nor sleep, having an immortall substance emediately return to God who gave them. The souls of the Righteous being then made perfect in holiness and emediately received in to Heaven and the souls of the wicked are cast into Hell.

18ly—That the Bodyes of ye Just and unjust shall be raised at the Last Day.

19ly—That God hath appointed a daye wherein he will judge the world in Righteousness by Jesus Christ in which all persons that have lived upon the Earth shall appear before the Judgment seat of Christ to give an account of their thoughts, words and deeds, and to receive according to what they have done in ye body whether it be good or evil, etc."

THE CHURCH COVENANT

For as much as it has pleased God who hath commanded us to pray dayly that his kingdom may come and be advanced and hath given directions in his holy word and manifold incoragment to his poore servants to seek and sett fourth his worship and the conserments of his Glory. Wee do therefore personally present ourselves this day in the holy Affair of his Kingdom and Glory and our own salvation.

And humbling ourselves before the Lord for all our sins and the sinns of oures earnestly praying for parddoning Mercy and Reconsilliation with God through the blood of our Lord Jesus Christ and for his Glorious presence and assistance of his holy spirit under a deep sense of our own weakness, unworthiness and with a humble confidence of his faverable adoption each owne for ourselves and all as one jointly together enter into a holy covenant with God and one with another; that is to say we do according to the terms and tenor of Everlasting Covenant first give up ourselves and our offspring to the Lord God, father, Sone and Holy Ghost as the only true and living God, all sufficient and our God in Covenant and to our Lord Jesus Christ our only Savior and Prophet, Priest and King and the only Mediator of the Covenant of Grace, promissing and covenanting through the help of his Grace to cleave to God and to our Lord Jesus Christ by faith in a waye of Gospell obedience with full purpose of heart as his covenant people; And do also by this act of consideration give up our selves one to another in ye Lord according to the will of God; promising and engaging to cleave and walk together in a holly union and communion as members of the Misticall Body and instituted church of Christ rightly instituted and established in ye true faith and order of the Gospell; further obliging our selves by this, our holy covenant to keep and maintain the holy word and worship of God committed unto us, and to endeavor faithfully to transmit it to our posterity to cleave unto and uphold the true gospell ministry established by Jesus Christ in his church to have it in due honour and esteem for ye works sake—and to submit ourselves fully and sincearly to the ministration of the word and administration of the Sacraments, the Lord's supper to those in full communion and without offence, baptism to vissible church members and their infant seed, as allso for the due application of dissiplins with Love, care and faithfulness, watching one over another and over all our children of the covenant, growing up with us and all obedience to the blessed Rule and government of our Lord Jesus Christ, the alone head of the church.

And withall we further ingage ourselves to walk orderly in a waye of fellowship and communion with all neighboring churches according to ye rule of the Gospel that the name of ye Lord Jesus Christ may be one throughout all the churches to the Glory of God the Father, our holly covenant we doe in most solemn manner take upon ourselves in all the parts of it with full purpose of heart as the Lord shall help us and according to the measure of Grace received, we will walk before God fully and steadfastly and constantly in the discharge of all covenant duties; and the Lord keep this forever in the thoughts and emaginations of the hearts of us his poor servants to establish our hearts unto him and the good Lord pardon every one of us that prepareth his heart to seek the Lord God of his Fathers. Amen.

* * *

"The precedent confession of Faith and Covenant as acknowledged by all that were the members and joined together in full communion,—whose names are as followeth:"—

To the foregoing creed and covenant were attached the names of fourteen males at the head of which was "Mr. Isaac Cushman;" and twenty females, at the head of which was "Mrs. Rebeckah Cushman," his wife.

The record continues: "And those of the persons above said, which were not baptized in their infancy, were baptized at their admission and that we make our Rule to go by in that thing."

We give the foregoing "Creed and Confession of Faith" entire, for the purpose of showing something of the state of dogmatic theology of that day, as held by the first generation from the Pilgrims, and also for the purpose of illustrating the literature of that age and the ability of the writer of them,—the Rev. Isaac Cushman.

At the time of his ordination as Pastor at Plympton, he was in the prime of life, (about fifty years of age), and we may therefore suppose his maturest judgment and best thoughts were called into requisition in the preparation of that Creed and Confession of Faith.

And it is a curious and historical fact that that Creed and Covenant are precisely the same that are now used by the Congregational Church at Plympton.

In the year 1793, under the ministry of Rev. Ezra Sampson, it was changed and its ultra-calvanism somewhat modified, but in the year 1808, the original, as prepared by our ancestor, was again adopted and has since remained unchanged. Stability must certainly be a marked characteristic of the people of Plympton.

On Sunday the 27th of November, 1698, the deacons of this new church were ordained—and the first sacrament administered by their recently ordained Pastor, on the 4th day of December, 1698.

For a period of nearly thirty seven years, until he was "gathered to his Fathers" he continued in the ministry at Plympton; though it is probable that he became infirm and superannuated during the latter years of his life, as a colleague was ordained over his church about a year before his death.

Of his talents as a preacher we know but little. None of his sermons were ever printed, so far as we can learn, and none of them in manuscript are now extant, but "judging the tree by its fruit" we must place him among the most useful and valuable members of his profession.

During his ministry of thirty seven years, two hundred and forty seven persons became members of his church—viz. 103 females and 144 males averaging nerely seven per annum. In a small and sparsely settled community like that, a church so numerous shows very conclusively the deeply prevailing religious sentiment of the people, and the faithful and unremitting labors of its Pastor.

He solemnized during his ministry 144 marriages. The number of children baptized is not stated, but from the fact that in a few cases the children of parents who were church members that were *not* baptized, were recorded, we may infer that it was a universal custom for all children of members of the church, at an early day after their birth, to receive that initiatory ceremonial of the Pilgrim Church.

An example of the foregoing is found on page 14 of the Plymouth Church records: "Memorandum, that Israel Maye, son of Dorcas Maye hath not been baptized here."

A few of the last pages of the Plympton Church records contain a history of that church and its ministers, written by Deacon Lewis Bradford,[1] Speaking of Rev. Isaac Cushman, it says: He was a pious and Godly man. He had not a college education. He used to preach without notes, but studied his sermons beforehand and committed them to memory. It is said that those who worked with him could generally tell where his text would be the Sabbath following. I have heard my grandfather, Gideon Bradford, Esq. say that when the Rev. Mr. Cushman met with children or youth, he always had something to say to them of a religious nature, and at parting, gave them his blessing; that he himself, had received many a blessing from him.

The Rev. Mr. Cushman, on Sabbath days, instead of a wig, used to wear a black velvet cap. His dwelling house, which had what was called a dormon roof, stood near the easterly end of a small piece of fresh meadow, the water from which,

---

[1] I am indebted to Deacon Bradford, late of Plympton (a lineal descendant of Governor Bradford, the second Governor of Plymouth Colony), whose lamented decease took place so suddenly August 10, 1851, for much genealogical information respecting the Cushmans who settled early in the Old Colony. Mr. Bradford was killed instantly by being thrown from a wagon in Plympton, on Sunday, as he was about to return home from divine worship, at the age of 83. He had been Town Clerk of Plympton for nearly forty years; a Representative in the Legislature from that town, and was a highly respected and excellent citizen, and a devout member of the Congregational Church at Plympton, of which he was Clerk for many years. He was a most laborious and persevering genealogist and antiquarian. As a friend remarked: "He was the living embodiment of genealogy—having made it almost the business of his life."

when it runs, crosse the road about forty rods northward of the Burying Ground in Plympton.[1]

His Salary in the year 1701 was 35£ and it was increased from time to time till in 1728 it was 85£ a year as money was then reckoned.

He died Oct. 21st, 1732 in the 84th year of his age, and the 37th of his ministry. He was buried, in the burying yard at Plympton, next to the road, about middle way between the north and south end of the yard. He is said to have been a sound Calvanist and a faithful preacher. His memory has been much respected in Plympton.

It was a practice among our fore-fathers, in days of yore, on the occasion of the decease of eminent and good men, to express their feelings, or in other words, to write their obituaries in poetry. It did not always show the greatest degree of artistic skill and excellence, or the highest flights of fancy imagination; but it suited their purpose and was a part of the literature of the day.

Claiming to be wiser than our ancestors, it may, perhaps, be called "Machine Poetry" by some poetasters who may not be, possibly, the most perfect judges of poetic excellence. But in form their obituary poetry was not always the most superior, the sentiments were always good and true.

The death of Rev. Isaac Cushman received more than ordinary attention from the poets of his day. Two "poems" and two "Epitaphs" were written respecting him, eulogising his virtues, his talents and his usefulness, and pointing out the moral and the improvement to be derived from their bereavement.

This concludes the material as taken direct from Henry Wyles Cushman's Historical and Biographical Genealogy of the Cushmans.

[For further information concerning General-Cushman-History than that already encompassed herein, relating to the

---

[1] He owned a large farm, extending from the Burying Ground northwardly, on the east side of the present highway, on which his house was located. The land was given to him by his father's will "on both sides of Colchester Brook" and was after owned and occupied by his brother Thomas.

descent from the names recorded, except those descended from Thomas Cushman and Ruth (Howland) Cushman, Thomas Cushman and Sarah (Strong) Cushman, Thomas and Mary Cushman and their two sons, Thomas Cushman and Isaac Cushman of the sixth (6th.) generation, the writer refers you to the "Henry Wyles Cushman's, Historical and Biographical Genealogy of the Cushmans" published in 1855 by Messrs. Little, Brown and Company of Boston, Mass., which volume you will most likely find in the public library of your city.]

THOMAS CROCHEMAN, OF ROLVENDEN, COUNTY KENT

EXECUTOR OF HIS BROTHER JOHN'S WILL, WHICH HE PROVED 10 MAY, 1524, WAS PROBABLY FATHER OF:

Thomas Couchman, of Rolvenden, husbandman, the testator of 1585/6, who was born about 1538 and was buried at Rolvenden 10 February, 1585/6. He married there 18 July, 1568, Elinor Hubbarde, whose ancestry has not been found. She married secondly 17 October, 1587, Emanuel Evernden of Rolvenden, the testator of 1589, who was buried at Rolvenden, 3 December, 1589.

Robert Cutchman or Cushman, baptized at Rolvenden, County Kent, 9 February 1577/8 was probably identical with Robert Cushman, the agent of the Leyden Pilgrims in England. In 1603 we find him in Canterbury, England, County Kent, as servant to George Maisters. He was presented 14 November, 1603, by the churchwardens of St. Andrew's Parish, "For that he doth say he will not come to his parish church because he cannot be edified and saith he can and will defend it by the word of God." He not doing the penance imposed upon him by the ecclesiastical court, he was excommunicated 12 November, 1604, but on June 28, 1605, he appeared before the Court and asked for absolution which was granted to him on 7 July, 1605, when he was received again into the Church.

In the same year, 1605, he became a freeman of Canterbury, the record of his admission describing him as Robert Couchman "Grosser" a freeman by apprenticeship to George Maisters.

---x---

ELDER THOMAS CUSHMAN (Robert I), of Plymouth in New England, baptized in the parish of St. Andrew, Canterbury, County Kent, England, 8th February, 1607/8, came to New England with his father in the Fortune, arriving at Plymouth in November, 1621, and died at Plymouth 10th or 11th December, 1691, near the end of the 84th year of his life. He married at Plymouth, probably about 1636, Mary Allerton, born at Leyden, Holland, about 1610, died at Plymouth 28th November, 1699; daughter of Isaac and Mary (Norris) Allerton, and the last female survivor of those who came in the Mayflower in 1620. Children born:

Thomas, born at Plymouth, 16th Sept., 1637.

Sarah, married 11th April, 1661, John Hawks; eight children.

Lydia, married William Harlow, Jr.

Rev. Isaac, born at Plymouth, 8th Feb., 1648/9; died at Plympton, Mass., 21st October, 1732; married about 1675 Rebecca Rickard, born about 1654; died at Plympton, 3rd September, 1727, in her 73rd year. Six children born.

Deacon Elkannah, of Plympton, Mass., born at Plymouth 1st June, 1651; died at Plympton 4th September, 1727; married (1st) at Plymouth 10th February, 1677/8, Elizabeth Cole, who died there 4th January, 1681/2; married (2nd) at Plymouth 2nd March, 1683/4, Martha Cooke, born at Plymouth 16th March, 1659/60; died at Plympton 17th Sept., 1722—three children by first wife and five by second.

Fear, born at Plymouth 20th June, 1653; died young.

Eleazar, of Plympton, Mass., born at Plymouth, 20th Feb., 1656/7; married at Plymouth, 12th January, 1687/8, Elizabeth Combes; five children born.

Mary, died before 22nd Oct., 1690; married ———— Hutchinson, of Lynn, Mass.

———————x———————

THOMAS CUSHMAN (Elder Thos.[2], Robert[1]), of Plymouth and Plympton, Mass., born at Plymouth 16th Sept., 1637; died at Plympton 23rd August, 1726. He married first, 1664, Ruth Howland, who died between 29th May, 1672, and 16th Oct., 1679; daughter of John Howland and Elizabeth (Tilley) Howland, both of whom came to New England in the Mayflower in 1620. Secondly, married 16th Oct., 1679, Abigail Fuller, of Rehoboth, in New England. He and his wife were members of the church at Plympton of which his brother, Rev. Isaac Cushman, was the pastor. Children by his first wife:

1. Robert, of Kingston, Mass., born Oct. 4, 1664; died at Kingston, 7th September, 1757; married first, Persis ————, who died at Kingston 14th Jan., 1743/4, in her 73rd year; married secondly, in Feb., 1744/5, when he was 80 years of

CUSHMAN GENEALOGY AND GENERAL HISTORY 203

age, Prudence Sherman, of Marshfield, Mass., a maiden turned of 70. Seven children by first wife.
2. Thomas Cushman, born about 1670.
3. Desire, living 17th Dec., 1686. Her name and bequest mentioned in the will of her grandmother, Elizabeth Tilley Howland, widow of John Howland (See "Mayflower Descendants," vol. 3, pp. 54-57).
Children by second wife:
1. *Job*, born about 1680; died prior to 21st May, 1740. Married Lydia Arnold, who died prior to 27th Sept., 1746.
2. *Bartholomew*, of Plympton, Mass., born about 1684/5; baptized 13th March, 1684/5; died at Plympton 21st Dec., 1721.
3. *Samuel*, of Plympton and Attleboro, Mass., born 16th July, 1687. Married at Plympton 8th Dec., 1709, Fear Corsser, who died at Attleboro in 1727. (Six children.)
4. *Benjamin*, of Plympton, Mass., born about 1690/1; baptized 1st March, 1690/1; died at Plympton 17th Oct., 1770, in his 80th year. Married first at Plympton, 8th Jan., 1712/3, Sarah Eaton, who died at Plympton 13th Sept., 1737, in her 42nd year. Married second, 14th March, 1738/9, Sarah Bell, widow, who died at Plympton 16th Jan., 1783, in her 89th year. (Ten children by first wife.)

―――――x―――――

ROBERT CUSHMAN (4th Gen.), son of Thomas Cushman and Ruth (Howland) Cushman; born about 1664; died at Kingston 7th Sept., 1757. Married Persis ――――― Cushman, who died Jan., 14, 1743/4, in her 73rd year. Children born:
1. Robert Cushman, born July 2, 1698.
2. Ruth Cushman, born March 25, 1700.
3. Abigail Cushman, born July 3, 1701.
4. Hannah Cushman, born Dec. 25, 1704.
5. Thomas Cushman, born Feb. 14, 1706.
6. Joshua Cushman, born Oct. 14, 1708.
7. Jonathan Cushman, born July 28, 1712.
Robert Cushman married secondly, Feb., 1744/5, when he was 80 years of age, Prudence Sherman, of Marshfield, Mass., a maiden turned of 70 years.

―――――x―――――

ROBERT CUSHMAN (5th Gen.), son of Robert Cushman and

Persis ———— Cushman, born July 2, 1698; died about 1751.
He published for marriage April 17, 1725, to Mary Washburn.
He gave all of his property to his wife. Children born:
1. Lydia Cushman, born Sept. 29, 1726.
2. Jerusha Cushman, born Jan., 15, 1728.
3. Rebekah Cushman, born April 9, 1730.
4. Mercy Cushman, born June 5, 1731; died January 19, 1770.
5. Hannah Cushman, born July 2, 1732.
6. Thankful Cushman, born March 10, 1734.
7. Ruth Cushman, born Dec. 22, 1735.
8. Abigail Cushman, born April 3, 1737.
9. Robert Cushman, born Oct. 27, 1738.
10. Elkanah Cushman, born Dec. 29, 1740.
11. Martha Cushman, born Sept. 14, 1742.
12. Isaac Cushman, born March 10, 1745.

———x———

RUTH CUSHMAN (5th Gen.), daughter of Robert Cushman and Persis ———— Cushman, born March 25, 1700. Married, Jan. 28, 1716/7, Luke Perkins, Junior, at Plympton, Mass. He was the son of Luke Perkins, Sr., of Plympton, and brother of Deacon Josiah Perkins, of that town. The marriage was performed by the Rev. Isaac Cushman. Children born:
1. Ignatius Perkins, born July 15, 1720.
2. Hannah Perkins, born May 27, 1723.
3. Mary Perkins, born June 28, 1726.

———x———

HANNAH CUSHMAN (5th Gen.), daughter of Robert Cushman and Persis ———— Cushman, born Dec. 25, 1704. Married, August 17, 1731, John Waterman, of Plymouth, Mass.

———x———

THOMAS CUSHMAN (5th Gen.), son of Robert Cushman and Persis ———— Cushman, born Feb. 14, 1706; died June 13, 1768. Married Mehitable Faunce, born April 11, 1722; died June 19, 1761. He resided at Kingston and was a farmer.

———x———

JOSHUA CUSHMAN (5th Gen.), son of Robert Cushman and Persis ———— Cushman, born Oct. 14, 1708; died March 25, 1764, at Marshfield, Mass. Married first, Jan. 2, 1733, Mary Soule, born Dec. 6, 1706; daughter of Josiah Soule, of Duxbury, Mass. He married second, March 5, 1752, Deborah Ford, of Marshfield, Mass., born 1718; died July 1, 1789; aged 71 years.

JONATHAN CUSHMAN (5th Gen.), son of Robert Cushman and Persis ——— Cushman, born July 28, 1712. Married in 1736, Susannah Benson, of Kingston, Mass., daughter of John and Elizabeth Benson.

LYDIA CUSHMAN (6th Gen.), daughter of Robert Cushman and Mary Washburn Cushman, born Sept. 29, 1726. Married Capt'n Josiah Fuller, of Kingston. They had 10 children, five of whom had families:
1. Josiah Fuller, married ——— Holmes; lived in Kingston.
2. Zephaniah Fuller, married ——— Loring, of Kingston.
3. Lydia Fuller, married Elisha Cushman.
4. Charlotte Fuller, married Sylvanus Everson.
5. Joanna Fuller, married ——— Sumner.

JERUSHA CUSHMAN (6th Gen.), daughter of Robert Cushman and Mary Washburn Cushman, born Jan. 15, 1728. Married Ebenezer Cobb, of Kingston, and had seventeen children:
1. Sylvanus Cobb, married ——— Chandler and moved to New Gloucester, Maine.
2. Ruth Cobb, married Job Cobb, of Plymouth, Mass.
3. Eleanor Cobb, married John Honarel, of Plymouth, Mass.
4. Molly Cobb, married Gershom Drew, of Kingston, Mass.
5. Francis Cobb, married Phoebe Hob.
6. Ebenezer Cobb, married Mercy Porter.
7. Mattia Cobb, married Rebeacca Brewster, of Kingston.
8. Jerusha Cobb, married Barnabas Cobb, of Carver.
9. Mercy Cobb, married Paul Tinkham.
10. William Cobb, married Charlotte Coffin, of Nantuckett.
11. Fear Cobb, married Ariel Brewster, of Kingston.
12. Joseph Cobb, married Jerusha Loring.
13. Zenas Cobb, married ——— Rowe.
Four (4) children died young.

REBEKAH CUSHMAN (6th Gen.), daughter of Robert Cushman and Mary (Washburn) Cushman, born April 9, 1730. Married Barnabus Fuller, of Kingston; moved to Hebron, Maine. They had seven children.

———x———

MERCY CUSHMAN (6th Gen.), daughter of Robert Cushman and Mary (Washburn) Cushman, born June 5, 1731; died Jan. 19, 1770. Married James Harlow, of Plympton, Mass.

———x———

HANNAH CUSHMAN (6th Gen.), daughter of Robert Cushman and Mary (Washburn) Cushman, born July 2, 1732. Married John Cobb, of Kingston, Mass. Six children born:
1. Hannah Cobb, born June 17, 1756; unmarried.
2. Patience Cobb, born April 29, 1758; married Samuel Atwood, of Carver, Mass.
3. Joanna Cobb, born Dec. 4, 1759; married Thomas Morton, of Plymouth, Mass.
4. Lydia Cobb, born Nov. 3, 1761; married Wm. Pettingall, of NoBridgewater.
5. Sarah Cobb, born Nov. 5, 1763; unmarried.
6. Abigail Cobb, born Nov. 30, 1765; married Jonathan Rickard, of Buckfield, Maine.

———x———

RUTH CUSHMAN (6th Gen.), daughter of Robert Cushman and Mary (Washburn) Cushman, born Dec. 22, 1735. Married Samuel Rickard, of Plympton, Mass., and died there Nov. 2, 1826. No issue.

———x———

ABIGAIL CUSHMAN (6th Gen.), daughter of Robert Cushman and Mary (Washburn) Cushman, born April 3, 1737. Married, first, Benjamin Robbins. They removed to Yarmouth, Nova Scotia, where he was drowned. They had one son, who returned with his mother, to Kingston, Mass. She married, secondly, Benjamin Crocker, of Carver. Her son was in the Revolutionary War, at the close of which, he went to Yarmouth, Nova Scotia, and died there in 1840.

———x———

ROBERT CUSHMAN (6th Gen.), son of Robert Cushman and Mary (Washburn) Cushman, born Oct. 27, 1738; died at Woolwich, Maine, in 1799. Married, 1759, Martha Delano, born about 1738; died in 1820; aged 82 years.

ELKANAH CUSHMAN (6th Gen.), son of Robert Cushman and Mary (Washburn) Cushman, born Dec. 29, 1740.

———————x———————

ISAAC CUSHMAN (6th Gen.), son of Robert and Mary (Washburn) Cushman, born March 10, 1745. Married ————, and removed to Sumner, Maine, where he was deacon, and a pious and worthy man. He later moved to Hebron, Maine. He had children by his first wife:
1. Lovisa Cushman.

———————x———————

LOVISA CUSHMAN (7th Gen.), daughter of Isaac Cushman and ———— Cushman. Married, April 8, 1808, Stephen Washburn, of Paris, Maine. Children born:
1. Ruth Washburn, born July 22, 1809. Married, first, Benjamin Washburn; lived in Cumberland, Maine, and had nine children. She married, second, Zachariah Field.
2. Roxalana Washburn, born Feb. 28, 1811. Married Richard J. Elder; had nine children and lived in Windham, Maine.
3. Isaac Cushman Washburn, born Dec. 23, 1812; died January 28, 1852. He was a lawyer. He married Cynthia Stevens; lived at Damariscotta, Maine, and had three children.
4. Lovisa Washburn, born Oct. 22, 1814. Married James Hadlock and lived in Westbrook, Maine.

———————x———————

LYDIA FULLER (7th Gen.), daughter of Lydia Cushman and Josiah Fuller, of Kingston, Mass., born Aug. 21, 1759. Married Elisha Cushman May 13, 1780. He was born Jan. 15, 1755. They were married by William Drew, Esq. She was a member of the Church at Kingston and died there July 17, 1842. He was a cordwainer by trade, and died at Kingston May 17, 1790. She married, secondly, in 1798, Perez Bradford.

Having had a very pleasant correspondence with Mrs. Ivanilla Dunham Ball (Mrs. Fred Ball, Sr.), of Clinton, Ill., who is a descendant of Robert Cushman (4th Generation), the son of Thomas Cushman and Ruth Howland Cushman, which Robert, was the elder brother of Thomas Cushman, who married Sarah Strong and from whom I descend, I feel grateful to her for the following data and detail of her family lineage:

ROBERT CUSHMAN (1st Gen.), married Sarah Reder.

ELDER THOMAS CUSHMAN (2nd Gen.), married Mary Allerton who came in the Mayflower.

THOMAS CUSHMAN (3rd Gen.), married Ruth Howland.

ROBERT CUSHMAN (4th Gen.), married Persis ———.

JOSHUA CUSHMAN (5th Gen.), married Mary Soule. He was born Oct. 14, 1708; died March 25, 1764. Mary Soule, born Dec. 6, 1706. Married Jan. 2, 1733; was the daughter of Josiah Soule. Her Line: Josiah Soule, 3rd Gen.; John, 2nd; George Soule, 1st Gen., came over in the Mayflower.

———————x———————

CEPHAS CUSHMAN (6th Gen.), born 1746; died 1815. Married 1767, Judith Clark, born 1750; died 1833. Cephas Cushman served as a Revolutionary soldier (see Massachusetts Archives, Vol. IV, p. 207). He served in Capt. Nathaniel Hammond's Company, 4th Plymouth Co. Regiment, commanded by Colonel White; enlisted July 30, 1780; discharged August 8, 1780; service nine days on alarm at R. I. Roll certified at Rochester. Copy furnished by Mrs. Amos G. Draper, Washington, D. C.

———————x———————

EZEKIEL CUSHMAN (7th Gen.), born Nov. 5, 1768; died Dec. 2, 1831. Married, Oct. 4, 1792, Abigail Tobey, born Nov. 8, 1770; died Aug. 26, 1832.

———————x———————

JAMES HARVEY CUSHMAN (8th Gen.), son of Ezekiel Cushman and Abigail Tobey Cushman, born Oct. 24, 1795; died 1860. He was one of a family of fourteen children. It is said that James Harvey Cushman was not interested in family history and would not give his items to the compiler of the Cushman book, this last referring of course to the Henry Wyles Cushman publication of 1855. He married Lucy Lucinda (Bennett) Sears, a widow. Children born:

1. Frank Cushman, married Susan Gifford, of Woodstock, Ohio; Charles Cushman; Julius Cushman; Warren Cushman; all born in Woodstock, Ohio.

2. A daughter of James Harvey Cushman married John Slack; two children were born near Waynesville, Illinois.

3. George Bartlett Cushman, born Sept., 1847. Married Tabitha Parker and lived in Woodstock, Ohio; had children.
4. Abiel Pierce Cushman, born May 15, 1820, at Woodstock, Ohio.

———————x———————

ABIEL PIERCE CUSHMAN (9th Gen.), son of James Harvey Cushman and Lucy Lucinda (Bennett) (Sears) Cushman, born May 15, 1820 at Woodstock, Ohio; died March 3, 1895. Married, June 18, 1841, Julia Elenor Sessions, born March 26, 1825; died April 1, 1894. (Ira Allen Sessions; Darius Sessions, Vermont.) Children born to Abiel Pierce Cushman and Lucy Lucinda (Bennett) (Sears) Cushman:
1. Ira Cushman, born Feb. 4, 1843, in Ohio; died in Kansas. Married Marilda Graham and lived in Illinois and in Kansas; one child born, Enola Cushman.
2. Harriet Cushman, born March 5, 1845. Married Wallace Graham; three children born, Clayton Graham, Frank Graham, Orville Graham.
3. Sarah Cushman, born Dec. 21, 1846.
4. Roxana Caroline Cushman, born March 27, 1848, at Woodstock, Ohio; died Sept. 23, 1875, near Waynesville, Ill.
5. Adora Cushman, born June 20, 1851; died young.
6. George H. Cushman, born Jan. 18, 1856; died young.
7. Charles Clayton Cushman, born Dec. 14, 1857.
8. G. Cary Cushman, born April 3, 1860. Married and has sons in Kansas.
9. Minnie Della Cushman, born Oct. 11, 1862; died about 1875, near Waynesville, Ill.
10. Addison Byron Cushman, born Sept., 1865. Married Vivinnie Estella Webb. They have one son, Don, who is married and who also has one child.
11. Ura Etta Cushman, born April 26, 1868, near Waynesville, Ill; died at Humbolt, Kansas, about 1890. She married William Burton. Two girls were born and one died young.

———————x———————

ROXANNA CAROLINE CUSHMAN (10th Gen.), daughter of Abiel Pierce Cushman and Julia Elenor Sessions Cushman, born March 27, 1848, at Woodstock, Ohio; died Sept. 23, 1875, near Waynesville, Ill. Married, March 1, 1867, William Williams Dunham II. Children born:

1. Ivanilla Dunham, born June 13, 1869, at Waynesville, Ill.

———————x———————

IVANILLA DUNHAM (11th Gen.), daughter of Roxanna Caroline Cushman Dunham and William Williams Dunham II, born June 13, 1869, at Waynesville, Ill. Married, Oct. 9, 1893, Fred Ball, born Nov. 17, 1862, in Morgan County, Ohio; died May 29, 1938, at Clinton, Ill. He was an attorney at law and was the son of James Rosser Ball and Ann Bell Ball. One child born to Ivanilla Dunham Ball and Fred Ball:

1. Frederic Dunham Ball.

She was educated at Waynesville, Illinois, public schools, at Oxford College, Oxford, Ohio; was graduated from Illinois Women's College, Jacksonville, Ill., and attended Waynesville, Illinois, Academy.

She is a member of P. E. O. Society; Daughters of the American Revolution, nine bars for ancestors services (others eligible); and resigned membership in United States Daughters of 1812; Daughters of Magna Charta Dames; Society of Mayflower Descendants in Illinois; Daughters of Colonial Wars, in Illinois; Descendants of Knights of the Garter.

From March, 1917 to March, 1920, state historian of National Society Daughters of the American Revolution in Illinois.

Originated securing and filing of services in World War I of members of National Society D. A. R. in Illinois (and their husbands and sons and daughters, direct lineage). This service was adopted by the historian general of the National Society D. A. R. and was made by all chapters in the National Society D. A. R., both here and abroad. Such records were filed in States where services were rendered and in the National Society D. A. R. Library in Memorial Continental Hall in Washington, D. C. Illinois records are on file in Centennial Hall, on State House grounds, at Springfield, Ill. Our "Honor Roll."

Ivanilla Dunham Ball served later for a period of two years as state librarian in Illinois National Society D. A. R.

Fred Ball, Sr., attorney at law, master in chancery, DeWitt County, Ill., was educated at Beverly College, Beverly, Ohio; Illinois Wesleyan University, Bloomington, Ill. Fred Ball[1] lineage: James Rosser Ball[2], James Rosser Ball[3], Edward Ball[4], Capt. William Ball[5], Rev. Spencer Ball[6], Joseph Ball[7], Capt. William Ball[8], Col. William Ball[9], of Millenbeck Plantation, Lancaster, Virginia.

———————x———————

FREDERIC DUNHAM BALL (12th Gen.), son of Ivanilla Dunham Ball and Fred Ball, born March 23, 1895, at Clinton, Ill. Married Odell Shehane. Children born:

1. Frederic Dunham Ball, 2nd, born April 9, 1923, at Dallas, Texas.

Frederic Dunham Ball married, secondly, Lois Gregory.

Frederic Dunham Ball enlisted May 15, 1917, at Fort Sheridan, Illinois, First Officers' Training School; was appointed Aug. 15, 1917, Infantry Reserve Corps, National Army (U. S.); trained and stationed before going to Europe. Second Training School; also instructor at Camp Custer, Michigan. Third Officers' Training School, Jan. 5 to April 19, 1918. Attached to Company A., 85th Center Division, Jan. 5, 1918, Camp Custer, 328th Machine Gun Company.

A. E. F. 4th Infantry Machine Gun Company, Regular Army U. S. A., Gondrecourt, France. Promoted: vacated captaincy (I. F. C.), Infantry Reserve Corps, pending provisional 2nd lieutenancy in Regular Army, Nov. 27, 1917. Embarked for over seas from New York, July 21, 1918, arriving at Liverpool, England, August 3, 1918; proceeded from Liverpool, England, to Southampton, England, and from there to Cherbourg, France; to Les Aix De Allions to Gondrecourt, where he joined the 4th Infantry Regiment; assigned to 4th Infantry Machine Gun Company.

Trained abroad First Machine Gun School, Laugres, France, Sept. 29 to Oct. 29, 1918. Third School for Care of Animals, Coblentz, Lützel, Germany, Jan. 1-10, 1919. Went into action with 4th Infantry Machine Gun Company Sept. 12, 1918, St. Mihiel, France; participated in engagement, St. Mihiel drive, Meuse offensive, the Argonne. Started for Metz but the Armistice brought him back; was in the Army of Occupation.

From mustard gas effect and from many small wounds, he received medical care:
1. Field Hospital No. 7, Andernach, Germany, April 12, 1919.
2. Field Hospital No. 5, Maria Laache, Germany.
3. Evacuation No. 30, Mayen, Germany.
4. Evacuation No. 27, Coblenz, Germany.
5. Base Hospital No. 118, Saveney, France.
6. Embarkation Hospital No. 4, New York City, N. Y., U. S. A., June 13, 1919.
7. General Hospital No. 28, Fort Sheridan, Illinois, June 20, 1919.

Arrived at New York pier from St. Nazaire, France, June 12, 1919, and stayed in General Hospital No. 28 until discharged Sept. 8, 1919.

October, 1920, appointed psychiatrist, Public Health Service, U. S. Army; resigned.

Sept. 1, 1920, U. S. vocational training for disabled soldiers. Journalism—Assigned to the *Dallas Journal*, Dallas, Texas. Served on *Dallas Journal, News* and etc., after training publicity for Baylor Hospital, Dallas, Texas.

Educated at: Clinton Ill., public high school; Wesleyan University, Bloomington, Ill.; University of Illinois, Liberal Arts Degree, majoring in sociology, minor psychology. Transferred to University of Texas, Austin, Texas. Returned to University of Illinois for Liberal Arts Degree; taught in University of Illinois School of Journalism; took Masters Degree at University of Illinois; member of 21 honor societies. Created service of community gardens in Clinton and was helpful in planning community gardens in the entire state. Head of Bureau for Care of the Poor in DeWitt County, Ill.; head of old age pension service in DeWitt County, Ill.; served on draft board in Clinton, Ill.; district commander American Legion, State of Illinois (He held all offices in local Legion up to this office).

He was for many years on State Board of American Legion Welfare. July 12, 1942, he was appointed major in the Sixth Illinois Reserve (which took the place of State Militia and is now in the Regular U. S. Army). He was justice of the peace, Clinton, Ill., 1940-1942.

He lives one mile south of Clinton, Ill.

———x———

Lineage: Henry Wyles Cushman Genealogy (1855):
1. Robert Cushman, page 2.
2. Thomas (Elder), page 84.
3. Thomas, married Ruth Howland, page 100.
4. Robert, page 125.
5. Joshua, page 131.
6. Cephas, page 149.
7. Ezekiel, page 233.
8. James Harvey, page 417.

Family Records:
9. Abiel Pierce.
10. Roxanna Carolina.
11. Ivanilla Dunham.
12. Frederic Dunham Ball.
13. Frederic Dunham Ball, 2nd.

[Here ends the contribution of Mrs. Ivanilla Dunham Ball.]

———x———

THOMAS CUSHMAN (Thomas[3], Elder Thomas[2], Robert[1]), of Duxbury, Mass., and Lebanon, Conn., son of Thomas Cushman and Ruth Howland Cushman, born about 1670; died at Lebanon 9th Jan., 1726/7, aged 57 years. He married Sarah Strong, born about 1674; died at Lebanon, Conn., 25th December, 1726, aged 52 years; daughter of Jedediah Strong, of Coventry, Conn.

The will of Thomas Cushman, dated 9th Jan., 1726/7, is on record at the court house, Willimantic, Windham County, Conn. The testator appointed his sons, William and Thomas, as executors. (Windham Probate Records, vol. 1, pp. 167/169.)

Children mentioned in will of their father:
1. William.
2. Thomas, born probably at Lebanon about 1705.
3. Eleazar, baptized at Lebanon 18th Dec., 1720; under 21 on 9th Jan., 1726/7.
4. Zibiah, eldest daughter, married 9th March, 1727/8, Josiah Cook.

5. Ruth, under 18 on 9th Jan., 1726/7. Married 24th May, 1732, Jonathan Hunt.

6. Lydia, baptized at Lebanon 18th July, 1730; under 18 on 9th Jan., 1726/7.

---x---

THOMAS CUSHMAN (Thomas[4], Thomas[3], Elder Thomas[2], Robert[1]), of Lebanon, Conn., and Elizabeth, N. J., was born probably at Lebanon, about 1705. He married, first, Mary ————, and secondly, at New Providence, N. J., 17th June, 1764, Susannah Johnson.* He removed from Lebanon, Conn., to Elizabeth, N. J. Prior to June 19, 1759, when as Thomas Cushman, Yeoman, he was administrator of the estate of his son, Oliver.

Children by his first wife were all born at Lebanon, Conn., New London County, except the last and eighth child, Isaac, who was born at New Providence, Essex County, N. J., July 16, 1752.

In the early days of New Jersey there were no Public Health Records kept, nor church records of marriages, births, deaths and baptisms as are now kept today. There has been found in the records in one of the old minute books of the First Presbyterian Church of New Providence, fragmentary mention of the Frazee family which is recorded herein under the Isaac Cushman descent. The earliest records made and in existence, at this time, in either Essex County or in Union County, New Jersey, are dated 1848. In Union County they supplement by saying, ''to 1848 but, of course, we do not have every one.''

In Preston County, West Virginia, the court house burned in 1869 and therefore they have no records prior to that date.

The children of Thomas Cushman and Mary Cushman follow:

1. Oliver, of Elizabeth, N. J., carpenter, born Nov. 24, 1729; died prior to 19th June, 1759, when his father appears as administrator of his estate. He was a soldier and his name is found in Joseph Camp's account book in 1753, pages 28-29.

2. Sybil, born 7th April, 1732.

3. Rhoda, born 4th Feb., 1733/4.

4. Mercy, born 23rd Oct., 1735.

5. Mary, born 16th May, 1737.

6. Thomas, born 19th Dec., 1739.
7. Sarah, born 6th Nov., 1743. Married at New Providence, N. J., 27th Dec., 1763, David Jennings.
8. Isaac, born July 16, 1752, at New Providence, Essex County, N. J.

The family moved from Lebanon, Conn., consisting of seven children (two sons, five daughters). Recorded in the Archives of the town clerk of Lebanon, New London County, Conn. The family, therefore, moved down to Essex County, N. J., after 1743, as the last child was born in New Providence, Essex County, N. J., in 1752.

SIXTH GENERATION

THOMAS CUSHMAN (Thomas[5], Thomas[4], Thomas[3], Elder Thomas[2], Robert[1]), of Lebanon, Conn., and Elizabeth, N. J., born at Lebanon, Conn., 19th Dec., 1739; died probably after 11th April, 1787.

According to family tradition he was, while camping out with his father-in-law, accidentally shot and killed by the latter, who, in the darkness, mistook him for an Indian. (Information in affidavit of William David Cushman, of Richmond, Va., a descendant of Thomas Cushman.)

He married, at New Providence, N. J., 5th June, 1764, Mary Frazee, born April 3, 1744. He married, secondly, ———— Abbott, who was living in 1797 as Mary Abbott, and died in Kentucky.

Thomas Cushman, together with his younger brother, Isaac, attracted by the great possibilities of the new country westward, with their families, moved from New Jersey westward, settling in Fayette County, Penn., and Monongalia County, Va. (now West Virginia), Isaac settling in Wharton Township, Fayette County, Penn., and Thomas in Monongalia County, Virginia. After the War of the Revolution, both men having served as soldiers of the American Revolution, Thomas entered, on divers dates, his claims to Monongalia County, Va., lands, parts of his preemption warrant, these acres adjoining and abutting the land so acquired by his younger brother, Isaac, in Wharton Township, Fayette County, Penn., the two counties abutting, one in Virginia and one in Pennsylvania. The latest entry being dated April 11, 1787; whether he actually settled on these lands does not appear.

Proof notes, relating to the above entry of lands, found in New England Historical and Genealogical Register, Vol. 72, page 15.

Children born to Thomas Cushman and Mary Frazee Cushman:

1. David, born 3rd Oct., 1764; died 13th Dec., 1839. Married, June 22, 1788, Dorcas Morris; he lived the latter part of his life in Mason County, Ky. (He had issue.)
2. Sarah, married Morris Morris. They lived in Mason

County, Ky., removing thence to where Indianapolis now stands.

3. Thomas, born at Elizabeth, N. J., 31st July, 1781.

———————x———————

Records in entry book number 2, pages 8, 36, 239, 288, in the office of the county clerk of Monongalia County, West Va., show that on June 11, 1783, Thomas Cushman entered two hundred acres, part of a preemption warrant of 1,000 acres, exchange No. 189, dated April 18, 1782, on waters of Sandy Creek, near by adjoining the westward of David Frazee's lines. That on October 15, 1783, Mary Cushman entered 50 acres, etc., on the eastward of Thomas Cushman's claim and adjoining lands of Ephraim Frazee. That on June 13, 1785, Thomas Cushman entered 327 acres, part of the preemption warrant mentioned above, adjoining his settlement on the north side and extending to the Province lines. And that in April, 1787, Thomas Cushman entered 173 acres, part of the preemption warrant mentioned above, on Ashes Glade, on both sides of the main road, including the bridge.

David and Ephraim Frazee were probably brothers of Mary (Frazee) Cushman, wife of Thomas, as it is said she had two brothers so named, David, born about 1736 or '37, and Ephraim, named after his father, born about 1733 or '34.

Ephraim Frazee, father of Mary and Deborah Frazee, is said to have had a large family, nine children by his first marriage, two children by the second, and seven children by his third marriage. The grandfather and the father of the two Ephraims named above was Joseph Ephraim Frazee.

———————x———————

The writer highly appreciates the assistance afforded him by Prof. Oren E. Frazee in supplying Frazee family historical data which he has made use of:

Ephraim Frazee was born in New Jersey about 1700 and was the son or grandson of Joseph Ephraim Frazee. Record was made under date of April 29, 1730, mentioning his name in connection with a bond in inventory of the personal estate of John Blanchard, deceased, of Elizabethtown, N. J. (Ephraim was married three times, being the father of eighteen children.)

The following is given and taken from the history of Rush

County, Indiana, by Rev. E. S. Frazee: "In the early part of the eighteenth century two sons of Ephraim Frazer who resided in the western part of England emigrated to America, having obtained a grant of land from the English Crown. They settled near Elizabethtown, N. J. One of the sons was named Ephraim Frazee, born about 1700. He was married three times and the father of eighteen children, nine by his first wife, two by his second and seven by his third wife. He moved to Westmoreland County, Penn. in 1760 and died there in 1776."

One informant gives Garrett County Maryland, as his residence. Children born to Ephraim Frazee by his first wife (Rebecca Cutter):

1. Mariam Frazee, born March 29, 1729.
2. Martha Frazee, born April 6, 1731.
3. Ephraim Frazee, Jr., born Jan. 25, 1733.
4. David Frazee, born Oct. 9, 1737.
5. Rachel Frazee, born Nov. 1, 1739.
6. Hannah Frazee, born Jan. 25, 1742.
7. Mary Frazee, born April 3, 1744.
8. Elizabeth Frazee, born Jan. 13, 1747.
9. Jeremiah Frazee, born March 7, 1749.

Children born to Ephraim Frazee by his second wife (unknown):

10. Thurman Frazee, born March 20, 1752.
11. Samuel Frazee, born Nov. 5, 1753; died 1849.

Children born to Ephraim Frazee by his third wife, Anna Squier (Maxfield) Frazee:

12. Anna Frazee, born Oct. 19, 1757.
13. Deborah Frazee, born May 12, 1760.
14. Ephraim Frazee, born July 3, 1762.
15. Squier Frazee, born July 22, 1764.
16. Sarah Frazee, born Dec. 10, 1766.
17. Moses Frazee, born Sept. 8, 1770 } Twins.
18. Aaron Frazee, born Sept. 8, 1770 }

There is no special record concerning Mariam or Martha Frazee. Their brother, Ephraim Frazee, Jr., intestate and his father, Ephraim, administered the estate. David Frazee is reported to have settled on the Sandy River, near Bruceton,

Va., in 1769, and he and Jacob Judy are said to have been the first permanent settlers in Preston County, Va. (now West Virginia). There is no record concerning Rachel Frazee, who died June 11, 1748, nor Hannah Frazee. Mary Frazee, born April 3, 1744, married, June 5, 1764, Thomas Cushman, at New Providence, N. J. To this union three children were born, David, Sarah and Thomas. Elizabeth Frazee, born Jan. 13, 1747, married, in 1768, James Cole. Jeremiah Frazee, born March 7, 1749, moved from New Jersey to Shelbysport, Garrett County, Maryland, and settled on what is known as Frazee's Ridge. He lies buried in the Frazee graveyard on his former farm.

Children of Jeremiah Frazee and wis wife (unknown):
1. Elisha Frazee, 1800-1874.
2. Isaac Frazee, 1802-1881.
3. John Jerry Frazee, 1805-1879.
4. Jonathan Frazee, 1808-1865.
5. Polly Frazee, married John E. Frazee.
6. Another daughter, Frazee (given name unknown).

For a fuller account of Jeremiah Frazee's descendants, see Frazee Genealogy by Oren E. Frazee, filed with the Institute of American Genealogy, Chicago, Ill.; also for descendants of Thurman Frazee, 1797-1868.

Thurman Frazee, born March 20, 1752, in New Jersey, presumably in Essex County, N. J., removed to Frazee's Ridge, Maryland, where he died April 19, 1844. He married first, Anna Edwards, born 1755, and buried in Preston County Va. (now West Virginia). They had six children. He married, secondly, (name not known), and had among other children: Squier Frazee, Samuel Frazee, Isaac Frazee, Ephraim Frazee, born Dec. 6, 1784, died Jan. 26, 1848; Matthias Frazee, Nancy Frazee, Patience Frazee, married John Wooley, of Portsmouth, Ohio; George Frazee, Thurman Frazee, born 1797 in Maryland, died Nov. 1, 1868, in Clinton County, Ind.

Ephraim Frazee, born Dec. 6, 1784; died Jan. 26, 1848. Married Barbara Stuck, born 1785; died 1857. Children born:

Mary Frazee, John Ephraim Frazee, Anne Frazee, Thurman Frazee, Susanna Frazee, Jacob Frazee, Billy Frazee, Elisha Frazee.

THURMAN FRAZEE, born 1797 in Maryland; died Nov. 1, 1868 in Clinton County, Ind. Married Frances Lasby, Sept. 30, 1820, near Portsmouth, Ohio, and in 1835 he settled in Clinton County, Ind., as a farmer. Children born:
1. Salathiel B. Frazee, 1821-1868.
2. Martha Ann Frazee, 1825-1915.
3. Mary Margaret Frazee, 1827-1827.
4. Absalom D. Frazee, 1829-1834.
5. Margaret Frazee, 1832-1836.
6. Sarah Frazee, 1836-1867.
7. Samuel Frazee, 1838-1896.
8. John Frazee, 1840-1846.
9. William Frazee, 1846-1846.

Samuel Frazee, born in New Jersey, Nov. 6, 1753; died in Mason County, Ky., in 1849.

Anna Frazee, born Oct. 19, 1757. No further record.

Deborah Frazee, born May 12, 1760; died April 7, 1800. Married Isaac Cushman.

Ephraim Frazee, Jr., born July 3, 1762. No further record.

SQUIER FRAZEE, born July 22, 1764, with his mother, Anna Squier (Maxfield) Frazee, and twin brothers, Moses and Aaron Frazee, joined Samuel Frazee (half brother) in Kentucky in 1784, where he married Priscilla Forman, born 1778. Children born:

Rachel Frazee married, March 29, 1823, Buckner Black.
Ann Frazee married Jacob Frazee.
Samuel Frazee married, Nov. 12, 1832, Judith Hargott.
Hannah Frazee married Col. Jack Tabb.
David Frazee.
Squier Frazee.
Ira Frazee.

Diedema Frazee, born 1814. Married Isham Keith, born 1808. Children born: John Alexander Keith, Judith Ann Keith, Squier Asham Keith, Joseph Anderson Keith, and Diadema Frances Keith (called Pink Keith).

Diadema Frances Keith, born 1845. Married Thomas Benton Prather, born 1837. Children born: Baby Prather,

Thomas Isham Prather, Diadema Frances Prather, Carry May Prather, Mary Prather, Litta Prather, Yetta John Keith Prather, Benton Prather, and Fred Prather.

Diadema Frances Prather married Victor Louis Griser in 1893. Children born: Louis Keith Griser and Mary Elizabeth Griser.

Mary Elizabeth Griser married Chester Burnell Sanderson in 1927.

Sarah Frazee, born 1766, married Morris Morris. See Morris lineage in Frazee Genealogy by Oren E. Frazee, on file with the Institute of American Genealogy, Chicago, Ill.

———————x———————

DAVID CUSHMAN (7th Gen.), son of Thomas Cushman and Mary Frazee Cushman, born Oct. 3, 1764; died Dec. 13, 1839. Married, June 22, 1788, Dorcas Morris, born Aug. 15, 1765; died March 13, 1854. He lived the latter part of his life in Mason County, Kentucky. Children born:
1. Thomas Cushman, born Oct. 16, 1796; died Jan. 26, 1851.
2. Ann Cushman, born Oct. 12, 1798; died Aug. 11, 1851.
3. Joseph Cushman.
4. Mary Cushman.
5. Eliza Cushman.

———————x———————

THOMAS CUSHMAN (8th Gen.), son of David Cushman and Dorcas Morris Cushman, born Oct. 16, 1796; died Jan. 26, 1851. Married, Dec. 22, 1825, Mary M. Kilgour, born May 17, 1802; died June 7, 1880. Children born:
1. Preston O. Cushman, born Nov. 30, 1826.
2. Joseph David Cushman, born May 22, 1828; died Dec. 5, 1895.
3. Thomas K. Cushman, born Dec. 15, 1829; died March 4, 1859.
4. John Oscar Cushman, born Aug. 16, 1831; died Dec. 14, 1915.
5. Hartwell Boswell Cushman, born Oct. 5, 1833; died April 2, 1916.
6. Melissa M. Cushman, born Oct. 31, 1835; died June 27, 1864.
7. Mary M. Cushman, born Dec. 15, 1837.

ANN CUSHMAN (8th Gen.), daughter of David Cushman and Dorcas Morris Cushman, born in Mason County, Ky., Oct. 12, 1798; died Aug. 11, 1851. Married first, ———— Holliday; married, secondly, April 22, 1834, near Germantown, Mason County Ky., Joseph Frazee, born Sept. 15, 1794; died Aug. 7, 1870. Children born to second marriage:
1. Joseph Thomas Frazee, born Feb. 17, 1834; died Oct. 15, 1899.
2. Rebecca Frazee, died in childhood.
3. John Morris Frazee, born Aug. 13, 1838.
4. David Cushman Frazee, born Sept. 17, 1842.

————————x————————

JOSEPH THOMAS FRAZEE (9th Gen.), son of Ann (Cushman) Frazee and Joseph Frazee, born Feb. 17, 1834; died Oct. 15, 1899. Married, Oct. 20, 1857, Amanda Gordon, born Oct. 16, 1834. Children born:
1. Harriet (Hattie) Frazee, born March, 1860.

————————x————————

HARTWELL BOSWELL CUSHMAN (9th Gen.), son of Thomas and Mary M. (Kilgour) Cushman, born Oct. 5, 1833; died April 2, 1916. Married Martha Frances Frazee, in Mason County, Ky. Children born:
1. Anna Lutie Cushman, born Feb. 25, 1861; died Jan. 16, 1925.
2. Thomas Frazee Cushman, born Jan. 25, 1864.

————————x————————

ANNA LUTIE CUSHMAN (10th Gen.), daughter of Hartwell Boswell Cushman and Martha Frances (Frazee) Cushman, born Feb. 25, 1861; died Jan. 16, 1925. Married, April 7, 1880, Ira Frank Tabb, born February 22, 1856; died Aug. 10, 1936. Children born:
1. Mattie Elrod Tabb, born March 12, 1882.
2. Louise Cushman Tabb, born Aug. 10, 1885.
3. Mary VanSant Tabb, born Dec. 9, 1893.

————————x————————

MATTIE ELROD TABB (11th Gen.), daughter of Anna Lutie (Cushman) Tabb and Ira Frank Tabb, born March 12, 1882. Married, Oct. 29, 1902, Charles T. Hazelrigg, and lives at Mt. Sterling, Ky. Children born:
1. Frances Hartwell Hazelrigg, born Nov. 20, 1903.

2. Mary Dillard Hazelrigg, born Sept. 18, 1912.
3. Charles Tabb Hazelrigg, born Aug. 18, 1915.

———————x———————

LOUISE CUSHMAN TABB (11th Gen.), daughter of Anna Lutie (Cushman) Tabb and Ira Frank Tabb, born Aug. 10, 1885. Married, March 19, 1919, Al. M. Pulaski. Children born:
1. Frank Tabb Pulaski.

———————x———————

MARY VAN-SANT TABB (11th Gen.), daughter of Anna Lutie (Cushman) Tabb and Ira Frank Tabb, born Dec. 9, 1893. Married, Feb. 17, 1917, J. M. Hoffman, born April 26, 1880. Children born:
1. Jouett Miller Hoffman, Jr., born Oct. 1, 1919.
2. Anna Lou Hoffman, born Dec. 15, 1923.

———————x———————

FRANCES HARTWELL HAZELRIGG (12th Gen.), daughter of Mattie Elrod (Tabb) Hazelrigg and Charles T. Hazelrigg, born Nov. 20, 1903. Married, Oct. 18, 1928, John S. Carroll, of Frankfort, Ky.; married, secondly, June, 1938, Arthur G. Stevens, of Washington, D. C.

———————x———————

MARY DILLARD HAZELRIGG (12th Gen.), daughter of Mattie Elrod (Tabb) Hazelrigg and Charles T. Hazelrigg, born Sept. 18, 1912. Married, July 12, 1937, John Wesley Marr, of Lexington, Ky. Children born:
1. Nancy Carroll Marr, born June 6, 1938.
2. Martha Lee Marr, born Nov., 1939.

———————x———————

HARRIET (HATTIE) FRAZEE (10th Gen.), daughter of Joseph Thomas Frazee and Amanda (Gordon) Frazee, born March 18, 1860. Married, Nov., 1882, Raleigh Kendall Hart. Children born:
1. John Frazee Hart, born Feb. 3, 1886.
2. Arnold Robertson Hart, born Jan. 22, 1889.

———————x———————

ARNOLD ROBERTSON HART (11th Gen.), son of Harriett (Hattie) Frazee Hart and Raleigh Kendall Hart, born Jan. 22, 1889. Married, June 5, 1912, Lela Hurst. Children born:
1. Raleigh Kendall Hart, born Sept. 11, 1914.
2. Marshall Frazee Hart, born Oct. 24, 1917.

Mr. and Mrs. Arnold Robertson Hart have in their home at Flemingsburg, Kentucky, a number of fine old family portraits and other family antiques and treasures of interest. Their two sons, graduates of the University of the State of Kentucky, are both associated with the Commercial Credit Corporation at Charleston, West Virginia.

JOHN MORRIS FRAZEE (9th Gen.), son of Ann Cushman Frazee and Joseph Frazee, born Aug. 13, 1938; died July 31, 1923. Married, Nov. 18, 1869, Eliza Jennings Lusk, at Lancaster, Ky. Children born:
1. Ann Cushman Frazee, born Nov. 28, 1870, in Germantown, Ky.
2. Frances Lusk Frazee, born Dec. 19, 1874, in Germantown, Ky.

———————x———————

ANN CUSHMAN FRAZEE (10th Gen.), daughter of John Morris Frazee and Eliza Jennings Lusk Frazee, born Nov. 28, 1870; died Dec. 5, 1937, at the home of her daughter, Mrs. Frances Dixon Ball Goggin, near Germantown, Ky. She married Posey Dixon Ball, of Corydon, Ky., born Jan. 16, 1865, who died May 28, 1898, at Henderson, Ky. Children born:
1. Frances Dixon Ball, born Feb. 3, 1899.

After the death of her husband, Posey Dixon Ball, she devoted her life to teaching. She received her education at Hayswood Seminary and later entered Daughters College at Harrodsburg, Ky., from which she graduated, after which she was a member of Maysville, Kentucky, public school faculty, and taught the eighth grade.

She retired a few years after having received her Bachelor of Arts Degree from Transylvania College at Lexington, Ky.

She was a member of the Mayflower Society, a member of Limestone Chapter, Daughters of the American Revolution, and was chairman of the Correct Use of the Flag committee.

———————x———————

FRANCES DIXON BALL (11th Gen.), daughter of Ann Cushman Frazee and Posey Dixon Ball, born Feb. 3, 1899. Married, Nov. 18, 1924, at Maysville, Ky., Henry Reed Goggin. Children born:

1. Elizabeth Frazee Goggin, born Nov. 22, 1925.
2. Ann Cushman Goggin, born Nov. 15, 1928.

Mrs. Goggin, living at Germantown, Ky., is the proud possessor of "The Old Frazee Money Box," a highly prized memoir and antiquity, which it is said has been handed down from generation to generation from sometime in the early 1600's and was first owned by Ephraim Frazee.

She also has the old rocking chair, one of the prized possessions of Dorcas Morris Cushman, wife of David Cushman of the seventh generation from Robert Cushman, in which it was her habit to sit and read the bible to her children. She also has several of the old portraits, in oil, of the family, with other family treasures including a beautiful and massive mahogany side-board more than 100 years old.

———————x———————

FRANCES LUSK FRAZEE (11th Gen.), daughter of John Morris Frazee and Eliza Jennings Lusk Frazee, born Dec. 19, 1874, in Germantown, Ky. Married, May 28, 1912, Henry Lloyd born July 31, 1869; died May 15, 1926. Children born:
1. Henry Lloyd, Jr., born June 7, 1915, at Lexington, Ky., and now living at Cambridge, Mass.

———————x———————

JOSEPH CUSHMAN (8th Gen.), son of David Cushman and Dorcas Morris Cushman. Married Sallie Hess.

———————x———————

MARY CUSHMAN (8th Gen.), daughter of David Cushman and Dorcas Morris Cushman. Married Richard Kirk.

———————x———————

ELIZA CUSHMAN (8th Gen.), daughter of David Cushman and Dorcas Morris Cushman. Married Rudolph Black.

———————x———————

DAVID CUSHMAN FRAZEE (9th Gen.), son of Ann Cushman Frazee and Joseph Frazee, born Sept. 17, 1842. Married, Nov. 23, 1869, Maria Lee, born March 13, 1847.

———————x———————

MARY M. CUSHMAN (9th Gen.), daughter of Thomas Cushman and Mary M. (Kilgour) Cushman, born Dec. 15, 1837. Married A. J. McDougal March 4, 1862. Children born:
1. Harry McDougal.
2. Oscar McDougal.

3. Anna McDougal.
4. Minnie McDougal.

---x---

Preston O. Cushman (9th Gen.), son of Thomas Cushman and Mary M. (Kilgour) Cushman, born Nov. 30, 1826. Married, March 8, 1864, Lizzie M. Diltz. Children born:
1. Thomas Cushman.
2. Anna Cushman.

---x---

John Oscar Cushman (9th Gen.), son of Thomas Cushman and Mary M. (Kilgour) Cushman, born Aug. 16, 1831. Married, May 21, 1879, Eudora Hester. Children born.
1. Mary Eleanor Cushman, born Dec. 29, 1885.

---x---

Mary Eleanor Cushman (10th Gen.), daughter of John Oscar Cushman and Eudora (Hester) Cushman, born Dec. 29, 1885. Married, Nov. 18, 1914, Thomas Hunter Moss. Lives at 1304 Walnut street, Hopkinsville, Ky. Has an adopted son, Ben Tipton Moss, born June 1, 1926.

---x---

Thomas Frazee Cushman (10th Gen.), son of Hartwell Boswell Cushman and Martha Frances (Frazee) Cushman, born Jan. 25, 1864. Married Bettie Dudley. Children born:
1. James Dudley Cushman, born 1888.
2. Martha Frazee Cushman, born 1891.

---x---

Martha Frazee Cushman (11th Gen.), daughter of Thomas Frazee Cushman, born 1891. Married William Bowden June 5, 1917. Children born:
1. Bettie Ann Bowden, born March 19, 1919.
2. Billy Cushman Bowden, born June 13, 1926.

---x---

James Dudley Cushman (11th Gen.), son of Thomas Frazee Cushman and Bettie Dudley Cushman, born 1888. Married, 1907, Dorothy Martin. Children born:
1. Martha Jane Cushman, born March 1, 1916.
2. James Dudley Cushman, Jr., born May, 1923.

---x---

Martha Jane Cushman (12th Gen.), daughter of James Dudley Cushman and Dorothy (Martin) Cushman, born March 1, 1916. Married Gayle Oldroyd. Children born:

(Insert for page 217)

It is certified by the office of the Adjutant General of New Jersey that Thomas Cushman served as private, Bull's Troop, Second Regiment, Dragoons, Continental Army; enlisted March 2, 1777; discharged August 9, 1780, during the Revolutionary War.

(Page 226½—See Page 227)

RICHARD MORRIS

(The following used by consent of Mrs. William B. Ardery.)

Richard Morris, Revolutionary patriot, was probably born in New England, about 1729. He died intestate in Borubon County, Kentucky, in the year 1803, being far advanced in years. His wife, Mary (said to be second wife), survived him. He was the father of six children. Richard Morris built "Fort Morris," in which fortification the people from Morgantown took refuge during the battle of Point Pleasant, the accepted first battle of the Revolution. This fort was located in Monongalia County, that part of the county which later formed Preston County, Virginia, in 1818. Fort Morris enclosed an assemblage of cabins and was situated on Hog Run, tributary to Sandy Creek, in what is now Grant District. It was erected in 1774, immediately after the murder of Logan's relatives and was, no doubt, used not only during Dunmore's War but throughout the Revolution. In 1781, in a record filed in Bourbon County, Kentucky (file box 282, office of Circuit Clerk), Richard Morris styled himself "of Monongalia (Monongahala) County, State of Virginia." He received land grants in Kentucky territory. The known children of Richard Morris were:

1. Thomas Morris, born Feb., 1751; estate appraised Bourbon County, Kentucky, Nov. 2, 1818; left widow, Mary.
2. John Morris, died prior to 1800; left widow.
3. Morris (Maurice) Morris, born Feb. 17, 1761, died May 17, 1809, in Bourbon County, Kentucky. Married Sarah Cushman, born Sept. 10, 1766; died Jan. 10, 1842.
4. Rachel Morris, married Joseph Robinett.
5. Catherine Morris, married Samuel Spurgin.
6. Mary Morris, married Andrew McCreary.

1. Jimmie Oldroyd, born Feb., 1938.

———————x———————

The compiler and author is indebted to Mrs. Dayse (Whitecotton) Proctor, 7404 Mercier street, Kansas City, Mo., for the following history of descendants of Sarah Cushman.

———————x———————

SARAH CUSHMAN (7th Gen.), daughter of Thomas Cushman and Mary Frazee Cushman, born Sept. 10, 1766; died Jan. 10, 1842, aged 75 years, four months. Married Morris Morris, of Monongalia County, Va., third child of Richard and Mary Morris, born Feb. 17, 1751, probably in vicinity of Philadelphia, Penn. He died May 17, 1809, aged 58 years and three months. Children born:
1. Thomas Morris, born May 3, 1783.
2. Rachel Morris, born Jan. 20, 1786.
3. Daniel Cushman Morris, born April 14, 1788, at Bryan Station, Ky.
4. Mary Morris, born April 20, 1791; died in Kentucky.
5. John Morris, born Feb. 10, 1793.
6. Rebecca Morris, born Oct. 17, 1794.
7. Betsy Morris, born Oct. 10, 1798.
8. Horatio Morris, born Sept. 12, 1800.
9. Preston Morris, born Aug. 7, 1802.
10. Albert Famous Morris, born Dec. 4, 1804. Settled near Payson, Ill.
11. Beauford V. Morris, born June 10, 1807.

The above list of children of Morris Morris and Sarah Cushman Morris, copied from the bible of Nancy Turney and now owned by Amos Turney, Paris, Ky.

Richard Morris and Mary Morris, father and mother of Morris Morris, and also Morris Morris and his wife, Sarah Cushman Morris, all died in Kentucky.

———————x———————

RACHEL MORRIS (8th Gen.), daughter of Sarah Cushman Morris and Morris Morris, born Jan. 20, 1786. Married, Aug. 7, 1803, her cousin, Morris Morris, in Bourbon County, Ky. Children born:
1. Thomas Morris, born in Nicholas County, Ky., was a graduate from West Point in 1834; resigned from the Army. In 1836 became president of the Indianapolis & Cincinnati

Railroad. He died in Indianapolis in 1904. His family lived in Indianapolis for many years.

---x---

DANIEL CUSHMAN MORRIS (8th Gen.), son of Sarah Cushman Morris and Morris Morris, born April 14, 1788, at Bryan Station, Ky.; died April, 1852, at Cloverdale, Ind. Married, April 25, 1811, Anna Meenack (Minnich). She died at Greenfield, Mo., July, 1854. Children born:
1. Morris Robenet Morris (9th Gen), born Jan., 1812; died single.
2. Dulcina Morris, born July 26, 1819.
3. Thomas Morris.
4. Catherine Elizabeth Morris, born Oct. 22, 1822; died 1880.
5. Albert Famous Morris, born at Cloverdale, Ind.
6. Samuel Morris.
7. Almanza Palmyra Morris, born in Nicholas County, Ky.
8. Rebecca Ann Morris, born Jan. 24, 1836, in Nicholas County, Ky.

---x---

HORATIO MORRIS (8th Gen.), son of Sarah Cushman Morris and Morris Morris, born Sept. 12, 1800. Married ——— Hughes.

---x---

PRESTON MORRIS (8th Gen.), son of Sarah Cushman Morris and Morris Morris, born Aug. 7, 1802. Married (unknown).

---x---

ALBERT FAMOUS MORRIS (8th Gen.), son of Sarah Cushman and Morris Morris, born Dec. 4, 1804. Settled near Payson, Ill.

---x---

BEAUFORD V. MORRIS (8th Gen.), son of Sarah Cushman and Morris Morris, born June 10, 1807. Married ——— Bowles and settled in Illinois.

---x---

DULCINA MORRIS (9th Gen.), daughter of Daniel Cushman Morris and Anna Minnich Morris, born July 26, 1819. Married ——— Lane and lived at Cloverdale, Ind. Children born:
1. Thomas Lane.
2. John Lane.
3. Ella Lane married Mr. McCoy, of Cloverdale, Ind.

(Page 228½)

MORRIS MORRIS

In the early settlement of Virginia, three brothers, James, John, and Morris, came from Wales. The subject of this sketch was the grandson of James Morris, was born in Virginia in 1780. In his young days his parents moved to Fleming County, Kentucky, where he was brought up, and lived until he was 40 years old. He received an English education, read law, and for many years practiced it. In 1803 he married Rachel Morris, a descendant of John Morris, one of the three brothers mentioned above. The future capitol of the new State of Indiana had just been fixed at Indianapolis, and the settlement was only in the second year of existence when he came to it. He bought land largely within and without its limits and was among those foremost in its active life. In 1828 he was elected Auditor of State and successively re-elected to that office for sixteen years. In 1832 he was one of the three commissioners who had in charge the building of the State House. His son, Thomas A. Morris, as civil engineer, laid out the grounds. Nearly a half century later that son, General Thomas A. Morris, is now in charge of the building of the new State House, on the same spot where the old one stood, and his (Morris Morris) grandson, Morris M. Defrees, as civil engineer, laid out the grounds for the new. He died in 1864, in his eighty-fourth year. General Thomas A. Morris, born in Nicholas County, Kentucky, December 26, 1811, began to learn the printer's trade in 1823; after three years at the printer's trade, he then had one year at Ebeneezer School. After four years he was appointed Cadet at West Point.

For reference: "Representative Men of Indiana," 1880, Volume 2. Published by Western Biographical Publishing Co., Cincinnati, Ohio. Indiana Room Genealogical Department, Indianapolis, pages 258-260.

MARY MORRIS (8th Gen.), daughter of Sarah Cushman Morris and Morris Morris, born April 20, 1791. Married ———— McIntire. Children born:
1. Lucinda McIntire.

———————x————————

LUCINDA MCINTIRE (9th Gen.), daughter of Mary (Morris) McIntire and ———— McIntire. Married Amos Turney. Children born:
1. Mary Turney.
2. Sallie Turney, never married.
3. Betty Turney.
4. Amos Turney.
5. Dan Turney.
6. Jesse Turney.
7. Henry Turney.

———————x————————

MARY TURNEY (10th Gen.), daughter of Lucinda (McIntire) Turney and Amos Turney. Married, first, ———— Colville. Children born:
1. May Colville.
2. Lucy Colville.
Mary married, secondly, Mr. Neely.

———————x————————

AMOS TURNEY (10th Gen.), son of Lucinda (McIntire) Turney and Amos Turney. Married Lizzie ————. Children born:
1. Jessie Turney. Married Zeke Arnold.

———————x————————

DAN TURNEY (10th Gen.), son of Lucinda (McIntire) Turney and Amos Turney. Married Mollie Mitchell. Children born:
1. Margaret Turney.
2. Lucille Turney.
3. Nellie Turney.
4. Edna Turney. Married Charles McMillan (No issue).

———————x————————

MARGARET TURNEY (11th Gen.), daughter of Dan Turney and Mollie (Mitchell) Turney. Married Harry B. Clay. Children born:
1. Mary Mitchell Clay.

2. John Clay.
   3. Nell Clay.

---x---

LUCILLE TURNEY (11th Gen.), daughter of Dan Turney and Mollie (Mitchell) Turney. Married J. Frank Clay. Children born:
1. Frances Clay.
2. Dan Turney Clay.
3. ——— Clay.

---x---

NELLIE TURNEY (11th Gen.), daughter of Dan Turney and Mollie (Mitchell) Turney. Married Sam Willis. Children born:
1. Margaret Willis. Married Vaughan Drake.

---x---

JESSE TURNEY (10th Gen.), son of Lucinda (McIntire) Turney and Amos Turney. Married Lizzie Ewing. Children born:
1. Clell Ewing Turney.
2. Jack Turney.
3. Amos Turney. Married Edna Earl Hinton (No issue).
4. Lizzie Manning Turney. Married Robert Winn.
5. Leslie Turney. Married Lois Taylor.

---x---

CLELL EWING TURNEY (11th Gen.), son of Jesse Turney and Lizzie (Ewing) Turney. Married Betty Brent Johnson. Children born:
1. McClelland Turney.

---x---

HENRY TURNEY (10th Gen.), son of Lucinda (McIntire) Turney and Amos Turney. Married Lizzie Stitt. Children born:
1. Alfred Turney, died in childhood.
2. Lucy Turney.

---x---

LUCY TURNEY (11th Gen.), daughter of Henry Turney and Lizzie (Stitt) Turney. Married Bob Tucker. Children born:
1. Henry Tucker.
2. Gideon Tucker.

---x---

CAPTAIN JOHN MORRIS (8th Gen.), son of Sarah (Cushman) Morris and Morris Morris, born Feb. 10, 1793, at Paris, Ky.

Married, first, (Unknown); married, secondly, Mrs. Payne, a widow; married, thirdly, Katherine Turney.

His daughter, Mrs. Lee Morris Sconce, living in Broomfield in 1906, now deceased, gave Mrs. Daisy Whitecotton Proctor this family record of the descent of Sarah Cushman; and her daughter, Mrs. Sallie Sconce Peak, now lives at Cypress, Calif., Box 123.

Children born to Captain John Morris by his first marriage:
1. Perry Morris.
2. Elizabeth or Lizzie Morris.

Children by his second marriage to Mrs. Payne, widow:
1. Henry Morris.

Children by his third marriage to Katherine Turney:
1. Lucinda Morris, who married James Sconce.
2. Susan Morris.
3. Nancy Morris.
4. John Graves Morris.
5. William Amos Morris.
6. Allen Gano Morris.

―――――x―――――

LUCINDA MORRIS (9th Gen.), daughter of Captain John Morris and Katherine (Turney) Morris. Married James Sconce. Children born:
1. John Sconce.
2. Robert Sconce.
3. Sallie Sconce. Married ――――― Peak.

―――――x―――――

SUSAN MORRIS (9th Gen.), daughter of Captain John Morris and Katherine (Turney) Morris. Married Robert Soper. Children born:
1. Claine Soper.
2. Catharine Soper.

―――――x―――――

NANCY MORRIS (9th Gen.), daughter of Captain John Morris and Katherine (Turney) Morris. Married John L. Soper. Children born:
1. Louella Soper.
2. Willie Kate Soper.
3. Sue Soper.

LOUELLA SOPER (10th Gen.), daughter of Nancy (Morris) Soper and John L. Soper. Married J. M. Hughes. Children born:
1. Leslie Hughes.
2. William Hughes.

---x---

WILLIE KATE SOPER (10th Gen.), daughter of Nancy (Morris) Soper and John L. Soper, born 1864. Married Dr. George Grimes. No issue.

---x---

SUE SOPER (10th Gen.), daughter of Nancy (Morris) Soper and John L. Soper, born in 1870. Married John F. Young. Children born:
1. Chester M. Young married Ruth Chandler; one daughter born.
2. Nancy M. Young, married Roy J. Roy; one son, Walter Roy.
3. Katherine Young married Reynolds Bell; two daughters born.
4. John F. Young married Ruby ———; one child.

---x---

JOHN GRAVES MORRIS (9th Gen.), son of Captain John Morris and Katherine (Turney) Morris, born 1839. Married Hepsibaugh Ricketts. Children born:
1. Robert E. Lee Morris, born April 27, 1866.
2. Hazel Morris.
3. Bobby Morris.
4. John Allen Morris, born Nov. 14, 1867.
5. Nancy Turney Morris, born Oct. 10, 1869.
6. Catharine Morris, born Nov. 23, 1873.
7. James Sconce Morris, born Dec. 19, 1875.
8. Sallie Peak Morris, born Dec. 3, 1878.
9. Henrietta Morris, born Nov. 15, 1880.
10. Mitchell Morris, born July 1, 1883; died June 5, 1941.
11. Hugh Henry Morris, born April 15, 1885.
12. Adelaide Morris, born March 10, 1887.
13. Susan Rebecca Morris, born March 14, 1889.

---x---

ROBERT E. LEE MORRIS (10th Gen.), son of John Graves

Morris and Hepsibaugh (Ricketts) Morris, born April 27, 1866. Married Myrtle Allison. Children born:
1. Guy Morris. Married ——— and has a family.

———x———

HAZEL MORRIS (10th Gen.), daughter of John Graves Morris and Hepsibaugh (Ricketts) Morris. Married first Thomas Higgins. One child born:
1. Volney Higgins.
Hazel married, secondly, Toby Jacoby (no issue).

———x———

BOBBY MORRIS (10th Gen.), daughter of John Graves Morris and Hepsibaugh (Ricketts) Morris. Married, first, John Stuart (no issue); married, secondly, Bob Hamilton (no issue).

———x———

JOHN ALLEN MORRIS (10th Gen.), son of John Graves Morris and Hepsibaugh (Ricketts) Morris, born Nov. 14, 1867. Married Laura Strausbaugh. Children born:
1. Walter Morris.
2. Lillian Morris.
3. John Morris.
4. Raymond Morris.
5. Louis Morris.

———x———

NANCY TURNEY MORRIS (10th Gen.), daughter of John Graves Morris and Hepsibaugh (Ricketts) Morris, born Oct. 10, 1869. Married, first, William Strausbaugh. Children born:
1. Allene Strausbaugh, born Mar. 25, 1893. } twins
2. Eugene F. Strausbaugh, born Mar. 25, 1893 }
Allene Strausbaugh married Darby W. Doyle. Eugene Franklin Strausbaugh married Mary Quisenbury.
Nancy Turney Morris married, secondly, ——— Van Deren (no issue).

———x———

CATHARINE MORRIS (10th Gen.), daughter of John Graves Morris and Hepsibaugh (Ricketts) Morris, born Nov. 23, 1873. Married Albert Sidney Collins. Children born:
1. Albert Marvin Collins, born Nov. 21, 1891. Married Martha Snowden (no issue).
2. Clara Collins, born Oct. 16, 1893.

———x———

CLARA COLLINS (11th Gen.), daughter of Catharine Morris

and Albert Sidney Collins, born Oct. 16, 1893. Married Bailey P. Wooten. Children born:
1. Kitty Janie Wooten, born Aug. 31, 1917.
2. Alice Rebecca Wooten, born March 30, 1920.

———————x———————

KITTY JANIE WOOTEN (12th Gen.), daughter of Clara Collins and Bailey P. Wooten, born Aug. 31, 1917. Married Wm. H. Beck. Children born:
1. Kitty Anne Beck, born May 26, 1940.

———————x———————

JAMES SCONCE MORRIS (10th Gen.), son of John Graves Morris and Hepsibaugh (Ricketts) Morris, born Dec. 19, 1875. Married Ethel Ball, first. Children born:
1. Margaret Morris. Married Robert Erd; two children.
2. Russell Morris (married).
3. Kitty Morris (married).
James Sconce Morris married, secondly, Pearl Turner. Children born:
1. John Morris.
2. James Morris.
3. Enid Morris.

———————x———————

SALLIE PEAK MORRIS (10th Gen.), daughter of John Graves Morris and Hepsibaugh (Ricketts) Morris, born Dec. 3, 1878. Married W. T. Robertson (no issue).

———————x———————

HENRIETTA MORRIS (10th Gen.), daughter of John Graves Morris and Hepsibaugh (Ricketts) Morris, born Nov. 15, 1880. Married Charles B. Johnson (no issue).

———————x———————

MITCHELL MORRIS (10th Gen.), son of John Graves Morris and Hepsibaugh (Ricketts) Morris, born July 1, 1883; died June 5, 1941. Married Gertrude Miller. Children born:
1. Gertrude Morris. Married ————.
2. Edward Morris.
3. Dora Mitchell Morris. Married ———— Clever.

———————x———————

HUGH HENRY MORRIS (10th Gen.), son of John Graves Morris and Hepsibaugh (Ricketts) Morris, born April 15, 1885. Married Elida Roberts. Children born:

1. Mary Morris. Married and has two or three children.
2. John Morris.

---x---

ADELAIDE MORRIS (10th Gen.), daughter of John Graves and Hepsibaugh (Ricketts) Morris, born March 10, 1887. Married Frank Warren. Children born:
1. Marjorie Warren married Wm. Herring and has one daughter.
2. Jane Graves Warren.
3. Cleora Warren.

---x---

SUSAN REBECCA MORRIS (10th Gen.), daughter of John Graves Morris and Hepsibaugh (Ricketts) Morris, born March 14, 1889. Married H. R. Cox.

---x---

WILLIAM AMOS MORRIS (9th Gen.), son of Captain John Morris and Katherine (Turney) Morris. Married Mollie Snivens. Children born:
1. Dan Turney Morris, born about 1866; died 1941.
2. Lula Morris, born 1869; died 1900.
3. Katharine Morris, born 1871.
4. William Morris, born 1876.
5. Tom Morris.

---x---

DAN TURNEY MORRIS (10th Gen.), son of William Amos Morris and Mollie (Snivens) Morris, born about 1866; died 1941. Married Ellen Gividen. Children born:
1. Margaret Morris.

---x---

KATHARINE MORRIS (10th Gen.), daughter of William Amos Morris and Mollie (Snivens) Morris, born 1871. Married Tom Chandler. Children born:
1. Nancy Chandler.
2. Doris Chandler.

---x---

WILLIAM MORRIS (10th Gen.), son of William Amos Morris and Mollie (Snivens) Morris, born 1876. Married Gertrude ———. Children born:
1. Turney Morris.
2. William Morris, Jr.

Tom Morris (10th Gen.), son of William Amos Morris and Mollie (Snivens) Morris. Married Marie Rash (no issue).

———x———

Allen Gano Morris (9th Gen.), son of Captain John Morris and Katherine (Turney) Morris. Married Hattie Rodman. Children born:
1. Thomas Rodman Morris.

———x———

Henry Morris (9th Gen.), son of Captain John Morris and his second wife, Mrs. Payne (widow) Morris. Married Mary Layson. They had a large family; the names of some follow:
John Morris.
Tobe Morris.
Rodman Morris.
Emma Morris.

———x———

Perry Morris (9th Gen.), son of Captain John Morris and his first wife (name unknown), married and had a family; their names not known.

———x———

Lizzie Morris or Elizabeth Morris (9th Gen.), daughter of Captain John Morris and his first wife, also married but no record of this marriage has been found.

———x———

Thomas Morris (9th Gen.), son of Daniel Cushman Morris and Anna Minnich Morris, born about 1820. Married Celinda Hart. Children born:
1. Thomas Morris.
2. Ann Morris. Married ——— Davis and lived at Arkansas City, Kansas.

———x———

Albert Famous Morris (9th Gen.), son of Daniel Cushman Morris and Anna Minnich Morris. Married ———. Children born:
1. Dr. A. O. Morris. Lived on Washington street, Indianapolis, Ind.
2. Ella Morris. Married ——— Truesdale. One son born.

———x———

Rebecca Morris (8th Gen.), daughter of Sarah Cushman Morris and Morris Morris, born Oct., 1784. Married, Feb. 5, 1812, Jess Turney, in Bourbon County, Ky.

BETSY MORRIS (8th Gen.), daughter of Sarah Cushman Morris and Morris Morris, born Oct. 10, 1798. Married William Brown. Children born:
1. James H. Brown, born Oct. 15, 1816.
2. Thomas Brown, born Dec. 6, 1819.
3. Kitty Ann Brown. Married ——— Tanner.
4. Rachel Brown. Married ——— Bowles and moved to Quincy, Ill.

———————x———————

CATHERINE ELIZABETH MORRIS (9th Gen.), daughter of Daniel Cushman and Anna (Minnich) Morris, born Oct. 22, 1822, in Nicholas County, Ky.; died at Whitesboro, Texas, 1880. Married, Sept. 12, 1839, Richard Lindsay Hart, born Jan. 21, 1815, in Bath County, Ky.; died near Center, Ralls County, Mo., July 19, 1898, being 84 years old. Children born:
1. Mary Ann Hart, born June 9, 1840, at Cloverdale, Ind.; died 1924.

———————x———————

MARY ANN HART (10th Gen.), daughter of Catherine Elizabeth (Morris) Hart and Richard Lindsay Hart, born June 9, 1840, at Cloverdale, Ind.; died at Paris, Mo., 1924. Married first, Andrew Henderson Wilson, born 1832, in Clay County, Mo.; died 1868, at Bentonville, Ark. Children born:
1. Zora Almanza Wilson, born Feb. 4, 1858.
2. Mortimer Hart Wilson, born in 1864 in Red River County, Tex.

Mary Ann Hart Wilson married, secondly, William Graves. Children born:
1. Berta Graves, born 1875; died 1892, at Paris, Mo.
2. Frances L. Graves, born Jan. 25, 1877.

———————x———————

ZORA ALMANZA WILSON (11th Gen.), daughter of Mary Ann (Hart) Wilson and Andrew Henderson Wilson, born Feb. 4, 1858. Married, 1870, James Henry Whitecotton, in Albany, Ralls County, Mo. He was a lawyer and state senator from Paris, Mo. Children born:
1. Dayse Mary Whitecotton, born Oct. 28, 1881.
2. Andrew Tilden Whitecotton, born Nov. 25, 1883.
3. Elizabeth Morris Whitecotton, born Oct. 20, 1888, in Paris, Mo.

4. James Henry Whitecotton, born Aug. 8, 1893; died Dec. 12, 1918, at Moberly, Mo.

DAYSE MARY WHITECOTTON (12th Gen.), daughter of Zora Almanza (Wilson) Whitecotton and James Henry Whitecotton, born Oct. 28, 1881. Married, in Paris, Mo., David Milton Proctor, born April 2, 1881, in Monroe City, Mo. Children born:
1. David Milton Proctor, Jr., born Jan. 10, 1909.
2. Zora Wilson Proctor, born Aug. 18, 1913.
3. Elizabeth Ellen Proctor, born June 6, 1919.

ANDREW TILDEN WHITECOTTON (12th Gen.), son of Zora Almanza (Wilson) Whitecotton and James Henry Whitecotton, born Nov. 25, 1883. Married, June, 1924, Lola Alverson; lives at Santa Fe, Mo.

ELIZABETH MORRIS WHITECOTTON (12th Gen.), daughter of Zora Almanza (Wilson) Whitecotton and James Henry Whitecotton, born Oct. 20, 1889, in Paris, Mo. Unmarried and living at Paris, Mo.

JAMES HENRY WHITECOTTON (12th Gen.), son of Zora Almanza (Wilson) Whitecotton and James Henry Whitecotton, born Aug. 8, 1893; died Dec. 12, 1918, in Moberly, Mo., where he was in business.

MORTIMER HART WILSON (11th Gen.), son of Mary Ann (Hart) Wilson and Andrew Henderson Wilson, born 1864, in Red River County, Tex. Married, 1884, Lillie Holloway. Children born:
1. George Hart Wilson.
2. Zora Wilson.
3. Mortimer Hart Wilson, Jr. Married. Lives in Hannibal, Mo. (no issue).
4. Cleo Wilson. Married Dr. Campbell, Hanibal, Mo. (no issue).
5. Morris Wilson.

FRANCES L. GRAVES (11th Gen.), daughter of Mary Ann

Hart (Wilson) Graves and William Graves, born Jan. 25, 1877. Married Dr. M. S. Bodine, of Paris, Mo. Children born:
1. M. Stapleton Bodine, born Oct., 1908, at Paris, Mo.
2. Mary Ann Bodine, born July 10, 1910, at Paris, Mo. Lives at 7428 Summit Street, Kansas City, Mo.

DAVID MILTON PROCTOR, JR. (13th Gen.), son of Dayse Mary (Whitecotton) Proctor and David Milton Proctor, born Jan. 10, 1909. Married Mary Jane Dodge, in Kansas City, Mo. He is employed in the legal Department of Elections, Kansas City, Mo. Children born:
1. Virginia Dodge Proctor, born July 14, 1933.
2. David Milton Proctor III, born Feb. 4, 1935.

ZORA WILSON PROCTOR (13th Gen.), daughter of Dayse Mary (Whitecotton) Proctor and David Milton Proctor, born Aug. 18, 1913. Married Richard Currie Montague, of Norfolk, Va. They live in Salisbury, North Carolina. One child born:
1. John Currie Montague, born April 25, 1942.

ELIZABETH ELLEN PROCTOR (13th Gen.), daughter of Dayse Mary (Whitecotton) Proctor and David Milton Proctor, born June 6, 1919. Married Robert Ellsworth Jenks, of Kansas City, Mo. One child born:
1. Susan Hamilton Jenks, born March 12, 1942.

M. STAPLETON BODINE (12th Gen.), son of Frances L. (Graves) Bodine and Dr. M. S. Bodine, born Oct., 1908. Married Josephine Brandon, in Kansas City, Mo. He is an electrical engineer for the Missouri Public Service Company of Jefferson City, Mo.

REBECCA ANN MORRIS (9th Gen.), daughter of Daniel Cushman Morris and Anna (Minnich) Morris, born Jan. 24, 1836, in Nicholas County, Ky. Married, Nov. 20, 1851, Andrew McDowell in Cloverdale, Ind. Died Nov. 20, 1909. Children born:
1. Ora Ann McDowell, born Oct. 3, 1852 (Deceased).
2. Lula McDowell, born Nov. 26, 1855.

ORA ANN McDOWELL (10th Gen.), daughter of Rebecca Ann

(Morris) McDowell and Andrew McDowell, born Oct. 3, 1852. Married, Oct. 12, 1873, William Winfield Seibert. Children born:
1. Bess McDowell Seibert, born May 27, 1876, at Galesburg, Ill.

LULA McDOWELL (10th Gen.), daughter of Rebecca Ann (Morris) McDowell and Andrew McDowell, born Nov. 26, 1855. Married, Oct. 12, 1878, Melvin L. Walker. Children born:
1. Ora Zoe Walker, born Feb. 6, 1880.

ORA ZOE WALKER (11th Gen.), daughter of Lula (McDowell) Walker and Melvin L. Walker, born Feb. 6, 1880. Married John Leo Roach, Aug. 14, 1912 (no issue).

GEORGE HART WILSON (12th Gen.), son of Mortimer Hart Wilson and Lillie (Holloway) Wilson. Married ———— Hale, at Omaha, Neb. Children born:
1. George Wilson.
2. Ann Wilson.

ZORA WILSON (12th Gen.), daughter of Mortimer Hart Wilson and Lillie (Holloway) Wilson. Married Clarence Haynes and lives in Jefferson City, Mo. Children born:
1. Clarence Haynes, Jr.
2. Jack Haynes.

MORTIMER HART WILSON, JR. (12th Gen.), son of Mortimer Hart Wilson and Lillie (Holloway) Wilson. Married; lives in Hannibal, Mo., and has no children.

CLEO WILSON (12th Gen.), daughter of Mortimer Hart Wilson and Lillie (Holloway) Wilson. Married Dr. Campbell, of Hannibal, Mo. (no issue).

MORRIS WILSON (12th Gen.), son of Mortimer Hart Wilson and Lillie (Holloway) Wilson. Married ————. Has one son.

[End of contribution by Mrs. Dayse (Whitecotton) Proctor.]

CUSHMAN GENEALOGY AND GENERAL HISTORY   241

THOMAS CUSHMAN (7th Gen.), son of Thomas Cushman and Mary Frazee Cushman, was born July 31, 1781, at Elizabeth, N. J., and died Jan. 27, 1870. Married, Aug. 12, 1803, Polly Hieatt, who was born 1788, and who died Aug. 21, 1858. Thomas died at Middletown, Mo. He lived in Monongalia County, Va., now subdivided into Monongalia and Preston counties of W. Va.; afterwards lived in Kentucky and in 1853 moved to Missouri. Children born and raised on a farm near Newport, Ky.:

1. Lucinda Cushman, born Nov. 6, 1804. Married Samuel Mason; lived in Kentucky.
2. Hiett Cushman, born May 19, 1806; died unmarried at Louisiana, Mo., March 23, 1853.
3. Sallie Cushman, born Aug. 19, 1808. Married Calvin Jack and lived in Indiana.
4. Rachel Cushman, born Oct. 19, 1810; died Dec. 20, 1890. Married Thomas Stephens and lived in Kentucky.
5. Thomas Cushman, born Oct. 27, 1812; died Jan. 23, 1899, at Middletown, Mo. Married Mary Pew and lived in Missouri.
6. America Cushman, born June 12, 1815. Married Frank Calvert and lived in Missouri.
7. Mary Cushman, born Sept. 9, 1817; died 1886 at Montgomery City, Mo. Married John Paxton and lived in Missouri.
8. Harvey Cushman, born Nov. 10, 1819; died, unmarried, June 18, 1835.
9. Julian Cushman, born Nov. 5, 1821; died, unmarried, July 17, 1845.
10. Parkerson Gardner Cushman, born Nov. 12, 1823.

―――――x―――――

PARKERSON GARDNER CUSHMAN (8th Gen.), son of Thomas Cushman and Polly (Hieatt) Cushman, born Nov. 12, 1823. Married, Sept. 2, 1852, Phoebe Jane Rogers, born in Nelson County, Ky., Dec. 21, 1832; died at Montgomery City, Mo., Jan. 1, 1911. Children born:

1. Harvey Cushman, born July 2, 1853; died Sept. 1, 1855.
2. Estella Ellen Cushman, born Oct. 7, 1854. Married, Dec. 3, 1872, George L. Hewitt.
3. Mary Elizabeth Cushman, born Dec. 11, 1857; died Jan.

1, 1908, at Liberty, Mo. Married, July 10, 1878, Martin Luther Bibb.

4. William Presley Cushman (twin), born Jan. 27, 1863. Married, Aug. 6, 1894, Louise Bloomer.

5. *James Thomas Cushman* (twin), born Jan. 27, 1863. *Married*, June 30, 1855, at Montgomery City, Mo., Martha Bennett Jackson. Children born:
  1. Charlotte May Cushman (10th Gen.), born May 3, 1886.
  2. Thomas James Jackson Cushman, born June 27, 1895.

———————x———————

CHARLOTTE MAY CUSHMAN (10th Gen.), daughter of James Thomas Cushman and Martha Bennet (Jackson) Cushman, born May 3, 1886. Married, Oct. 15, 1907, Thomas Bon Durant Taylor.

LINEAGE

The THOMAS CUSHMAN 6th generation family descent follows:

1. Isaac Allerton married Mary Norris. Their daughter, Mary Allerton (2), married Thomas Cushman (2), later Ruling Elder of the First Church of Plymouth, Mass. Isaac Allerton, with his wife and daughter, Mary, came over in the Mayflower.
1. John Howland married Elizabeth Tilley, daughter of John Tilley; their daughter, Ruth Howland (2), married Thomas Cushman (3), son of Elder Thomas Cushman and Mary Allerton Cushman. John Howland and his wife, Elizabeth Tilley Howland, and also John Tilley and his wife, Bridget Van Der Velde Tilley, all came over in the Mayflower.
1. Robert Cushman married Sarah Reder.
2. Elder Thomas Cushman married Mary Allerton.
3. Thomas Cushman married Ruth Howland.
4. Thomas Cushman married Sarah Strong.
5. Thomas Cushman, of Lebanon, Conn., Essex County, New Jersey, married Mary ―――――.
6. Thomas Cushman, of Lebanon, Conn., Essex County, New Jersey, and Monongalia County, Va., married Mary Frazee, daughter of Ephraim Frazee by his first wife. He was the father of 18 children by three marriages.
7. David Cushman married, June 22, 1788, Dorcas Morris, and lived the latter part of his life in Mason County, Kentucky.

From this point it will be easy for one to trace their line down to their present.

Father and Mothers Ages

Isaac Cushman was born July the 16 in the year of our Lord 1752

Deborah Cushman was born May the 12 in the year AD 1760

A List of Ages Copied B Moses 64

Moses Cushman was born Decemb the 19 – 1776

Rachel Cushman was born July the 18 – 1778

Thomas Cushman was born March the 18 – 1782

Mary Cushman was born February the 1 1782

Sary Cushman was born March the 17 – 1788

Ribecah Cushman was born February the 14 – 1792

Squier Cushman was born March the 2 – 1794

Levi Cushman was born July the 17 – 1796

Ephraim Cushman was born September the 6 – 1798

Frazee Cushman was born on Munday Aprile the 7 – 1800

The preceding photographs were made from brown and aged sheets of paper, very fragile with age, and the writing thereon faded and dim.

These original papers are the property of Mrs. Rosa E. Pence, of Rossville, Illinois (a Cushman descendant).

The following is as true a copy of their content, in writing, as the use of a strong reading glass makes possible:

Father and Mother's Ages

Isaac Cushman was born July the 16 in the year of our Lord 1752

Deborah Cushman was born May the 12 in the year A. D. 1760.

A List of Ages Copied by Moses Cushman
Moses Cushman was born December the 19—1776
Rachel Cushman was born July the 18—1778
Thomas Cushman was born March the 18—1782
Mary Cushman was born February the 11th, 1784
Sary Cushman was born March the 17—1788
Rebeccah Cushman was born February the 14—1792
Squier Cushman was born March the 2—1794
Levi Cushman was born July the 17—1796
Ephraim Cushman was born September the 6—1798
Frazee Cushman was born on Munday Aprile the 7—1800

STATE OF OHIO } SS.
HAMILTON COUNTY }

I, Alvah W. Burt, hereby certify that the foregoing is as true a copy of the content in writing made from brown and aged sheets of paper, fragile with age, as is possible with the us of a strong reading glass.

(signed)　ALVAH W. BURT.

Sworn to and subscribed before me this 29th day of January, 1941.

(signed)　W. H. ZIEVERINK,　(Seal)
Notary Public.

My commission expires March 31, 1943.

―――x―――

ISAAC CUSHMAN (6th Gen.), son of Thomas Cushman and Mary Cushman, of Lebanon, Conn., and Essex County, New

Jersey, born July 16, 1752, at New Providence, Essex County, N. J. Married Deborah Frazee, born May 12, 1760, daughter of Ephraim Frazee by his third wife. Children born:
1. Isaac or Moses Cushman, born Dec. 19, 1776.
2. Rachel Cushman, born July 18, 1778.
3. Thomas Cushman, born March 18, 1782.
4. Mary Cushman, born Feb. 11, 1784.
5. Sary Cushman, born March 17, 1788.
6. Rebecca Cushman, born Feb. 14, 1792.
7. Squier Cushman, born March 2, 1794.
8. Levi Cushman, born Feb. 17, 1796.
9. Ephraim Cushman, born Sept. 6, 1798.
10. Frazee Cushman, born April 7, 1800.

Isaac Cushman was the eighth child born to Thomas Cushman and Mary Cushman; his elder brothers and sisters, Oliver, Sybil, Rhoda, Mercy, Mary, Thomas and Sarah, all having been born at Lebanon, New London County, Conn., and Sarah, the seventh child, born Nov. 16, 1743; the family therefore moved after that date to Essex County, N. J., where on July 16, 1752, Isaac, the eighth child, was born at New Providence, Essex County, N. J.

Isaac Cushman died late in the fall time of 1837 or in the winter time, early in 1838. The last pension payment being made Sept. 11, 1837, covering a period from March 4, 1837 to Sept. 4, 1837.

Heeding the call of "Westward Ho!" he and his elder brother, Thomas, born Dec. 19, 1739, left Essex County, N. J., heading westward to Pennsylvania and Virginia; both men served as soldiers of the American Revolution and later, through rights of preemption warrants, entered their claims to lands adjoining each other; Isaac acquiring acreage in Fayette County, Wharton Township, Pennsylvania, at a point known as Gibson Glade, and on the State line and adjoining across the State line in Monongalia County, Virginia, now the State of West Virginia, and in what is now Preston County, W. Va. (the County of Monongalia, since that early period, having been subdivided into Monongalia [west portion] and Preston County [east portion]).

Thomas Cushman, the brother, laid claim to his acreage adjoining that of Isaac, and on the Virginia side also contiguous to lands acquired by Mary Cushman, David Frazee and Ephraim Frazee.

Isaac Cushman and his brother, Thomas Cushman, married half sisters; Isaac married Deborah Frazee, born May 12, 1760, daughter of Ephraim Frazee by his third wife, and Thomas Cushman married Mary Frazee, born April 3, 1744, daughter of Ephraim Frazee by his first wife.

The foundation upon which stood the Isaac Cushman home, or Stand, is yet to be seen, by leaving Uniontown, Penn., traveling eastward on Route Number 40, reaching the top of the mountain at Summit Hotel, then starting down the hill, east side, take the black-top road, first to the right up the sharp or steep hill to Gibbon Glade; at Gibbon Glade ask the way to the "old George Thomas farm with the big barn," which Harry E. Hinebaugh now owns and on which he lives. To the right of this home, as you face it, you will note the milk house, and about 20 feet to the right of the milk house is the old foundation upon which stood the Isaac Cushman home and Stand.

It is interesting to note that Essex County, New Jersey, was a large one in the early history of the State and at a later date it was subdivided into Essex (with Newark as a county seat), and Union (with Elizabeth as its county seat) and, too, that no public record was required or made concerning vital statistics, especially births, and if made the records have been destroyed by the court house fire. Such record as was made was done in jotting down in church Minute Books, here and there, but not with equal regularity, but rather in fragmentary form; in the old Minute Books of the First Presbyterian Church at New Providence, New Jersey, some record was made and from this the New Jersey Historical Society of Newark, N. J., made its record.

It is recorded in an old Minute Book of the First Presbyterian Church at New Providence, in a brief statement of members prior to 1764, that there was an Ephraim Frazee.

Mary Frazee, born 3rd April, 1744, married Thomas Cushman at New Providence, 5th Jan., 1764.

David Cushman married Dorcas Morris.
Ann Cushman married Holliday, secondly, Joseph Frazee.
Elizabeth Frazee, born 13th Jan., 1747.
The third marriage of Ephraim Frazee.
Anna Frazee, born 1757.
Deborah Frazee, born 1760.
Ephraim Frazee, born 1762.
Squier Frazee, born 1764.
At the State Library at Harrisburg, Pa., the following records are found:
From the census of 1790; Monongalia County, Va., page 35:
Samuel Frazee, head of family of 7.
David Frazee, head of family of 5.
No Cushmans in census of Monogalia County in 1790.
From census of 1790: Fayette County, Pa., page 112:
Isaac Cushman, Wharton Township; 2 sons under 16—3 daughters and wife.

Earlier record of Wharton Township, Fayette County, Pa., shows that Wharton Township was one of nine into which Fayette County was originally divided by the first court for the County, at its December session, 1783. After naming eight of the townships, the record mentions Wharton, the ninth, as follows:

The residue of the County, being chiefly mountainous, is included in one township, known as Wharton Township, it being first in size, and fifth in order of age, and ninth in that of designation of the 23 townships into which the County is now divided.

The surface of Wharton Township is broken. It has an elevation of 1800 to 2000 feet above the sea level and on the west a deep cut is made by the waters of Big Sandy, preventing Laurel Hill Ridge from becoming a part of the high hills of the centre of the Township.

In the south-central and eastern portion of the Township is the unwooded elevation and plain known as the Glades.

The Township in its early period had an abundance of timber on the hills, mostly oak; on the mountain ridges chestnut and oak; and on the creek bottoms a diversified growth of poplar, pine, sugar, cherry, and some oak.

In the early days of the furnace this timber was cut off to a great extent and probably needlessly so; there were also a number of tanneries in the Township which required oak bark for tanning.

There is a variety of soil: On the hills, mostly clay-loam; and on the streams, chestnut ridges and glades, mostly sand loam; the Township being well suited to stock and sheep raising.

The Township has an abundance of limestone, sandstone, and iron ore; also some fire clay; and the county is rich in coal deposits.

Fayette County is a very historical spot, especially turning to the left at the top of the mountain on which is situated Summit Hotel, and proceeding on this road about three and one-half miles, one comes to a large bronze plate, standing about 10 feet high, with three arrows pointing to the right, reading:

WASHINGTON'S FIRST BATTLEFIELD →
WASHINGTON'S ROCKS →
JUMONVILLE'S GRAVE →

And at this point, standing about four feet high, another bronze tablet on which is stated:

"WASHINGTON'S FIRST BATTLEFIELD

THE WASHINGTON-BRADDOCK ROAD 1764-1765
WAS SITUATED ABOUT ONE HUNDRED FIFTY
YARDS TO THE EASTWARD.
WASHINGTON'S FIRST BATTLEFIELD; WASHINGTON'S
ROCKS AND JUMONVILLE'S GRAVE ARE LOCATED
ABOUT THREE HUNDRED YARDS TO THE EASTWARD
OF THIS FAMOUS ROAD.
HORACE WALPOLE SAID IT WAS THE VOLLEY
FIRED BY A YOUNG VIRGINIAN (WASHINGTON)
IN THE BACK WOODS OF AMERICA THAT SET
THE WORLD ON FIRE.
DUNBAR'S CAMP WAS SITUATED ABOUT FOUR
HUNDRED YARDS TO THE NORTHWARD"

Jumonville's Camp is about a half-mile south of the Old Dunbar Spring; and about one-quarter mile from the Spring, (about 10 feet from the right bank), is the spot supposed to be Jumonville's Grave; and then west approximately 20 yards is the Camp, thus situated in a deep hollow and almost entirely concealed from observation; and at this point in the dawn of morning light, Washington fired the first gun here of a great war that swept New France from the map of the New World and established the supremacy of the English speaking people in North America.

Some authorities credit Jumonville with having inspired Washington with the belief that America should be free and independent of English rule.

Going back to the main road, No. 40, facing Summit Hotel, and turning left and proceeding eastward, one travels a short distance and comes to a replica of old Fort Necessity. There seems to have been quite a difference of opinion as to the shape of the Fort, however, the maps and curios, that one finds in the Fort Necessity Museum at the top of the hill, are of sufficient interest to engage one in browsing around.

Farther eastward one comes to a bronze tablet at the left of the road, descriptive of General Braddock and Braddock's Run; and looking to the left, in the field, one sees a monument amidst a surrounding of pine trees and enclosed by an iron fence. History records that in re-building the road in 1812, the workmen dug up, on Braddock's Run, human bones together with some military trappings, which indicated an officer of rank, and as General Braddock was known to have been buried on this Run, the bones were supposed to be his. Part of the bones were sent to Peale's Museum in Philadelphia.

Abraham Stewart gathered the bones together, as well as he could, and placed them under a tree, marking the spot with a board reading: "Braddock's Grave." In 1872 Mr. J. King, editor of the *Pittsburgh Gazette*, came to Chalk Hill, and enclosed the spot with a neat fence and planted the pine trees now standing around the grave.

In 1780 Daniel McPeck lived near Gibbon's Glades; in 1783 Tom Fossit lived on the old road, the junction of Dunlap's Road and Braddock's Road, near the Great Rock; he kept a house for travelers. Next came Isaac Cushman, he kept the Cushman Stand, one mile south of Fossit's. Early in November, 1787, we find him taking out a patent for 423 acres of land on Gibbon Glade. He was a great hunter and during one winter when a hard crust was on the snow and the deer broke through and could not run, Cushman and others killed them nearly all off. Cushman had two sons, Thomas and Isaac.

The Cushman tavern stood one mile north of Downers. It was a log cabin, kept about 1784 by Cushman. About 1787 Tom Fossit (the Old Soldier, who as some said killed General Braddock) kept here.

The following letter will be of interest to most all readers:

COMMONWEALTH OF PENNSYLVANIA
DEPARTMENT OF PUBLIC INSTRUCTION
STATE LIBRARY AND MUSEUM
HARRISBURG

October 3, 1940

Mr. Alvah W. Burt
3031 Temple Avenue
Cincinnati,
Ohio

Dear Mr. Burt:

The first denomination to effect an organization in Wharton Township, Fayette County was the Presbyterian. The Presbytery of Redstone, on March 24, 1842, organized the Church of Mount Washington. In May, 1842, fifteen of these organizers established Brown's Church near Elliottsville. Both churches were log buildings, but in 1857 at Mount Washington a neat frame church was erected.

Very truly yours,
ALBERT DECKER KEATOR,
Director State Library and Museum.

By (signed) JESSICA C. FERGUSON,
Genealogical Librarian.

The foregoing is of interest because for many years after Isaac Cushman had settled in Wharton Township, Fayette

County, Pa., there was no established church of any denomination, and in the early days before the organization of an established church, religious services were held at and in the homes of the believers from time to time, as the services of an itinerant preacher could be obtained; and it was not until 1842 that an organization by the Presbyterian denomination established the first church. The Presbytery of Redstone on March 24, 1842, organized the Church of Mt. Washington, and in May of 1842, fifteen of these organizers established Brown's Church near Elliottsville; both churches were of log construction, but in 1857 a neat frame church was erected at Mount Washington.

Taking into consideration the history that Fayette County, Pa., has made, especially as relates to the coal industries, mining, etc., one can easily understand the natural early inducement this area offered to the pioneer and the reason why Thomas Cushman and Isaac Cushman selected this particular locality for a stopping place and the establishment of a home.

It is believed that Isaac Cushman died early in the year 1838; records of legal transaction by him, recorded in Book V, page 205, in the court house of Fayette County, at Uniontown, Pa., dated December 29, 1837, together with record of the cessation of his pension as a soldier of the American Revolution, as shown by the copy hereafter of letter, that the last pension check covered the period from March 4, 1837 to Sept. 4, 1837, is evidence of the fact of his death at that time.

There is in the possession of Mr. Harry E. Hinebaugh, Gibbon Glade, Fayette County, Pa., written with lead-pencil on school tablet paper or similar paper, and somewhat dim, by one of the local or home folk, a brief recording of events of the past, wherein it is stated that Isaac Cushman, in his eighties, old and blind, was living in a cabin back of George Thomas' wood-yards. The exact date of his death or where he was buried is unknown.

Also a curious and interesting note relating to the early-day superstitions is also recorded therein, that a certain family had been scourged or plagued by fever and to break the spell of the plague, old Mrs. Cushman, assisted the mother of this fever-plagued family in digging up of one of the children that had died from the effect of fever and re-interred the body in the belief that this act would break the spell or the plague.

I herewith enter copies of legal transactions taken from court house records made by Isaac Cushman, Thomas Cushman, Levi Cushman and others for the reader's perusal:

From Surveyor's Record Book No. 1, page 274, in court house at Morgantown, West Virginia:

―――――――――x―――――――――

Nov. 17, 1785

Surveyed for Isaac Cushman, assignee of Martin Judy—250 acres of land in Monongalia County on part of a Preemption Warrant of 1000 Acres No. 2185 dated Aug. 14, 1782 and entered Sept. 13th, 1785 on little Sandy Creek including an improvement he bought of Elisha Frazee, bounded as followeth—viz: etc., etc., etc. Platted by a scale of 100 poles to the inch—Variation 20 Min. east

Henry Martin, Asst. to Sam'l Hanaway

S. M. C.

―――――――――x―――――――――

Nov. 20, 1781

Surveyed for Thomas Cushman—400 Acres of land in Monongalia Co. on waters of Little Sandy Creek in the Glades of Sandy Creek—including his settlement made thereon in the year 1770—bounded agreeable to a certificate from the Commissioners for the district of Monongalia and Ohio dated March 8th 1781—and bounded as followeth: Viz & & & to White Oaks Corner to Ephraim Frazee and thence to etc etc etc to beginning corner of Ephraim and David Frazee—Platted by scale 100 poles to inch. Variation 20 Min. West.

James French, Ass't to
John Madison.

―――――――――x―――――――――

At Uniontown, Pa., court house, Fayette County, Deed Book T, page 495, dated April 12, 1836:

Wharton Township, Fayette County, Pennsylvania. This Article of Agreement made and entered into June 19th, 1835 between Isaac Cushman of the first part and Levi Cushman of the second part

Witnesseth: that the said Isaac Cushman doth agree to let the said Levi Cushman have his farm to where the said Isaac now lives for to work, and the said Levi in consideration thereof is to keep or cause to be kept the said Isaac Cushman and his wife with a comfortable living and to provide for them in sickness and in health such things as shall be necessary for their suport as long as they both shall live and the said Isaac doth further agree for the before mentioned consideration that at his death he will give unto the said Levi Cushman the aforesaid farm or plantation containing three hundred acres all right and title unto the said Levi and his heirs forever and we do hereby bind ourselves in the penal sum of one thousand dollars to do as before mentioned.

In Witness whereof we hereunto set our hands and seals this day and year above written.

(Signed, Sealed and delivered in presence of us)

           his
John Henry) Isaac X Cushman
)   mark
Fayette County SS) Levi Cushman

Personally appeared before me a Justice of the Peace in and for the said County; John Henry, Esq. who deposeth and saith that the above is his genuine signature as witness and that he seen the parties sign and seal the same as their act and deed, that he wrote Isaac Cushman's name at his request and he made his mark to it in presence of this deponant.

                  John Henry

Sworn and subscribed before me the ninth day of April, 1836.

                 James Piper

Recorded and compared April 12th, 1836

---x---

At Uniontown, Pa., court house, Fayette County, Deed Book U, pages 182 and 183:

A purchase of 163 Acres two quarters and one perch of land through joint purchase of 496-1/8 Acres of land by Conrad W. Show, Levi Cushman, Alexander Stewart, Samuel Lain, and on Sept. 7th, 1836 Levi received his portion of above purchase of land which in description joined up to the land belonging to Isaac Cushman, and which Isaac and Margaret sold on Sept. 26th, 1836 for the sum of $147.00 to Robert Stewart.

At Uniontown, Pa., court house, Fayette County, Deed Book 315, page 138:

The Commonwealth of Pennsylvania To All to Whom these presents shall come, Greeting:

Know ye that in consideration of the Monies paid by Isaac Cushman at the granting of the warrant hereinafter mentioned, and the further sum of five dollars and twenty cents now paid into the Treasury office of this Commonwealth, there is granted by the said Commonwealth, unto the said Isaac Cushman a certain tract of land containing Four Hundred twenty three acres and the usual allowance situate in Wharton township in the County of Fayette beginning at a dogwood, thence by land of John McLean north 50 degrees east forty four perches and five tenths to a beach, thence south 31 degrees east, forty nine perches and six tenths to a linn east twenty nine perches and nine tenths to a post, thence south sixty eight and a half degrees east twenty nine perches and four tenths to stones, thence south eighty nine and half degrees east one hundred and twenty perches and nine tenths to a post, thence by vacant land south one hundred and eighty three perches and nine tenths to stones, thence south sixty four degrees west one hundrd and sixty two perches to stones, thence south fifty seven degrees west ninety two perches to a white oak, thence south forty nine perches and nine tenths to a post, thence by State Line south eighty nine degrees west forty six perches to stones; thence by vacant land claimed by Thomas Cushman north eighteen degrees west one hundred and twenty eight perches and three tenths to a white oak, and thence north one hundred and twenty perches to the beginning. Which said tract of land was surveyed in pursuance of warrant dated November 14th, 1787 and a decree of the Board of Property of the 7th February, 1787, to the said Isaac Cushman to have and to hold the said tract or parcel of land with the appurtenances, unto the said Isaac Cushman his heirs, to the use of the said Isaac Cushman, his heirs and assignes forever. Free and Clear of All Restrictions and Reservations as to mines, Royalties, Quit Rents or otherwise, excepting and reserving only the fifth part of all gold and silver ore, for the use of the Commonwealth, to be delivered at the Pit's Mouth clear of all charges. In Witness ,Whereof, John Gebhart, secretary of the Land Office of the said Commonwealth, hath hereunto set his hand and the Seal of the Land Office of Pennsylvania hath been affixed, the seventeenth day of October, in the year of our Lord One Thousand Eight hundred and Thirty Six and of the Commonwealth the Sixty First.

      Attest Jos. Henderson, Dep'y Sec. Land Office
In Testimony—That the within is a copy of a Patent as recorded in Patent Book H, Volume 36—Page 485 remaining in the Department of Internal Affairs of Pennsylvania, I have hereunto set my hand and caused the seal of said Department to be affixed, at Harrisburg, this third day of May, A. D. 1911.
            James H. Craig
      Deputy Secretary of Internal Affairs
Seal of Internal Affairs
 Compared by J. C. Kirk
     R. C. De Wald
   Recorded & Compared June 22, 1911
    Chas. O. Schroyer, Recorder

At Uniontown, Pa., court house, Fayette County, Deed Book U, page 283, dated Feb. 2, 1837:

This Indenture made this 2nd day of February, A. D. 1837 between Isaac Cushman, Levi Cushman and Margaret his wife of Wharton Township, Fayette County and State of Pennsylvania of the one part and Michael Thomas, Jr. of the same County and State of the other part; Witnessed that the said Isaac Cushman, Levi Cushman and Margaret his wife for and in consideration of the sum of one hundred and fifty dollars lawful money to them in hand paid by the said Michael before the delivery hereof the receipt whereof they do hereby acknowledge have granted bargained and sold and by these presents do grant, bargain and sell unto the said Michael Thomas; Jr. his heirs or assigns, the following described tract of land lying in said Township County and State adjoining lands of Samuel Morton, Jacob Fiske, Conrad ,W. Show and others on which is erected a small log cabin, log barn about forty acres cleared containing two hundred and twenty acres be the same, more or less, to have and to hold the before described premises with the appurtenances, rights liberties and privileges, woods ways waters water courses and hereditaments thereunto belonging or in any wise appertaining to the only proper use and behoff of the said Michael Thomas, Jr. his heirs or assigns forever. This to be not regarded as a mortgage but as an absolute deed, depending on this condition only, that if the said Isaac or Levi Cushman or their heirs or assigns shall and do pay the above consideration, money back to the said Michael his heirs or assigns within three years from the time of the sealing and delivery of this deed with lawful interest thereon then the same to be void and of no effect In Testimony whereof the granting parties, have hereunto set their hands and the day first above written,

signed, sealed and delivered in
           Isaac Cushman (Seal)
presence of:
           Levi Cushman (Seal)
Attest Alexander Stewart
          Margaret X Cushman (Seal)
          her mark

Received on the day of the date of the foregoing indenture of Michael Thomas, Jr. one hundred and fifty dollars the consideration in full

Test:—Isaac Umbell)   Levi Cushman
)
 Alexander Stewart)   Isaac Cushman

Fayette County, S. S.

Personally appeared before me a Justice of the Peace in and for said County Isaac Cushman, Levi Cushman and Margaret his wife and acknowledged the foregoing indenture to be their act and deed, she the said Margaret being of full age and by me examined separate and apart from her husband and made fully acquainted with the contents and object of the same acknowledged that she signed and sealed the same as her own act and deed of her own free will and accord without any coercion or compulsion of her said husband, In testimony whereof I have hereunto set my hand and seal this 2nd day of February, A. D. 1837.

Isaac Umbel (Seal)

Recorded and Compared February 3rd, 1837

———————x———————

At Uniontown, Pa., court house, Fayette County, Book V, page 205:

Recorded and compared in January 17th, 1838.
This Indenture made the 29th day of December in the year of our Lord one thousand eight hundred and thirty-seven between Isaac Cushman of Wharton Township, Fayette County and State of Pennsylvania of the one part and Levi Cushman of the County and State aforesaid, of the other part, WITNESSETH:—

That the said Isaac Cushman for and in consideration of the sum of $600.00 to me paid by the said Levi Cushman at or before the ensealing and delivery hereof the receipt whereof I do hereby acknowledge and thereof acquit and forever discharge the said Levi Cushman his heirs, executors, and administrators by these presents have granted, bargained, sold, alienated, enefeoffed, released, and confirmed and confirmed by these presents do grant, bargain and sell, alien, enfeoff, release and confirm unto the said Levi Cushman and to his heirs and assigns all that message and tract of land where I now live containing 225 acres more or less adjoining lands on the East by H. Wysong and Robert Stewart, on the South by Creps (Kreps) and Grind, on the West by Fike, on the North by Morton together with all and singular other the houses and barns stables ways, woods, waters, water courses, rights, libertys, privileges, hereditaments and appurtenances whatsoever thereunto belonging or in anywise appurtaining and the revertions and remainders, rents, issues and profits thereof, and also all the estate, right, title, interest, property claim and demand whatsoever the said Isaac Cushman in law or equaty, and otherwise howsoever of or in to or out of the same to have and to hold the said message, or tenement and tract containing 225 acres more or less of land hereditaments and premises hereby granted or mentioned or intended so to be with the appurtenances unto the said Levi Cushman his heirs and assigns to the only proper use and behoof of the said Levi Cushman his heirs or assigns forever. In Witness whereof, the said parties to these presents have hereunto set my hand and seal the day and year above written.

Signed, Sealed, Delivered   Isaac X Cushman   (Seal)

his / mark

in the presence of: : FAYETTE COUNTY, S. S.
DAVID GADDIS : the 29th day of December in the
MATTHEW McNEAL : year of our Lord 1837 personally
: appeared before me the subscriber
: one of the Justices of the Peace
: in and for the County aforesaid the
above named Isaac Cushman and acknowledged the above written indenture to be his act and deed and desired the same as such might be recorded according to law.
Witness my hand and seal.

      ISAAC UMBEL (SEAL)

Received on the day of the date of the above written Indenture of the above named Levi Cushman the sum of six hundred ($600.00) dollars in full for the consideration money for the above premises as witness my hand and seal.

    ISAAC X CUSHMAN
    (his mark.)   (SEAL)

At Uniontown, Pa., court house, Fayette County, Book X, page 135:

RECORDED AND COMPARED THE THIRD DAY OF JUNE, 1839.

    THIS INDENTURE,

Made and entered into the 15th day of February in the year 1839, between Levi Cushman and Margaret Cushman, his wife of Fayette County, Pennsylvania, of the one part, and John Conner of the same County and State aforesaid of the other part.

WITNESSETH:— That the said Levi Cushman and Margaret, his wife for and in consideration of the sum of $600.00 to them in hand paid by the said John Conner (the receipt whereof is hereby acknowledged) have granted, bargained, aliened, infeoffice, sold, released and confirmed and by these presents do grant, bargain, sell, alien, infeoff, release and confirm and convey all the right, title, interest, claim and demand in and to the following described tract or parcel of ground lying in Wharton Township, Fayette County, Pennsylvania to the said John Conner, his heirs and assigns forever to wit :—

BEGINNING at stones by a corner in land of Jacob Fike, Dec'd. to him by Isaac Cushman in a line of Samuel Morton's land, thence with said Samuel Morton's line interesected line of Harrison Whysong and thence with said line of Harrison Whysong till it intersected the line of Robert Stewart, thence with said Robert Stewart's line till it intersects the line of Francis Krebs formerly of C. W. Show's thence with said Krebs till it intersects the line of Joseph Thomas thence with said Thomas line till it intersects the line of Jacob Fike at a corner of his land and Col. Andrew Moore, thence with said Fike's line to the place of beginning so as to include all the land with said boundaries, containing by estimation 225 acres by the same more or less which said tract of land is the same as deeded by Isaac Cushman to Levi Cushman and warranted in name of Isaac Cushman in date warrant 14th day of November, 1787 and patented 17th October 1836, the patent calling for 423 acres and allowance to have and to hold the same clear of all demands whatsoever of the said Levi Cushman or his wife or their heirs or assigns forever and the said Levi Cushman and Margaret his wife for themselves and their heirs do further covenant and agree and hereby bind themselves and their heirs and assigns to warrant and forever defend the said land and premises aforesaid unto the said John Conner his heirs and assigns forever against and free from all claims and against all titles and persons claiming the same whatsoever.

IN WITNESS WHEREOF the said Levi Cushman and Margaret his wife have each hereunto set their

hands and affixed their seals the date first above
written.

        Levi Cushman (Seal)
          her
      Margaret X Cushman (Seal)
          mark

Signed, sealed and delivered : Received the 15th day of
in the presence of: : February, 1839, all the full
John Henry   : amount of $600.00 in full
James Goodwin   : it being the consideration
William Tisi.   : money above named.
              Levi Cushman

FAYETTE COUNTY, SS:

 Be it known that before me the subscriber a Justice of the Peace in and for said County personally came Levi Cushman and Margaret, his wife and severally acknowledged the foregoing indenture to be their act and the said Margaret being by me examined separate and apart from her said husband and having the contents fully made known to her acknowledged the same to be done by her freely and of her own accord without any compulsion or coercion of her said husband in the testimony whereof I have hereunto set my hand and seal this 15th day of February, 1839.

         John Baker, (Seal)
         Justice of the Peace.

 From the above records at Uniontown, Fayette County, Pennsylvania, it would seem there was ample substance to have cared for this old father to his end; but agreeable to the local scribe, that living all alone in his last days, old and blind, in a little cabin on the hillside back of the George Thomas wood yards, as the place has been pointed out to me, such a description inclines the writer to a sympathetic feeling and belief that there had been neglect of pledge and duty as well.

———————x———————

In reply refer to
Rev. & 1812 Wars Section 3-1865   M. E. E.

UNITED STATES
DEPARTMENT OF THE INTERIOR
Bureau of Pensions
Washington

August 27, 1928

Mrs. Lenore C. Jones
250 Littleton Street
West Lafayette, Indiana

Madam:

I advise you that from the papers in the Revolutionary War pension claim, S. 8263, it appears that Isaac Cushman was born in 1752 in Essex County, New Jersey.

While a resident of Wharton Township, Fayette County, Pennsylvania, he enlisted and served at various times during the years 1775, 1776, 1777 and 1778, in Captain James Daugherty's Pennsylvania Company, as a spy guarding the frontier. The entire length of his service was between two and three years.

He was allowed pension on his application executed June 4, 1833, while a resident of Wharton Township, Fayette County, Pennsylvania.

There are no data on file relative to his family.

Respectfully,

(Signed) E. W. Morgan

E. W. MORGAN
Acting Commissioner.

STATE OF OHIO } ss.
HAMILTON COUNTY

Virginia Noll, being duly sworn, deposes and says that she has compared the above with the original letter and finds the same a true and correct copy thereof.

(Signed) Virginia Noll

Sworn to before me and subscribed in my presence at Cincinnati, Ohio, this 18th day of October 1939.
    (Signed) W. H. Zieverink
         W. H. Zieverink, Notary Public
         Hamilton County, Ohio
         My commission expires Apr. 1, 1940

VETERANS ADMINISTRATION
WASHINGTON

         November 2, 1939.

        YOUR FILE REFERENCE:

        IN REPLY REFER TO
        BA-J/ILL
        Isaac Cushman
        S. 8263

Alvah W. Burt
3031 Temple Avenue
Cincinnati, Ohio

Dear Sir:

  Reference is made to your letter in which you request information in regard to Thomas Cushman and his brother, Isaac Cushman, who served in the Revolutionary War.

  There is no claim for pension or bounty land on file based upon service in the Revolutionary War of a Thomas Cushman, under any spelling of that surname. The record has been found of an Isaac Cushman, who was born in New Jersey. The data which follow were found in the papers on file in his claim for pension, S. 8263, based upon his service in the Revolutionary War. This record may aid you in your research.

  Isaac Cushman was born in the year 1752, in Essex County, New Jersey; the names of his parents and exact day of his birth are not given.

  While a resident of Wharton Township, Fayette County, Pennsylvania, Isaac Cushman enlisted very early in the Revolutionary War and served as a scout or spy in Captain James Daugherty's company of Pennsylvania troops, stationed a part of the time at Morris Fort and was on expeditions down the waters of Cheat River in defense of the frontier. He served on various tours in the years 1776, 1777 and 1778 as private in Captain James Daugherty's company under Colonel Gaddis in the Pennsylvania troops, engaged principally on the frontier. His service amounted in all to at least thirteen months.

Isaac Cushman was allowed pension on his application executed June 4, 1833, at which time he resided in Wharton Township, Fayette County, Pennsylvania; he had resided there ever since the Revolutionary War.

Isaac Cushman referred to one of his sons, but did not give his name, nor the names of any other children. The name of the soldier's wife and date and place of their marriage were not given.

In order to obtain the date of last payment of pension, name and address of person paid and, possibly, the date of death of this pensioner, you should apply to The Comptroller General, General Accounting Office, this city, and furnish the following data:

    Isaac Cushman
    Certificate #26314
    Issued May 2, 1834
    Rate $43.33 per annum
    Commenced March 4, 1831
    Act of June 7, 1832
    Pennsylvania Agency.

        Very truly yours,
            (signed) A. D. Hiller
            A. D. HILLER,
            Executive Assistant
            to the Administrator.

      GENERAL ACCOUNTING OFFICE
          WASHINGTON

        November 28, 1939.
RECORDS DIVISION
  In Reply Please Quote
  R-128505-AFH

Alvah W. Burt,
3031 Temple Avenue,
Cincinnati, Ohio.

Sir:

In reply to your letter of November 6, 1939, wherein you request information concerning Isaac Cushman, a pensioner of the Revolutionary War, Certificate No. 26314, Pennsylvania Agency, you are advised the records of this office show that the last payment of pension, covering the period from March 4, 1837 to September 4, 1837, was made on September 11, 1837, at the Pension Agency in Philadelphia, Pennsylvania, to James McKean, as attorney for the pensioner.

On September 4, 1837, the pensioner certified that he had resided in Fayette County, Pennsylvania, for a period of fifty years, and previous thereto he had resided in New Jersey.

No further information has been found of record in this office.

Respectfully,
(signed) P. D. Fallon
Asst. Chief, Records Division.

THE NAME SQUIER given to the seventh child born to Isaac Cushman and Deborah (Frazee) Cushman, appears as a given name in the Isaac Cushman family, for the first time in Cushman record, that I find. It is accounted for in that Ephraim Frazee, father of Deborah Frazee Cushman, married for his third wife, about 1755 at Elizabethtown, New Jersey, Anna (Squier) Maxfield, widow of Samuel Maxfield and the daughter of Thomas Squier and Rachel (Ludlam) Squier, of Westfield, Essex County, New Jersey.

Thomas Squier, born in 1701, died February 14, 1778 in Westfield, New Jersey. He married, in 1739, Rachel Ludlam, born in 1707, died December, 1753. Thomas Squier was born in East Hampton, Long Island, and served as a Minute-Man in the Essex County, New Jersey, Militia during the American Revolution, although a very old man at that time.

Children:
David Squier.

Thomas Squier.
Rachel Squier.
Deborah Squier.
Anna Squier.
Phoebe Squier.
Eleazar Squier.
Rachel married John Darby; Deborah married Thomas Marsh.
(Above information on Squier family furnished by Mrs. Lenore Chumlea Jones.)

ISAAC (CALLED MOSES) CUSHMAN (7th Gen.), son of Isaac Cushman and Deborah (Frazee) Cushman, born Thursday, December 19, 1776, in Pennsylvania.

No further record has been found of Moses Cushman; the last knowledge of his whereabouts was his being in Trumbull and Mahoning Counties, Ohio, with his brother, Ephraim Cushman.

The above picture is a reproduction, in copper-plate half-tone, from an oil painting of
RACHEL CUSHMAN, WIFE OF DANIEL WOODMANSEE
The original portrait is now in the possession of Mrs. Floyd T. Jones, West Lafayette, Indiana.

The above picture is a reproduction, in copper-plate half-tone, from
an oil painting of
DANIEL WOODMANSEE
The original portrait is now in the possession of Mr. and Mrs. Michael
Gibbons, of Dayton, Ohio.

STATE OF NEW JERSEY,
OFFICE OF THE ADJUTANT GENERAL
Trenton, December 11, 1919.

It is CERTIFIED, THAT the records of this office show that
JAMES WOODMANSEE
was commissioned Lieutenant, Captain John Stout's Company, Second Regiment Monmouth County New Jersey Militia, 1776—One month—during the Revolutionary War. * * *

* * *

SEAL

Frederick Gilkyson,
The Adjutant General.

(The original of this record is in the possession of Mrs. Floyd T. Jones, 212 East Lutz Avenue, West Lafayette, Indiana.)

To Mr. Ralph Burdsal Woodmansee the writer owes much in appreciation, since the greater part of the Woodmansee family history, recorded herein, has been copied from the "Old Woodmansee Family Records" now in his possession. The writer using that portion relating to Cushman descent:

———————x———————

RACHEL CUSHMAN (7th Gen.), daughter of Isaac Cushman and Deborah (Frazee) Cushman, born July 18, 1778; died Sept. 20, 1875. Married, 1801, in Pennsylvania, Daniel Woodmansee, born Sept. 22, 1777; died May 28, 1842, about 65 years of age. Children born:

1. Hannah Woodmansee, born March 1, 1802, in Pennsylvania; died Feb. 16, 1889, in Dayton, Ohio. Unmarried.
2. Asa C. Woodmansee, born July 12, 1804, in Pennsylvania; died Sept. 18, 1845.
3. Lorenzo Dow Woodmansee, born Nov. 16, 1806, in Pennsylvania; died Dec. 11, 1894.
4. Julia Woodmansee, born March 27, 1809, in Butler County, Ohio; died Sept. 23, 1893.
5. Sarah Woodmansee, born Sept. 18, 1811, in Butler County, Ohio; died 1853.
6. James Woodmansee, born April 20, 1814, in Butler County, Ohio; died 1887.
7. Mary Woodmansee, born March 15, 1818; died Nov. 22, 1892.

Rachel Cushman was the second child born to Isaac Cushman and Deborah (Frazee) Cushman. She was born in Fayette County, Wharton Township, Pennsylvania. She married, in 1801, Daniel Woodmansee, son of James Woodmansee; Daniel Woodmansee was born in New Jersey. James Woodmansee was born on Tuesday, Aug. 26, 1732, at 8 o'clock in the morning in New Jersey; he died in Butler County, Ohio, January 29, 1818. Hannah Woodmansee, his wife, was born January 18, 1738, and died in Butler County, Ohio, April 16, 1824. They were married on the 5th day of October, in the year 1758. Their children were all born in New Jersey.

James Woodmansee was a farmer and owned a large tract of land in New Jersey, which he exchanged for land in Pennsylvania, near Brownsville, to which he removed; in 1808 he removed to Butler County, Ohio, with his son Daniel, who bought land about 25 miles north of Cincinnati, and six miles east of Fort Hamilton.

James Woodmansee lived with his son, Daniel, and wife, Rachel, until his death, Jan. 29, 1818. His remains lie in the family cemetery on the farm of Daniel Woodmansee.

Rachel Cushman and her husband, Daniel, made their removal by way of flat-boat, which was built on the Monongahela River and, which when complete, was loaded with hollowware (cast-iron kettles, cooking utensils, etc.), together with household goods.

They floated down the Ohio River to Cincinnati, which was then a small village and military post, where he disposed of the hollow-ware. The land bought was in heavy timber; he built a log house and cleared the land for a farm. A few years later he built, what was then considered, a large house of hewn logs, having seven rooms, four downstairs and three upstairs, which was afterwards covered with sawed weatherboard.

The kitchen was much the largest of the rooms being about 20 x 25 feet in size. In this kitchen was a large fireplace about seven feet wide and three feet deep, in which a huge fire of wood was kept burning in cold weather. Beside the fireplace was the bake oven, built of brick, large enough to bake the bread and pies for a week. All the daily cooking was done by the open fireplace, boiling in kettles hung by chains and hooks on the crane over the fire. Baking and frying was done in Dutch ovens and skillets heated by coals drawn out on the hearth, and placed on the lids or covers of the cooking utensils; hoe cake was baked on a board set at an angle before the fire; meats were roasted by being suspended by a cord before the fire and allowed to turn slowly by the twist in the cord, a vessel being placed underneath to catch the drippings. Potatoes were roasted by being covered with hot ashes and coals on the hearth. Buckwheat cakes were baked on a griddle about 20 inches in diameter which was suspended from a crane and swung over the fire.

The writer has some vivid recollections of the toothsome food cooked as above in that old kitchen. That kitchen was for many years the preaching place for the itinerant Methodist preachers. Once in two weeks the preacher came and all the people of the neighborhood would be there to hear him; long oaken benches were placed in the kitchen to seat all who came.

After the service, dinner was prepared and all from a considerable distance remained to dinner. This continued until about 1840 when a church was built.

The people would generally go to these meetings on horseback; the father with a boy or girl behind him and the mother with probably one behind and the baby in her lap; the young man with his best girl riding behind him. Of carriages or buggies there was none, the only wheeled vehicle was the farm wagon.

On his farm was a very fine grove of sugar maples through which ran a small stream; from these trees was made all the sugar and syrup needed by the family and from this grove the farm got its name, Sugar Valley.

Daniel Woodmansee was a thrifty farmer and so much respected that in 1830 he was elected to the State Legislature on the Whig ticket; he lived on his farm until his death, May 28, 1842. His widow remained on the farm until her death, Sept. 20, 1875, aged 97 years.

In the files of Lane Public Library, Hamilton, Ohio, "A History and Biographical Cyclopedia of Butler County, Ohio" published in 1882, the following is recorded:

The first of the Woodmansee's who came to Butler County was Daniel; he was born Sept. 22nd, 1777 in New Jersey and was married in 1801 in Pennsylvania to Rachel Cushman who was born in Pennsylvania, July 18th, 1778. They had seven children: Hannah was born March 3rd, 1802; Asa, July 12th, 1804; Lorenzo Dow, Nov. 16th, 1806; Julia, March 25th, 1809; Sarah, Dec. 18th, 1811; James, April 20th, 1814; Mary, March 15th, 1818.

The last born is the wife of Charles Ferguson and lives in Clinton County; Lorenzo Dow is married and lives in Minnesota; Julia is the widow of Hiram Jones and lives in Illinois; and Asa is dead.

Mr. Woodmansee came to Butler County in 1809 and settled

in Liberty Township; he purchased 160 acres of land where he lived till the time of his decease and which his son James now owns.

He and his wife were prominent members of the Methodist Church and in fact during its early years in their neighborhood, were its chief support. Their house was used as a meeting house, and also for entertaining the ministers and congregation afterward. He was a very hospitable man and prominent in political circles. He represented the County both in the lower house and the Senate for a period of ten years; He was also a very prominent man in his own district, acting as law advisor for all of the neighborhood and doing the work of a "Justice of the Peace" although refusing to be elected.

He also held several other important offices in the County and Township and in fact held office all his life long. He came down the river to Cincinnati in a flat boat which he loaded with iron castings, sugar, kettles, etc., which he disposed of in Cincinnati.

His father, James Woodmansee (Born August 15th, 1732—Died January 29th, 1818) and his mother, Hannah Wordin (Born January 18th, 1738, Died April 16th, 1824) came with him, and in a few years he sent for his brothers and sister to come; they were Samuel, James, Thomas, and Hannah, with her husband, James Gray, and their children; They all came and settled in Butler County except the Gray's, who went to Preble County.

James Woodmansee, the father, was a soldier of the American Revolutionary War; he went out with the first hostilities and was soon made a Corporal; he was afterward promoted to Lieutenant, serving all through the war.

Daniel, the son, died in 1842: his last vote was cast for Harrison; his wife died Sept. 7th, 1875 and both lie buried in the Woodmansee cemetery at Sugar Valley.

The following memorial to Rachel Cushman Woodmansee was written by her daughter, Mary Woodmansee Ferguson, born March 15, 1818, who first married Rev. William R. Anderson, and secondly married Rev. Charles Ferguson.

AN AGED PILGRIM

"Thou shalt come to thy grave in full age, like as a shock of corn cometh in his season."

My Dear Mother, Rachel, widow of Daniel Woodmansee, finished her earthly sojourn of ninety-seven years and two months, Sept. 20, 1875 at the old homestead in Butler County, Ohio, where she had lived sixty-six years, beloved by all who knew her.

She was the mother of seven children, had twenty-nine grandchildren and several great grandchildren; she was born in Pennsylvania, July 18th, 1778, and moved to Ohio with her husband and four children in 1809.

Their house at once became the welcome home of the weary itinerant; and there the Gospel was preached regularly for more than twenty years. She and her husband were converted early in life, and joined the Methodist Church, in which they remained faithful until called to their reward.

Her religion shone brightest in the quiet walks of life, never demonstrative, but always ready to give a reason of the hope within. She was a devout student of the Bible, and practiced reading the New Testament through several times every year, until age so weakened her eyes that she had to forego that pleasure; but she had so much of it treasured in her memory, the loss was scarcely felt: instead of reading she would repeat chapter after chapter, as daily food for her soul. She greatly loved the hymns of John and Charles Wesley and Watts; many of them she had committed to memory, and would often rejoice with joy unspeakable while repeating them.

Always at her post of duty, and never willingly absent from class, prayer meeting or public worship, her faith was unwavering and took into its vision immortality and a crown of life, which enabled her to see the bow of promise in every dark cloud of sorrow, and when the devoted husband of her youth, a noble son and a cherished daughter, preceded her to the heavenly home, though her sensitive nature felt keenly the pang of separation, she was enabled to say without a murmur, "The Lord gave and the Lord hath taken away, Blessed be the name of the Lord."

Well do I remember with what deep feeling and humble resignation, the evening of the sepulture of my father, she gathered her family together and said, "Children, when the standard-bearer falls, some one must raise the colors; Our family Altar must not go down. I will try as best I can, to fill your father's place," and for forty-three years of widowhood she stood at the head of her household, shedding a quiet, serene radiance, imparted by an indwelling Savior.

Not a word of impatience ever escaped her lips; though for years anxious to depart and join those gone before, she was willing to wait and suffer God's will, and would often say, "All the days of my appointed time will I wait till my change comes."

Her christian course has been a steady, shining light; since God converted her, she was never known to be angry, so completely did grace enable her to triumph and bear with patience the toils and trials of life.

More than thirty years since, after relating to me her Christian experience, she added: "I shall not be satisfied with anything less than an experience that will enable me to rejoice evermore, pray without ceasing, and in everything give thanks."

As old age came on, her mental powers were but little affected, and there was no abatement of her zeal and efforts to do the will of God. Her faith and hope were always in youthful vigor, "Her leaf did not wither." We arrived just in time to receive her blessing and hear her parting words. All her children were present except a daughter living in Illinois. She was greatly rejoiced at seeing us, and said, "I am glad to have you come, that I may see you once more, but I can't see you very well, I can only discern you." Mr. Ferguson replied, "But mother, you can see Jesus." "O! yes, bless his holy name. He is with me all the time." These were among her last words.

Gradually the crumbling tabernacle was taken down without pain, while the soul gathered celestial vigor, with drafts from the fountain of life and gleams of eternal glory. When faith was being lost in sight, she tried to speak, stretch forth her arm as though reaching toward an object, then closed her eyes and accompanied the heavenly messengers to the mansions of bliss. Her warfare has terminated in a glorious victory, and she rests from her labors.

May her children and grandchildren, and those who knew her well, imitate her fidelity, heed her Godly counsel, and at last obtain a crown of life with loved ones on the other shore.

Mary W. Ferguson

The following picture of Mrs. Lenore Chumlea Jones, a descendant of Rachel Cushman Woodmansee, in whose home the oil portrait of Rachel now hangs, contributes this poem under her picture:

MRS. LENORE CHUMLEA JONES

TO GREAT-GREAT-GRANDMOTHER

There you sit so calm and still
    Upon my parlor wall,
And never tell us what you think—
    If you approve of us at all.

Your eyes so clear, your lips so firm,
    No smile upon your wrinkled face;
You look at us so very stern,
    From out your cap, edged round with lace.

Was life so hard when you were young
  That you never danced at all,
Were your long days so filled with toil
  You had no time for pleasure's call?

Yet love you found—you left your home—
  On a river flat-boat sought the west,
To make a new home here for us
  You must have loved grandfather best.

You had to work from dawn to dark,
  You spun and baked, and taught to sew
The little children in your home,
  One hundred fifty years ago.

We've not forgot, grandmother dear,
  What all we owe to you;
We really wish that you were here
  To have a good time too.

ASA C. WOODMANSEE (8th Gen.), son of Rachel Cushman Woodmansee and Daniel Woodmansee, born July 12, 1804, in Pennsylvania. He was four years of age when his parents emigrated from Pennsylvania to Butler County, Ohio, where he lived on the farm until he married, November 20, 1828, Anna Ross, born Feb. 15, 1808, at Monroe, Butler County, Ohio.

He bought a farm, two miles east of his father's home, where he lived until his death, Sept. 18, 1845, when he was accidentally killed.

Near the barn was a well, surrounded by a low rail fence, where water was drawn by a bucket and rope. From the fence extended a trough at which stock was watered, and while watering a number of young horses that were running loose in the barnyard it is supposed that one of them, in play, kicked a top rail from the fence, which, as he stooped to draw water, struck him back of the ear, dislocating his neck.

He was a successful farmer and had sold his farm intending to go to Illinois and buy land on the prairies. He and his wife were members of the Methodist Episcopal Church and to their home the traveling preachers were always welcome.

He was an ardent Whig, politically, and took a very active part in the memorable campaign of 1840. He had six sons, all born on the farm three miles west of Monroe, Butler County, Ohio:

1. Joseph Hough Woodmansee, born March 24, 1830.
2. Daniel Benson Woodmansee, born Oct. 31, 1831.
3. James Ross Woodmansee, born Sept. 10, 1833.
4. William Augustus Woodmansee, born Sept. 14, 1835.
5. George Clinton Woodmansee, born Nov. 17, 1837.
6. Frank Asa Woodmansee, born June 29, 1845.

Anna Ross Woodmansee, widow of Asa C. Woodmansee, removed to Monroe, Butler County, Ohio, in the spring of 1846, where she lived until all her boys had left home but Frank A., when she married Thomas Boyd, a farmer living one mile west of Monroe, with whom she lived until his death. She then moved to Middletown, Ohio, where she lived until 1867, when she removed to Urbana, Champaign County, Illinois, and lived with her son, George C. Woodmansee.

In 1872 she removed to Davenport, Iowa, and lived with her sons, James Ross and George C., until after the death of both. She then removed to Danville, Illinois, and lived with her son, Joseph H., until her death, Jan. 7, 1892, age 84 years, and was buried on his lot in Spring Hill Cemetery, Danville, Illinois.

On Sept. 30, 1830, under Governor Allen Trimble, of the State of Ohio, Asa C. Woodmansee, was commissioned second lieutenant, of the First Cavalry Company, in the First Regiment, Third Brigade, and First Division, in the Militia of the State.

―――――――――x―――――――――

JOSEPH HOUGH WOODMANSEE (9th Gen.), son of Asa C. Woodmansee and Anna (Ross) Woodmansee, born March 24, 1830, on his father's farm in Butler County, Ohio, was named for his mother's uncle, who was a pioneer merchant at Hamilton, Ohio (and who also bought farm produce and shipped it in flat boats down the Miami, Ohio, and Mississippi Rivers to New Orleans, returning on foot or on horseback; this was before there were any steamboats on the rivers).

His educational advantages were limited to periods of six months a year in the country school, which taught spelling, reading, arithmetic, writing, geography and grammar. In 1847 he went to Hamilton, Ohio, to learn the trade of machinist with Martin Lemon, manufacturer of cotton machinery.

In 1849 he went to Cincinnati, Ohio, and completed his apprenticeship in 1850, as machinist in the locomotive shops of A. Harkness. He then went home and attended school one term at the Monroe Academy (Rev. Noah Bishop, principal), where he reviewed his former studies and acquired some knowledge of algebra and geometry.

He married, May 24, 1854, Susan Maria Horr, of Cincinnati, at the home of her father in Aurora, Indiana.

In the fall of 1854 he removed from Cincinnati to Paris, Illinois (Edgar County), and, in January, 1856, to Urbana, Champaign County, Illinois.

Aug. 6, 1862, he enlisted in Company G, 76th Regiment, Illinois Vol. Infantry for three years or duration of the war. In the same month he was detailed as Armorer to Ordinance

Department at Columbus, Kentucky, and moved with the army to Jackson, Tennessee, during the winter, and in the spring of 1863, to Memphis, Tenn., where he had charge of a large shop for the repair of arms, until March, 1865. He then joined the regiment at New Orleans and went with the expedition to Pensacola, Florida, and Mobile, Alabama. After the storming and taking of Fort Blakely, east of Mobile, April 9, 1865, he went, in charge of the wounded, to Sedgewick Hospital, New Orleans, where he remained as Chief Wardmaster, until mustered out of the service May 31, 1865, by reason of order from War Department.

Returning to Urbana he accepted a position in the circuit court clerk's office and completed for O. O. Alexander, clerk, a set of abstract of title books of Champaign County. In 1870 he was appointed assistant assessor of internal revenue and held the office until it was abolished. In 1873 he bought a half interest in a job printing office with George W. Flynn and, in 1874, removed to Danville, Illinois, and established the Illinois Printing Company of which he was secretary and treasurer. In 1881 he sold his interest and accepted the positions of secretary, treasurer and superintendent of the Danville Gas, Light and Coke Company, which he held for eight years.

He died Oct. 9, 1909, and was buried at Spring Hill Cemetery, Danville, Illinois.

Susan M. Horr, his wife, was born of New England parents, Nov. 22, 1832, at Montreal, Canada. The family moved to Cincinnati, while she was quite young, where her mother died and was buried in the cemetery which is now Washington Park.

Joseph Hough Woodmansee and Susan (M. Horr) Woodmansee had five children:

1. Charles Horr Woodmansee, born at Monroe, Ohio, March 7, 1855; died March 27, 1877, at Danville, Illinois. Unmarried.

2. Kate Ann Woodmansee, born May 24, 1857, at Urbana, Illinois; died Jan. 13, 1883, at Danville, Illinois. Unmarried.

3. George Asa Woodmansee, born Oct. 5, 1860, at Urbana, Illinois; died Nov. 25, 1863, at Memphis, Tennessee.

4. William Ross Woodmansee, born Nov. 1, 1867, at Urbana, Illinois; died Jan. 11, 1915.

5. Windsor Augustus, born Feb. 7, 1870; died June 23, 1917.

Susan Maria Horr Woodmansee died at Danville, Ill., Aug. 13, 1888. She became a member of the Methodist Episcopal Church at Paris, Ill., in 1855, and lived a consistent Christian life until her death; respected by all who knew her.

---x---

Katie Ann, her daughter, was a very active member of the Methodist Episcopal Church, especially in Sunday School work as a teacher, and in all the social interests and Young People's meetings; she was a leader among them.

She was organist for Church and Sunday School for several years and was always in her place, when possible.

As a member of W. M. B. (We Mean Business) Society of Young People, she, with many others, did good and successful work in organizing and leading the young members to united effort in raising means to help build and furnish the new Kimber Church building, in 1882, at the corner of Franklin and Seminary Streets, in Danville, Ill.

Those were busy times when all worked together with hearty good will and accomplished great things. She did not live to see the building completed but when done her name appeared in the large south window placed there by the W. M. B. Society as a memorial to her.

She died at Danville, Ill., Jan., 13, 1883, and is buried on the family lot in Spring Hill Cemetery.

---x---

JOSEPH HOUGH WOODMANSEE (9th Gen.), son of Asa C. Woodmansee and Anna (Ross) Woodmansee, married, a second time, Nov. 28, 1890, Rachel B. Woodmansee, daughter of Lorenzo Dow Woodmansee, at Covington, Ky. No children.

Joseph Hough Woodmansee united with the Methodist Episcopal Church, Dec., 1854, at Paris, Ill., and, in 1899, was still a member in good standing in Kimber Methodist Episcopal Church of Danville, Ill., and expected to remain an acceptable member as long as he lived. He was a member of the official board for thirty-three years.

He was a member of Olive Branch Lodge No. 38, F. and A. M., Danville, Ill.; also a member of Kenesaw Post No. 77, G. A. R., Danville, Ill., and a Republican (politically) from the organization of the "Grand Old Party" in 1856. Long may it rule our country.

Joseph Hough Woodmansee died Oct. 3, 1909, at Norwood, Ohio, and was buried in Spring Hill Cemetery, Danville, Ill.

―――――――x―――――――

WILLIAM ROSS WOODMANSEE (10th Gen.), son of Joseph Hough Woodmansee and Susan M. (Horr) Woodmansee, born Nov. 1, 1867, at Urbana, Ill.; died Jan. 11, 1915, at Los Angeles, Calif. Married, June 7, 1893, Jessie Pottenger, born Dec. 30, 1868, at Danville, Ill. Children born:

1. Katie Adele Woodmansee, born Jan. 10, 1895, at Danville, Ill.

2. Windsor Ross Woodmansee, born Nov. 27, 1896, at Pullman, Ill.; died July 26, 1913, at Los Angeles, Calif., of pneumonia.

―――――――x―――――――

WINDSOR AUGUSTUS WOODMANSEE (10th Gen.), son of Joseph Hough Woodmansee and Susan Maria Horr, born Feb. 7, 1870, at Urbana, Ill.; died Feb. 22, 1939, at the home of his son, Ralph Burdsal Woodmansee, 1636 Beacon Street, Mt. Washington, Ohio; buried in Spring Grove Cemetery, Cincinnati, Ohio.

He was married, June 1, 1892, to Martha W. Burdsal, in Cincinnati, Ohio, by Dr. Edw. S. Lewis, pastor of Trinity M. E. Church. She was born April 28, 1874; died June 23, 1917; buried in Spring Grove Cemetery, Cincinnati, Ohio.

He spent several years with the Woodmansee Ink Company and later as salesman with the Eagle Picher Lead Company.

Children born to Windsor Augustus Woodmansee and Martha W. (Burdsal) Woodmansee:

1. Marguerite Josephine Woodmansee, born Wednesday, Aug. 30, 1893, at Cincinnati, Ohio.

2. Susan Marie Woodmansee, born Thursday, Dec. 19, 1895, at Cincinnati, Ohio.

3. Ralph Burdsal Woodmansee, born Jan. 19, 1901, at Cincinnati, Ohio.

Marguerite Josephine Woodmansee (11th Gen.), daughter of Windsor Augustus Woodmansee and Martha W. (Burdsal) Woodmansee, born Aug. 30, 1893, at Cincinnati, Ohio. Married, March 27, 1913, Louis Richmond Hollmeyer, at Lebanon, Ohio. Children born:
1. Harriet Hollmeyer, born Oct. 30, 1913, at Chicago, Ill.
2. Louis Richmond Hollmeyer, Jr., born April 23, 1917, at Norwood, Ohio.
3. Jane Hollmeyer, born April 3, 1920, at Cincinnati, Ohio.

———x———

Harriet Hollmeyer (12th Gen.), daughter of Marguerite Josephine Woodmansee Hollmeyer and Louis Richmond Hollmeyer, born Oct. 30, 1913. Married, March 29, 1941, Andrew Mehan.

———x———

Louis Richmond Hollmeyer (12th Gen.), son of Marguerite Josephine Woodmansee Hollmeyer and Louis Richmond Hollmeyer, born April 23, 1917. Married, Sept. 21, 1940, Audrey Wagner. Children born:
1. Louis Richmond Hollmeyer III, born March 22, 1942.

———x———

Susan Marie Woodmansee (11th Gen.), daughter of Windsor Augustus Woodmansee and Martha W. (Burdsal) Woodmansee, born Dec. 19, 1895, at Cincinnati, Ohio. Married, Dec. 1, 1922, Edgar E. Muller, at Dayton, Ohio, in the Episcopal Church, by Rev. Robert Porter. Children born to Susan Marie Woodmansee Muller and Edgar E. Muller:
1. Edgar E. Muller, Jr., born Feb. 29, 1924.
2. Susanne Muller, born June 8, 1925. } Twins
3. Joanne Muller, born June 8, 1925. }

———x———

Ralph Burdsal Woodmansee (11th Gen.), son of Windsor Augustus Woodmansee and Martha W. (Burdsal) Woodmansee, born Jan. 19, 1901, at Cincinnati, Ohio. Married, Oct. 13, 1923, Margaret Helen Asbury, at the Church of the Epiphany (Episcopal), by Rev. Robert Hogarth. Children born:
1. Robert Asbury Woodmansee, born March 6, 1926.
2. Ralph Windsor Woodmansee, born Jan. 1, 1929.
3. Peggy Ann Woodmansee, born Aug. 5, 1930.

He left high school to enter the navy where he spent two years, during which time he graduated from the Naval Electrical School, then followed seven months as instructor in the same school; after being discharged he entered the University of Cincinnati, and was a member of Sigma Alpha Epsilon fraternity.

Later he was connected with a local Cincinnati electrical firm as sales engineer.

Three years later he bought the Woodmansee Ink Manufacturing business, started by Frank Woodmansee. It had suffered poor management since his death, which prevailing condition he was not able to overcome, and in August, 1928, he became connected with Piper and Piper, real estate, after which he went to Georgia, in 1931, to operate his father's orchard properties, where he remained four years. Returning to Cincinnati, he became connected with the Thomas Emery Sons Company.

―――――――x―――――――

DANIEL BENSON WOODMANSEE (9th Gen.), son of Asa C. Woodmansee and Anna (Ross) Woodmansee, born Oct. 2, 1831, in Butler County, Ohio. Married, ―――――, 1855, Sarah Margaret Boyd at Monroe, Ohio. He died Oct. 28, 1896, at Danville, Ill., and was buried at Hamilton, Ohio. She, Sarah Margaret (Boyd) Woodmansee, died Sept. 16, 1905. They had one child.

Thomas Boyd Woodmansee, born May 25, 1856, at Monroe, Ohio, who married but had no children.

Daniel Benson Woodmansee, an active member of the Masonic Lodge, became Eminent Commander of Athalstan Commandery, Knights Templar, at Danville, Ill.

He enlisted in Company G, 167th Regiment, Ohio Volunteers Infantry, at Middletown, Ohio, in 1864, and was honorably discharged in 1865 at the close of the war.

They both were members of the Presbyterian Church.

―――――――x―――――――

JAMES ROSS WOODMANSEE (9th Gen.), son of Asa C. Woodmansee and Anna (Ross) Woodmansee, born Sept. 10, 1833, in Butler County, Ohio. Married, Sept. 13, 1887, Jessie Torrington, at Davenport, Iowa. Both were members of the

Protestant Episcopal Church. He died Dec. 12, 1890. He was a member of F. and A. M., the Knights Templar and Scottish Rite 32nd Degree Masonic bodies, and he was a Republican. One child born:
1. Ross Woodmansee, born March 5, 1889; died June 10, 1894, at Davenport, Iowa.

———————x———————

WILLIAM AUGUSTUS WOODMANSEE (9th Gen.), son of Asa C. Woodmansee and Anna (Ross) Woodmansee, born Sept. 14, 1835, in Butler County, Ohio. Married, May 22, 1866, Harriet Storms, at Middletown, Ohio. Both members of the Presbyterian Church. Children born:
1. Martha Ann Woodmansee, born Dec. 25, 1866, at Middletown, Ohio.
2. Corrinne Woodmansee, born Feb. 15, 1876, at Middletown, Ohio.

He enlisted, in 1864, in Company G. 167th Regiment, Ohio Volunteer Infantry, and was honorably discharged, in 1865, at the close of the war.

———————x———————

GEORGE CLINTON WOODMANSEE (9th Gen.), son of Asa C. Woodmansee and Anna (Ross) Woodmansee, born Nov. 17, 1837, in Butler County, Ohio; died June 19, 1880. He was unmarried. He was a member of the Methodist Episcopal Church and Free and Accepted Masons.

———————x———————

FRANK ASA WOODMANSEE (9th Gen.), son of Asa C. Woodmansee and Anna (Ross) Woodmansee, born June 29, 1845, in Butler County, Ohio; died Feb. 21, 1897. Married, first, Kate Butler, of Cincinnati, Ohio. Children:
1. Kate B. Woodmansee, died in infancy at Newport, Ky.

He married, secondly, Sarah May Lape. No children born.

He and both wives were members of the Protestant Episcopal Church. He is buried in Spring Grove Cemetery, Cincinnati, Ohio. He was a Republican.

———————x———————

LORENZO DOW WOODMANSEE (8th Gen.), son of Rachel Cushman Woodmansee and Daniel Woodmansee, born Nov. 16, 1806, in Pennsylvania; died Dec. 11, 1894, in Illinois; buried at Perryville, Ind. Married, March 20, 1827, Hanna Vangordon, born Aug. 3, 1812; died Sept. 29, 1842; buried in

cemetery on Woodmansee home farm. Children born to Lorenzo Dow Woodmansee and Hanna Maria (Vangordon) Woodmansee:
1. Andrew Jackson Woodmansee, born Aug. 18, 1828.
2. Daniel Webster Woodmansee, born Jan. 22, 1830.
3. Elizabeth Ann Woodmansee, born Feb. 6, 1832.
4. Amy Jane Woodmansee, born June 28, 1834.
5. Benjamin DeWitt Woodmansee, born Feb. 9, 1840.

He grew to manhood on his father's farm in Butler County, Ohio, and, after marriage, bought a farm one mile north of his father's farm, where all his children were born. He was a Republican and a man of exemplary habits, temperate in all things.

He married, secondly, in 1840, Mrs. Lydia Williamson (nee Barkalow), who died Aug. 31, 1856, and was buried at Franklin, Ohio. Children born:
1. George Woodmansee, born Oct. 11, 1844; died April 7, 1845.
2. Lydia Maria Woodmansee, born July 6, 1846.
3. Rachel Barkalow Woodmansee, born May 6, 1848; died July, 1935.
4. Mary Anderson Woodmansee, born July 25, 1850.
5. Rebecca Eleanor Woodmansee, born June 20, 1853.

―――――x―――――

ANDREW JACKSON WOODMANSEE (9th Gen.), son of Lorenzo Dow Woodmansee and Hannah Maria (Vangordon) Woodmansee, born Aug. 18, 1828, in Butler County, Ohio; died at Chester, Ohio, July 9, 1903. Married, ―――――, 1849, Sarah Ayers, died Feb. 4, 1874, daughter of Col. Ayers, of Butler County, Ohio. Children born:
1. Julia Woodmansee, born April 8, 1850.
2. Laura Woodmansee, born April 10, 1856; died June 4, 1906. Unmarried.

He married, secondly, Mrs. ――――― Cox. No issue.

―――――x―――――

JULIA WOODMANSEE (10th Gen.), daughter of Andrew Jackson Woodmansee and Sarah (Ayers) Woodmansee, born April 8, 1850. Married William Vinnedge. No issue.

DANIEL WEBSTER WOODMANSEE (9th Gen.), son of Lorenzo Dow Woodmansee and Hannah Maria (Vangordon) Woodmansee, born Jan. 22, 1830, in Butler County, Ohio; died in Minneapolis, Minn., April 25, 1908, and was buried in Lakewood Cemetery, Minneapolis, Minn. Married, December 7, 1859, Kate King, at Glendale, Hamilton County, Ohio. Children born:
1. Blanche Woodmansee, born July 2, 1862, in Urbana, Ohio.
2. Charles Woodmansee, born May 22, 1866, in Dayton, Ohio; died in San Diego, Calif.
3. Kate Woodmansee, born April 9, 1876, at St. Paul, Minn.; died March 14, 1883, at Minneapolis, Minn.

―――――x―――――

BLANCHE WOODMANSEE (10th Gen.), daughter of Daniel Webster Woodmansee and Kate (King) Woodmansee, born July 12, 1862, in Urbana, Ohio. Married, March 13, 1884, Henry L. Martin, in Hamilton, Ohio. Children born:
1. Dean Woodmansee Martin, born Nov. 13, 1887, in Minneapolis, Minn.
2. Ruth Vangordon Martin, born March 8, 1890, in San Diego, Calif.
3. Kate King Martin, born Dec. 17, 1891, in Minneapolis, Minn.
4. John Marsh Martin, born Feb. 18, 1894, in Minneapolis, Minn.
5. Mary Roberta Martin, born June 25, 1897, in Minneapolis, Minn.
6. Blanche Helena Martin, born March 26, 1900, in Minneapolis, Minn.
7. Henry L. Martin, Jr., born Sept. 21, 1903, in Minneapolis, Minn.

―――――x―――――

ELIZABETH ANN WOODMANSEE (9th Gen.), daughter of Lorenzo Dow Woodmansee and Hannah Maria (Vangordon) Woodmansee, born Feb. 6, 1832, in Butler County, Ohio. Married, ―――――, 1860, William Collins, who died Sept. 4, 1893, at Perrysville, Ind. Children born:
1. Imogene Roselle Collins, born Oct. 21, 1863.
2. Zadah Collins. } Born Jan. 30, 1872.
3. Naidah Collins, died March 20, 1872.

IMOGENE ROSELLE COLLINS (10th Gen.), daughter of Elizabeth Ann Woodmansee Collins and William Collins, born Oct. 21, 1863. Married, Dec. 11, 1889, William Daniel Chumlea, at Perrysville, Ind. He died at West Lebanon, Ind., 1901. Children born:
1. Zadah Lenore Chumlea, born April 23, 1892, at Oakland, Ill.
2. Esther Genevieve Chumlea, born Nov. 13, 1895.
3. Leon William Chumlea, born May 1, 1897.

———x———

ZADAH LENORE CHUMLEA (11th Gen.), daughter of Imogene Roselle Collins and William Collins, born April 23, 1892. Married, Oct. 3, 1912, Floyd Thomas Jones, born July 18, 1891, at Ft. Wayne, Ind. Children:
1. Betty Jane Jones, born Oct. 5, 1916, at Chicago, Ill.

———x———

BETTY JANE JONES (12th Gen.), daughter of Zadah Lenore Chumlea Jones and Floyd Thomas Jones, born Oct. 5, 1916. Married, Sept. 1, 1940, Claude Alexander Leet.

———x———

ZADAH COLLINS (10th Gen.), daughter of Elizabeth Ann Woodmansee Collins and William Collins, born Jan. 30, 1872. Married, June 25, 1895, James Henry Black, at Perrysville, Ind. Children born:
1. Ian Collins Black, born Oct. 6, 1898, at Crawfordsville, Ind.; died March 8, 1937; buried at San Diego, Calif.
2. Jean Everett Black, born April 6, 1901, at Crawfordsville, Ind.
3. James Gerald Black, born March 27, 1909, at Lebanon, Ind.
4. Margaret Elizabeth Black, born April 13, 1917, at Lebanon, Ind.

———x———

IAN COLLINS BLACK (11th Gen.), son of Zadah (Collins) Black and James Henry Black, born Oct. 6, 1898, at Crawfordsville, Ind. Married, Aug. 27, 1922, at Lebanon, Ind., Ruth Hunt. Children born:
1. Gareth Black, born Oct. 5, 1924.

———x———

JEAN EVERETT BLACK (11th Gen.), son of Zadah (Collins) Black and James Henry Black, born April 6, 1901, at Craw-

fordsville, Ind. Married, July 18, 1928, at Lebanon, Ind.,
Louise Wiseheart. Children born:
1. Judith Black, born Jan. 7, 1938.

---x---

JAMES GERALD BLACK (11th Gen.), son of Zadah (Collins)
Black and James Henry Black, born March 27, 1909, at Lebanon, Ind. Married, Nov. 2, 1940, Ruth Mills Finlayson.

---x---

LEON WILLIAM CHUMLEA (11th Gen.), son of Imogene Roselle (Collins) Chumlea and William Daniel Chumlea, born
May 1, 1897, at West Lebanon, Ind. Married, June 1, 1921,
Roxanna Dilley, at Lafayette, Ind. Children born:
1. Patricia Ruth Chumlea, born Aug. 9, 1922, at West
Lafayette, Ind.
2. Judith Ann Chumlea, born Nov. 5, 1936, at Lebanon,
Ind.

---x---

AMY JANE WOODMANSEE (9th Gen.), daughter of Lorenzo
Dow Woodmansee and Hannah Maria (Vangordon) Woodmansee, born June 28, 1834, in Butler County, Ohio; died
July 15, 1892. Married, Dec. 4, 1850, Daniel Elliott, died
July 15, 1862. Children born:
1. Elizabeth Marie Elliot, born Oct. 22, 1852.
2. Flora May Elliot, born Jan. 27, 1858; died Oct. 26, 1861.
Amy Jane Woodmansee Elliot married, secondly, Barton
Stone Hays. One child born:
1. Naomi Hays.

---x---

ELIZABETH MARIE ELLIOT (10th Gen.), daughter of Amy
Jane (Woodmansee) Elliot and Daniel Elliot, born Oct. 22,
1852. Married, Aug. 30, 1870, Isaac Morse. Children born:
1. Charles Elliot Morse, born Aug. 8, 1871.
2. Bertha Beatrice Morse, born Aug. 29, 1873.
Elizabeth Marie (Elliot) Morse married, secondly, Sept.
10, 1896, Marcus A. Bogie. She died Jan. 4, 1903. No issue.

---x---

BENJAMIN DEWITT WOODMANSEE (9th Gen.), son of Lorenzo
Dow and Hannah Marie (Vangordon) Woodmansee, born
Feb. 9, 1840, in Butler County, Ohio; died April 9, 1897. Married, Oct. 16, 1866, Harriet Davis. Children born:
1. Algernon Woodmansee, born Oct. 12, 1867.

2. Leon Woodmansee, born March 29, 1878; died April 30, 1878.

―――――――x―――――――

LYDIA MARIA WOODMANSEE (9th Gen.), daughter of Lorenzo Dow Woodmansee and Lydia (Barkalow) Williamson Woodmansee, born July 6, 1846, in Butler County, Ohio. Married, June 11, 1868, Rudolph Herr Reist, at Dayton, Ohio. One child born:
1. Robert Woodmansee Reist, born July 26, 1871, at Lafayette, Ind.

All are members of the Methodist Episcopal Church and all are Republicans.

―――――――x―――――――

ROBERT WOODMANSEE REIST (10th Gen.), son of Lydia Maria (Woodmansee) Reist and Rudolph Herr Reist, born July 26, 1871, at Lafayette, Ind. Married, Oct. 2, 1908, Grace McKinley Githens. Children born:
1. Edythe Lydia Reist, born Dec. 9, 1909, and now Sister Mary Theophane Venard, O. S. B., Mt. Angel, Oregon.

―――――――x―――――――

RACHEL BARKALOW WOODMANSEE (9th Gen.), daughter of Lorenzo Dow Woodmansee and Lydia (Barkalow) Williamson Woodmansee, born May 6, 1848, in Butler County, Ohio. Married, Nov. 28, 1890, Joseph H. Woodmansee, at Covington, Ky. Died March 14, 1935. No issue.

―――――――x―――――――

MARY ANDERSON WOODMANSEE (9th Gen.), daughter of Lorenzo Dow Woodmansee and Lydia (Barkalow) Williamson Woodmansee, born July 25, 1850, in Butler County, Ohio; died, unmarried, Nov. 23, 1909. She was an artist and teacher and was superintendent of art in the public schools at Dayton, Ohio. She was a member of the Methodist Episcopal Church.

―――――――x―――――――

REBECCA ELEANOR WOODMANSEE (9th Gen.), daughter of Lorenzo Dow Woodmansee and Lydia (Barkalow) Williamson Woodmansee, born June 20, 1853, in Butler County, Ohio; died Feb. 7, 1839. Married, Dec. 30, 1874, Samuel Eden Kemp, born Feb. 5, 1848; died May 22, 1905. Children born:
1. Mary Aden Kemp, born Nov. 12, 1876, in Dayton, Ohio.
2. Rachel Edith Kemp, born April 1, 1880, in Dayton, Ohio; died, single, Aug. 26, 1897.

3. Bertha Lydia Kemp, born Dec. 19, 1881, in Dayton, Ohio.

John Sanford Kemp, born July 11, 1897, in Dayton, Ohio.

---x---

"Another Teacher Gone" (Matrimonially)
(December 30, 1874)

A very happy event occurred yesterday morning at nine o'clock, at the residence of R. H. Reist, No. 91 North Eighth Street, in the marriage of Miss Ella R. Woodmansee of this city, and Mr. Samuel E. Kemp of Dayton, Ohio.

Miss Woodmansee was one of the most popular and efficient teachers in our city schools and among the most talented and accomplished young ladies of our city, and her departure from our midst is universally regretted. Mr. Kemp is an attorney in Dayton, and is well reported of. The happy couple left on the afternoon train on the Indianapolis, Cincinnati and Lafayette Railroad for Dayton, Ohio, followed by the hearty good wishes of many true and tried friends. The bridal presents were numerous and valuable.

Rev. I. W. Joyce officiated on the occasion.

"Matrimonial"

Hymen has again entered the ranks of the LaFayette teachers. Miss Ella Woodmansee although but a few months in the profession, proved herself to be one of the most efficient workers, and won for herself many laurels in her calling.

But while she will be much missed in the corps, the social and home circle miss her most; There she was always ready with her bright smile, her sweet happy face, casting sunshine wherever she went.

The winner of this most valuable prize was Mr. S. E. Kemp of Dayton, Ohio. They were united in Matrimony at the residence of the bride's sister this morning, by Rev. I. W. Joyce, of Trinity Church.

Mr. and Mrs. Kemp went directly to Dayton, at which place they will make their home for the future.

---x---

Mary Aden Kemp (10th Gen.), daughter of Rebecca Eleanor Woodmansee Kemp and Samuel Eden Kemp; born Nov. 12, 1876, in Dayton, Ohio. Married, Dec. 16, 1901, Harvey S.

Gruver, born Nov. 29, 1874, at Reliance, Va. Children born:
1. Edith Eleanor Gruver, born Jan. 28, 1909, at Cambridge, Mass.
2. John Kemp Gruver, born Sept. 1, 1910; died Sept. 1, 1910, at Methuen, Mass.
Harvey S. Gruver was the oldest son of Benjamin Franklin Gruver and Margaret Snyder Gruver.

―――――――――x―――――――――

EDITH ELEANOR GRUVER (11th Gen.), daughter of Mary Aden (Kemp) Gruver and Harvey S. Gruver, born Jan. 28, 1909, at Cambridge, Mass. Married, May 25, 1941, Russell Ryan.

―――――――――x―――――――――

BERTHA LYDIA KEMP (10th Gen.), daughter of Rebecca Eleanor (Woodmansee) Kemp and Samuel Eden Kemp, born Dec. 19, 1881. Married, June 12, 1907, Michael Gibbons, at Dayton, Ohio. Children born:
1. John Gibbons, born March 15, 1908; died March 17, 1908, in Dayton, Ohio.
2. Michael J. Gibbons, Jr., born Feb. 2, 1911.
3. Samuel J. Gibbons, born Aug. 4, 1913.
4. Edith Catherine Gibbons, born Nov. 8, 1914.
5. Mary Patricia Gibbons, born Aug. 7, 1919.
6. Julia Rose Gibbons, born July 17, 1923; died June 29, 1941.

―――――――――x―――――――――

MICHAED J. GIBBONS, JR. (11th Gen.), son of Bertha Lydia (Kemp) Gibbons and Michael J. Gibbons, born Feb. 2, 1911. Married, Nov. 28, 1934, Kathleen Quennan, at Dayton, Ohio. Children born:
1. Michael Gibbons III, born Aug. 29, 1935.
2. Thomas Q. Gibbons, born April 7, 1939.
3. David Kemp Gibbons, born July 27, 1942.

―――――――――x―――――――――

SAMUEL GIBBONS (11th Gen.), son of Bertha (Kemp) Gibbons and Michael J. Gibbons, born Aug. 4, 1913. Married, Jan. 4, 1939, Celeste Saavedra, at Dayton, Ohio. Children born:
1. Kathleen Ann Gibbons, born March 3, 1940.
2. Mary Margaret Gibbons, born May 4, 1942.

EDITH CATHERINE GIBBONS (11th Gen.), daughter of Bertha Lydia (Kemp) Gibbons and Michael J. Gibbons, born Nov. 8, 1914. Married, Oct. 30, 1934, J. Howard Sachs, at Dayton, Ohio. Children born:
1. Mary Lynne Sachs, born Jan. 27, 1936.
2. Jeanne Sachs, born March 4, 1938.
3. Karen Virginia Sachs, born Oct. 5, 1939; died Oct. 7, 1939.
4. Catherine Edith Sachs, born April 3, 1941.

---x---

MARY PATRICIA GIBBONS (11th Gen.), daughter of Bertha Lydia (Kemp) Gibbons and Michael J. Gibbons, born Aug. 7, 1919. Married, Oct. 25, 1935, Robert H. Miller. Children born:
1. Robert H. Miller, Jr., born Oct. 16, 1936.
2. Timothy K. Miller, born Feb. 21, 1940.

---x---

JOHN SANFORD KEMP (10th Gen.), son of Rebecca Eleanor (Woodmansee) Kemp and Samuel Eden Kemp, born July 11, 1897, at Dayton, Ohio. Married, July 25, 1941, Mrs. Ruth Scott Casterton, born April 4, 1902, at Flagstaff, Ariz.

---x---

JULIA WOODMANSEE (8th Gen.), daughter of Rachel Cushman Woodmansee and Daniel Woodmansee, born March 22, 1809, in Butler County, Ohio; died Sept. 23, 1893, at Brimfield, Peoria County, Ill. Married, in 1834, Hiram Jones, and located in Eaton, Ohio. He died Sept. 29, 1862, at Brimfield, Ill. Children born:
1. Romeo Woodmansee Jones, born May 28, 1835, at Lebanon, Ohio.
2. Rachel Ann Jones, born 1838; died in infancy, 1838.
3. Montague John Jones, born 1840, at Eaton, Ohio.
4. Almon Cushman Jones, born 1843, at Eaton, Ohio; died 1861, at Galesburg, Ill.
5. Corydon Daniel Jones, born 1850, at Eaton, Ohio.

In 1851, they removed to Brimfield, Ill., Peoria County, where they bought 640 acres of land, and where they spent the rest of their lives.

---x---

ROMEO WOODMANSEE JONES (10th Gen.), son of Julia (Woodmansee) Jones and Hiram Jones, born May 28, 1835.

Married, May 5, 1865, Arabella Guyer, at Brimfield, Ill. Children born:
1. Nettie Guyer Jones, born Jan. 24, 1866.
2. Romeo Guyer Jones, born Sept. 21, 1870; died Aug. 17, 1881.
3. Almon Roscoe Jones, born Nov. 17, 1871.
4. Mary Louisa Jones, born Feb. 26, 1874; died Feb. 29, 1896.
5. Paul Jones, born Sept. 15, 1876.
6. Julia Elizabeth Jones, born Nov. 5, 1878.
7. Ernest Jones, born April 3, 1881.

———x———

NETTIE GUYER JONES (11th Gen.), daughter of Romeo Woodmansee Jones and Arabella (Guyer) Jones, born Jan. 24, 1866; died June 23, 1890. Married, June 5, 1889, William Emery. Children born:
1. Nettie Emery, born Feb. 26, 1890.

———x———

MONTAGUE JOHN JONES (9th Gen.), son of Julia (Woodmansee) Jones and Hiram Jones, born in 1840, at Eaton, Ohio. Married Mary Lauder, at Hamilton, Ohio. Children born:
1. Lauder Jones.
2. Nellie Jones.

———x———

CORYDON DANIEL JONES (9th Gen.), son of Julia (Woodmansee) Jones and Hiram Jones, born in 1850, at Eaton, Ohio. Married, Aug. 17, 1881, Julia Wiley, at Brimfield, Ill. Children born:
1. George W. Jones, 1882.

———x———

SARAH WOODMANSEE (8th Gen.), daughter of Rachel Cushman Woodmansee and Daniel Woodmansee, born Dec. 18, 1811, in Butler County, Ohio. Married, in 1830, Joseph Randolph. Children born:
1. Columbus Randolph.
2. Daniel Randolph.
3. William Randolph.
4. Benjamin Randolph, born in Greenville, Ohio; died, in 1864, in hospital at St. Louis. He was a soldier in the Civil War, 1861/65.

5. Julia Randolph, born in Greenville, Ohio; died at Salem, Iowa, 1870.

---x---

JAMES WOODMANSEE (8th Gen.), son of Rachel Cushman Woodmansee and Daniel Woodmansee, born April 20, 1814, in Butler County, Ohio; died in Butler County, Ohio, in 1887, in his 74th year, and is buried there in Sugar Valley Cemetery on the Old Sugar Valley Farm. Married, Oct. 27, 1874, Miss Fannie Sampson McGowan, born Feb. 24, 1844, in Urbana, Ohio. They were married at the residence of the bride's sister, Mrs. E. D. Swampstead, Cincinnati, Ohio, by Rev. D. H. Moore. Children born:

1. Cicero McGowan Woodmansee, born Aug. 29, 1876, at Sugar Valley, Butler County, Ohio (near Trenton and Princeton).
2. Pauline Brown Woodmansee, born March 25, 1879, at Sugar Valley, Butler County, Ohio; died at Urbana, Ohio.
3. Letha Clark Emma Sullivant Woodmansee, born July 16, 1881, at Urbana, Ohio.
4. Ada Leigh Woodmansee, born Nov. 8, 1883, at Urbana, Ohio.

The Centennial History of Butler County, Ohio, by Hon. Bert S. Bartlow, N. H. Todhunter, Stephen D. Cone, Jos. J. Pater, Frederick Schneider and others, in the files of Lane Public Library at Hamilton, Ohio, says of James Woodmansee:

He was born in Liberty Township, of Butler County, Ohio, in 1814. His father was Daniel Woodmansee, a native of New Jersey, who settled in Butler County in 1809. The son received a good education and was brought up to agricultural pursuits, but this life did not have attraction for him. In his early years he showed a fondness for verse and he developed into a literary character of ability and, in the selection of the topics for his muse, was of unusual eccentricity. He called himself the bard of Sugar Valley, and was sometimes denominated the Milton of America.

James Woodmansee was the Author of two Epic poems, "The Closing Scene: a Poem in 12 Books," and "Religion: a Poem in 12 Books." The subject of the first named is the great war between Gog and Magog, ending with the wreck of

The above picture is a reproduction, in copper-plate half-tone, from an oil painting of
MARY WOODMANSEE
The original portrait in the possession of Mr. and Mrs. Michael J. Gibbons, of Dayton, Ohio.

matter and the crash of the worlds. The second shows religion from the time the "Spirit Brooded O'er the Water's Space" to the millenium.

Besides these, he wrote, "Wrinkles from the Brow of Experience," "Poetry of the Seasons," a poem in four books, descriptive of every month in the year, and "The Prodigal Son: a Drama in Five Acts."

The "Closing Scene" and "Wrinkles," published many years ago, received much praise, both in America and Europe. Thomas Noon Talford, the great critic and judge of Westminister, said "The Closing Scene" rivals the "Divina Commedia" of Dante, and Samuel Rogers, author of "Pleasures of Memory," called it the "Paradise Lost" of America.

Mr. Woodmansee had traveled considerably in Europe and all over America. He died in December, 1887, in his 74th year, in Butler County.

An interesting story is told by Mr. A. J. Augspurger, of Trenton, Butler County, Ohio: Years ago it was the habit of the country schools to devote the last Friday afternoon of each school month to entertainment; and as James Woodmansee was recognized as poet, author and humorist, he was invited to these Friday afternoon recreations as an entertainer. Upon one of these occasions he told them that within the 20th century, great machines would be perfected that would fly through the air and carry passengers, and others that would carry freight. He also envisioned and spoke of an instrument that would take music and conversation out of the air.

Following this speech, causing much comment concerning such talk in the presence of, and within the hearing of little children, some of the prominent elders in the community voiced their objections and said such nonsense should not be spoken before, or in the presence or hearing of children.

And now at the present time, the date of this publication, the flying machine and the radio are common and essential production for use, both in peacetime and in war.

---------x---------

MARY WOODMANSEE (8th Gen.), daughter of Rachel Cushman Woodmansee and Daniel Woodmansee, born March 15, 1818, in Butler County, Ohio; died Nov. 22, 1893, at Dayton,

Ohio. Married, March 15, 1843, Rev. William R. Anderson, of Methodist Episcopal Church, born June 21, ——; died Feb. 25, 1846. Children born:
1. Calvary B. Anderson, born July 27, 1844, at Portsmouth, Ohio, in the Methodist Parsonage; died Oct. 8, 1882.

Mary (Woodmansee) Anderson married, secondly, Oct. 23, 1860, Rev. Charles Ferguson, of Methodist Episcopal Church. No issue.

———————x———————

CALVARY B. ANDERSON (9th Gen.), son of Mary (Woodmansee) Anderson and Rev. William R. Anderson, born July 27, 1844, in Butler County, Ohio; died Oct. 8, 1882. Married, Nov. 28, 1872, on Thanksgiving Day, Margaret Louise Zupp, born Sept. 30, 1850. Children born:
1. George Woodmansee Anderson, born Dec. 8, 1873, at Belle Center, Ohio.

———————x———————

MARY WOODMANSEE FERGUSON

(*By* REV. MIGHILL DUSTIN, D. D.)

"A Pioneer Crusader—A Model Pastor's Wife—
A Noble Character"

Mrs. Mary W. Ferguson was born to Daniel and Rachel Woodmansee, in Butler County, March 15, 1818. A Christian home furnished the foundation principles upon which her beautiful character was builded and her useful life regulated.

In the twelfth year of her age she was converted, united with the Methodist Episcopal Church and became a living witness.

Besides an unblemished Christian character, she possessed rare intellectual gifts and a pleasing personality. These qualities attracted the attention of William R. Anderson, of Ohio Conference, and, quite naturally, he thought they were such as befitted the character and position of an itinerant's wife.

That the attraction was mutual is evidenced by the fact that, on March 15, 1843, they were united in marriage. But they were permitted to be "workers together" in the itinerant field for only three years, when the Lord called the husband from labor to reward.

For fourteen years Mrs. Anderson lived in widowhood devoting her time chiefly to the care and education of her son.

On the 23rd of October, 1860 she was united in marriage to the Rev. Charles Ferguson of the Cincinnati Conference.

During the twenty-four years of their married life, Brother Ferguson served some of the most important charges in the Conference. In all of these Mrs. Ferguson's helpfulness was manifest in every department of Christian labor.

Her solid Christian character, her faithfulness in all religious duties, and her kindly spirit contributed in no small degree to that success which uniformly accompanied the labors of her husband.

Her clear view of the truth and duty led her naturally into these lines of moral reform that tend to make the world better.

Hence, when the Woman's Crusade against the drink traffic was in progress, she gave of her hearty sympathies and active co-operation.

Her residence at that time was in Cincinnati. A large number of the best women of that city united in an organization for the purpose of carrying on more efficiently their crusade against the dramshop. Mrs. Ferguson was chosen president of that organization.

It was not in her nature to desire leading positions, but her high sense of moral duty impelled her to accept them when proffered and urged by those in whom she had confidence.

It was well that she accepted the presidency of the "Woman's Christian Temperance League, of Cincinnati;" for, at the bidding of the liquor interest, the city authorities undertook to stop the Crusade.

The Mayor and Chief of Police wrote to Mrs. Ferguson, as president of the organization and tried to persuade her to desist from the work in which she and her associates were engaged, threatening the direst consequence if they refused. But the gifted, cultured, and refined leader of that temperance band replied so effectually to the appeals and threatenings of the city authorities that they abandoned diplomacy, and resorted to force, as many will still remember.

It is well known that for several years Mrs. Ferguson filled the office of District Secretary of the "Woman's Foreign Missionary Society." That office was not of her seeking, though the objects and aims of the Society had her heartiest sympathies. It was expected that the secretary would travel through the district, deliver public missionary addresses, and organize societies in the several charges. This work called for qualifications which every one did not possess and Mrs. Ferguson was obviously chosen to that position because it was known she was qualified for its duties, in fact, her moral and intellectual prominence determined the question of her leadership in that as well as other organizations.

Mrs. Ferguson's literary attainments were much above the average. To a strong and active intellect there was added careful and painstaking study. Her public addresses evidenced the possession of a trained intellect, as well as natural gifts of a high order. They were clear in statement, logical in arrangement, and strikingly accurate and beautiful in language and style.

Her contributions both in prose and poetry, to the "Ladies Repository," many years ago, show that, if she had continued to cultivate literature as an art, in all probability, she would have achieved large success in that field.

But in her mature womanhood her desire to save souls, and her position as a pastor's wife, led her to renounce every ambition that was not distinctly religious. Her work in the missionary cause was precisely in the line of her aspirations. Hence in that work, and all soul-saving work, she continued to be interested to the very close of her life.

About seven years ago she had a slight stroke of paralysis, from which she never fully recovered. After that she was almost wholly disabled from any sphere.

For two years prior to her death she was entirely helpless, needing the constant care and attention of friends. But she was always patient and submissive, and could even "joy in tribulation," because the Divine Comforter was ever present. Her favorite theme of conversation was the riches of grace in Christ Jesus. No clouds obscured her sky; no doubts or fears interrupted her communion with God; no assault of the enemy disturbed or weakened in the least degree her early and steadfast faith in the Lord Jesus Christ. That faith, with its rich fruitage of peace and joy and hope, continued to the end. At twelve o'clock meridian, November 22nd, 1893 she sweetly fell asleep in Jesus. DAYTON, OHIO.

GEORGE WOODMANSEE ANDERSON (10th Gen.), son of Calvary B. Anderson and Margaret Louise (Zupp) Anderson, born Dec. 8, 1873, at Belle Center, Ohio. Married, Aug. 14, 1912, Nellie Josephine Sharpe, of Troy, New York. Children born:
1. Robert Cushman Anderson, born June 9, 1922.
2. Jane Wyckham Anderson, born Feb. 18, 1926.

Rev. George Wood (Woodmansee) Anderson was ordained a Methodist Episcopal Minister, serving as such for several years; he later became an evangelist and lecturer. He is the author of a number of books.

THOMAS CUSHMAN (7th Gen.), third child, son of Isaac Cushman and Deborah Frazee Cushman, born March 18, 1782; died about 1837. Married, May 12, 1808, Elizabeth Jenkins, born March 3, 1791. Children born:
1. Delilah Cushman, born Feb. 22, 1809; died Jan. 15, 1888.
2. Deborah Cushman, born Feb. 2, 1811.
3. Isaac Cushman, born May 20, 1813; died March 7, 1898.
4. Rachael Cushman, born July 30, 1815.
5. Louisa Cushman, born Jan. 9, 1818.
6. Rebecca Cushman, born May 10, 1820; died single.
7. Maryann Cushman, born Aug. 16, 1822; died Nov. 29, 1880.
8. Jonathan Cushman, born Dec. 30, 1824.
9. Elizabeth Cushman, born Aug. 20, 1827.
10. Sarah Cushman, born Sept. 5, 1833; died March 19, 1926.

The above names and dates of birth taken from the family Bible in the possession of Mrs. Mary Bolander and family at Fortville, Ind.

According to the record of the family, in possession of Clara Jane Lane, living at 1008 Orchard Street, Ottumwa, Iowa,

Thomas Cushman Born March 18th 1782

Elisabeth Jenkins Born March 3rd 1791

Married

On the 12th May 1806

Delilah Cushman Daughter of Thomas and Elisabeth Cushman Born February 22nd 1809

Deborah Cushman Daughter of Thomas and Elisabeth Cushman Born February 2nd 1811

Isaac Cushman Son of Thomas and Elisabeth Cushman Born May 20th 1813

Rachel Cushman Daughter of Thomas and Elisabeth Cushman Born July 30th 1815

Louisa Cushman Daughter of Thomas and Elisabeth Cushman Born January 9th 1818

Rebecah Cushman Daughter of Thomas and Elisabeth Cushman Born May 10th 1820

Maryann Cushman Daughter of Thomas and Elisabeth Cushman Born August 6th 1822.

Jonathan S Cushman son of Thomas and Elisabeth Cushman Born December 30th 1824.

Elisabeth Cushman Daughter of Thomas and Elisabeth Cushman Born August 20th 1827

Sarah Cushman Daughter of Thomas and Elisabeth Cushman was Born September 5th 1835

daughter of Evangeline Wynn, who was the daughter of Sarah Cushman Wynn, the tenth child of Thomas Cushman (7th Gen.), her great-grandfather, Thomas Cushman (7th Gen.), died when his daughter, Sarah, was four years old; agreeable to this record he was going to a mill and had a four-bushel sack of grain on the back of one horse which he was leading and a two-bushel sack on the horse he was riding. The sack, on the horse he was leading, fell off and in trying to lift the sack back on the horse again he burst a blood vessel in the struggle, and laid a long while before any one found him. He lived only a short time after they brought him home. Sarah had a brother, Isaac, older than herself, and had a brother, Jonathan.

DELILAH CUSHMAN (8th Gen.), daughter of Thomas Cushman and Elizabeth (Jenkins) Cushman, born Feb. 22, 1809; died Jan. 15, 1888. Married Jacob Larue. Children born:
1. John Larue.
2. Hannah Larue.

HANNAH LARUE (9th Gen.), daughter of Delilah Cushman and Jacob Larue. Married Thomas Wynn. Children born:
1. Samuel Wynn, born June 8, 1852; died March 30, 1919.
2. Jacob Wynn, born about 1854; died, unmarried, about 1877.
3. William Morgan Wynn, born Feb. 20, 1857; died March 1, 1938.
4. Mary D. Wynn, born 1858.
5. John Wynn, born April 10, 1860.
6. Sarah Elizabeth Wynn, born June 6, 1863; died Sept. 28, 1934.
7. Louisa J. Wynn, born 1868.
8. Ida E. Wynn, born June 16, 1876; died Oct. 10, 1919.
9. Thomas Edward Wynn, born Feb. 19, 1873; died June 21, 1934.

SAMUEL WYNN (10th Gen.), son of Hannah Larue Wynn and Thomas Wynn, born June 8, 1852; died March 30, 1919. Married, March 4, 1880, Margaret Albert, born ————; died Feb. 3, 1930. Children born:

1. Ernest Wynn, born July 31, 1882; died Nov. 10, 1940.

ERNEST WYNN (11th Gen.), son of Samuel Wynn and Margaret (Albert) Wynn, born July 31, 1882; died Nov. 10, 1940. Married, June 27, 1906, Eugenia Hunton Barnes. Children born:
1. Nathan Eldrige Wynn, born Oct. 16, 1907.
2. Walter Samuel Wynn, born Jan. 11, 1911.
3. Norval Owen Wynn, born July 15, 1914.

NATHAN ELDRIDGE WYNN (12th Gen.), son of Ernest Wynn and Eugenia Hunton (Barnes) Wynn, born Oct. 16, 1907. Married, Dec. 4, 1936, Flora Albert (widow of David Fowler). No issue.

WALTER SAMUEL WYNN (12th Gen.), son of Ernest Wynn and Eugenia Hunton (Barnes) Wynn, born Jan. 11, 1911. Married, June 25, 1934, Eva Jo Gentry. No issue.

NORVAL OWEN WYNN (12th Gen.), son of Ernest Wynn and Eugenia Hunton (Barnes) Wynn, born July 15, 1914. Married, Dec. 4, 1936, Beulah White. No issue.

The following is from the family record of Mrs. Tacy Stovall and Mrs. Dora Makemson, daughters of William Morgan Wynn and Valina Frances (Clem) Wynn:

WILLIAM MORGAN WYNN (10th Gen.), son of Thomas Wynn and Hannah (Larue) Wynn, born Feb. 20, 1857; died March 1, 1938. Married, first, Oct. 11, 1882, Valina Frances Clem, daughter of Jonas and Valina Jane Clem, born Jan. 26, 186—; died Jan. 11, 1892; buried in Pentecost Cemetery, N. W. Danville, Ill. Children born:
1. Samuel Smith Wynn, born July 24, 1883.
2. Dora Frances Wynn, born Nov. 1, 1884.
3. Laura Edna Wynn, born Feb. 25, 1887.
4. Tacy Ann Wynn, born March 28, 1889.
5. George Henry Wynn, born Jan. 17, 1891.

William Morgan Wynn (10th Gen.), of Glenburn, Ill., age 38 years, farmer, son of Thomas Wynn and Hannah (Larue) Wynne, married, secondly, Jan. 26, 1896, Ruthanna Lovett, widow, age 34 years, of Glenburn, Ill., daughter of Isaac Downing and Mary Ann Blowers. Married by Robert M. Rogers; witnesses, Charles Downing and Frank Downing. Following the death of Valina Frances, first wife of William Morgan Wynn, Tacy Ann and George Henry Wynn were reared by foster parents; Tacy Ann by Jarrett and Hattie Davis, of Danville, Ill.; George Henry by Mr. and Mrs. Stunn, farmers, near Oakwood, Ill.

---x---

SAMUEL SMITH WYNN (11th Gen.), son of William Morgan Wynn and Valina Frances (Clem) Wynn, born July 24, 1883. Married, first, Dec. 20, 1902, Ethel May Stanfield, daughter of Thomas and Manda Stanfield, born April 24, 1884; died May 20, 1926. Children born (to Samuel Smith Wynn and Ethel May [Stanfield] Wynn):
1. Edna Vera Wynn, born Aug. 4, 1904.
2. Grace May Wynn, born Nov. 26, 1905.
3. Samuel Clifford Wynn, born Dec. 12, 1907.
4. Clyde Morgan Wynne, born Oct. 3, 1913.
5. Ora Earl Wynn, born May 24, 1916.
6. Ethel Eileen Wynn, born July 9, 1919.
7. Beverly Sidonia Wynn, born July 2, 1921.
8. Eva Bernice Wynn, born May 14, 1923.
9. Glen William Wynn, born Dec. 19, 1925; died April 9, 1926.

---x---

EDNA VERA WYNN (12th Gen.), daughter of Samuel Smith Wynn and Ethel May (Stanfield) Wynn, born Aug. 4, 1904. Married, first, Loren Earnest Eddy, born Nov. 19, 1919; died April 16, 1926; he was the son of Laban and Araminta Eddy. Children born:
1. Opal Eileen Eddy, born April 15, 1921.
2. Evelyn Juanita Eddy, born May 21, 1923.

Edna Vera Wynn married, secondly, May 26, 1928, Elsney Ray Gay, son of John and Alvira Gay; he died Aug. 31, 1936.

Edna Vera Wynn married, thirdly, July 28, 1937, Alonzo Thomas Lappin, son of Alonzo and Elizabeth Lappin.

---x---

OPAL EILEEN EDDY (13th Gen.), daughter of Edna Vera Wynn and Loren Earnest Eddy, born April 15, 1921. Mar-

ried, Sept. 28, 1937, Oscar Stearns, son of John and Jessie Stearns. Children born:
1. Larry Wayne Sterns, born June 20, 1939.

GRACE MAY WYNN (12th Gen.), daughter of Samuel Smith Wynn and Ethel May (Stanfield) Wynn, born Nov. 26, 1905. Married, March 13, 1923, Bernice Graves, born Oct. 23, 1896. Children born:
1. Samuel Albert Graves, born March 29, 1924.
2. Jess Robert Graves, born July 30, 1926.
3. William Rankin Graves, born Feb. 1, 1933.

———————x———————

SAMUEL CLIFFORD WYNN (12th Gen.), son of Samuel Smith Wynn and Ethel May (Stanfield) Wynn, born Dec. 12, 1907. Married, July 27, 1935, Mrs. Mary Agnes (Roger) Duke, daughter of Robert Thomas and Georgia Lee Roger, born May 28, 1910. Children born:
1. Ethel Marveen Wynn, born March 7, 1936.
2. Clifford Lee Wynn, born Jan. 21, 1940.

———————x———————

CLYDE MORGAN WYNN (12th Gen.), son of Samuel Smith Wynn and Ethel May (Stanfield) Wynn, born Oct. 3, 1913. Married, Oct. 30, 1935, Inez Greer, born Dec. 30, 1918. Children born:
1. Patsy Mae Wynn, born March 17, 1937.
2. Edna Bernice Wynn, born July 12, 1938.

———————x———————

ORA EARL WYNN (12th Gen.), son of Samuel Smith Wynn and Ethel May (Stanfield) Wynn, born May 24, 1916. Married Elma Greer Howard (widow), born Jan. 3, 1921. License issued Dec. 7, 1940.

———————x———————

ETHEL EILEEN WYNN (12th Gen.), daughter of Samuel Smith Wynn and Ethel May (Stanfield) Wynn, born July 9, 1919. Married, Aug. 31, 1935, James Greer, born Oct. 31, 1912. Children born:
1. Shirley E. Greer, born May 3, 1936.
2. Doris Jean Greer, born Sept. 21, 1937.
3. James Earl Greer, born Jan. 28, 1940.

BEVERLY SIDONIA WYNN (12th Gen.), daughter of Samuel Smith Wynn and Ethel May (Stanfield) Wynn, born July 2, 1921. Married, Sept. 14, 1939, Elmer Quick, son of Ralph Cleo and Lucy Quick. Children born:
1. Barbara Jo Quick, born May 2, 1940.

———————x———————

EVA BERNICE WYNN (12th Gen.), daughter of Samuel Smith Wynn and Ethel May (Stanfield) Wynn, born May 14, 1923. Married Howard Abbott, son of Ruel and Hazel E. Abbott. Children born:
1. Howard Eugene Abbott.

———————x———————

DORA FRANCES WYNN (11th Gen.), daughter of William Morgan Wynn and Valina Frances (Clem) Wynn, born Nov. 1, 1884, in Blount Township, Vermillion County, Ill. Married, Sept. 2, 1901, Wilbur Darius Makemson, born Aug. 10, 1880, at Oakwood, Ill., son of Hiram Bradshaw Makemson. Children born:
1. Louetta Hazel Makemson, born Dec. 1, 1902, at Danville, Ill.; died March 12, 1904.
2. Ruby Elizabeth, born Sept. 19, 1904, in Oakwood, Township, Vermillion County, Ill.

———————x———————

RUBY ELIZABETH MAKEMSON (12th Gen.), daughter of Dora Frances (Wynn) Makemson and Wilbur Darius Makemson, born Sept. 19, 1904. Married, Aug. 29, 1925, Clay Carter Campbell, born in 1897 at Farmer City, Ill., son of Albert O. Campbell. Children born:
1. Jack Donald Campbell, born Nov. 9, 1926.
2. Myra Frances Campbell, born June 18, 1927.
3. Robert Clay Campbell, born Sept. 14, 1940.

———————x———————

LAURA EDNA WYNN (11th Gen.), daughter of William Morgan Wynn and Valina Frances (Clem) Wynn, born Feb. 25, 1887. Married, Nov. 27, 1903, Samuel Edward Winn, born Jan., 1885, son of Thomas and Emma Winn, of Oakwood Township. Fifteen children born:
1. Elma Ellen Winn, born Oct. 27, 1904.
2. Russell Merl Winn, born Feb. 20, 1907, in Danville Township.

3. Oscar Edward Winn, born Aug. 22, 1909, in Danville Township.
4. Vernice Raymond Winn, born June 13, 1911, in Danville Township; died Aug. 2, 1933.
5. Marion T. Winn, born Sept. 16, 1913, in Danville Township.
6. Cleo Harrison Winn, born Aug. 29, 1915, in Danville Township.
7. Farris Richard Winn, born Aug. 27, 1917, in Danville Township.
8. Alta Bernice Winn, born Dec. 19, 1919, in Danville Township.
9. Doris Laverne Winn, born Aug. 1, 1921, in Oakwood Township.
10. Norman Edwin Winn, born April 4, 1923, in Oakwood Township.
11. Melvin William Winn, born May 1, 1924, in Danville Township.
12. Ruth Marie Winn, born June 30, 1925, in Danville Township; died May 11, 1926.
13. Ralph Eugene Winn, born July 7, 1926, in Danville Township; died Sept. 24, 1926.
14. Mary Lou Winn, born Sept. 24, 1927, in Danville Township.
15. Genevieve Gertrude Winn, born May 19, 1931, in Danville Township.

———————x———————

TACY ANN WYNN (11th Gen.), daughter of William Morgan Wynn and Valina Frances (Clem) Wynn, born March 28, 1889. Married, June 12, 1908, James Oras Stovall, born Oct. 16, 1885, in Douglas County, Ill.; son of William Stovall. Children born:

1. Cleota Fern Stovall, born July 12, 1910.
2. Juanita LaVone Stovall, born Aug. 12, 1912.
3. Guinevere Maxine Stovall, born Dec. 21, 1914.
4. James Milford Stovall, born July 12, 1920.

———————x———————

JUANITA LAVONE STOVALL (12th Gen.), daughter of Tacy Ann Wynn and James Oras Stovall, born Aug. 12, 1912. Married, July 25, 1933, at Newport, Ind., Vernon Wilfred Epperson, born Nov. 7, 1913, son of William Epperson. No issue.

———————x———————

ELMA ELLEN WINN (12th Gen.), daughter of Laura Edna (Wynn) Winn and Samuel Edward Winn, born Oct. 27, 1904. Married, March 10, 1923, Harry Todd, born Jan. 21, 1903. Children born:
1. Charles Edgar Todd, born Nov. 22, 1923.
2. Perry Edward Todd, born Aug. 31, 1925.
3. Harry Lyndol Todd, born April 14, 1927.
4. Lois Jeane Todd, born March 27, 1932.

———————x———————

GEORGE HENRY WYNN (11th Gen.), son of William Morgan Wynn and Valina Frances (Clem) Wynne, born Jan. 17, 1891. Married, Aug. 21, 1915, Anna Wilson, born Sept. 21, 1895, daughter of Charles and Margarette E. Wilson. Children born:
1. Dorothy Vivian Wynn, born Dec. 10, 1916, in Oakwood Township.
2. Norma Winifred Wynn, born Oct. 19, 1919, in Oakwood Township.

———————x———————

DOROTHY VIVIAN WYNN (12th Gen.), daughter of George Henry Wynn and Anna (Wilson) Wynn, born Dec. 10, 1916. Married, Dec. 20, 1933, Forrest Thurman Williams, son of Irving and Ochel Williams; born April 15, 1913. Children born:
1. Wayne Allen Williams, born Sept. 19, 1936.
2. Carl Leonard Williams, born Feb. 11, 1940.

———————x———————

NORMA WINIFRED WYNN (12th Gen.), daughter of George Henry Wynn and Anna (Wilson) Wynn, born Oct. 19, 1919. Married, April 9, 1936, in Covington, Ind., by Rev. Lawrence Green, Edward Orville Dalbey, son of Winfred and Isla Florence Dalbey. Children born:
1. William Phillip Dalbey, born May 18, 1938.

———————x———————

MARY D. WYNN (10th Gen.), daughter of Hanna (Larue) Wynn and Thomas Wynn, born in 1858. Married, Sept. 8, 1881, James Reeder, at Mr. Wynn's residence in Vermillion

County, Ill., by the Rev. Thomas Snyder. James Reeder, of Blount, Ill., was a farmer, age 31, born in Ohio, son of George Reeder and R. Crators Reeder. Witnesses, Frank Buck and John R. Davis. Children born:
1. Bessie Reeder, born Nov. 2, 1886.

---x---

BESSIE REEDER (11th Gen.), daughter of Mary D. (Wynn) Reeder and James Reeder, born Nov. 2, 1886. Married, Nov. 23, 1909, George H. Thomas, who died Oct. 17, 1918. Children born:
1. Robert H. Thomas, born June 23, 1911.
2. Leonard R. Thomas, born Jan. 10, 1914.
Bessie Reeder Thomas (widow) married, secondly, May 4, 1935, George Senft, and has no children (Jan. 20, 1941).

---x---

ROBERT H. THOMAS (12th Gen.), son of Bessie (Reeder) Thomas and George H. Thomas, born June 23, 1911. Married, Jan. 12, 1935, Rita Curts. They have no children.

---x---

LEONARD THOMAS (12th Gen.), son of Bessie (Reeder) Thomas and George H. Thomas, born Jan. 10, 1914. Married, May 10, 1936, Lena May Smith. Children born:
1. Freda Joan Thomas, born Nov. 11, 1937.

---x---

JOHN WYNN (10th Gen.), son of Hannah (Larue) Wynn and Thomas Wynn, born April 10, 1860. Married, first, Grace Greer. Children born:
1. Blanche Wynn, died in fall of 1929.
2. Earl Wynn, born March 12, 1889.
3. Benton Wynn, born in Danville, Ill.
4. Omer Wynn, born Oct. 5, 1893.
5. Laura Wynn.
John Wynn married, secondly, Ivy ————. No issue.

---x---

BLANCHE WYNN (11th Gen.), daughter of John Wynn and Grace (Greer) Wynn, died in fall of 1929. Married John Tolson. Children born:
1. Carl Tolson.
2. Orville Tolson.

EARL WYNN (11th Gen.), son of John Wynn and Grace (Greer) Wynn, born March 12, 1889. Married, Oct. 21, 1920, Mille Montgomery, born Aug. 28, 1891. Children born:
1. Harold Arnold Wynn, born Aug. 2, 1921.
2. Richard Eugene Wynn, born June 9, 1923.
3. John Edward Wynn, born Nov. 23, 1924.
4. James Robert Wynn, born Feb. 15, 1926.
5. Kenneth Dale Wynn, born Jan. 23, 1931.

BENTON WYNN (11th Gen.), son of John Wynn and Grace (Greer) Wynn. Married Merritt McPherson. Children born:
1. George Ishmail Wynn, born March 30, 1915.
2. Alice Lorraine Wynn, born May 10, 1917.
3. Abbie Wilma Wynn, born May 1, 1919.
4. Mary Eileen Wynn, born Aug. 22, 1923. } Twins
5. Marion Eugene Wynn, born Aug. 22, 1923. }

OMER WYNN (11th Gen.), son of John Wynn and Grace (Greer) Wynn, born Oct. 5, 1893. Married Grace Mauck. Children born:
1. Gerald Wynn.
2. Doris Wynn.
3. Paul Raymond Wynn.

LAURA WYNN (11th Gen.), daughter of John Wynn and Grace (Greer) Wynn, born Nov. 22, 1896. Married, June 22, 1916, James Hinckley. Children born:
1. June Hinckley, born May 18, 1917.
2. Johnine Hinckley, born Sept. 30, 1933.

GEORGE ISHMAIL WYNN (12th Gen.), son of Benton Wynn and Merritt (McPherson) Wynn, born March 30, 1915. Married, June 6, 1937, Laura Laurene Kidd, born Oct. 16, 1917. Children born:
1. Thomas Earle Wynn, born March 4, 1938.
2. Donnie Jean Wynn, born June 11, 1941.

ALICE LORRAINE WYNN (12th Gen.), daughter of Benton Wynn and Merritt (McPherson) Wynn, born May 10, 1917. Married, Oct. 24, 1936, Squire Wesley Stewart, born May 10, 1911. Children born:

1. Marion Duane Stewart, born March 9, 1939.
2. Sandra Lynn Stewart, born March 22, 1942.

———x———

MARY EILEEN WYNN (12th Gen.), daughter of Benton Wynn and Merritt (McPherson) Wynn, born Aug. 22, 1923. Married, June 2, 1940, Clarence Woodrow Johnson, born July 4, 1917.

———x———

SARAH ELIZABETH WYNN (10th Gen.), daughter of Hannah (Larue) Wynn and Thomas Wynn, born June 6, 1863; died Sept. 28, 1934. Married, Oct. 23, 1884, George Allen, age 32 years; died Dec. 11, 1899. Children born:
1. Grace May Allen, born Aug. 8, 1885; died June 6, 1886.
2. Clarence Allen, born Jan. 27, 1887; died Sept. 15, 1896.
3. Georgia Dexter Allen, born Nov. 6, 1897.

Sarah Elizabeth (Wynn) Allen married, secondly, Dec. 21, 1902, Rollie Edward Wheatley. Children born:
1. Raleigh Raymond Wheatley, born Nov. 1, 1903.

———x———

GEORGIA DEXTER ALLEN (11th Gen.), daughter of Sarah Elizabeth (Wynn) Allen and George Allen, born Nov. 6, 1897. Married, Nov. 27, 1932, Roy Lee Case. Children born:
1. William Allen Case, born Aug. 24, 1936.

———x———

LOUISA J. WYNN (10th Gen.), daughter of Hannah (Larue) Wynn and Thomas Wynn, born Dec. 5, 1867, in Vermillion County, Ill.; died Nov. 23, 1912; buried in Pleasant Grove Cemetery, Vermillion County, Ill. Married, Aug. 2, 1886, at the age of eighteen years, Eli Williams, a farmer, age 24 years, and of English parentage, the son of Huston Williams and Catharine (Vualls or Cualls) Williams. Witnesses, R. P. West and George Allen. Children born:
1. Grace Ethel Williams, born Jan. 15, 1888; died Oct. 19, 1892.
2. Guy Williams, born July 23, 1889, at Pinckneyville, Ill.
3. Harry Williams, born Oct. 29, 1893.
4. Bessie Pearl Williams, born June 21, 1896; died in infancy.
5. Everett Williams, born June 11, 1897, at Pinckneyville, Ill.; died June 16, 1929.

6. Herschel Williams, born Dec. 24, 1901; died Sept. 17, 1903.

———————x———————

GUY WILLIAMS (11th Gen.), son of Louisa J. (Wynn) Williams and Eli Williams, age 29, born in Perry County, Ill., July 23, 1889. Married, first, Oct. 2, 1912, at Storm Lake, Iowa, Mayme O'Neill, born May 17, 1890. Children born:
1. Mernie Williams, born June 19, 1915, at Rembrandt, Iowa.

Guy Williams married, secondly, March 16, 1918, Rosa Martens, of Danville, Ill., born Nov. 10, 1890, a daughter of Charles Martens and Sophia Weinke Martens; married by Rev. Franklin C. Reed; witnesses, Robert J. Prast and Mrs. Lillian Prast. Children born:
1. Garnet Williams, born Aug. 21, 1925, at Danville, Ill.

———————x———————

MERNIE WILLIAMS (12th Gen.), son of Guy Williams and Mayme (O'Neill) Williams, born June 19, 1915, at Rembrandt, Iowa. Married, June 13, 1936, Ruth Catharine Kizer, born June 4, 1918. Children born:
1. Rosalie Pearl Williams, born Jan. 16, 1937.
2. Cleo Edward Williams, born Dec. 29, 1939.

———————x———————

EVERETT WILLIAMS (11th Gen.), son of Louisa J. (Wynn) Williams and Eli Williams, born June 11, 1897, at Pinckneyville, Ill.; died June 16, 1929, age 32 years and 12 days. Married, Sept. 6, 1924, Mrs. Lavern Grimes Webber. No issue.

———————x———————

HARRY WILLIAMS (11th Gen.), son of Louisa J. (Wynn) Williams and Eli Williams, born Oct. 29, 1893; died April 15, 1935. Married, Oct. 1, 1913, Eva Pichon, widow. Children born:
1. Carl Williams, born Dec. 25, 1915.
2. Hershel Williams, born Jan. 13, 1918.
3. Myrtle Lou Williams, born Dec. 8, 1921.

———————x———————

IDA E. WYNN (10th Gen.), daughter of Hannah (Larue) Wynn and Thomas Wynn, born June 16, 1871, at Newton, Ill.; died Oct. 10, 1919. Married, Feb. 28, 1889, William M. Harter, age 30, of Muncie, Ill. (From Marriage Records of Vermillion County, Ill., Reg. 11, page 113). Children born:

1. Leslie Harter, born March 22, 1894; died Dec. 10, 1918.
2. Elsie Harter, born 1907 or 1908; died, age about 19.
3. Edith Harter, b. Jan. 1, 1901; d. in infancy. } Twins
4. Esther Harter, b. Jan. 1, 1901; d. Aug. 1, 1903. }
5. Oscar Harter, born in 1902.

―――――x―――――

Death Certificate, Vermillion County, Ill., No. 3171:
Leslie Harter, born March 22, 1894; died Dec. 10, 1918. Cause of death, gassed while in action with the United States Army.

―――――x―――――

Death Certificate No. 5003:
Ida Harter, born June 16, 1871, at Newton, Ill.; died Oct. 10, 1919, 48 years, 4 months, 7 days.

―――――x―――――

Death Certificate No. 5641:
Wilson M. Harter, born Dec. 18, 1857; died May 15, 1920, 62 years, 4 months, 17 days. Informant, Oscar Harter.

After the death of Leslie Harter and his parents, the whereabouts of Oscar being unknown, the money due Leslie Harter was divided between his living relatives. Oscar went to the Southwest, and he is now believed to be dead.

Concerning William Harter, note that his name is here given as both William and Wilson. His relatives call him, "Uncle Will," "Uncle Wils" and "Uncle Wilt."

Oscar's relatives say that he was at home at the time of Leslie's death, and that he died in New York City, on the streets, sometime after his parents had died.

Taken from old newspaper files in Danville Public Library:
"*Danville Morning Press*, Dec. 11, 1918:

"Leslie Harter, soldier of the United States Army, a member of Battery A, 149th Field Artillery, has lost his brave battle with death.

"The young soldier, sent home from France three months ago that he might receive better treatment in his fight against tuberculosis, contracted while in the service of his country, passed away yesterday morning, Dec. 10, at the home of his parents, Mr. and Mrs. W. M. Harter, 409 Cunningham Avenue, West Side.

"The death of Leslie Harter occurred just seventeen months

to the day after Battery A left Danville on the first lap of their trip to France. He was with the Battery when it left Danville, during the time the boys were in training at Fort Sheridan, and at Camp Mills, N. Y., and when it faced the Huns after its arrival on the firing lines. He participated in all the big battles and shared all the hardships of war with his comrades.

"Three months ago during one of the Allied drives, in northern France, he was severely gassed and was removed to a base hospital. Shortly after, tuberculosis of the throat developed and at his request he was sent home, arriving in New York six weeks ago. From New York he was transferred to Fort Bayard, New Mexico. There his condition became critical and his mother was summoned to his bedside. He pleaded to come home to spend his last days among his relatives, so accompanied by his mother and a young army surgeon, he arrived in Danville last Thursday. He was born in Danville, March 22, 1894, and all his life was spent in Danville. Besides his parents, William M. and Ida Wynn Harter, he is survived by a brother, Oscar, sixteen years old. Previous to his enlistment in the service of his country, he was employed by the Danville Street Railway and Light Company.

"Leslie Harter will be buried with full military honors. The funeral to be held at two o'clock tomorrow from the Fourth Church of Christ, Vermillion Heights. Interment at Spring Hill Cemetery."

In the same paper appeared a notice to Spanish American War veterans to attend as military escorts, taps, etc.

There was a Battery A, organized at Danville long before the Spanish American War.

During the World War, Danville was proud to have sent the "Initial Battery" in the 149th Field Artillery, 42nd or Rainbow Division. Danville boys in this unit won many honors and medals for distinguished service in action, including the "Order of the Purple Heart."

———————x———————

THOMAS EDWARD WYNN (10th Gen.), son of Hannah (Larue) Wynn and Thomas Wynn, born Feb. 19, 1873; died June 21, 1934, age 61 years, four months and two days; buried at

Pleasant Grove Cemetery, Oakwood, Ill. Married, Jan. 29, 1898, Mattie Pritchard, of Newtown, Ill., age 22 years, daughter of Gilbert and Elizabeth (Downing) Pritchard; married by G. F. Coburn, J. P.; witnesses, J. A. Bantz and G. B. Dunn. (Death Certificate No. 10197 confirms above marriage. See Vermillion County Register 111, page 185.)

---x---

DEBORAH CUSHMAN (8th Gen.), daughter of Thomas Cushman and Elizabeth (Jenkins) Cushman, born Feb. 2, 1811; died Aug. 6, 1898. Married James Gorman, born April 16, 1813; died Dec. 5, 1907. Children born:

1. Thomas C. Gorman, born April 6, 1838; died Jan. 5, 1896.
2. Absalom Gorman, born June 28, 1840; died in childhood.
3. John B. Gorman, born July 7, 1842; died Dec. 22, 1928.
4. Henry Clay Gorman, born Aug. 10, 1844 ⎫ died in infancy
5. Theodore F. Gorman, born Aug. 10, 1844 ⎭
6. Joseph Hilt Gorman, born Jan. 17, 1847; died June 6, 1926.
7. Mary Elizabeth Gorman, born Feb. 23, 1849; died Nov. 8, 1872.
8. Milbert Gorman, born June 8, 1851.

---x---

THOMAS C. GORMAN (9th Gen.), son of Deborah and James Gorman, was born April 6, 1838, and died Jan. 7, 1896. He married Sarah M. Parris Larue Sept. 20, 1865. She was born Jan. 23, 1842 and died Nov. 15, 1932. She first married William Larue, who was the son of Delilah Cushman Larue, in 1860. William Larue was killed in the Civil War. The following children were born to Thomas C. Gorman and Sarah M. Parris Larue Gorman:

1. Anna L. Gorman, born June 18, 1868.
2. Orpha J. Gorman, born Feb. 22, 1870; died March 15, 1915.
3. Deborah Gorman, born Feb. 26, 1876.
4. Zoa Gorman, born May 20, 1880. Unmarried.

---x---

ANNA L. GORMAN (10th Gen.), daughter of Thomas C. Gorman and Sarah M. Parris Larue Gorman, was born June 18,

1868. Married, March 27, 1886, Guilford Crayne. Children born:
1. Maggie Crayne, born June 11, 1887. Married H. D. Oakley, Dec. 24, 1905.
2. Thomas Crayne, born May 4, 1891. Married Mabel Traxyler, July 1, 1917.
3. Charles Crayne, born May 20, 1894. Married Lena Russell, Oct. 26, 1919.

———————x———————

ORPHA J. GORMAN (10th Gen.), daughter of Thomas C. Gorman and Sarah M. Parris Larue Gorman, born Feb. 22, 1870. Married, in 1887, H. V. Cardiff. Children born:
1. Sarah E. Cardiff, born May 25, 1888. Married J. L. Stayton.
2. Albert P. Cardiff, born Nov. 25, 1889. Married Pearl Davis.
3. Ethel Cardiff, born Sept. 26, 1892. Married W. I. Bell.
4. John Cardiff, born Sept., 1894.
5. Deborah Cardiff, born Nov. 17, 1898. Married D. Garver.

———————x———————

DEBORAH GORMAN (10th Gen.), daughter of Thomas C. Gorman and Sarah M. Parris Larue Gorman, born Feb. 26, 1876. Married, Dec. 28, 1898, Rev. Emory J. Rees. Children born:
1. Dorothy Rees, born April 15, 1910.
2. E. Keith Rees, born Aug. 2, 1915.

———————x———————

DOROTHY REES (11th Gen.), daughter of Deborah (Gorman) Rees and Rev. Emory J. Rees, born April 15, 1910. Married C. Hagenson. Children born:
1. Karen Jean Hagenson, born Jan. 20, 1936.
2. Keith Roald Hagenson, born April 7, 1937.

———————x———————

ZOA GORMAN (10th Gen.), daughter of Thomas C. and Sarah M. Parris Larue Gorman, born May 20, 1880. She lives at Urbana, Ill., and has kindly furnished the following information:

Her mother's father, William Parris (her grandfather), was one of the first settlers of Vermillion County, Illinois; her mother was the seventh child born into the family, so it must have been 1826 or 1827 that he settled at Muncie, Illinois. Later on, in 1850, he moved to a farm three miles north of Ogden, Illinois, and was one of the first settlers there; some of this farm remains in their family to this day.

She further states, that her grandfather Gorman was also one of the early settlers of Vermillion County, Illinois, and that the house which he built, and lived in, was still standing up to two years ago (present date 1941).

She writes that her sister, Deborah Gorman, who married Rev. Emory J. Rees, accompanied her husband as missionary to Natal, South Africa, in March of 1899. They were sent by the "Friend's Board" (Quaker Church); they stayed four years and were there during the Boer War.

Rev. Doctor and Mrs. Rees went to British East Africa in the spring of 1904. They retired from the missionary service in 1926. They were in East Africa during the World War, and crossed the ocean eight times.

Rev. Rees translated the New Testament in the "Luragoli" language, and is now engaged in revising a translation of the Old Bible prepared by another missionary.

The son of Rev. Emory J. Rees and Deborah Gorman Rees, Dr. E. Keith Rees, was born at Maragoli, British East Africa; he is now associate professor of German at Westmont College, Los Angeles, Calif.

———————x———————

SARAH E. CARDIFF (11th Gen.), daughter of Orpha J. (Gorman) Cardiff and H. V. Cardiff, was born May 25, 1888. Married J. L. Stayton. Children born:
1. Oren Stayton, born April 30, 1909.
2. Grace Stayton, born June 25, 1915.

———————x———————

OREN STAYTON (12th Gen.), son of Sarah E. (Cardiff) Stayton and J. L. Stayton, born April 30, 1909. Married ——— Children born:
1. John Stayton, born Oct., 1940.
2. Jane Stayton, born Oct., 1940.

———————x———————

GRACE STAYTON (12th Gen.), daughter of Sarah E. (Cardiff) Stayton and J. L. Stayton, born June 25, 1915. Married ——— Chappelle. Children born:
1. Janet E. Chappelle, born June 25, 1932.

2. Sharon E. Chappelle, born Aug., 1937.

ALBERT P. CARDIFF (11th Gen.), son of Orpha J. (Gorman) Cardiff and H. P. Cardiff, born Nov. 25, 1889. Married Pearl Davis. Children born:
1. Leon Cardiff, born March 27, 1913.
2. Albert Gorman Cardiff, born July 2, 1921.

ETHEL CARDIFF (11th Gen.), daughter of Orpha J. (Gorman) Cardiff and H. P. Cardiff, born Sept. 26, 1892. Married W. I. Bell.

DEBORAH CARDIFF (11th Gen.), daughter of Orpha J. (Gorman) Cardiff and H. P. Cardiff, born Nov. 17, 1898. Married D. Garver. Children born:
1. Vontella E. Garver, born March 1, 1916.

LEON CARDIFF (12th Gen.), son of Albert P. Cardiff and Pearl (Davis) Cardiff, born March 27, 1913. Married ———. Children born:
1. Albert Cardiff, born June, 1936.
2. Pearl T. Cardiff, born July 2, 1937.
3. David L. Cardiff, born ————, 1939.

MAGGIE CRAYNE (11th Gen.), daughter of Anna L. (Gorman) Crayne and Guilford Crayne, was born June 11, 1887. Married, Dec. 24, 1917, H. D. Oakley. Children born:
1. Dwight Oakley, born Oct. 23, 1911. Married Velva Stevenson.
2. Dorothy Oakley, born Dec. 24, 1913.
3. Mary Oakley, born March 1, 1916. Married (1934) G. Stamphill.
4. Lafayette Oakley, born Aug. 26, 1918. Married (1940) Hazel Hasty.
5. Daniel Gorman Oakley, born Nov. 26, 1924.

DWIGHT OAKLEY (12th Gen.), son of Maggie (Crayne) Oakley and H. D. Oakley, born Oct. 23, 1911. Married Velva Stevenson. Children born:
1. Leverne Oakley.

DOROTHY OAKLEY (12th Gen.), daughter of Maggie (Crayne) Oakley and H. D. Oakley, born Dec. 24, 1913. Married ———— Austin. Children born:
1. Larry Austin, born 1932.
2. Gene Knight Austin, born Jan., 1935.
3. Francis Austin, born April, 1938.

MARY OAKLEY (12th Gen.), daughter of Maggie (Crayne) Oakley and H. D. Oakley, born March 1, 1916. Married G. Stamphill, in 1934. No issue.

LAFAYETTE OAKLEY (12th Gen.), son of Maggie (Crayne) Oakley and H. D. Oakley, born Aug. 26, 1918. Married Hazel Hasty, ————, 1940.

THOMAS CRAYNE (11th Gen.), son of Anna L. (Gorman) Crayne and Guilford Crayne, born May 4, 1891. Married, July 1, 1917, Mabel Traxyler. Children born:
1. Elmer G. Crayne, born Oct. 15, 1920.
2. Myrle C. Crayne, born July 8, 1923.
3. Willis M. Crayne, born Oct. 23, 1925.
4. Jerry W. Crayne, born Oct. 25, 1933.

CHARLES CRAYNE (11th Gen.), son of Anna L. (Gorman) Crayne and Guilford Crayne, born May 20, 1894. Married Lena Russell, Oct. 26, 1919. Children born:
1. Ruby M. Crayne, born Nov. 11, 1921.
2. Florence M. Crayne, born July, 1923.
3. Charles H. Crayne, born March 14, 1926.
4. Martha Sue Crayne, born Jan. 7, 1934.

RUBY M. CRAYNE (12th Gen.), daughter of Charles Crayne and Lena (Russell) Crayne, born Nov. 11, 1921. Married ———— Milem. Children born:
1. Jule Ruby Milem, born May 14, 1938.
2. Donale Ray Milem, born April 30, 1940.

FLORENCE M. CRAYNE (12th Gen.), daughter of Charles Crayne and Lena (Russell) Crayne, born July, 1923. Married ———— DeVault. Children born:
1. Charles H. DeVault, born March 14, 1926.

2. Martha Sue DeVault, born Jan. 7, 1934.
3. James E. DeVault, born Nov. 7, 1939.

---x---

JOHN B. GORMAN (9th Gen.), son of Deborah Cushman Gorman and James Gorman, born July 7, 1842; died Dec. 22, 1928. Married, Dec. 24, 1865, America Jane Norton, born Dec. 24, 1844. Children born to Deborah Cushman Gorman and James Gorman:
1. Emma Gorman, born 1866; died in infancy.
2. Ella Gorman, born April 20, 1867; died in 1938.
3. Mattie Gorman, born 1868; died in infancy.
4. Dora Gorman, born Feb. 3, 1870.
5. James Gorman, born Oct. 7, 1871.
6. Minnie Gertrude Gorman, born Feb. 13, 1873.
7. Lucy Mae Gorman, died in infancy.
8. Nellie Pearl Gorman, born Aug. 17, 1885.

---x---

ELLA GORMAN (10th Gen.), daughter of John B. Gorman and America Jane (Norton) Gorman, born April 20, 1867; died in 1938. Married, Aug. 8, 1896, Jonathan Mendenhall. Children born:
1. Ralph Mendenhall, born Oct. 30, 1897.
2. Charity Jane Mendenhall, born Feb. 23, 1899.
3. Minnie Emily Mendenhall, born July 2, 1901.
4. Carl M. Mendenhall, born April 24, 1903.
5. Mary Dorothy Mendenhall, born Sept. 5, 1905; died Nov. 4, 1933.
6. Lawrence N. Mendenhall, born June 7, 1908. } Twins.
7. Lillian Nellie Mendenhall, born June 7, 1908. }

---x---

RALPH MENDENHALL (11th Gen.), son of Ella (Gorman) Mendenhall and Jonathan Mendenhall, born Oct. 30, 1897. Married, June 11, 1922, Mabel Lyman. No issue.

---x---

CHARITY JANE MENDENHALL (11th Gen.), daughter of Ella (Gorman) Mendenhall and Jonathan Mendenhall, born Feb. 23, 1899. Married, July 23, 1929, Orville DeHaven. No issue.

---x---

MINNIE EMILY MENDENHALL (11th Gen.), daughter of Ella (Gorman) Mendenhall and Jonathan Mendenhall, born July 2, 1901. Married, Dec. 24, 1926, Paul Propst. Children born:

1. Wanda May Propst, born May 18, 1928.

———x———

CARL M. MENDENHALL (11th Gen.), son of Ella (Gorman) Mendenhall and Jonathan Mendenhall, born April 24, 1903. Married, March 3, 1934, Martha Driskell. Children born:
1. Donna Lee Mendenhall, born Dec. 16, 1934.

———x———

MARY DOROTHY MENDENHALL (11th Gen.), son of Ella (Gorman) Mendenhall and Jonathan Mendenhall, born Sept. 5, 1905; died Nov. 4, 1933. Married, Nov. 29, 1929, Everett Offutt. Children born:
1. Doris Jean Offutt, born Sept. 6, 1930.

———x———

LILLIAN NELLIE MENDENHALL (11th Gen.), daughter of Ella (Gorman) Mendenhall and Jonathan Mendenhall, born June 7, 1908. Married, June 17, 1929, Walter Hess. Children born:
1. Mary Jane Hess, born Feb. 2, 1937.

———x———

DORA GORMAN (10th Gen.), daughter of John B. Gorman and America Jane (Norton) Gorman, born Feb. 3, 1870. Married, July 4, 1892, Joseph E. Doughty. Children born:
1. Ruth Doughty.
2. John Doughty.
3. Paul Doughty.
4. Mary Doughty.

———x———

JAMES GORMAN (10th Gen.), son of John B. Gorman and America Jane (Norton) Gorman, born Oct. 7, 1871. Married, Sept. 21, 1899, Annie Banta. Children born:
1. Ernest Gorman, born Dec. 18, 1900; died Dec. 31, 1900.
2. Thelma Gorman, born July 15, 1903.
3. Elsie Gorman, born April 26, 1906.

———x———

THELMA GORMAN (11th Gen.), daughter of James Gorman and Anna (Banta) Gorman, born July 15, 1903. Married, Dec. 6, 1922, Paul Ritter. Children born:
1. Anna Jane Ritter, born Dec. 29, 1923.
2. Ervin Ritter, born Nov. 7, 1924; died Jan. 26, 1929.
3. Mearle Gorman Ritter, born May 8, 1926.
4. Max Paul Ritter, born Dec. 30, 1929.
5. Connie Jo Ritter, born Sept. 10, 1937.

CUSHMAN GENEALOGY AND GENERAL HISTORY   335

ELSIE GORMAN (11th Gen.), daughter of James Gorman and Anna (Banta) Gorman, born April 26, 1906. Married, Jan. 12, 1925, Bert O. Callahan. Children born:
 1. Esther Virginia Callahan, born April 4, 1926; died March 19, 1929.
 2. Howard Lee Callahan, born March 9, 1930.
 3. Gilbert Ray Callahan, born March 10, 1932.
 4. Linda Janet Callahan, born Dec. 9, 1933.
 5. Gary Deane Callahan, born Aug. 21, 1938.

---x---

MINNIE GERTRUDE GORMAN (10th Gen.), daughter of John B. Gorman and America Jane (Norton) Gorman, born Feb. 13, 1873, at Fithian, Vermillion County, Ill. Married, Sept. 29, 1904, John Arnold Callaway, of Brown County, Texas, born Nov. 15, 1857; died Oct. 17, 1930. Children born:
 1. James Gorman Callaway, born Aug. 13, 1905, at Woodward County, Okla.
 2. Minnie Callaway, born Feb. 11, 1907, at Woodward County, Okla.
 3. Fred Dickerson Callaway, born Aug. 17, 1909, at Woodward County, Okla.
 4. Nellie Luella Callaway, born March 28, 1911, at Woods County, Okla.
 5. Enid America Callaway, born April 10, 1913, at Woods County, Okla.
 6. Arnold Lafayette Callaway, born May 15, 1917, at Woods County, Okla.

---x---

JAMES GORMAN CALLAWAY (11th Gen.), son of Minnie Gertrude (Gorman) Callaway and John Arnold Callaway, born Aug. 13, 1905, in Woodward County, Okla. Married, Aug. 22, 1931, Naomi Laverne Hutchinson, in Woods County, Okla., born Feb. 24, 1912. Children born:
 1. Mary Lynn Callaway, born July 26, 1934.
 2. Jimmie Darrell Callaway, born Feb. 10, 1936.
 3. Naomi Kay Callaway, born Nov. 6, 1939.

---x---

FRED DICKERSON CALLAWAY (11th Gen.), son of Minnie Gertrude (Gorman) Callaway and John Arnold Callaway, born

Aug. 17, 1907, in Woodward County, Okla. Married, Dec. 12, 1932, Jean Ingelow McNeely, born Aug. 12, 1914. Children born:
1. Patricia Jean Callaway, born July 11, 1934.
2. Jo Anne Callaway, born Sept. 20, 1936.
3. Minerva Lue Callaway, born Feb. 10, 1940.

———x———

ENID AMERICA CALLAWAY (11th Gen.), daughter of Minnie Gertrude (Gorman) Callaway and John Arnold Callaway, born April 10, 1913. Married, Jan. 16, 1937, in Oklahoma City, Okla., Delos George Reynolds, born Dec. 28, 1914. Children born:
1. Rex Arnold Reynolds, born Oct. 14, 1938.
2. Ray Neil Reynolds, born Jan. 19, 1940.

———x———

NELLIE PEARL GORMAN (10th Gen.), daughter of John B. Gorman and America Jane (Norton) Gorman, born Aug. 17, 1885. Married Alvin Floid Andrews, born Nov. 16, 1891. Children born:
1. Floid Gorman Andrews, born Oct. 4, 1916.
2. Lloyd Wilson Andrews, born June 28, 1918.
3. Clifford Brooks Andrews, born Dec. 13, 1919.
4. Lynn Ernest Andrews, born Nov. 19, 1921.
5. Phillip Royal Andrews, born Jan. 31, 1924.
6. Jean Jackson Andrews, born June 21, 1926.

———x———

FLOID GORMAN ANDREWS (11th Gen.), son of Nellie Pearl (Gorman) Andrews and Alvin Floid Andrews, born Oct. 4, 1916. Married, March 19, 1939, Mary Koch, born Sept. 25, 1914. No issue.

———x———

JOSEPH HILT GORMAN (9th Gen.), son of Deborah Cushman Gorman and James Gorman, born Jan. 17, 1847; died May 6, 1926. He was enrolled in Company K., 150th Illinois Regiment and served as guard for Northern prison camps. He married Emma Foster, born Feb. 16, 1854; died May 12, 1931. They had no children, but raised John G. Sargeant.

———x———

MARY ELIZABETH GORMAN (9th Gen.), daughter of Deborah Cushman Gorman and James Gorman, born Feb. 23, 1849;

died Nov. 8, 1872. Married John McGee. One child born:
1. Hattie McGee, born about Oct. 16, 1872.

―――――x―――――

HATTIE MCGEE (10th Gen.), daughter of Mary Elizabeth (Gorman) McGee and John McGee, born about Oct. 16, 1872. Married Emory Bowman. No issue.

MILBERT GORMAN (9th Gen.), son of Deborah Cushman Gorman and James Gorman, born June 8, 1851. Married Sarah Marie Harter. Children born:
1. Hattie Gorman, born 1875.
2. Cora Alice Gorman, born March 8, 1877.
3. Sarah Catharine Gorman, born April 14, 1879.
4. James Henry Gorman, born Sept. 14, 1881.
5. Leander Wm. Gorman, born May 23, 1885.
6. Bertha Gorman.
7. Benjamin Harrison Gorman.
8. Dean Gorman.

―――――x―――――

CORA ALICE GORMAN (10th Gen.), daughter of Milbert Gorman and Sarah Marie (Harter) Gorman, born March 8, 1877. Married, Oct. 10, 1897, Elmer Florence Plymire. Children born:
1. Clarence James Plymire, born July 28, 1898.

―――――x―――――

CLARENCE JAMES PLYMIRE (11th Gen.), son of Cora Alice (Gorman) Plymire and Elmer Florence Plymire, born July 28, 1898. Married Florence Smith June 16, 1920, born July 20, 1900. Children born:
1. Cora Anna Plymire, born Dec. 15, 1921.
2. Margaret May Plymire, born May 3, 1923.
3. Jane Eleanore Plymire, born March 6, 1925.
4. James Elmer Plymire, born Aug. 4, 1926.
5. David G. Plymire, born Oct. 15, 1933.

―――――x―――――

SARAH CATHARINE GORMAN (10th Gen.), daughter of Milbert Gorman and Sarah Marie (Harter) Gorman, born April 14, 1879. Married James W. Boots. Children born:
1. Hazel Gorman Boots.

LEANDER WILLIAM GORMAN (10th Gen.), son of Milbert Gorman and Sarah Maria (Harter) Gorman, born May 23, 1885. Married, Oct. 4, 1905, Ida Baker, of Blue Island, Ill. Children born:
1. Marie Gorman, born June 13, 1906.
2. Clelland Gorman, born Dec. 25, 1908.
3. Kenneth Gorman, born June 27, 1915.
4. Virgil Gorman, born Nov. 13, 1922.
5. Robert Lee Gorman, born Oct. 3, 1926.

Leander died July 28, 1940. He and his son, Kenneth, both served as Elders of Blue Island Christian Church. Leander met death in an automobile accident, at which time, his son, Kenneth, was taking him to a Sunday School picnic.

———————x———————

MARIE GORMAN (11th Gen.), daughter of Leander William Gorman and Ida (Baker) Gorman, born June 13, 1906. Married Andrew Frederico. Children born:
1. Leon Frederico, born Dec. 7, 1925.
2. Ruby Aileen Frederico, born Oct. 3, 1926.
3. Elizabeth Marie Frederico, born Jan. 3, 1927; died Jan. 15, 1940.
4. Ida Leah Frederico, born Feb. 20, 1930.
5. Norma Maxine Frederico, born April 16, 1933.
6. Milbert Gordon Frederico, born June 6, 1935.
7. Frank Eldon Frederico, born Jan. 29, 1940.

———————x———————

CLELLAND GORMAN (11th Gen.), son of Leander William Gorman and Ida (Baker) Gorman, born Dec. 25, 1908. Married, April 16, 1933, Mary Danner. Children born:
1. Carol Gorman, born Aug. 9, 1934.
2. Paul Gorman, born Sept. 14, 1938.

———————x———————

ISAAC CUSHMAN (8th Gen.), son of Thomas Cushman and Elizabeth (Jenkins) Cushman, born May 20, 1813; died March 7, 1898. Married, July 16, 1842, Sarah Jane Prickett, born Feb. 4, 1821; died Jan 30, 1911. Children born:
1. Louisa Cushman, born March 28, 1843; died Aug. 18, 1860.
2. Nancy Cushman, born Nov. 20, 1844; died Aug. 17, 1851.
3. John Frazy Cushman, born March 2, 1847; died Aug. 30, 1934.

CUSHMAN GENEALOGY AND GENERAL HISTORY   339

4. Diana Cushman, born Sept. 3, 1852; died Oct. 27, 1934.
5. Mary Cushman, born July 1, 1857.

———————x———————

JOHN FRAZY CUSHMAN (9th Gen.), son of Isaac Cushman and Sarah Jane (Prickett) Cushman, born March 2, 1847; died Aug. 30, 1934. Married Mary Catharine Moon. Children born:
1. William Isaac Cushman, born Jan. 21, 1873.
2. Sarah Hetti Cushman, born Feb. 14, 1875.
3. Harvey Kyle Cushman, born Jan. 24, 1877.
4. Anna Mary Cushman, born Aug. 18, 1881; died Nov. 3, 1918.

Mary Catharine (Moon) Cushman died Feb. 13, 1889. John Frazy Cushman married, secondly, June 30, 1890, Mary Jane Price. Children born to second marriage:
1. Ila F. Cushman, born April 17, 1891; died Dec. 28, 1891.
2. John E. Cushman, born June 1, 1893; died Sept. 1, 1901.
3. James Russell Cushman, born March 8, 190—.

Mary Jane (Price) Cushman died Nov. 18, 1929.

———————x———————

WILLIAM ISAAC CUSHMAN (10th Gen.), son of John Frazy Cushman and Mary Catharine (Moon) Cushman, born Jan. 21, 1873. Married, Dec. 9, 1894, Mary Alice Wiggins. Children born:
1. Julia Mildred Cushman, born 1895.
2. Catharine Melroy Cushman, born Dec. 8, 1907.

———————x———————

JULIA MILDRED CUSHMAN (11th Gen.), daughter of William Isaac Cushman and Mary Alice (Wiggins) Cushman, born 1895. Married, Dec. —, 1917, Raymond L. Johnson. Children born:
1. Marietta Johnson, born Jan. 6, 1919.
2. William Johnson, born Dec. 3, 1923.

———————x———————

CATHARINE MELROY CUSHMAN (11th Gen.), daughter of William Isaac Cushman and Mary Alice (Wiggins) Cushman, born Dec. 8, 1907. Married, July ————, 1942, James Lynch.

———————x———————

SARAH HETTI CUSHMAN (10th Gen.), daughter of John Frazy Cushman and Mary Catharine (Moon) Cushman, born

Feb. 14, 1875. Married Daniel Sitton. Children born:
1. Irene Sitton.

IRENE SITTON (11th Gen.), daughter of Sarah Hetti Cushman Sitton and Daniel Sitton. Married, Sept. 24, 1915, Floyd Brown. Children born:
1. Eugene Brown, born Oct. 5, 1916; died Nov. 7, 1922.
2. Russel Melvin Brown, born Sept. 18, 1918.
3. Richard Calvin Brown, born Feb. 17, 1922.
4. Marjorie Edwina Brown, born April 29, 1926.
5. Edwin Leroy Brown, born Feb. 20, 1928.
6. Willadene Brown, born Aug. 7, 1930.

HARVEY KYLE CUSHMAN (10th Gen.), son of John Frazey Cushman and Mary Catharine (Moon) Cushman, born Jan. 24, 1877. Married, Aug. 8, 1897, Maggie Brown. Children born:
1. Ralph Cushman, born Jan. 1, 1905.

Maggie Brown Cushman died May 11, 1919, and Harvey Kyle Cushman married, secondly, Nov. 26, 1919, Nellie Fort.

RALPH CUSHMAN (11th Gen.), son of Harvey Kyle Cushman and Maggie (Brown) Cushman, born Jan. 1, 1905. Married, Dec. 29, 1932, Leone Ross. Children born:
1. Donald Ross Cushman, born May 27, 1934.
2. Peggy Anne Cushman, born April 9, 1937.

ANNA MARY CUSHMAN (10th Gen.), daughter of John Frazy Cushman and Mary Catharine (Moon) Cushman, born Aug. 18, 1881; died Nov. 3, 1918. Married, April 3, 1905, Edward Shull. Children born:
1. Blanche Shull, born Feb. 17, 1906.
2. Bernice Shull, born Feb. 17, 1907.
3. Frances Shull, born May 8, 1908.
4. Laila Shull, born May 24, 1910.
5. Gladys Shull, born Aug. 26, 1913.

BLANCHE SHULL (11th Gen.), daughter of Anna Mary Cushman Shull and Edward Shull, born Feb. 17, 1906. Married Jesse Combs. Children born:
1. Hugh Lemoine Combs, born ————, 1936.

CUSHMAN GENEALOGY AND GENERAL HISTORY   341

BERNICE SHULL (11th Gen.), daughter of Anna Mary Cushman Shull and Edward Shull, born Feb. 17, 1907. Married Richard Martindale. Children born:
1. Lehla Shull Martindale.
Bernice Shull married, secondly, Aug., 1941, Edward Pruitt, of Indianapolis, Ind.

———x———
FRANCES SHULL (11th Gen.), daughter of Anna Mary Cushman Shull and Edward Shull, born May 8, 1908. Married Loren Albae.

———x———
LAILA SHULL (11th Gen.), daughter of Anna Mary Cushman Shull and Edward Shull, born May 24, 1910. Married, ———, 1942, Charles George.

———x———
JAMES RUSSEL CUSHMAN (10th Gen.), son of John Frazy Cushman and Mary Jane (Price) Cushman, born March 8, 1900. Married, April, 1919, Ethel Johnson.

———x———
DIANA CUSHMAN (9th Gen.), daughter of Isaac Cushman and Sarah Jane (Prickett) Cushman, born Sept. 3, 1852; died Oct., 27, 1934. Married, Dec. 25, 1871, John Houk. Children born:
1. Maud E. Houk, born Oct. 13, 1873.
2. Charles Houk, born Dec., 1875; died Feb. 22, 1877.

———x———
MAUD E. HOUK (11th Gen.), daughter of Diana Cushman Houk and John Houk, born Oct. 13, 1873. Married, in 1895, John Wiggins. Children born:
1. Bessie E. Wiggins, born Sept., 1895.
2. Ione Wiggins, born Sept., 1896; died April, 1928.

———x———
BESSIE E. WIGGINS (12th Gen.), daughter of Maud E. (Houk) Wiggins and John Wiggins, born Sept., 1895. Married Ernest Ellingwood. Children born:
1. John O. Ellingwood, born Jan. 24, 1924.
2. Frances Ellingwood, born May 19, 1927.
3. Elizabeth Ellingwood, born Aug., 1930.

———x———
IONE WIGGINS (12th Gen.), daughter of Maud E. (Houk) Wiggins and John Wiggins, born Sept., 1896; died April,

1928. Married, Dec. 24, 1917, Donald Chappel. Children born:
1. Maudellen Chappel, born Nov. 24, 1918.
2. Maybelle Chappel, born Feb., 1920.
3. Aaron Chappel, born Sept., 1921.
4. Marylee Chappel, born Sept., 1923.
5. Glenn Lloyd Chappel, born Sept., 1925.

―――――x―――――

MARY CUSHMAN (9th Gen.), daughter of Isaac Cushman and Sarah Jane (Prickett) Cushman, born July 1, 1857. Married, March 15, 1876, William Bolander. Children born:
1. Sarah Frances Bolander, born April 7, 1877.
2. Guy Elmore Bolander, born June 8, 1887.

―――――x―――――

GUY ELMORE BOLANDER (10th Gen.), son of Mary Cushman Bolander and William Bolander, born June 8, 1887. Married, March 11, 1908, Mattie Alford. Children born:
1. Floyd Alford Bolander, born Feb. 13, 1910.
2. Marthellen Bolander, born March 11, 1917.
3. Stuart Hervey Bolander, born May 12, 1920.

―――――x―――――

MARTHELLEN BOLANDER (11th Gen.), daughter of Guy Elmore Bolander and Mattie Alford Bolander, born March 11, 1917. Married, May 5, 1940, Robert Hogue.

―――――x―――――

STUART BOLANDER (11th Gen.), son of Guy Elmore Bolander and Mattie Alford Bolander, born May 12, 1920. Married, March 23, 1940, Helen Sylvester.

―――――x―――――

RACHEL CUSHMAN (8th Gen.), daughter of Thomas Cushman and Elizabeth (Jenkins) Cushman, born July 30, 1815; died Jan. 29, 1905. Married, March 18, 1841, George Hoagland, born May 15, 1802; died 1892. Children born:
1. Angeline Hoagland, born March 14, 1842; died in childhood.
2. Mary Elizabeth Hoagland, born May 12, 1844; died in 1884.
3. Jonathan Cushman Hoagland, born April 24, 1846.
4. Minnah Simason Hoagland, born March 2, 1849; died Jan. 30, 1883.
5. William Hoagland, born April 30, 1854; died in 1855.

MARY ELIZABETH HOAGLAND (9th Gen.), daughter of Rachel Cushman Hoagland and George Hoagland, born May 12, 1844; died in 1884. Married John Barcus, who died in 1908. Children born:
1. James William Barcus, born Oct. 18, 1861; died Feb. 26, 1942.
2. Charles Morton Barcus, born May 23, 1866.
3. Anna Barcus, born in 1867; died in childhood.
4. George Warner Barcus, born April 17, 1869.
5. Luella Barcus, born May 19, 1875; died April, 1904.

―――――――x―――――――

JAMES WILLIAM BARCUS (10th Gen.), son of Mary Elizabeth (Hoagland) Barcus and John Barcus, born Oct. 18, 1861; died Feb. 26, 1942. Married, Nov. 27, 1888, Marie Trusheim, born July 3, 1864. Children born:
1. George Benjamin Barcus, born Sept. 18, 1889.
2. Adaline Beatrice Barcus, born Sept. 4, 1891.
3. Lawrence William Barcus, born June 29, 1896.

―――――――x―――――――

GEORGE BENJAMIN BARCUS (11th Gen.), son of James William Barcus and Marie (Trusheim) Barcus, born Sept. 18, 1889. Married, 1912, Candace McCormick. Children born:
1. Candace Marie Barcus, born June 24, 1913; died June 12, 1933.
2. Katharine Elizabeth Barcus, born Feb., 1917.
3. Robert Reesman Barcus, born April 23, 1919.
4. Ben Philip Barcus, born Nov. 3, 1922.

George Benjamin Barcus married, secondly, Ruth Righter Reick Young, in 1935. No issue.

―――――――x―――――――

CANDACE MARIE BARCUS (12th Gen.), daughter of George Benjamin Barcus and Candace (McCormick) Barcus, born June 24, 1913; died June 12, 1933. Married Joseph Cleggett Wiles. Children born:
1. Rachel Ann Wiles, born June 5, 1933.

―――――――x―――――――

KATHARINE ELIZABETH BARCUS (12th Gen.), daughter of George Benjamin Barcus and Candace (McCormick) Barcus, born Feb., 1917. Married Truman Knutson. Children born:
1. Candace Ann Knutson, born May 26, 1938.

ADALINE BEATRICE BARCUS (11th Gen.), daughter of James William Barcus and Marie (Trusheim) Barcus, born Sept. 4, 1891. Married, first, Clarence Brooks, now deceased. Children born:
1. William Brooks, born Feb. 22, ——.
She married, secondly, in 1918, Jesse Bennett. Children born:
1. Sylvia Marie Bennett, born July 8, 1920.
2. Louise Bennett, born March 11, 1922.
3. Jesse Bennett, Jr., born Dec. 9, 1925.
4. Margarite Melvina Bennett, born May 17, 1928.

———x———

SYLVIA MARIE BENNETT (12th Gen.), daughter of Adaline Beatrice (Barcus) Bennett and Jesse Bennett, born July 8, 1920. Married, ————, 1938, Lester Ellis. Children born:
1. Carol Marie Ellis, born March 29, 1942.

———x———

LAWRENCE WILLIAM BARCUS (11th Gen.), son of James William Barcus and Marie (Trusheim) Barcus, born June 29, 1896. Married Anna Trill. Children born:
1. Florence Elmanda Barcus, born Feb. 27, 1926.

———x———

CHARLES MORTON BARCUS (10th Gen.), son of Mary Elizabeth (Hoagland) Barcus and John Barcus, born May 23, 1866. Married, Oct. 23, 1890, Bessie Lee Cox, born March 30, 1871. Children born:
1. William Oscar Barcus, born Nov. 22, 1891.
2. Infant son not named.
3. Bonnie May Barcus, born Nov. 30, 1894; died Dec. 25, 1923.
4. Chauncey Hobert Barcus, born March 14, 1896.
5. Rolla Dewey Barcus, born Jan. 10, 1898.
6. Ollie Daisy Marie Barcus, born Oct. 18, 1900.
7. Charles Ward Barcus, born June 22, 1902.
8. Ann Frances Barcus, born March 15, 1905.
9. Harold Eugene Barcus, born Oct. 18,. 1910.

———x———

WILLIAM OSCAR BARCUS (11th Gen.), son of Charles Morton Barcus and Bessie Lee (Cox) Barcus, born Nov. 22, 1891. Married, Dec. 1, 1918, Lucy Julie Culpin, at Sioux Falls,

South Dakota. Children born:
1. Helen Luciella Barcus, born Sept. 4, 1920, at Lincreek, Mo.
2. John Martin Barcus, born Aug. 5, 1922, at Springfield, Ill.; died Nov. 22, 1923, at Rhinelander, Wis.
3. Bonnie Lee Barcus, born Dec. 3, 1923, at Rhinelander, Wis.
4. Betty Lou Barcus, born Oct. 26, 1925, at Mankato, Minn.
5. Donald Raymond Barcus, born May 5, 1928, at Minneapolis, Minn.
6. Wanetta June Barcus, born June 17, 1930, at Lemmon, S. Dakota; died April 7, 1931.

―――――x―――――

HELEN LUCIELLA BARCUS (12th Gen.), daughter of William Oscar Barcus and Lucy Julie (Culpin) Barcus, born Sept. 4, 1920. Married, March 30, 1937, at Urbana, Ill., Neil Harvey Burgen, born May 1, 1915. Children born:
1. Sharon Lee Burgen, born Nov. 20, 1939.

―――――x―――――

CHAUNCEY HOBERT BARCUS (11th Gen.), son of Charles Morton Barcus and Bessie Lee (Cox) Barcus, was born March 14, 1896. Married Edna Rose, born March 10, 1901, at Durham, England. Children born:
1. Chauncey Harold Barcus, born Sept. 9, 1921.
2. Ethel Bernice Barcus, born July 16, 1924.
3. Francis Earl Barcus, born Feb. 1, 1927.
4. Armetta Claudine Barcus, born April 1, 1931.
5. Shirley May Barcus, born May 5, 1933; died Jan. 21, 1934.

―――――x―――――

ROLLA DEWEY BARCUS (11th Gen.), son of Charles Morton Barcus and Bessie Lee (Cox) Barcus, born Jan. 10, 1898. Married, Jan. 31, 1925, Dora Lee Henegar, born July 16, 1906. Children born:
1. Virginia Lee Barcus, born Jan. 23, 1926.
2. Dora June Barcus, born July 10, 1929.
3. Norma Jean Barcus, born Jan. 31, 1931.
4. Richard Dale Barcus, born Dec. 15, 1933.
5. Ronald Dean Barcus, born Oct. 6, 1935.

OLLIE DAISY MARIE BARCUS (11th Gen.), daughter of Charles Morton Barcus and Bessie Lee (Cox) Barcus, born Oct. 18, 1900; died July 7, 1935. Married Sylvester Queen, born Feb. 6, 1890. Children born:
1. Walter Eugene Queen, born Aug. 31, 1922.
2. Joseph Charles Queen, born Oct. 28, 1923.
3. Billie Louise Queen, born Jan. 18, 1926.

———————x———————

CHARLES WARD BARCUS (11th Gen.), son of Charles Morton Barcus and Bessie Lee (Cox) Barcus, born June 22, 1902. Married, July 4, 1925, Cecil Kapp, born June 5, 1897. Children born:
1. Frances Lucille Barcus, born Aug. 1, 1928.
2. Barbara Alleene Barcus, born Oct. 16, 1929.
3. Ward Earl Barcus, born May 5, 1937.

———————x———————

ANN FRANCES BARCUS (11th Gen.), daughter of Charles Morton Barcus and Bessie Lee (Cox) Barcus, born March 15, 1905. Married, Aug. 21, 1939, Howard Olliverson. No issue. They adopted one daughter, Patricia Ann Howard.

———————x———————

HAROLD EUGENE BARCUS (11th Gen.), son of Charles Morton Barcus and Bessie Lee (Cox) Barcus, born Oct. 18, 1910. Unmarried.

———————x———————

GEORGE WARNER BARCUS (10th Gen.), son of Mary Elizabeth (Hoagland) Barcus and John Barcus, born April 17, 1869. Married, Dec. 27, 1896, Nora Etta Courtney. Children born:
1. Sylvia Ada Barcus, born March 6, 1898.
2. Russel Ethelbert Barcus, born Nov. 6, 1900.
3. Eula Amanda Barcus, born July 17, 1903.
4. Rachel Elizabeth Barcus, born Dec. 28, 1905.
5. Kenneth Lloyd Barcus, born Feb. 12, 1907; died March, 1914.
6. Georgetta Barcus, born March 29, 1910.
7. Virgil William Barcus, born Sept. 30, 1912.
8. Earl Courtney Barcus, born Sept. 13, 1915.
9. Wallace Frazier Barcus, born June 3, 1917.

SYLVIA ADA BARCUS (11th Gen.), daughter of George Warner Barcus and Nora Etta (Courtney) Barcus, born March 6, 1898. Married, June 6, 1926, Melvin Duerre. Children born:
1. Duanne Eugene Duerre, born Sept. 20, 1927.
2. Kenneth Harold Duerre, born Dec. 8, 1931.
3. Melvin Gerald Duerre, born March 8, 1933.
4. Danny Jim Duerre, born Oct. 26, 1939.

RUSSEL ETHELBERT BARCUS (11th Gen.), son of George Warner Barcus and Nora Etta (Courtney) Barcus, born Nov. 6, 1900. Married, Nov. 12, 1921, Dagmar Earsen. Children born:
1. Frances Lorain Barcus, born May 11, 1925; died June, 1931.
2. Richard Elmer Barcus, born Oct. 6, 1932.

EULA AMANDA BARCUS (11th Gen.), daughter of George Warner Barcus and Nora Etta (Courtney) Barcus, born July 17, 1903. Married, June 1, 1932, Lee Steeves, who died Dec. 28, 1939. Children born:
1. Joan Yvonne Steeves, born June 25, 1935.

RACHEL ELIZABETH BARCUS (11th Gen.), daughter of George Warner Barcus and Nora Etta (Courtney) Barcus, born Dec. 28, 1905. Married, March 21, 1926, Leslie Aune. Children born:
1. Cecil Ross Aune, born Aug. 1, 1927.
2. Carol Audrey Aune, born June 19, 1931.

GEORGETTA BARCUS (11th Gen.), daughter of George Warner Barcus and Nora Etta (Courtney) Barcus, born March 29, 1910. Married, July 9, 1937, Vaughn Ehlers. No issue.

VIRGIL WILLIAM BARCUS (11th Gen.), son of George Warner Barcus and Nora Etta (Courtney) Barcus, born Sept. 30, 1912. Married, Aug. 8, 1936, Margie Engl. Children born:
1. Virgie Mae Barcus, born Dec. 9, 1938.
2. Velva Lee Barcus, born March 27, 1940.

LUELLA BARCUS (10th Gen.), daughter of Mary Elizabeth (Hoagland) Barcus and John Barcus, born May 19, 1875; died April, 1904. Married, Jan. 14, 1904, Joseph Brazil. No issue.

JONATHAN CUSHMAN HOAGLAND (9th Gen.), son of Rachel Cushman Hoagland and George Hoagland, born April 24, 1846; died March 6, 1913. Married, Dec. 24, 1874, Rebecca Jane Sanders, born Jan. 31, 1851; died April 21, 1920. Children born:
1. Rosa Ellen Hoagland, born Sept. 28, 1875.
2. Mary Melvina Hoagland, born Sept. 5, 1878; died Sept. 21, 1898.
3. Flora Bell Hoagland, born Aug. 1, 1881; died Sept. 9, 1895.

---x---

ROSA ELLEN HOAGLAND (10th Gen.), daughter of Jonathan Cushman Hoagland and Rebecca Jane (Sanders) Hoagland, born Sept. 28, 1875. Married, Nov. 26, 1913, Albert R. Pence, born Sept. 26, 1873; died Sept. 27, 1924. Children born:
1. Francis Hoagland Pence, born Dec. 31, 1914; died April 26, 1928.
2. Anna Rose Pence, born Sept. 22, 1916.

---x---

LOUISA CUSHMAN (8th Gen.), daughter of Thomas Cushman and Elizabeth (Jenkins) Cushman, born Jan. 9, 1818, in Pennsylvania; died July 29, 1901. Married Azel Dearth. Children born:
1. John A. Dearth, died in Civil War.
2. William H. Dearth, born Jan. 1, 1844; died Feb. 2, 1894. Married Sarah Stein.
3. Hannah D. Dearth, born Sept. 20, 1845, in Pennsylvania; died June 3, 1928.

It is said that Louisa Cushman Dearth rode out to Illinois from Pennsylvania, on horseback, carrying her little son in her arms, to their new home. She and Azel Dearth are buried near Fithian, Ill.

---x---

HANNAH D. DEARTH (9th Gen.), daughter of Louise Cushman Dearth and Azel Dearth, born Sept. 20, 1845, in Pennsylvania; died June 3, 1928. Married Jesse Upperman. Children born:
1. Walter W. Upperman, born July 13, 1872.
2. Chloe E. Upperman, born Aug. 5, 1874.

3. Charity A. Upperman, born Jan. 7, 1877; died Sept. 28, 1936.
4. Sarah L. Upperman, born March 12, 1880; died Aug. 4, 1881.
5. Tabitha Upperman, born March 16, 1883, in Vermillion County, Ill., and still living Feb. 10, 1941, in Decatur, Ill.

———————x———————

WALTER W. UPPERMAN (10th Gen.), son of Hannah D. (Dearth) Upperman and Jesse Upperman, born July 13, 1872. Married Laura ————. Children born:
1. Genevieve Upperman, born Dec. 30, 1908.

———————x———————

CHLOE UPPERMAN (10th Gen.), daughter of Hannah D. (Dearth) Upperman and Jesse Upperman, born Aug. 5, 1874. Married ———— Cosant. Children born:
1. Evert Cosant, born Aug. 15, 1894.
2. Glen Cosant, born June 3, 1900; died Dec. 12, 1902.

———————x———————

TABITHA UPPERMAN (10th Gen.), daughter of Hannah D. (Dearth) Upperman and Jesse Upperman, born March 16, 1883. Married, June 4, 1899, Henry David Fletcher, born Feb. 3, 1876; died Aug. 10, 1933, at Decatur, Ill., and was buried at Cowden, Ill., in Mud Run Cemetery. Children born:
1. Cecil Duward Fletcher, born March 27, 1900, in Shelby County, Ill.
2. Jessie Chloe Fletcher, born Feb. 27, 1906.

———————x———————

CECIL DUWARD FLETCHER (11th Gen.), son of Tabitha (Upperman) Fletcher and Henry David Fletcher, born March 27, 1900. Married, April 7, 1919, Elsie K. Wallard, born June 30, 1900; died Aug. 21, 1938; buried at Price Cemetery, Oconee, Ill. Children born:
1. Cecil Eugene Fletcher, born June 16, 1923, at Shelby County, Ill.

Cecil Duward Fletcher married, secondly, Oct. 20, 1938, at St. Louis, Mo., Mamie G. Thompson, born May 27, 1904, by whom he has three step-children.

———————x———————

JESSIE CHLOE FLETCHER (11th Gen.), daughter of Tabitha (Upperman) Fletcher and Henry David Fletcher, born Feb.

27, 1906. Married, Nov. 30, 1929, Daniel Gafford, born Oct. 31, 1903, at Forrest, Tex. No issue.

———————x———————

MARYANN CUSHMAN (8th Gen.), daughter of Thomas Cushman and Elizabeth (Jenkins) Cushman, born Aug. 16, 1822, in Fayette County, Pa.; died Nov. 20, 1880. Married, Jan., 1845, John Henry Hiday. Children born:
1. Thomas Hiday, born Dec. 10, 1846; died March 14, 1923.
2. Rebecca Hiday, born Oct. 6, 1848; died Feb. 9, 1874.
3. Elizabeth Hiday, born Dec. 29, 1849; died, unmarried, Feb. 10, 1874.
4. John Hiday, born Oct. 5, 1852.
5. Melissa Ann Hiday, born Nov. 20, 1854; died May 25, 1865.
6. Charles William Hiday, born Dec. 9, 1855; died Feb. 5, 1856.
7. Mary Ellen Hiday, born Feb. 26, 1857; died April 27, 1913.
8. Calder Hiday, born April 9, 1858; died Nov. 30, 1940.
9. George Henry Hiday, born Oct. 19, 1859; died, unmarried, Feb. 26, 1933.
10. Louisa Hiday, born Dec. 17, 1860; died, unmarried, Nov. 15, 1886.
11. James Monroe Hiday, born Dec. 8, 1862; died Jan. 23, 1864.
12. Calvin Hiday, born Feb. 12, 1865; died March 17, 1933.

———————x———————

THOMAS HIDAY (9th Gen.), son of Maryann Cushman Hiday and John Henry Hiday, born Dec. 10, 1846; died March 14, 1923. Married, June 11, 1896, Annie M. Clements, in Pittsburgh, Pa. Children born:
1. Mary Lois Hiday, born July 20, 1900, at Anderson, Ind.

———————x———————

MARY LOIS HIDAY (10th Gen.), daughter of Thomas Hiday and Annie M. (Clements) Hiday, born July 20, 1900. Married, Sept. 9, 1930, Thomas Rees. Children born:
1. Margaret Louise Rees, born Nov. 29, 1932.

———————x———————

JOHN HIDAY (9th Gen.), son of Maryann Cushman Hiday and John Henry Hiday, born Oct. 5, 1852; died Dec. 30, 1926.

Married, March 9, 1874, Mary Jane Bolen, born April 5, 1858; died Aug. 15, 1915. Children born:

---x---

1. Rosa Hiday, born Dec. 2, 1874, in Madison County, Ind.
2. William Hiday, born March 27, 1877, in Madison County, Ind.; died Sept. 23, 1934.
3. Minnie Hiday, born Dec. 21, 1878, in Madison County, Ind.
4. Jesse R. Hiday, born April 5, 1881, in Madison County, Ind.
5. Bessie V. Hiday, born Nov. 8, 1884, in Madison County, Ind.; died July 31, 1936.
6. Alonzo V. Hiday, born Dec. 13, 1889, in Madison County, Ind.
7. Cecil L. Hiday, born March 27, 1892, in Madison County, Ind.
8. Virgil F. Hiday, born May 14, 1895, in Madison County, Ind.

---x---

ROSA HIDAY (10th Gen.), daughter of John Hiday and Mary Jane (Bolen) Hiday, born Dec. 2, 1874, in Madison County, Ind. Married, Dec. 31, 1895, near Anderson, Ind., Horace McCord, born Aug. 2, 1875. Children born:
1. Elsie McCord, born April 13, 1898.
2. Kenneth McCord, born March 18, 1900.
3. Claudie McCord, born Aug. 14, 1901.
4. Opal McCord, born March 26, 1910.

---x---

ELSIE MCCORD (11th Gen.), daughter of Rosa (Hiday) McCord and Horace McCord, born April 13, 1898. Married, Oct., 1916, at Anderson, Ind., Kenneth Allen, born Dec. 3, 1896. Children born:
1. Robert Allen, born May 9, 1919.
2. Dorothy Allen, born March 2, 1920.
3. Mary Allen, born Sept. 2, 1922.
4. Richard Allen, born Dec. 12, 1925.
5. Phyllis Allen, born Sept. 22, 1927.

KENNETH MCCORD (11th Gen.), son of Rosa (Hiday) McCord and Horace McCord, born March 18, 1900. Married Bernice Webster, born Nov. 14, 1902.

———————x———————

CLAUDIE MCCORD (11th Gen.), son of Rosa (Hiday) McCord and Horace McCord, born Aug. 14, 1901. Married Edith Hall, born June 6, 1907. Children born:
1. Robert McCord, born Dec. 17, 1920.
2. Rosemary McCord, born May 21, 1922.
3. Albert McCord, born Feb. 8, 1929.

———————x———————

OPAL MCCORD (11th Gen.), daughter of Rosa (Hiday) McCord and Horace McCord, born March 20, 1910. Married, Sept. 22, 1928, at Alexandria, Ind., Loren A. Brobst. Children born:
1. Marilyn Brobst, born Feb. 2, 1932.
2. Gerald Brobst, born July 17, 1934.

———————x———————

WILLIAM HIDAY (10th Gen.), son of John Hiday and Mary Jane (Bolen) Hiday, born March 27, 1877, in Madison County, Ind.; died Sept. 23, 1934. Married, 1901, Cella Brown. Children born:
1. Landis Hiday.
2. Erma Hiday.

———————x———————

MINNIE HIDAY (10th Gen.), daughter of John Hiday and Mary Jane (Bolen) Hiday, born Dec. 21, 1878, in Madison County, Ind. Married John Poet. Children born:
1. Granville Lee Orlando Poet.
2. Juanita Ethel Lavonne Poet.
3. Mary Margaret Poet.
4. John Junior Poet.
5. Glenn Poet.

———————x———————

JUANITA ETHEL LAVONNE POET (11th Gen.), daughter of Minnie (Hiday) Poet and John Poet. Married Elbert Walling. Children born:
1. Alberon Walling.

———————x———————

MARY MARGARET POET (11th Gen.), daughter of Minnie (Hiday) Poet and John Poet. Married Earl Crittenden. Children born:

1. Lois Crittenden.
2. Lavonne Crittenden.
———x———

CHARLES C. HIDAY (10th Gen.), born Feb. 18, 1870. Married, April 8, 1900, Fannie Wilson, born Feb. 23, 1882. Children born:
1. Forrest J. Hiday, born Nov. 14, 1900.
2. Viola Fay Hiday, born Aug. 15, 1902; died Sept. 23, 1919.
3. Lena May Hiday, born March 11, 1905.
4. Frances Isabell Hiday, born Jan. 17, 1908.
5. Pearl Ann Hiday, born April 8, 1910.
6. Vivian Lois Hiday, born May 1, 1913.
7. Clarence Albert Hiday, born March 12, 1916.
8. Ruby Lucille Hiday, born Dec. 5, 1920.
———x———

FORREST J. HIDAY (11th Gen.), son of Charles C. Hiday and Fannie (Wilson) Hiday, born Nov. 14, 1900. Married, April 30, 1920, Lucille Lewis. Children born:
1. David Hiday, born Oct. 7, 1937.
———x———

LENA MAY HIDAY (11th Gen.), daughter of Charles C. Hiday and Fannie (Wilson) Hiday, born March 11, 1905. Married, Feb. 14, 1925, Gerald Noblitt. Children born:
1. Irmalee Noblitt, born Sept. 20, 1925.
2. Sandra Noblitt, born Jan. 22, 1940.
———x———

FRANCES ISABELL HIDAY (11th Gen.), daughter of Charles C. Hiday and Fannie (Wilson) Hiday, born Jan. 17, 1908. Married, Aug. 26, 1930, Guy Davenport. Children born:
1. Blair Davenport, born Nov. 28, 1931.
2. Kay Frances Davenport, born May 8, 1939.
———x———

PEARL ANN HIDAY (11th Gen.), daughter of Charles C. Hiday and Fannie (Wilson) Hiday, born April 8, 1910. Married, July 4, 1931, Marsee Beckett. Children born:
1. Marilyn Beckett, born Oct. 11, 1932.
2. Marsee Oliver Beckett, born Sept. 10, 1937.
———x———

JESSE R. HIDAY (10th Gen.), son of John Hiday and Mary Jane (Bolen) Hiday, born April 5, 1881, in Madison County,

Ind. Married, in 1901, Ethel Stanley. Children born:
1. Tracy Hurble Hiday, born May 6, 1903.
2. Mary Margaret Hiday, born Oct. 15, 1905.

———————x———————

TRACY HURBLE HIDAY (11th Gen.), son of Jesse R. Hiday and Ethel (Stanley) Hiday, born May 6, 1903, in Madison County, Ind. Married, April 5, 1925, Frances Hunt. Children born:
1. Joseph Richard Hiday, born Sept. 12, 1926.
2. David Lindley Hiday, born Oct. 7, 1935.

———————x———————

MARY MARGARET HIDAY (11th Gen.), daughter of Jesse R. Hiday and Ethel (Stanley) Hiday, born Oct. 15, 1905, in Madison County, Ind. Married, July 12, 1922, Perry Edgar James. Children born:
1. Norma Louise James, born Oct. 22, 1924.
2. Philis Joan James, born Oct. 21, 1926.
3. Donald Robert James, born Oct. 10, 1928.

———————x———————

BESSIE V. HIDAY (10th Gen.), daughter of John Hiday and Mary Jane (Bolen) Hiday, born Nov. 8, 1884, in Madison County, Ind.; died July 31, 1936. Married, Dec. 24, 1902, Fred Badgley. Children born:
1. Edith Pauline Badgley, born May 12, 1905.
2. Freda Marie Badgley, born Sept. 10, 1906.
3. Earl Webster Badgley, born June 14, 1908.
4. Vere Badgley, born Sept. 27, 1909.
5. Loren Eugene Badgley, born Sept. 10, 1910.
6. Katherine Badgley, born Dec. 18, 1911.

———————x———————

EDITH PAULINE BADGLEY (11th Gen.), daughter of Bessie V. (Hiday) Badgley and Fred Badgley, born May 12, 1905. Married, April 17, 1927, Clay Kenneth Ulmer, born Dec. 25, 1902. Children born:
1. Margaret Louise Ulmer, born July 29, 1928, in Madison County, Ind.
2. Helen Nadine Ulmer, born Jan. 12, 1934, in Madison County, Ind.

———————x———————

FREDA MARIE BADGLEY (11th Gen.), daughter of Bessie V. (Hiday) Badgley and Fred Badgley, born Sept. 10, 1906.

Married, Nov. 17, 1926, Fred H. Stewart, born Oct. 16, 1907. Children born:
1. Harry Mervin Stewart, born Sept. 25, 1927.

———x———

EARL WEBSTER BADGLEY (11th Gen.), son of Bessie V. (Hiday) Badgley and Fred Badgley, born June 14, 1908. Married, Sept. 29, 1929, Geneva Stephens, born April 9, 1911.

———x———

VERE BADGLEY (11th Gen.), son of Bessie V. (Hiday) Badgley and Fred Badgley, born Sept. 27, 1909, in Anderson, Ind. Married, Sept. 2, 1933, Edith Baker.

———x———

LOREN EUGENE BADGLEY (11th Gen.), son of Bessie V. (Hiday) Badgley and Fred Badgley, born Sept. 10, 1910, at Anderson, Ind.; died Feb. 12, 1939. Married, June 30, 1934, Mary Bell Levi. One child born:
1. Jack Eugene Badgley, born Dec. 18, 1937.

———x———

KATHERINE BADGLEY (11th Gen.), daughter of Bessie V. (Hiday) Badgley and Fred Badgley, born Dec. 18, 1911, in Anderson, Ind. Married George Bernard Hexamer. Children born:
1. Gloria May Hexamer, born Jan. 4, 1933.
2. George Bernard Hexamer, born Nov. 18, 1934.
3. Earl Edward Hexamer, born Dec. 18, 1936.
4. Mary Jeannine Hexamer, born June 16, 1938.

———x———

CECIL L. HIDAY (10th Gen.), son of John Hiday and Mary Jane (Bolen) Hiday, born March 27, 1892, in Madison County, Ind. Married, in 1941, Cleo Robinette. Children born:
1. Velma Irene Hiday, born March 5, 1915.
2. Grace Bernice Hiday, born June 4, 1916.
3. John Franklin Hiday, born Oct. 24, 1918.
4. Lloyd Donald Hiday, born Feb. 11, 1920.
5. Vera Mae Hiday, born Dec. 27, 1921.
6. Minnie Belle Hiday, born Jan. 30, 1925.
7. Inez Louise Hiday, born Nov. 28, 1926.
8. Gilbert Paul Hiday, born Sept. 12, 1928.
9. Robert David Hiday, born July 15, 1930.
10. Mary Bernadine Hiday, born Feb. 5, 1933.

VIRGIL F. HIDAY (10th Gen.), son of John Hiday and Mary Jane (Bolen) Hiday, born May 14, 1895, in Madison County, Ind. Married, in 1917, Sarah Smith. Children born:
1. Doris Maxine Hiday, born Oct. 6, 1919.

———————x———————

DONNA GAY SEIBERT (11th Gen.), daughter of Minnie Hiday and Ernst Seibert, born Sept. 6, 1899. Married Virgil Lawler. Children born:
1. Betty Jean Lawler, born Jan. 22, 1923.

———————x———————

MARY ELLEN HIDAY (9th Gen.), daughter of Maryann Cushman Hiday and John Henry Hiday, born Feb. 26, 1857; died April 27, 1913. Married, Jan. 8, 1887, Phillip Carroll, born March 29, 1837; died Feb. 26, 1898. Children born:
1. Emma Lee Carroll, born April 9, 1886.
2. Minnie Blanche Carroll, born Feb. 14, 1888.
3. Anna Belle Carroll, born Oct. 12, 1889.
4. Clarison John Carroll, born March 3, 1891.
5. Lawrence Carroll, born Sept. 23, 1893; died Dec. 27, 1898.
6. Leatha May Carroll, born March 3, 1894.
7. Emerson Carroll, born Nov. 24, 1895; died Nov. 29, 1908.

———————x———————

EMMA LEE CARROLL (10th Gen.), daughter of Mary Ellen (Hiday) Carroll, and Phillip Carroll, born April 9, 1886. Married, Nov. 15, 1903, Tony Pickett, born July 14, 1878. Children born:
1. Elva Marie Pickett, born April 29, 1904, at Holton, Ind.
2. Harry Pickett, born March 15, 1906, at Leroy, Ind.
3. Nancy Pickett, born Sept. 26, 1908, at New Salem, Ind.
4. Clifford Pickett, born Aug. 26, 1911, at Panola, Ill.
5. Nellie Pickett, born Sept. 26, 1915, at Dewitt, Ark.
6. Robert Pickett, born May 27, 1920, at Lexington, Ill.

———————x———————

ELVA MARIE PICKETT (11th Gen.), daughter of Emma Lee (Carroll) Pickett and Tony Pickett, born Nov. 29, 1904, at Holton, Ind. Married, Aug. 27, 1924, Ira Ray Andress, of Woolstock, Iowa. He was born Jan. 21, 1892, and they were married at Iron Mountain, Mich. Children born:

1. Helen Marie Andress, born March 23, 1926, at Iron Mountain, Mich.
2. June Maxine Andress, born June 3, 1928, at Iron Mountain, Mich.
3. Myrtle Agnes Andress, born Nov. 5, 1930, at Iron Mountain, Mich.
4. Ira Raymond Andress, born Aug. 2, 1931, at Iron Mountain, Mich.; died March 27, 1932.
5. Norman Ray Andress, born Sept. 13, 1935, at Waucedah, Mich.

―――――――x―――――――

HARRY PICKETT (11th Gen.), son of Emma Lee (Carroll) Pickett and Tony Pickett, born March 15, 1906, at Leroy, Ind. Married, Sept. 25, 1929, at Bloomington, Ill., Verna ―――――, born Sept. 25, 1907, at Colfax, Ill. Children born:
1. Josephine Pickett, born June 15, 1930, at Chenoa, Ill.
2. Joseph Pickett, born Dec. 6, 1931, at Chenoa, Ill.
3. Gerald Pickett, born June 25, 1934, at Peoria, Ill.
4. LaVerne Pickett, born Nov. 9, 1938, at Chenoa, Ill.

―――――――x―――――――

NANCY PICKETT (11th Gen.), daughter of Emma Lee (Carroll) Pickett and Tony Pickett, born Sept. 26, 1908, at New Salem, Ind. Married, May 16, 1927, at Bloomington, Ill., Lee Newkirk, born May 20, 1905, at English, Ind. Children born:
1. Dorothy Newkirk, born April 3, 1928, at Chenoa, Ill.
2. Mary Newkirk, born June 20, 1930, at Chenoa, Ill.
3. Shirley Newkirk, born Aug. 30, 1935, at Chenoa, Ill.

―――――――x―――――――

CLIFFORD PICKETT (11th Gen.), son of Emma Lee (Carroll) Pickett and Tony Pickett, born Aug. 26, 1911, at Panola, Ill. Married, Oct. 17, 1933, at Chenoa, Ill., Zazel Belle, born Oct. 10, 1914, at Chenoa, Ill. Children born:
1. Betty Mae Pickett, born Oct. 5, 1934, at Chenoa, Ill.
2. Kenneth Elwood Pickett, born July 24, 1938, at Chenoa, Ill.

―――――――x―――――――

NELLIE PICKETT (11th Gen.), daughter of Emma Lee (Carroll) Pickett and Tony Pickett, born Sept. 26, 1915, at DeWitt, Ark. Married, Dec. 23, 1931, at Kankakee, Ill., Emmet

Leonard, born Oct. 15, 1905, at Colfax, Ill. Children born:
1. Emmet B. Leonard, born Oct. 6, 1932, at Colfax, Ill.
2. Harold Leonard, born Feb. 12, 1933, at Cooksville, Ill.
3. Evelyn Leonard, born Nov. 10, 1935, at Chenoa, Ill.
4. Donald Leonard, born July 8, 1937, at Weston, Ill.
5. Richard Leonard, born Oct. 12, 1938, at Weston, Ill.

———————x———————

MINNIE BLANCHE CARROLL (10th Gen.), daughter of Mary Ellen (Hiday) Carroll and Phillip Carroll, born Feb. 14, 1888. Married, Dec. 23, 1906, at Perkinsville, Ind., Otto McCarty, born May 6, 1880. Children born:
1. Thelma Bettina McCarty, born Jan. 21, 1908, at Hamilton County, Ind.
2. Opal Louise McCarty, born July 17, 1915, at Hamilton County, Ind.; died Nov. 13, 1923.
3. Dorothy Helen McCarty, born March 28, 1918, at Hamilton County, Ind.

———————x———————

THELMA BETTINA MCCARTY (11th Gen.), daughter of Minnie Blanche (Carroll) McCarty and Otto McCarty, born Jan. 21, 1908, in Hamilton County, Ind. Married, June 4, 1938, at Noblesville, Ind., George Hawkins, born Aug. 1, 1905, in Madison County, Ind.

———————x———————

DOROTHY HELEN MCCARTY (11th Gen.), daughter of Minnie Blanche (Carroll) McCarty and Otto McCarty, born March 28, 1918, in Hamilton, County, Ind. Married, Dec. 24, 1937, at Elwood, Ind., James Wesley Baker, born Feb. 24, 1916, in Howard County, Ind. Children born:
1. Marcella Carol Baker, born June 15, 1939, in Hamilton County, Ind.

———————x———————

ANNA BELLE CARROLL (10th Gen.), daughter of Mary Ellen (Hiday) Carroll and Phillip Carroll, born Oct. 2, 1889, in Henry County, Ind. Married, July 8, 1905, Herbert E. Summers, born Nov. 21, 1882. Children born:
1. Florence M. Summers, born Aug. 5, 1906, in Ripley County, Ind.
2. Orval Glen Summers, born Nov. 19, 1909, in Ripley County, Ind.

3. Mary Cecil Summers, born March 7, 1913, in Madison County, Ind.

―――――x―――――
FLORENCE M. SUMMERS (11th Gen.), daughter of Anna Belle (Carroll) Summers and Herbert E. Summers, born Aug. 5, 1906. Married, Jan. 2, 1926, Robert R. Crook, born July 9, 1905. Children born:
1. Marian A. Crook, born Sept. 12, 1926.
2. Jimmie R. Crook, born March 24, 1930.
3. Melvin G. Crook, born Feb. 21, 1933; died Jan. 29, 1937.

―――――x―――――
ORVAL GLEN SUMMERS (11th Gen.), son of Anna Belle (Carroll) Summers and Herbert E. Summers, born Nov. 19, 1909. Married, Sept. 2, 1929, Elva M. Kimball, born Sept. 12, 1908, in Minnesota. Children born:
1. Audrey Lee Summers, born Feb. 6, 1931, in Minnesota.
2. Elizabeth Anne Summers, born Sept. 4, 1933, in Minnesota.

―――――x―――――
MARY CECIL SUMMERS (11th Gen.), daughter of Anna Belle (Carroll) Summers and Herbert E. Summers, born March 7, 1913, in Madison County, Ind. Married, Oct. 24, 1935, in Minnesota, Lawrence C. Uker, born Jan. 22, 1914, in Minnesota. Children born:
1. Jerald Lawrence Uker, born Oct. 17, 1939, in Minnesota.

―――――x―――――
CLARISON JOHN CARROLL (10th Gen.), son of Mary Ellen (Hiday) Carroll and Phillip Carroll, born March 3, 1891. Married, April 6, 1910, Mabel Bowers, who died April 11, 1919. Children born:
1. Virgil Henry Carroll, born Sept. 8, 1911, in Ripley County, Ind.
2. Esther Agatha Carroll, born Jan. 3, 1914, in Ripley County, Ind.

Clarison John Carroll married, secondly, in 1923, Luella Burtsch. Children born:
1. Mary Elizabeth Carroll, born Feb. 17, 1926, in Ripley County, Ind.

―――――x―――――
LEATHA MAY CARROLL (10th Gen.), daughter of Mary Ellen (Hiday) Carroll and Phillip Carroll, born March 3, 1894.

Married, Aug. 13, 1912, Allen Metzger, born March 9, 1893. Children born:
1. Irvin Metzger, born March 19, 1913, in Madison County, Ind.

---x---

CALVIN HIDAY (9th Gen.), son of Maryann Cushman Hiday and John Henry Hiday, born Feb. 17, 1865; died March 17, 1933. Married, Sept. 9, 1883, Ellen Nibarger, at Beech Grove, Ind. Children born:
1. Ethel Hiday, born July 16, 1884.
2. Emza Rettie Hiday, born Nov. 3, 1888, in Madison County, Ind.
3. Hershel H. Hiday, born Sept. 12, 1895, at Wilkinson, Ind.
4. Forrest Hiday, born Dec. 4, 1897, at Pendleton, Ind.
5. Everett Hiday, born March 14, 1904, at Alexandria, Ind.

---x---

ETHEL HIDAY (10th Gen.), daughter of Calvin Hiday and Ellen (Nibarger) Hiday, born July 16, 1884. Married, April 26, 1908, Medarie S. Wall, born Oct. 17, 1885, in Ohio. Children born:
1. Emza Edna Wall, born Aug. 23, 1914, at Summitville, Ind.

---x---

EMZA EDNA WALL (11th Gen.), daughter of Ethel (Hiday) Wall and Medarie S. Wall, born Aug. 23, 1914, at Summitville, Ind. Married Ralph W. Thurston, born July 15, 1914, at Aberdeen, Saskatchewan, Canada. Children born:
1. Joyce Ann Thurston, born April 3, 1939.

---x---

CALDER HIDAY (9th Gen.), son of Maryann Cushman Hiday and John Henry Hiday, born April 9, 1858; died Nov. 30, 1940. Married, first, Feb., 1881, Lucretia Jarrett. Children born:
1. Ernst O. Hiday, born June 25, 1883.
2. Estella Hiday, born Nov. 28, 1884.

Calder Hiday married, secondly, Clara Beechler. Children were born, but have been unable to ascertain names and dates.

---x---

ERNST O. HIDAY (10th Gen.), son of Calder Hiday and Lucretia (Jarrett) Hiday, born June 25, 1883, in Madison

County, Ind. Married, Jan. 6, 1907, Virgie Day, at Oklahoma City, Okla. Children born:
1. Janie Beattrice Hiday, born Dec. 23, 1907, in Anderson, Ind.
2. Robert Calder Hiday, born Feb. 12, 1912, in Anderson, Ind.
3. Bruce Roland Hiday, born Sept. 19, 1920, at Forsyth, Mont.

―――――――x―――――――

JANIE BEATTRICE HIDAY (11th Gen.), daughter of Ernst O. Hiday and Virgie (Day) Hiday, born Dec. 23, 1907, in Anderson, Ind. Married, June 2, 1923, Lewis J. Vanderhoof. Children born:
1. Leroy Gene Vanderhoof, born Feb. 29, 1924.
2. Virginia Vanderhoof, born March 6, 1925.

―――――――x―――――――

ROBERT CALDER HIDAY (11th Gen.), son of Ernst O. Hiday and Virgie (Day) Hiday, born Feb. 12, 1912, in Anderson, Ind. Married, April 8, 1939, Annabell Lovelace. Children born:
1. Robert Wayne Hiday, born June 28, 1940.

―――――――x―――――――

EMZA HIDAY (10th Gen.), daughter of Calvin Hiday and Ellen (Nibarger) Hiday, born Nov. 3, 1888, in Madison County, Ind. Married, Sept. 18, 1909, William Godsey, born Oct. 3, 1878, in Missouri; died Dec. 23, 1933. Children born:
1. Doris Etheleen Godsey, born July 16, 1910, at Lind, Wash.
2. Bernis Emza Godsey, born Nov. 1, 1911, at Pomeroy, Wash.
3. Reta Leone Godsey, born March 16, 1913, at Fairmount, Ind.
4. William Godsey, born Oct. 14, 1915, at Pomeroy, Wash.; died Oct. 18, 1915.
5. Wilma Ellen Godsey, born Dec. 27, 1916, at Pomeroy, Wash.
6. Carol Hiday Godsey, born Sept. 20, 1920, at Garfield, Wash.

Doris Etheleen Godsey (11th Gen.), daughter of Emza Rettie (Hiday) Godsey and William Godsey, born July 16, 1910, at Lind, Wash. Married, Jan. 1, 1933, at Tia Juana, Mexico, Daniel John Buchley, born Oct. 5, 1904, at San Francisco, Calif. Children born:
1. Michael John Buchley, born Dec. 9, 1935, at Long Beach, Calif.
2. Patrick Stanton Buchley, born Aug. 28, 1937, at Long Beach, Calif.
3. Susan Maurine Buchley, born Dec. 31, 1938, at Long Beach, Calif.

―――――x―――――

Bernis Emza Godsey (11th Gen.), daughter of Emza Rettie (Hiday) Godsey and William Godsey, born Nov. 1, 1911, at Pomeroy, Wash. Married, May 17, 1941, at Longview, Wash., Paul Grush, born Feb. 13, 1914, at Falls City, Neb.

―――――x―――――

Reta Leone Godsey (11th Gen.), daughter of Emza Rettie (Hiday) Godsey and William Godsey, born March 16, 1913, at Fairmount, Ind. Married, April 29, 1935, at Laguna Beach, Calif., John Robert Moreatt, born March 12, 1911, at Kansas City, Kansas.

―――――x―――――

Wilma Ellen Godsey (11th Gen.), daughter of Emza Rettie (Hiday) Godsey and William Godsey, born Dec. 27, 1916, at Pomeroy, Wash. Married, June 27, 1937, at Pasadena, Calif., Willard Homer Spiegel, born Oct. 29, 1911, at Pasadena, Calif.

―――――x―――――

Carol Hiday Godsey (11th Gen.), son of Emza Rettie (Hiday) Godsey and William Godsey, born Sept. 20, 1920, at Garfield, Wash. Married, May 31, 1941, at Vancouver, Wash., Lillian Marie Ware, born May 11, 1923, at Lakeview, Oregon.

―――――x―――――

Herschel H. Hiday (10th Gen.), son of Calvin Hiday and Ellen (Nibarger) Hiday, born Sept. 12, 1895, at Wilkinson, Ind. Married, Aug. 3, 1917, at Pomeroy, Wash., Mina Fay Mann, born March 19, 1898, at Jonesboro, Ind. Children born:
1. Ernest Hiday, born Jan. 13, 1919, at Pomeroy, Wash.
2. Leah Hiday, born Dec. 18, 1927, at Missoula, Mont.

ERNEST HIDAY (11th Gen.), son of Herschel H. Hiday and Mina Fay (Mann) Hiday, born Jan. 13, 1919, at Pomeroy, Wash. Married, Jan. 2, 1941, at Gas City, Ind., Donna Jean Peterson.

———————x———————

FORREST HIDAY (10th Gen.), son of Calvin Hiday and Ellen (Nibarger) Hiday, born Dec. 4, 1897, at Pendleton, Ind. Married, July 19, 1925, at Missoula, Mont., Clara Crow, born Nov. 12, 1906, at Crawford, Neb. Children born:
1. Robert F. Hiday, born July 7, 1927, at Missoula, Mont.
2. Donald C. Hiday, born Dec. 3, 1934, at Missoula, Mont.

———————x———————

EVERETT HIDAY (10th Gen.), son of Calvin Hiday and Ellen (Nibarger) Hiday, born March 15, 1904, at Alexandria, Ind. Married, May 11, 1926, Hazel C. Hinds, at Cowallis, Oregon. Children born:
1. Olive May Hiday, born July 3, 1927.

———————x———————

JONATHAN CUSHMAN (8th Gen.), son of Thomas Cushman and Elizabeth (Jenkins) Cushman, born Dec. 30, 1824. He was a Union soldier and served through much of the Civil War. He died, unmarried, and is probably buried in a country cemetery near Hoopston, Ill. He was one of those who followed "Sherman to the Sea."

Also Jonathan C. Hogland, Thomas Gorman, Joseph Gorman and John Gorman.

Thomas Gorman was taken captive and held in a Rebel prison and when he was released, at the close of the war, he was so starved he was unable to stand alone and was brought home on a stretcher.

———————x———————

ELIZABETH CUSHMAN (8th Gen.), daughter of Thomas Cushman and Elizabeth (Jenkins) Cushman, born Aug. 20, 1827. Married Calder Snodgrass. Children born:
1. Charles Snodgrass.

———————x———————

SARAH CUSHMAN (8th Gen.), daughter of Thomas Cushman and Elizabeth (Jenkins) Cushman, born Sept. 5, 1833, in Pennsylvania; died March 19, 1926, at 1008 Orchard Street, Ottumwa, Iowa. Married, March 14, 1857, Morgan Wynn; the marriage ceremony was performed by Rev. L. A. Baird.

Children born:
1. William Jackson Wynn, born 1858.
2. Evangeline Wynn, born Dec. 20, 1860; died Oct. 7, 1936.
3. Oliver Wynn, born 1863; died at Albia, Ia., unmarried.
4. Winafred Wynn, born 1865; died July 20, 1918.
5. Mary Jane Wynn, born 1867.
6. Ona Maud Wynn, born 1869; died Dec. 28, 1919.
7. Blanche Wynn, born 1870; died 1888.

―――――x―――――

WILLIAM JACKSON WYNN (9th Gen.), son of Sarah Cushman Wynn and Morgan Wynn, born in 1858. Married, Feb. 24, 1881, Margaret Ann Phipps. Children born:
1. James Arthur Wynn, born April 13, 1882, at Lovilia, Monroe County, Ia.
2. Morgan M. Wynn, born Oct. 1, 1883, at Lovilia, Monroe County, Ia.
3. Ira Wynn, born Sept. 9, 1886, at Lovilia, Monroe County, Ia.
4. Benjamin Wynn, born Aug. 26, 1889, at Lovilia, Monroe County, Ia.

―――――x―――――

JAMES ARTHUR WYNN (10th Gen.), son of William Jackson Wynn and Margaret Ann (Phipps) Wynn, born April 13, 1882, at Lovilia, Monroe County, Ia. Married, in 1910, Carrie Stevenson, at Albia, Ia. Children born:
1. Bonnie Odeah Wynn, born July 25, 1918, at Melrose, Ia.

―――――x―――――

BONNIE ODEAH WYNN (11th Gen.), daughter of James Arthur Wynn and Carrie (Stevenson) Wynn, born July 25, 1918, at Melrose, Ia. Married, in 1937, at Lancaster, Mo., Russell Pickins, of Ottumwa, Ia.

―――――x―――――

MORGAN M. WYNN (10th Gen.), son of William Jackson Wynn and Margaret Ann (Phipps) Wynn, born Oct. 1, 1883, at Lovilia, Monroe County, Ia. Married, May 7, 1912, Bessie Welch, of Knoxville, Ia., at Yuma, Colo. Children born:
1. Josephine Wynn, born Jan. 29, 1922.

―――――x―――――

IRA WYNN (10th Gen.), son of William Jackson Wynn and Margaret Ann (Phipps) Wynn, born Sept. 9, 1886, at Lovilia,

Monroe County, Ia. Married, June, 1914, at Ottumwa, Ia., Jessie Clear, of Lovilia, Ia. Children born:
1. William Edgar Wynn, born Dec. 3, 1916, at Melrose, Ia.
2. Gladys Geraldine Wynn, born April 16, 1922, at Melrose, Ia.

WILLIAM EDGAR WYNN (11th Gen.), son of Ira Wynn and Jessie (Clear) Wynn, born Dec. 3, 1916. Married, Feb. 11, 1937, at Lancaster, Mo., Catherine Richmond. Children born:
1. William Edgar Wynn, born 1937.
2. Jerrold Wynn, born 1939.

GLADYS GERALDINE WYNN (11th Gen.), daughter of Ira Wynn and Jessie (Clear) Wynn, born April 16, 1922, at Melrose, Ia. Married, Jan. 13, 1940, at Chariton, Ia., Ross Keeton. Children born:
1. Saundra Keeton, born 1940.

BENJAMIN WYNN (10th Gen.), son of William Jackson Wynn and Margaret Ann (Phipps) Wynn, born Aug. 26, 1889, at Lovilia, Monroe County, Ia. Married, May, 1924, at Chariton, Iowa, Frances O'Brien.

EVANGELINE WYNN (9th Gen.), daughter of Sarah Cushman Wynn and Morgan Wynn, born Dec. 20, 1860; died Oct. 7, 1936. Married L. M. Lane, born March 7, 1853; died April 7, 1888. Children born:
1. Blanche Lane, born 1882. Married ———— Randall.
2. Etta Lane, born 1885. Married ———— Mitchell.
3. Clara J. Lane, born 1887.

MARY JANE WYNN (9th Gen.), daughter of Sarah Cushman Wynn and Morgan Wynn, born 1867. Married Garrett Tutor. Seven children were born to this union.

ONA MAUD WYNN (9th Gen.), daughter of Sarah Cushman Wynn and Morgan Wynn, born 1869; died Dec. 28, 1919. Married, at Lovilia, Ia., Clum Foutch. Children born:
1. Dollie May Foutch.

MARY CUSHMAN (7th Gen.), daughter of Isaac Cushman and Deborah Frazee Cushman, born Feb. 11, 1784. The writer has never been able to secure information further than the date of her birth.

---x---

SARA CUSHMAN (7th Gen.), called Sallie, daughter of Isaac Cushman and Deborah Frazee Cushman, born March 17, 1788. Married Mr. Hayes and moved to Indianapolis. There were two sons born to this union, but the writer has never been successful in tracing the family.

---x---

REBECAH CUSHMAN (7th Gen.), daughter of Isaac Cushman and Deborah Frazee Cushman, born Feb. 14, 1792. Married, first, Daniel Voorhees. Further information concerning Rebecah and her family or marriages has never been obtained.

---x---

SQUIER CUSHMAN (7th Gen.), son of Isaac Cushman and Deborah Frazee Cushman, born in Fayette County, Wharton Township, Pa., on Sunday, March 2, 1794; died in May, 1855. Married, first, Hannah Humbert, who died in 1831.

He was a stone mason and builder, by trade, and the house the family lived in was constructed of stones which he and his sons picked up from the farm lands he owned.

A picture of this house is shown herewith.

A house of brick was first contemplated and a brick-maker was employed to make and kiln burn the brick, but the first batch of brick turned out faulty. The brick plans were abandoned and the large stone structure then undertaken.

Children born to Squier Cushman and Hannah Humbert Cushman:

1. Orlando Frazee Cushman, who died of typhus fever; unmarried.
2. Rebecca Woodmansee Cushman, married Mr. Kirkhart.
3. Adanaijah Ephraim Cushman, born Jan. 1, 1824; died Aug. 10, 1897.
4. Mary Numbers Cushman (called Aunt Polly), born Oct. 29, 1825; died Oct. 15, 1926.
5. Peter Humbert Cushman; deceased.
6. Malinda Robbins Cushman; deceased.
7. Rev. Isaac Jackson Cushman, born Sept. 19, 1831; died Aug. 26, 1881.

STONE HOUSE AND HOME OF THE SQUIRE CUSHMAN FAMILY, NEAR MAIDSVILLE, WEST VIRGINIA
Still standing in 1940 as shown in this picture.

Squier Cushman married, secondly, Mary Wing Conway. Children born to this second marriage:
1. Nancy Margaret Cushman, died, unmarried, in 1855.
2. Alcinda Jane Cushman, died, unmarried, in 1855.
3. Anna Mariah Cushman, born March 4, 1841; died June 15, 1934.
4. Eliza Rachel Cushman.
5. Amanda Ellen Cushman, born April 2, 1846; died July 21, 1911.
6. George Brown Cushman.

Squier Cushman, through his efforts, secured the first post office, and gave to his home community the name of Maidsville, Virginia (now West Virginia). The first church and school building, in Maidsville, were erected by Squier Cushman and the school building is still used as a residence (1940).

———x———

REBECCA WOODMANSEE CUSHMAN (8th Gen.), daughter of Squier Cushman and Hannah (Humbert) Cushman. Married Mr. Kirkhart.

———x———

ADANAIJAH EPHRAIM CUSHMAN (8th Gen.), son of Squier Cushman and Hannah (Humbert) Cushman, born Jan. 1, 1824; died Aug. 10, 1897. Married, first, 1852, Zanah Dean. Children born:
1. Mariah Lucinda Cushman, born June 19, 1853; died Jan. 21, 1932.
2. Erastus Montuville Cushman, born Dec., 1854; died June 19, 1932.

Zanah Dean Cushman died May, 1855. Adanaijah Ephraim Cushman married, secondly, Mary (Polly) Lazelle, who lived about three months after this marriage. After seven years Adanaijah Ephraim Cushman again married. This third wife, Kate Dean, a niece of his first wife. Children born to this third marriage:
1. Anna Lloyd Cushman, born Sept. 8, 1870.
2. Alpheus Cushman; deceased; unmarried.
3. Ella Cushman, born May 8, 1875.
4. Mary Estella Cushman, died at 16 years of age.
5. Della Leora Cushman, born Oct. 10, 1879.
6. Walter Humbert Cushman, born Nov. 14, 1881.

MARIA LUCINDA CUSHMAN (9th Gen.), daughter of Adanaijah Ephraim Cushman and Zanah (Dean) Cushman, born June 19, 1853; died Jan. 21, 1932. Married, April 18, 1876, John M. Garlow, in the Murdoch, Ohio, Presbyterian Church, near Loveland, Ohio, by her uncle, Rev. Isaac Jackson Cushman, who preached in that church until his death, and, in the cemetery close by, he lies buried, together with his wife and son, Charles. Children born:
1. Charles Lee Garlow, born Feb. 4, 1877. Unmarried.
2. Lucius Minor Garlow, born March 22, 1879.
3. Herbert Emmett Garlow, born April 18, 1881.
4. Cora L. Garlow, born Aug. 22, 1883.
5. William Whitfield Garlow, born Aug. 7, 1885.
6. Robert Garlow, born Aug. 22, 1887.
7. Bertha Florence Garlow, born Aug. 21, 1889.
8. Jesse Claude Garlow, born Aug. 24, 1893.

———x———

ERASTUS MONTUVILLE CUSHMAN (9th Gen.), son of Adanaijah Ephraim Cushman and Zanah (Dean) Cushman, born Dec., 1854; died June 19, 1932. Married, Feb., 1876, Delia A. Colebank. Children born:
1. Sarah Allie Cushman, born May 14, 1878; died March 22, 1908.
2. Mary Rosena Cushman, born March 30, 1879.
3. Nannie Lillian Cushman, born Oct. 3, 1880.

———x———

SARAH ALLIE CUSHMAN (10th Gen.), daughter of Erastus Montuville Cushman and Delia A. (Colebank) Cushman, born May 14, 1878; died March 22, 1908. Married, July 31, 1901, at Morgantown, W. Va., William Lee Graham, of Pittsburgh, Pa., born March 27, 1875. Children born:
1. Ione Claire Graham, born Feb. 23, 1908.

———x———

IONE CLAIRE GRAHAM (11th Gen.), daughter of Sarah Allie (Cushman) Graham and William Lee Graham, born Feb. 23, 1908. Married Lewis F. McClure, of Pittsburgh, Pa. Children born:
1. Lewis F. McClure, Jr., born 1929.
2. Wade Allen McClure, born 1941.

MARY ROSENA CUSHMAN (10th Gen.), daughter of Erastus Montuville Cushman and Adelia A. (Colebank) Cushman, born March 31, 1879. Married, April 22, 1909, William Brown. Children born:
1. Albert L. Brown, born March 7, 1910.
2. Roy S. Brown, born May 24, 1913.
3. William W. Brown, born Feb. 13, 1920.
4. Virginia Brown, born Sept. 16, 1922. } Twins
5. Vernon Brown, born Sept. 16, 1922.

———————x———————

NANNIE LILLIAN CUSHMAN (10th Gen.), daughter of Erastus Montuville Cushman and Adelia (Colebank) Cushman, born Oct. 3, 1880. Married, July 3, 1902, Harry Smith Johnson. Children born:
1. Howard Melvin Johnson, born May 13, 1904.

———————x———————

HOWARD MELVIN JOHNSON (11th Gen.), son of Nannie Lillian (Cushman) Johnson and Harry Smith Johnson, born May 13, 1904. Married, Aug. 29, 1922. Children born:
1. Thoron Johnson, born Nov. 11, 1923.

———————x———————

ANNA LLOYD CUSHMAN (9th Gen.), daughter of Adanaijah Ephraim Cushman and his third wife, Kate (Dean) Cushman, born Sept. 8, 1872. Married, 1905, William Milan Hopson. No issue.

———————x———————

ELLA MAY CUSHMAN (9th Gen.), daughter of Adanaijah Ephraim Cushman and his third wife, Kate (Dean) Cushman, born May 8, 1875. Married William Krepps Long, who died Oct. 18, 1918. Children born:
1. Alpheus P. Long, born April 10, 1894.
2. Sophie Elizabeth Long, born Sept. 30, 1896.

———————x———————

DELLA LEORA CUSHMAN (9th Gen.), daughter of Adanaijah Ephraim Cushman and his third wife, Kate (Dean) Cushman, born Sept. 30, 1879. Married John Harvey B. Simmons. No issue.

———————x———————

WALTER HUMBERT CUSHMAN (9th Gen.), son of Adanaijah Ephraim Cushman and his third wife, Kate (Dean) Cushman, born Nov. 14, 1881, at Rosedale, Greene County, Pa. Married,

Jan. 25, 1911, Lucille Evelyn Graham. Children born:
1. Lucille Evelyn Cushman, born Jan. 8, 1912.
2. Walter Humbert Cushman, Jr., born April 10, 1915.
3. Mary Kathryn Cushman, born June 18, 1920.

Walter Humbert Cushman, as an engineer, has been prominent in much of the improvement and progress made in northeastern Arkansas.

———————x———————

LUCILLE EVELYN CUSHMAN (10th Gen.), daughter of Walter Humbert Cushman and Lucille Evelyn (Graham) Cushman, born Jan. 8, 1912. Married, June 18, 1936, Richard Stephens Lynn, born Sept. 1, 1907. Children born:
1. Evelyn Pet Lynn, born March 22, 1937.

———————x———————

JAMES ALLEN CUSHMAN (9th Gen.), son of Adanaijah Ephraim Cushman and Kate (Dean) Cushman. Married, first, Ethel Graves. Children born:
1. Wilbur Cushman, born 1919.

James Allen Cushman married, secondly, Mary Jane Richards. Children born:
1. Dean Richards Cushman, born Feb. 8, 1926.

———————x———————

SOPHIE ELIZABETH LONG (10th Gen.), daughter of Ella May (Cushman) Long and William Krepps Long, born Sept. 30, 1896. Married, Jan. 7, 1913, Don Pardee Dowling, born Nov. 24, 1890. Children born:
1. Charlotte Jane Dowling, born Oct. 1, 1913; died in infancy.
2. Don Pardee Dowling, Jr., born Feb. 15, 1915.
3. William Morris Dowling, born Aug. 11, 1917.
4. Mary Jane Dowling, born Oct. 3, 1919.
5. Elaine Dowling, born March 13, 1923; died in infancy.
6. Maxine Annette Dowling, born Oct. 16, 1925.
7. Patricia Ann Dowling, born Jan. 8, 1927.
8. James Lincoln Dowling, born Feb. 12, 1930.
9. Barbara Ann Dowling, born March 6, 1932.

———————x———————

MARY JANE DOWLING (11th Gen.), daughter of Sophie Elizabeth (Long) Dowling and Don Pardee Dowling, born Oct. 3, 1919. Married, June, 1938, George Nichol. No issue.

WILLIAM MORRIS DOWLING (11th Gen.), son of Sophie Elizabeth (Long) Dowling and Don Pardee Dowling, born Aug. 11, 1917. Married Dorothy Bittner. Children born:
1. Deanna Rae Dowling, born Dec. 16, 1936.
2. Beverly Sue Dowling, born Jan. 17, 1938.
William Morris Dowling married, secondly, Sept., 1941, Dorothy Rhoades.

―――――――x―――――――

MARY KATHRYN CUSHMAN (10th Gen.), daughter of Walter Humbert Cushman and Lucille Evelyn (Graham) Cushman, born June 18, 1920. Married, Jan. 25, 1938, Dean Wakefield Christian, born Aug. 22, 1915. Children born:
1. Dean Wakefield Christian, Jr., born Dec. 9, 1939.

―――――――x―――――――

MARY NUMBERS CUSHMAN (8th Gen.), daughter of Squier Cushman and Hannah (Humbert) Cushman, born Oct. 29, 1825; died Oct. 15, 1926. She was called Aunt Polly. Married, March 2, 1847, Festus Hampton Tapp. Children born:
1. Velonia Tapp, born March 17, 1848; died in 1861.
2. Hannah Ethel Tapp, born Jan. 25, 1850; died Feb. 5, 1936.
3. Adelaide Florinda Tapp, born July 12, 1853; died Aug. 23, 1923.
4. William Whitfield Tapp, born June 25, 1856; died April 21, 1916.
5. Robert Westfall Tapp, born May 18, 1859. Unmarried and deceased.
6. Dicie Florence Tapp, born Dec. 18, 1861.
7. Sarah Tapp, born Sept. 30, 1864; died, unmarried, Sept., 1883.

Mary Numbers (Cushman) Tapp, usually referred to as Aunt Polly, reached the fine old age of (nearly) 101 years, and, up to the time of her death, was of clear mind and good memory. She was regarded as the family historian and was held in high esteem by all her friends.

―――――――x―――――――

REV. ISAAC JACKSON CUSHMAN (8th Gen.), son of Squier Cushman and Hannah (Humbert) Cushman, born Sept. 19, 1831; died Aug. 26, 1881. Married Martha Jane Dennis, born May 2, 1837; died Nov. 12, 1925. Children born:

1. Charles Cushman, born Feb. 14, 1860; died July 16, 1880.
2. John Spence Cushman, born April 12, 1862, at Murdock, Ohio.
3. Dr. George James Cushman, born March 19, 1866; died Sept. 29, 1916.
4. Isaac Newton Cushman, born Nov. 25, 1869.
5. Edward Lucius Cushman, born Jan. 15, 1872.
6. Mary Cushman, born Jan. 13, 1878.

Rev. Isaac Jackson Cushman was graduated from Miami University, Oxford, Ohio, and while attending there met Martha Jane Dennis, his future wife, who was attending Oxford Female College, or Oxford College for Women.

After finishing his theological work at the Seminary, then located at Oxford, Ohio, he served as principal of the South Salem Academy for a year, and then accepted the pastorate of the Murdock Presbyterian Church, located near Loveland, Ohio. He served as pastor of the Murdock Presbyterian Church the greater part of his life, where his family was born. He is buried in the church cemetery, located close by, and here, also, is buried his wife, Martha Jane (Dennis) Cushman, and their son, Charles Cushman. He served in the Army of the Civil War in the "90-day Service."

He never had but this one pastorate; at the celebration by the church of his 20th anniversary in service, he was presented with $100 by his parishioners; his wife with $20; and the baby, Mary Cushman, with $2.50; all was in gold coin and given as an expression of love and esteem for this family; former members of the congregation also sent beautiful gifts.

He had many calls from other churches and other places, but felt that the Lord had called him to Murdock and he remained faithful to his flock to the end.

The neighbors, at the late date of this publication, still speak kind words of this excellent family.

—x—

ANNA MARIA CUSHMAN (8th Gen.), daughter of Squier Cushman and Mary Wing (Conway) Cushman, born March 4, 1841; died June 15, 1934, at Sycamore, Greene County, Pa.

Married Lorenzo Dow Everly, who died December, 1911. Children born:
1. Dora Everly, born Jan. 22, 1862.
2. Jesse Claude Everly, born July 12, 1866.
3. Marcellus M. Everly, born Nov. 6, 1868.
4. Walter Elbert Everly, born Sept. 21, 1874.
5. Rose Mae Everly, born April 1, 1878.
6. Willis Francis Everly, born Feb. 23, 1881.
7. Robert E. Everly, born April 12, 1883.
8. Hal I. Everly, born Feb. 17, 1885.

―――――x―――――

ELIZA RACHEL CUSHMAN (8th Gen.), daughter of Squier Cushman and Mary Wing (Conway) Cushman. Married, June 30, 1864, Alonzo Everly. Children born:
1. Rev. Milton M. Everly; deceased.
2. Harry Everly.
3. Allie Everly.

―――――x―――――

AMANDA ELLEN CUSHMAN (8th Gen.), daughter of Squier Cushman and Mary Wing (Conway) Cushman, born April 2, 1846; died July 21, 1911. Married, June 30, 1864, Alpheus Keener. Children born:
1. Ida May Keener, born May 20, 1865.
2. William Edward Keener, born Jan. 20, 1867; died March 25, 1932.
3. Leonard Clark Keener, born Jan. 14, 1871.

―――――x―――――

GEORGE BROWN CUSHMAN (8th Gen.), son of Squier Cushman and Mary Wing (Conway) Cushman. Married, and it is reported had three children.

―――――x―――――

IDA MAY KEENER (9th Gen.), daughter of Amanda Cushman Keener and Alpheus Keener, born May 20, 1865. Married, May 18, 1887, Eric Jackson Everly. Children born:
1. Zella Alberta Everly, born June 5, 1888.
2. Leonard Lemoin Everly, born Nov. 17, 1889.

―――――x―――――

ZELLA ALBERTA EVERLY (10th Gen.), daughter of Ida May (Keener) Everly and Eric Jackson Everly, born June 5, 1888. Married William Ray. Children born:
1. Orvil Ray, born Sept. 25, 1908.

LEONARD LEMOIN EVERLY (10th Gen.), son of Ida May (Keene) Everly and Eric Jackson Everly, born Nov. 17, 1889. Married and has children.

———————x———————

WILLIAM EDWARD KEENER (9th Gen.), son of Amanda Ellen (Cushman) Keener and Alpheus Keener, born Jan. 20, 1867; died March 25, 1932. Married, Oct. 9, 1889, L. Lurena Everly. Children born:
1. Gladys Myrtle Keener, born Jan. 30, 1902.
2. Virginia Elizabeth Keener, born March 10, 1911.

———————x———————

GLADYS MYRTLE KEENER (10th Gen.), daughter of William Edward Keener and L. Lurena (Everly) Keener, born Jan. 30, 1902. Married, Sept. 1, 1920, Rev. Merle Lloyd Edwards. Children born:
1. William Bert Edwards, born Aug. 28, 1922.
2. Charles Edwards, born April 12, 1925.
3. Carol Tern Edwards, born Oct. 8, 1928.

———————x———————

VIRGINIA ELIZABETH KEENER (10th Gen.), daughter of William Edward Keener and L. Lurena (Everly) Keener, born March 10, 1911. Married, March 15, 1929, Emmet T. Cline. Children born:
1. Mary Lou Cline, born May 8, 1933.

———————x———————

LEONARD CLARK KEENER (9th Gen.), son of Amanda Ellen Cushman Keener and Alpheus Keener, born Jan. 14, 1871; died July 3, 1921. Married, Nov. 30, 1892, Mabel Willars, who died April 26, 1919. Children born:
1. Claudio Lester Keener, born Feb. 27, 1894.
2. John Calvin Keener, born Sept. 12, 1896.
3. Millard Grant Keener, born Nov. 13, 1907.

———————x———————

CLAUDIO LESTER KEENER (10th Gen.), son of Leonard Clark Keener and Mabel (Willars) Keener, born Feb. 27, 1894. Married, May 31, 1915, Pearl Harrington, born July 9, 1894. Children born:
1. Leonard Albert Keener, born Jan. 9, 1925.
2. Juanita May Keener, born Dec. 15, 1930.

———————x———————

JOHN CALVIN KEENER (10th Gen.), son of Leonard Clark Keener and Mabel (Willars) Keener, born Sept. 12, 1896.

Married, March 11, 1919, Essie Morler, born July 7, 1896. Children born:
1. Johnie Keener, Jr., born Oct. 12, 1921.
———————x———————
MILLARD GRANT KEENER (10th Gen.), son of Leonard Clark Keener and Mabel (Willars) Keener, born Nov. 13, 1907. Married, Nov. 14, 1928, Neva Marie Courtney, born Aug. 10, 1907. Children born:
1. Millard Donald Keener, born May 18, 1930.
———————x———————
HANNAH ETHEL TAPP (9th Gen.), daughter of Mary Numbers Cushman Tapp and Festus H. Tapp, born Jan. 25, 1850; died Feb. 5, 1936. Married, in 1873, Gibson Donley. Children born:
1. Oliver H. Donley, born July 10, 1874.
2. Luther M. Donley, born Oct. 8, 1882.
3. Dicie Evelyn Donley, born May 15, 1890.
———————x———————
ADELAIDE FLORINDA TAPP (9th Gen.), daughter of Mary Numbers Cushman Tapp and Festus H. Tapp, born July 12, 1853; died Aug. 23, 1923. Married Lorenzo D. Russell. Children born:
1. Benjamin W. Russell, born July 10, 1874.
2. Mary S. Russell, born Dec. 24, 1875.
3. Donley M. Russell, born July 19, 1878.
4. Eli H. Russell, born Jan. 22, 1890.
5. Robert W. Russell, born March 27, 1895.
———————x———————
WILLIAM WHITFIELD TAPP (9th Gen.), son of Mary Numbers Cushman Tapp and Festus H. Tapp, born June 25, 1856; died April 2, 1916. Married Leona Bartlett. Children born:
1. Mary Evelyn Tapp, born July, 1889.
2. Ethel Tapp, born March 2, 1892; died unmarried.
———————x———————
MARY EVELYN TAPP (10th Gen.), daughter of William Whitfield Tapp and Leona (Bartlett) Tapp, born July, 1889. Married Walter L. Reddick. No issue.
———————x———————
DICIE FLORENCE TAPP (9th Gen.), daughter of Mary Numbers Cushman Tapp and Festus H. Tapp, born Dec. 18, 1861.

Married, Nov., 1898, Spencer M. Donley. Children born:
1. David Edward Donley, born May 14, 1902.
2. Frank Benton Donley, born March 2, 1908.

Mrs. Dicie Florence (Tapp) Donley, of Carmichaels, Greene County, Pa., the oldest, now living of the 9th generation, avers, for our information, concerning her great grandfather, Isaac Cushman, who lived in Fayette County, Wharton Township, Pa., and his brother, Thomas Cushman, who was thirteen years older and owned adjoining land to her great grandfather but across the state line in Monongalia County, W. Va., that her mother, Mary Numbers (Cushman) Tapp, wife of Festus H. Tapp, often told her of her great grandfather, Isaac Cushman, and how he looked, so that she felt she would almost know him, from the description that her mother gave, could he come back. Her mother lived to be 101 years old, but for fourteen days, and with a clear memory until her death. She felt there was no doubt of Isaac Cushman and Thomas Cushman being brothers and that they had come down together to that country from Essex County, N. J., and both had married daughters of Ephraim Frazee. Her mother told her that Thomas was killed by the Indians.

———————x———————

JOHN SPENCE CUSHMAN (9th Gen.), son of Rev. Isaac Jackson Cushman and Martha Jane (Dennis) Cushman, born April 12, 1862, at Murdock, Warren County, near Loveland, Ohio. Married, Nov. 30, 1891, Susan Hollis. Children born:
1. Ruth Cushman, born Aug. 3, 1892, at Osborne, Ohio.
2. Kenneth Harland Cushman, born March 31, 1899, at Loveland, Ohio.
3. Alma Cushman, born Dec. 11, 1903, at Shelbyville, Ky.

———————x———————

MAJOR DAVID EDWARD DONLEY (10th Gen.), son of Dicie Florence (Tapp) Donley and Spencer M. Donley, born May 14, 1902, near Davistown, Pa. Married, Sept. 17, 1928, at Morgantown, W. Va., Cordelia Weaver, born Aug. 22, 1904, at Morgantown, W. Va. Children born:
1. Florence Patricia Donley, born Feb. 19, 1930, at Norfolk, Va.

Major David Edward Donley graduated from West Virginia University, Morgantown, W. Va., and received the degree of bachelor of science in civil engineering in 1926, and that of civil engineer (professional) in 1932.

Since graduating from the university he has been employed as a Government Engineer on river and harbor improvements in Kentucky and Illinois, 1926 to 1927; on sea coast defense work, from 1927 to 1930, and flood control investigations, from 1930 to 1933. During the winter of 1933-34 he was employed in the office of the Chief of Engineers, Washington, D. C.; and from March, 1934 to March, 1940 was engaged in flood control investigations for the Tennessee Valley Authority. He entered on active duty in the army as a Major in January, 1941; was transferred to the Ordnance Department and has served in divers ordnance plants since that time.

———————x———————

FRANK BENTON DONLEY (10th Gen.), son of Dicie Florence (Tapp) Donley and Spencer M. Donley, born March 2, 1908. Married Lucille Stephenson. Children born:
1. David Lee Donley, born Oct. 15, 1935.
2. Beverly Delores Donley, born March 2, 1937.
3. Errol Audrey Donley, born July 7, 1939.

———————x———————

RUTH CUSHMAN (10th Gen.), daughter of John Spence Cushman and Susan (Hollis) Cushman, born Aug. 3, 1892, at Osborne, Ohio. Married, May 8, 1912, Walter E. Snyder. Children born:
1. Edward W. Snyder, born May 13, 1913, at Hammond, Ind.
2. Delores Snyder, born April 26, 1916, at Hammond, Ind.

———————x———————

EDWARD W. SNYDER (11th Gen.), son of Ruth (Cushman) Snyder and Walter E. Snyder, born May 13, 1913, at Hammond, Ind. Married, first, ————. Children born:
1. Phyllis Snyder, born April 18, 1935.
Edward W. Snyder married, secondly, May 28, 1937, Cecelia Stalmac.

———————x———————

DELORES SNYDER (11th Gen.), daughter of Ruth (Cushman) Snyder and Walter E. Snyder, born April 26, 1916, at Hammond, Ind. Married, July 22, 1935, Charles P. Kelly. Children born:

1. James P. Kelly, born April 8, 1936.

———————x———————

KENNETH HARLAND CUSHMAN (10th Gen.), son of John Spence Cushman and Susan (Hollis) Cushman, born March 3, 1899, at Loveland, Ohio. Married, March 30, 1921, at Chicago, Ill., Elsie Aurora Bohlin. Children born:
1. Kenneth Dale Cushman, born June 23, 1927.

Kenneth Harland Cushman married, secondly, Aug. 8, 1931, at Chicago, Ill., Virginia Louise Stapley. Children born:
1. Willard Spence Cushman, born May 20, 1939.

———————x———————

ALMA CUSHMAN (10th Gen.), daughter of John Spence Cushman and Susan (Hollis) Cushman, born Dec. 11, 1903, at Shelbyville, Ky. Married Claude Mund. Children born:
1. Jackie Mund, born 1923.

———————x———————

DR. GEORGE JAMES CUSHMAN (9th Gen.), son of Rev. Isaac Jackson Cushman and Martha Jane (Dennis) Cushman, born March 19, 1866, at Murdock, Warren County, Ohio; died Sept. 29, 1916, in New York City. He was a dentist and practiced his profession in the city of Pittsburgh, Pa. Married Margaret Morey, born Sept. 13, 1876. Children born:
1. George Morey Cushman, born March 20, 1896, at Washington Court House, Ohio.

———————x———————

ISAAC NEWTON CUSHMAN (9th Gen.), son of Rev. Isaac Jackson Cushman and Martha Jane (Dennis) Cushman, born Nov. 25, 1869, at Murdock, Warren County, Ohio. Married, Oct. 20, 1892, Abbie Alice Dibble, born July 2, 1873, at Patriot, Ind. Children born:
1. Martha Mary Cushman, born Oct. 6, 1894, at Loveland, Ohio.
2. Joseph Dean Cushman, born Jan. 11, 1897, at Oxford, Ohio.
3. Edythe Thelma Cushman, born June 19, 1900, at Adams, Ind.
4. Ores Harold Cushman, born Nov. 24, 1906, at Greensburg, Ind.

———————x———————

EDWARD LUCIUS CUSHMAN (9th Gen.), son of Rev. Isaac Jackson Cushman and Martha Jane (Dennis) Cushman, born

Jan. 15, 1872. Married, Sept. 9, 1901, Blanche Jarvis, who died Oct. 2, 1905. Children born:
1. James Jarvis Cushman, born Aug. 6, 1902. } Twins
2. Lucius Jarvis Cushman, born Aug. 6, 1902. }
3. Martha Blanche Cushman, born Oct. 10, 1905; died Sept. 6, 1906.

Edward Lucius Cushman married, secondly, July 21, 1908, Waunita MacDonald, born March 9, 1884. Children born:
1. Edward Allen Cushman, born March 14, 1911.
2. Margaret Vernon Cushman, born June 11, 1914.
3. Elizabeth Ann Cushman, born June 5, 1919.

―――――x―――――

ORES HAROLD CUSHMAN (10th Gen.), son of Isaac Newton Cushman and Abbie Alice (Dibble) Cushman, born Nov. 24, 1906, at Greensburg, Ind. Married Erma Erickson. No issue.

―――――x―――――

JAMES JARVIS CUSHMAN (10th Gen.), son of Edward Lucius Cushman and Blanche Jarvis Cushman, born Aug. 6, 1902. Married, May, 1926, Alice Andrews. Children born:
1. Joan Blanche Cushman, born April 23, 1927.
2. Jan Marie Cushman, born Aug., 1931.
3. Judy Katharine Cushman, born Dec., 1939.

―――――x―――――

LUCIUS JARVIS CUSHMAN (10th Gen.), son of Edward Lucius Cushman and Blanche Jarvis Cushman, born Aug. 6, 1902. Married, March 10, 1939, Helen Kempe.

―――――x―――――

EDWARD ALLEN CUSHMAN (10th Gen.), son of Edward Lucius Cushman and Waunita (MacDonald) Cushman, born March 14, 1911. Married, June 7, 1937, Ann Frances Shinn. Children born:
1. Edward Allen Cushman, born April 2, 1938.
2. Michael Darby Cushman, born May 28, 1940.

―――――x―――――

MARGARET VERNON CUSHMAN (10th Gen.), daughter of Edward Lucius Cushman and Waunita (MacDonald) Cushman, born June 11, 1914. Married, Sept., 1937, Robert Truitt Hayes.

―――――x―――――

EMMET E. EVERLY (10th Gen.), son of Marcellus M. Everly and Mattie (Shafer) Everly, born Feb. 7, 1891. Married Katie Jordan. Children born:

1. Earl Everly.
2. Clifford Everly.
3. Jay Everly.

---x---

GEORGE MOREY CUSHMAN (10th Gen.), son of Dr. George James Cushman and Margaret (Morey) Cushman, born March 20, 1896, at Washington Court House, Ohio. Married, Feb. 13, 1918, Edith Anderson, born June 30, 1899, at Chicago, Ill. Children born:
    1. Charlotte Cushman, born May 12, 1919, at Hammond, Ind.
    2. George James Cushman, born Jan. 29, 1922, at Hammond, Ind.
    3. Arthur William Cushman, born Dec. 30, 1923, at Hammond, Ind.
    4. Richard Thomas Cushman, born Feb. 15, 1930, at Hammond, Ind.
    5. Margaret Dorothy Cushman, born Feb. 12, 1935, at Valparaiso, Ind.

---x---

MARTHA MARY CUSHMAN (10th Gen.), daughter of Isaac Newton Cushman and Abbie Alice (Dibble) Cushman, born Oct. 6, 1894, at Loveland, Ohio. Married, April 20, 1918, at Chicago, Ill., Frank Earl Baum. Children born:
    1. David Cushman Baum, born Nov. 11, 1921, at Chicago, Ill.
    2. Robert Earl Baum, born July 13, 1923, at Chicago, Ill.

---x---

JOSEPH DEAN CUSHMAN (10th Gen.), son of Isaac Newton Cushman and Abbie Alice (Dibble) Cushman, born Jan. 11, 1897, at Oxford, Ohio. Married, June 2, 1921, at Chicago, Ill., Kathryn R. Proctor. Children born:
    1. Jean Louise Cushman, born Dec. 17, 1922.
    2. William Dean Cushman, born Sept. 19, 1926.
    3. Marcella Mae Cushman, born Dec. 6, 1934.

---x---

EDYTHE THELMA CUSHMAN (10th Gen.), daughter of Isaac Newton Cushman and Abbie Alice (Dibble) Cushman, born June 19, 1900, at Adams, Ind. Married, Nov. 25, 1919, Anthony Schmillen. Children born:

1. June Rosalie Schmillen, born June 22, 1923.

———————x———————

MARY CUSHMAN (9th Gen.), daughter of Rev. Isaac Jackson Cushman and Martha Jane (Dennis) Cushman, born Jan. 13, 1878. Married Robert Foster Donnell. No issue. Mary Cushman Donnell has served as a trustee of Woman's Christian Temperance Union from 1924 to the present, 1942. She served W. C. T. U. as Recording Secretary from 1925 to 1936, and as Corresponding Secretary from 1936 to the present, 1942; like her Reverend father she commands the love and respect of all who know her.

———————x———————

DORA EVERLY (9th Gen.), daughter of Anna Maria (Cushman) Everly and Lorenzo Dow Everly, born Jan. 22, 1862. Married, first, Sept. 16, 1880, Jacob Ingraham Smith. Children born:
1. Thessie Smith, born Aug. 29, 1882.
2. Lena Smith, born March 31, 1886.

Dora Everly Smith married, secondly, Aug. 23, 1903, Joseph Taylor Garner. To this union no children were born.

———————x———————

THESSIE SMITH (10th Gen.), daughter of Dora (Everly) Smith and Jacob Ingraham Smith, born Aug. 29, 1882. Married Ward L. Ray. No issue.

———————x———————

LENA SMITH (10th Gen.), daughter of Dora (Everly) Smith and Jacob Ingraham Smith, born March 31, 1886. Married Fred L. Dunn. No issue.

———————x———————

JESSE CLAUDE EVERLY (9th Gen.), son of Anna Maria (Cushman) Everly and Lorenzo Dow Everly, born July 12, 1866. Married Louise Heavener. Children born:
1. Helen Everly, born Dec. 11, 1896, at New Kensington, Pa.
2. Dessie Everly, born June 19, 1899, at New Kensington, Pa.
3. Naomi Everly, born Jan. 8, 1905, at New Kensington, Pa.

———————x———————

HELEN EVERLY (10th Gen.), daughter of Jesse Claude Everly and Louise (Heavener) Everly, born Dec. 11, 1896, at

New Kensington, Pa. Married Jacob Elmer Kutz, born March 17, 1892, at Carlisle, Pa. Children born:
1. Evelyn Louise Kutz, born Dec. 19, 1923, in Carlisle, Pa.
2. Donna Mae Kutz, born May 8, 1930, in Carlisle, Pa.

———————x———————

DESSIE EVERLY (10th Gen.), daughter of Jesse Claude Everly and Louise (Heavener) Everly, born June 19, 1899, at New Kensington, Pa. Married Phillip Wagner, born Jan. 4, 1903, in New Kensington, Pa. Children born:
1. Dorothy Jean Wagner, born Nov. 3, 1925, at New Kensington, Pa.
2. Donald Roy Wagner, born June 21, 1933, at New Kensington, Pa.

———————x———————

NAOMI EVERLY (10th Gen.), daughter of Jesse Claude Everly and Louise (Heavener) Everly, born Jan. 8, 1905, in New Kensington, Pa. Married Paul Oliver White, born Jan. 15, 1906, at Mt. Union, Pa. Children born:
1. Lois Jone White, born Oct. 21, 1930, in New Kensington, Pa.
2. Paul Leon White, born July 15, 1936, in New Kensington, Pa.

———————x———————

MARCELLUS M. EVERLY (9th Gen.), son of Anna Maria (Cushman) Everly and Lorenzo Dow Everly, born Nov. 6, 1868. Married, 1890, Mattie Shafer. Children born:
1. Emmet E. Everly, born Feb. 7, 1891.
2. Ernest W. Everly, born Dec. 18, 1893.
3. Rev. William Niemon Everly, born Dec. 28, 1895.
4. Nova Negley Everly, born Feb. 8, 1898.
5. Jessie L. Everly, born July 12, 1901.

———————x———————

WALTER ELBERT EVERLY (9th Gen.), son of Anna Maria (Cushman) Everly and Lorenzo Dow Everly, born Sept. 21, 1874. Married. No issue.

———————x———————

ROSE MAE EVERLY (9th Gen.), daughter of Anna Maria (Cushman) Everly and Lorenzo Dow Everly, born April 1, 1878. Married, Dec. 17, 1903, Thomas J. Gabb. Children born:
1. Beulah Madeline Gabb, born July 7, 1905.

2. Thomas Gerald Gabb, born Sept. 24, 1906.

BEULAH MADELINE GABB (10th Gen.), daughter of Rose Mae (Everly) Gabb, and Thomas J. Gabb, born July 7, 1905. Married Albert Nelson Goslane.

THOMAS GERALD GABB (10th Gen.), son of Rose Mae (Everly) Gabb and Thomas J. Gabb, born Sept. 24, 1906. Married, 1933, Almeda Dinsmore, of Aleppo, Greene County, Pa. Children born:
1. Sarah Rose Gabb, born Jan. 16, 1934.

WILLIS FRANCIS EVERLY (9th Gen.), son of Anna Maria (Cushman) Everly and Lorenzo Dow Everly, born Feb. 23, 1881, at Sycamore, Greene County, Pa. Married, March 5, 1901, Bernadina Frances Lehman, born Oct. 29, 1883, in Carrick, Allegheny County, Pa. Children born:
1. Naomi Helen Everly, born Sept. 9, 1902.
2. Willis Francis Everly, Jr., born July 27, 1904.
3. Cameron Ray Everly, born July 4, 1911.

NAOMI HELEN EVERLY (10th Gen.), daughter of Willis Francis Everly and Bernadina Frances (Lehman) Everly, born Sept. 9, 1902. Married, 1925, Floyd Edward Wallace.

WILLIS FRANCIS EVERLY, JR. (10th Gen.), son of Willis Francis Everly and Bernadina Frances (Lehman) Everly, born July 27, 1904. Married, 1930, Hazel Violet Reid. Children born:
1. Joan Marlene Everly, born Oct. 23, 1931.
2. Carole Eileen Everly, born Aug. 12, 1933.

ROBERT E. EVERLY (9th Gen.), son of Anna Maria (Cushman) Everly and Lorenzo Dow Everly, born April 12, 1883. Married, first, Mayme Watton. Children born:
1. Robert Everly.
2. Valentine Everly.
3. Bernard Everly.

Robert E. Everly married, secondly, Anna Kerschner. Children born:
1. Patricia Everly.
2. Dora Bell Everly.

3. Alma Jean Everly.
4. Nancy Jane Everly.

---x---

HAL I. EVERLY (9th Gen.), son of Anna Maria (Cushman) Everly and Lorenzo Dow Everly, born Feb. 17, 1885. Married Winnie Provins. Children born:
1. Inez Everly.

---x---

HERBERT EMMETT GARLOW (10th Gen.), son of Maria Lucinda (Cushman) Garlow and John M. Garlow, born April 18, 1881. Married Lulabelle Corn Hoard. Children born:
1. Emma Lucinda Garlow.
2. Herbert Emmett Garlow, Jr.

---x---

JESSE CLAUDE GARLOW (10th Gen.), son of Maria Lucinda (Cushman) Garlow and John M. Garlow, born Aug. 24, 1893. Married ―――. Children born:
1. Roger Andrew Garlow.
2. Willard Stanley Garlow.
3. John Hollis Garlow.
4. Kenneth Adrian Garlow.

---x---

REV. WILLIAM NIEMON EVERLY (10th Gen.), son of Marcellus M. Everly and Mattie (Shafer) Everly, born Dec. 28, 1895. Married Myrtle Turley. Children born:
1. Della Lee Everly, born July 6, 1924.
2. David John Everly, born Nov. 27, 1937.

---x---

JESSIE LUELLA EVERLY (10th Gen.), daughter of Marcellus M. Everly and Mattie (Shafer) Everly, born July 12, 1899. Married, first, Nov. 1, 1921, at Pittsburgh, Pa., Herman W. Erbel. Children born:
1. Robert Everly Erbel, born April 29, 1923, at Detroit, Mich.

Jessie Luella Everly married, secondly, July 12, 1937, Clarence W. Terry, at Lewistown, Pa.

---x---

NOVA NEGLEY EVERLY (10th Gen.), daughter of Marcellus M. Everly and Mattie (Shafer) Everly, born Feb. 8, 1898. Married, April 13, 1918, Neil Christian Frederick Nielson, now Major Nielsen. Children born:

1. Frederick Owen Nielsen, born May 28, 1919.
2. Patricia Ruth Nova Nielsen, born July 24, 1920.

Major Nielsen served in World War I in the Air Corps, as Sergeant First Class. His son, Frederick Owen Nielsen, enlisted in June, 1941, in the Air Corps, and is now in active service in Australia.

Patricia Ruth Nova Nielsen, daughter of Major and Mrs. Nielsen, was married Thursday, April 16, 1942, at Las Vegas, New Mexico, to First Lieut. David Dorrington Kress-Muhlenberg, son of Colonel H. C. Kress-Muhlenberg. Mrs. Patricia Nielsen Kress-Muhlenberg has had two years experience flying; she also served as secretary to the Chief Test Pilot at Curtis-Wright Corporation. She was crowned "Miss Aviation of 1940," which coronation took place at the annual air show at Columbus, Ohio, her former home.

―――――――x―――――――

ALBERT L. BROWN (11th Gen.), son of Mary Rosena (Cushman) Brown and William Brown, born March 7, 1910. Married, Sept. 3, 1931, Garnet L. Titus, born Jan. 15, 1913. Children born:
1. Jerold Erwin Brown, born June 5, 1940.

―――――――x―――――――

LEVI CUSHMAN (7th Gen.), son of Isaac Cushman and Deborah (Frazee) Cushman, born Wednesday, Feb. 17, 1796; died 1840; buried at New Market, Va. Married Margaret Potter. Children born:
1. Ephraim Cushman.
2. Sarah Cushman, deceased and buried at New Market, Va.
3. Savilla Cushman.
4. Sarah Jane Cushman. Unmarried; deceased.

―――――――x―――――――

EPHRAIM CUSHMAN (8th Gen.), son of Levi Cushman and Margaret (Potter) Cushman. Married. Children born:
1. Ellen Elizabeth Cushman, born Aug., 1857; died Dec. 8, 1904.
2. James Cushman, unmarried and deceased.
3. Charles Cushman.
4. David Stephenson Cushman.

ELLEN ELIZABETH CUSHMAN (9th Gen.), daughter of Ephraim Cushman and ——— Cushman, born Aug., 1857; died Dec. 8, 1904. Married Abram Burkholder. Children born:
1. Casper David Burkholder, born April 26, 1874.
2. John William Burkholder.
3. James Burkholder, born 1881.
4. Abram Burkholder, born Dec. 12, 1879.
5. Albert Louis Burkholder, born Aug. 26, 1877.
6. Susan Burkholder.
7. Amanda Burkholder.
8. Israel Allen Burkholder, born Aug. 9, 1886.

———————x———————

CASPER DAVID BURKHOLDER (10th Gen.), son of Ellen Elizabeth (Cushman) Burkholder and Abram Burkholder, born April 26, 1874, at New Market, Va. Married, April 25, 1893, Mary Durr. Children born:
1. Emily May Burkholder, born Jan. 13, 1895, at New Market, Va.
2. Ernest Lee Burkholder, born May 7, 1896, at New Market, Va.
3. Julius Gorley Burkholder, born Aug. 27, 1897, at New Market, Va.
4. John William Burkholder, born July 22, 1899, at New Market, Va.
5. Welty Abram Burkholder, born Oct. 22, 1901, at New Market, Va.
6. Miller Eugene Burkholder, born Aug. 16, at New Market, Va.
7. Elmer Michael Burkholder, born Aug. 15, 1905, at New Market, Va.
8. Gardner Paxton Burkholder, born Sept. 21, 1907, at New Market, Va.
9. Harry Pastermac Burkholder, born Sept. 23, 1909, at New Market, Va.
10. Theodore Roosevelt Burkholder, born Aug. 9, 1911, at New Market, Va.
11. Nellie Virginia Burkholder, born May 3, 1913, at New Market, Va.

CUSHMAN GENEALOGY AND GENERAL HISTORY   389

12. Lenna Frances Burkholder, born July 10, 1915, at Lima, Ohio.
13. William Hoover Burkholder, born March 29, 1918, at Lima, Ohio.
14. James Polling Burkholder, born 1920, at Lima, Ohio.

———x———

EMILY MAY BURKHOLDER (11th Gen.), daughter of Casper David Burkholder and Mary (Durr) Burkholder, born Jan. 13, 1895, in New Market, Va. Married, Sept., 1915, William E. Reedy.

———x———

ERNEST LEE BURKHOLDER (11th Gen.), son of Casper David Burkholder and Mary (Durr) Burkholder, born May 7, 1896, at New Market, Va. Married Maud Wiggins. Children born:
1. Phyllis Burkholder, born Feb. 23, 1921.
2. June Burkholder, born Feb. 19, 1923.
3. Joseph Burkholder, born 1926.

———x———

JOHN WILLIAM BURKHOLDER (11th Gen.), son of Casper David Burkholder and Mary (Durr) Burkholder, born July 22, 1899, at New Market, Va. Married Gertrude Hasson. Children born:
1. William Burkholder.
2. John Burkholder.
3. Darrel Gene Burkholder.

———x———

WELTY ABRAM BURKHOLDER (11th Gen.), son of Casper David Burkholder and Mary (Durr) Burkholder, born Oct. 22, 1901, at New Market, Va. Married, July 10, 1921, Goldie Reeder, at Lima, Ohio. Children born:
1. Margaret Emily Burkholder, born June 20, 1923.
2. Welty Clayton Burkholder, born April 19, 1926.
3. Emma Colleen Burkholder, born Aug. 22, 1928.
4. Delores Virginia Burkholder, born June 5, 1930.
5. Lenna Lee Burkholder, born July 5, 1932.
6. Emiel Kess Burkholder (called Sonny), born Feb. 28, 1937.

———x———

MILLER EUGENE BURKHOLDER (11th Gen.), son of Casper David Burkholder and Mary (Durr) Burkholder, born Aug.

16, 1903, at New Market, Va. Married Gladys Burden. Children born:
1. Betty Jean Burkholder, born Dec. 26, 1925.
2. Mary Catharine Burkholder.
3. Catharine Burkholder.
4. Jerry Burkholder.

―――――――x―――――――

Elmer Michael Burkholder (11th Gen.), son of Casper David Burkholder and Mary (Durr) Burkholder, born Aug. 15, 1905, at New Market, Va. Married, March 10, 1941, Ruth Shockey.

―――――――x―――――――

Gardner Paxton Burkholder (11th Gen.), son of Casper David Burkholder and Mary (Durr) Burkholder, born Sept. 21, 1907, at New Market, Va. Married Rhoda Mann, at Lima, Ohio. Children born:
1. Joann Burkholder, born Feb. 1, 1932.

―――――――x―――――――

Harry Pasternac Burkholder (11th Gen.), son of Casper David Burkholder and Mary (Durr) Burkholder, born Sept. 23, 1909, at New Market, Va. Married Naomi Teters. Children born:
1. Wanda Maxine Burkholder, born Dec. 12, 1933.
2. Donald J. Burkholder, born Aug. 26, 1937.
3. Mary Lou Burkholder, born April 28, 1940.

―――――――x―――――――

Theodore Roosevelt Burkholder (11th Gen.), son of Casper David Burkholder and Mary (Durr) Burkholder, born Aug. 9, 1911, at New Market, Va. Married Florence Truesdale. Children born:
1. Crystal Evon Burkholder, born May 20, 1932.
2. Robert Earl Burkholder, born May 18, 1934.
3. Shirley Burkholder, born May 10, 1937.
4. Joyce Ann Burkholder, born Nov. 12, 1939.

―――――――x―――――――

Nellie Virginia Burkholder (11th Gen.), daughter of Casper David Burkholder and Mary (Durr) Burkholder, born May 3, 1913, at New Market, Va. Married Linwood Burkholder. Children born:
1. Ronald Dale Burkholder, born Dec. 24, 1934.

LENNA FRANCES BURKHOLDER (11th Gen.), daughter of Casper David Burkholder and Mary (Durr) Burkholder, born July 10, 1915, at Lima, Ohio. Married Walter Klinefetter. Children born:
1. Walter James Klinefetter, born June 26, 1940.

―――――――x―――――――
WILLIAM HOOVER BURKHOLDER (11th Gen.), son of Casper David Burkholder and Mary (Durr) Burkholder, born March 29, 1918. Married Ruth Cox. Children born:
1. Edith Catharine Burkholder, born Feb. 28, 1937.

William Hoover Burkholder married, secondly, Nina Stark. Children born:
1. Jerry David Burkholder, born 1940.

―――――――x―――――――
JOHN WILLIAM BURKHOLDER (10th Gen.), son of Ellen (Cushman) Burkholder and Abram Burkholder. Married Cora Shafer. Children born:
1. Linda Burkholder.
2. Frances Burkholder.
3. William Edward Burkholder, born Oct. 9, 1903.

John William Burkholder married, secondly, Charlotte Rice.

―――――――x―――――――
LINDA BURKHOLDER (11th Gen.), daughter of John William Burkholder and Cora (Shafer) Burkholder. Married Raymond Rice.

―――――――x―――――――
WILLIAM EDWARD BURKHOLDER (11th Gen.), son of John William Burkholder and Cora (Shafer) Burkholder, born Oct. 9, 1903, in New Market, Va. Married, Nov. 12, 1929, Anna Mary Burkholder. Children born:
1. Edward Eugene Burkholder, born June 21, 1930.
2. Rosemary Burkholder, born Oct. 22, 1931.
3. Richard Lee Burkholder, born May 14, 1934.
4. Thomas Walter Burkholder, born March 1, 1936.
5. James Earle Burkholder, born Jan. 5, 1938.

―――――――x―――――――
JAMES BURKHOLDER (10th Gen.), son of Ellen Elizabeth (Cushman) Burkholder and Abram Burkholder, born 1881, at New Market, Va. Married Emma Foley. Children born:
1. Viola Burkholder.
2. Mary Elizabeth Burkholder.

ABRAM BURKHOLDER (10th Gen.), son of Ellen Elizabeth (Cushman) Burkholder and Abram Burkholder, born Dec. 12, 1879, at New Market, Va. Married, Oct. 15, 1902, Edna Higgs, born May 11, 1885. Children born:
1. Claude Neff Burkholder, born Oct. 14, 1903.
2. Clarence Lee Burkholder, born Nov. 28, 1905.
3. Ralph Higgs Burkholder, born Jan. 28, 1908.
4. Linwood Jackson Burkholder, born March 28, 1910.
5. Pearl Leticia Burkholder, born April 13, 1912, at Lima, Ohio.
6. Frank Eugene Burkholder, born April 8, 1914.
7. Maxine Oweda Burkholder, born Dec. 17, 1919.

———x———

CLAUDE NEFF BURKHOLDER (11th Gen.), son of Abram Burkholder and Edna (Higgs) Burkholder, born Oct. 14, 1903, at New Market, Va. Married Ruth Frysinger. Children born:
1. William Wayne Burkholder, born June 10, 1928.

———x———

CLARENCE LEE BURKHOLDER (11th Gen.), son of Abram Burkholder and Edna (Higgs), Burkholder, born Nov. 28, 1905. Married Margarie Roselyn Bressler. Children born:
1. Richard Lee Burkholder, born June 14, 1928.
2. Thomas Arthur Burkholder, born May 3, 1930.
3. David Rodney Burkholder, born June 2, 1937.
4. Elizabeth Helen Burkholder, born April 20, 1939.

———x———

RALPH HIGGS BURKHOLDER (11th Gen.), son of Abram Burkholder and Edna (Higgs) Burkholder, born Jan. 28, 1908. Married Mary Kiser. Children born:
1. Robert Eugene Burkholder, born Aug. 6, 1927.
2. Donald Deane Burkholder, born March 20, 1930.
3. Phillip Roger Burkholder, born Jan. 2, 1933.
4. Jerry Lynn Burkholder, born Aug. 6, 1934.

———x———

LINWOOD JACKSON BURKHOLDER (11th Gen.), son of Abram Burkholder and Edna (Higgs) Burkholder, born March 28, 1910. Married Wanda Maury. Children born:
1. Imogene Burkholder, born Jan. 21, 1932.
Linwood Jackson Burkholder married, secondly, Nellie

Burkholder. Children born:
1. Ronald Dale Burkholder, born Dec. 24, 1933.

―――――x―――――

PEARL LETICIA BURKHOLDER (11th Gen.), daughter of Abram Burkholder and Edna (Higgs) Burkholder, born April 13, 1912, at Lima, Ohio. Married, April 9, 1932, George Fred Shrider. Children born:
1. James Russell Shrider, born Jan. 30, 1933.
2. Michael Lee Shrider, born June 23, 1934.
3. George Fred Shrider, Jr., born April 9, 1940.

―――――x―――――

FRANK EUGENE BURKHOLDER (11th Gen.), son of Abram Burkholder and Edna (Higgs) Burkholder, born April 8, 1914, at Lima, Ohio. Married, June 26, 1937, at Lima, Ohio, Maxine Catharine Morris.

―――――x―――――

MAXINE OWEDA BURKHOLDER (11th Gen.), daughter of Abram Burkholder and Edna (Higgs) Burkholder, born Dec. 17, 1919, at Lima, Ohio. Married, Feb. 17, 1937, at Lima, Ohio, Gerald Briley.

―――――x―――――

ALBERT LOUIS BURKHOLDER (10th Gen.), son of Ellen (Cushman) Burkholder and Abram Burkholder, born Aug. 26, 1877, at New Market, Va. Married, Nov. 24, 1904, Mildred Iona Newell. Children born:
1. Louis Albert Burkholder, born Dec. 2, 1905.
2. Violet Fern Burkholder, born March 22, 1907.
3. Ruth Opalite Burkholder, born Oct. 18, 1908.
4. Myrtle Ilanda Burkholder, born Oct. 11, 1909.
5. Anna Mary Burkholder, born Nov. 29, 1910.
6. Helen Lenora Burkholder, born March 5, 1913.
7. Harley Wilson Burkholder, born Oct. 11, 1914.
8. Florine Lecretia Burkholder, born Aug. 22, 1918.

―――――x―――――

LOUIS ALBERT BURKHOLDER (11th Gen.), son of Albert Louis Burkholder and Mildred Iona (Newell) Burkholder, born Dec. 2, 1905, in Lima, Ohio. Married, Aug. 11, 1926, Viola Bell Lehman, in Lima, Ohio. Children born:
1. Louis Albert Burkholder, Jr., born Jan. 25, 1928.

VIOLET FERN BURKHOLDER (11th Gen.), daughter of Albert Louis Burkholder and Mildred Iona (Newell) Burkholder, born March 22, 1907, at Lima, Ohio. Married, Sept. 25, 1926, at Lima, Ohio, Harold Ries. Children born:
1. Keith Burkholder Ries.
2. Burke Emmet Ries.

———————x———————

RUTH OPALITE BURKHOLDER (11th Gen.), daughter of Albert Louis Burkholder and Mildred Iona (Newell) Burkholder, born Oct. 18, 1908, in Lima, Ohio. Married, July 17, 1926, Ersell Elmer Layman. Children born:
1. Pearl Elizabeth Layman, born July 9, 1927.
2. Charles Albert Layman, born Oct. 2, 1929.

———————x———————

MYRTLE ILANDA BURKHOLDER (11th Gen.), daughter of Albert Louis Burkholder and Mildred Iona (Newell) Burkholder, born Oct. 11, 1909, in Lima, Ohio. Married Marion Ralph Fisher, at Woodstock, Va. Children born:
1. Robert Fisher.
2. Clarabell Fisher.
3. Margaret Fisher.
4. Donald Fisher, born Feb. 8, 1937.

———————x———————

HELEN LENORA BURKHOLDER (11th Gen.), daughter of Albert Louis Burkholder and Mildred Iona (Newell) Burkholder, born March 5, 1913, in Lima, Ohio. Married, Jan. 17, 1930, Arden Hess Schweinfurt. Children born:
1. Robert Franklin Schweinfurt, born Dec. 5, 1936.
Helen Lenora Burkholder married, secondly, Nov. 12, 1937, Clyde Robert Carden.

———————x———————

HARLEY WILSON BURKHOLDER (11th Gen.), son of Albert Louis Burkholder and Mildred Iona (Newell) Burkholder, born Oct. 11, 1914, at Lima, Ohio. Married, Dec. 25, 1938, Vilas Turner.

———————x———————

FLORINE LECRETIA BURKHOLDER (11th Gen.), daughter of Albert Louis Burkholder and Mildred Iona (Newell) Burkholder, born Aug. 22, 1918, at Lima, Ohio. Married Carl Kiester. Children born:
1. Wayne Edward Kiester, born June 11, 1939.

Cushman Genealogy and General History 395

ISRAEL ALLEN BURKHOLDER (10th Gen.), son of Ellen Elizabeth (Cushman) Burkholder and Abram Burkholder, born Aug. 9, 1886, at New Market, Va. Married, Aug. 20, 1910, Daisy Wiggins, in Lima, Ohio. Children born:
1. Waldo Eugene Burkholder, born May 19, 1911.
2. Clara Ruby Burkholder, born Nov. 21, 1912.
3. Florence Lucille Burkholder, born Oct. 5, 1914.
4. Ellen Mae Burkholder, born May 15, 1917.
5. Robert Donald Burkholder, born June 7, 1921.
6. Billy Kenneth Burkholder, born Nov. 15, 1924.
7. Thelma Elizabeth Burkholder, born Feb. 9, 1927.
8. Bernard Allen Burkholder, born March 21, 1928.

―――――――x―――――――

WALDO EUGENE BURKHOLDER (11th Gen.), son of Israel Allen Burkholder and Daisy (Wiggins) Burkholder, born May 19, 1911, in Lima, Ohio. Married, Jan. 20, 1931, Margaret Wilson. Children born:
1. Evelyn May Burkholder, born Nov. 1, 1931.
2. Dorothy Elinor Burkholder, born May 22, 1933.
3. Waldine Eugenia Burkholder, born Dec. 30, 1935.
4. Phillis Jane Burkholder, born Oct. 1, 1937.
5. Martha Lee Burkholder, born Aug. 13, 1940.

―――――――x―――――――

CLARA RUBY BURKHOLDER (11th Gen.), daughter of Israel Allen Burkholder and Daisy (Wiggins) Burkholder, born Nov. 21, 1912, in Lima, Ohio. Married, March 26, 1929, in Lima, Ohio, Leonard Tinney. Children born:
1. Robert Franklin Tinney, born Oct. 25, 1929.
2. Betty May Tinney, born Sept. 15, 1933.

―――――――x―――――――

FLORENCE LUCILLE BURKHOLDER (11th Gen.), daughter of Israel Allen Burkholder and Daisy (Wiggins) Burkholder, born Oct. 5, 1914, at Lima, Ohio. Married, May 10, 1930, George Amel Theis. Children born:
1. Leonard Theis, born July 1, 1933.
2. Charles Amel Theis, born Feb. 9, 1935.
3. Roger Eugene Theis, born May 5, 1937.

―――――――x―――――――

ELLEN MAE BURKHOLDER (11th Gen.), daughter of Israel Allen Burkholder and Daisy (Wiggins) Burkholder, born

May 15, 1917, at Lima, Ohio. Married, March 6, 1935, Earl Jerome Terflinger. Children born:
1. Barba Louise Terflinger, born Nov. 1, 1935.
2. Donald Lee Terflinger, born June 20, 1937.

———————x———————

DAVID STEPHENSON CUSHMAN (9th Gen.), son of Ephraim Cushman. Married Ella Mahoney. To this union no children were born; they have, however, to their credit, raised, educated and adopted other children; they live at New Market, Shenandoah Valley, Virginia.

———————x———————

SUSAN BURKHOLDER (10th Gen.), daughter of Ellen Elizabeth (Cushman) Burkholder and Abram Burkholder. Married Jacob Strickler and is reported as having two children.

———————x———————

AMANDA BURKHOLDER (10th Gen.), daughter of Ellen Elizabeth Burkholder and Abram Burkholder. Married Walter Frederick.

———————x———————

VIOLA BURKHOLDER (11th Gen.), daughter of James Burkholder and Emma (Foley) Burkholder. Married Wm. Steele.

MARY ELIZABETH BURKHOLDER (11th Gen.), daughter of James Burkholder and Emma (Foley) Burkholder. Married Mr. Lohr.

———————x———————

EPHRAIM CUSHMAN (7th Gen.), son of Isaac Cushman and Deborah (Frazee) Cushman, born Sept. 6, 1798; died Nov. 19, 1884. Married Nancy Fields, born 1806; died Oct. 6, 1886. Children born:
1. Frances Cushman, born 1868.
2. John Wesley Cushman, died unmarried.
3. Dianna Cushman, died young, unmarried.
4. Catharine Cushman (called Katie).
5. Louisiana Cushman, died Jan. 1, 1924.
6. Rouanna Cushman, died May 25, 1932.

Ephraim Cushman was born in Pennsylvania; his mother, Deborah (Frazee) Cushman, died when he was two years old, on the date of the birth of his younger brother, Frazier Frazee Cushman, April 7, 1800.

His father, Isaac, married a second time, and the last child born, Frazier Frazee Cushman, found, according to his statement left with his children, life so hard and burdensome and was so unhappy, that he felt it necessary to run away from his home; it, therefore, seems likely that such experiences prompted Ephraim to leave his home early as a boy, never returning, and losing all trace of his family.

The family of Ephraim still speak of his relating to them features concerning Isaac, called Moses Cushman, the first child born to Isaac and Deborah (Frazee) Cushman, and also Rachel Cushman, the second child, who married Daniel Woodmansee, and also a sister, Rebecca Cushman, who married Daniel Voorhees.

Ephraim Cushman was a farmer, a potter and, by trade, a carpenter.

Ephraim Cushman and Nancy (Fields) Cushman lived in Washington County, Ky., and six children born to them were all born in Washington County; later on their home in Washington County was destroyed by fire, after which they moved to Hardin County, Ky.

———————x———————

FRANCES CUSHMAN (8th Gen.), daughter of Ephraim Cushman and Nancy (Fields) Cushman, born 1868. Married, first, Gabriel Nichols. Frances Cushman Nichols, secondly, married Jesse Kerfoot. There is no record of any children born to Frances Cushman.

———————x———————

CATHARINE CUSHMAN (called "Katie") (8th Gen.), daughter of Ephraim Cushman and Nancy (Fields) Cushman. Married Archibald McGruder. No issue.

———————x———————

LOUISIANA CUSHMAN (8th Gen.), daughter of Ephraim Cushman and Nancy (Fields) Cushman, died Jan. 1, 1924. Married Ingram Blanks Collier, in 1869, who died 1879. Children born:
1. Nama Collier, born April 9, 1870; died Nov. 4, 1886.
2. Carmine Collier, born Feb. 20, 1872.
3. Ingram Blanks Collier, Jr., born Jan. 20, 1874; died Nov. 18, 1880.

ROUANNA CUSHMAN (8th Gen.), daughter of Ephraim Cushman and Nancy (Fields) Cushman, died May 25, 1932. Married Morgan Larue Hart. Children born:
1. James Morgan Hart, born Sept. 12, 1862; died April 22, 1929.
2. John Wesley Hart, born March 13, 1865.
3. Fannie Lou Hart, born April 19, 1868.
4. Nancy Katharine, or Katie, Hart, born Jan. 5, 1872.
5. Mary Elizabeth Hart, born 1875.
6. Henry Hart, born Aug. 24, 1878.
7. Blaine Hart, born April 2, 1882.

———————x———————

JAMES MORGAN HART (9th Gen.), son of Rouanna (Cushman) Hart and Morgan Larue Hart, born Sept. 12, 1862; died April 22, 1929. Married Mary Akers. Children born:
1. Roy Blanks Hart, born Aug. 24, 1897.
2. Lawrence Wesley Hart, born May 21, 1899.
3. Walter Thomas Hart, born April 21, 1901; died July 14, 1902.
4. Ethel May Hart, born Feb. 23, 1903.
5. James Oscar Hart, born Jan. 9, 1906.
6. Ressie May Hart, born May 19, 1908; died Oct. 7, 1910.
7. William Henry Hart, born July 20, 1911.
8. Stella Elizabeth Hart, born Aug. 4, 1914.
9. Phillip Giltner Hart, born Oct. 16, 1921.

———————x———————

JOHN WESLEY HART (9th Gen.), son of Rouanna (Cushman) Hart and Morgan Larue Hart, born March 13, 1865. Married Lillie Blandford. Lives in Elizabethtown, Ky., and has no children.

———————x———————

FANNIE LOU HART (9th Gen.), daughter of Rouanna (Cushman) Hart and Morgan Larue Hart, born April 19, 1868. Married William Lawson and lives at East View, Hardin County, Ky., near the old Cushman homestead, where Ephraim Cushman, her father, owned 500 acres of land. They have no children. ———————x———————

NANCY KATHARINE OR KATIE HART (9th Gen.), daughter of Rouanna (Cushman) Hart and Morgan Larue Hart, born Jan. 5, 1872. Married Walter S. Thomas, born Oct. 28, 1872.

Children born:
1. Walter Klinger Thomas, born Oct. 9, 1898.
2. Roma Thomas, born Sept. 6, 1901.
3. Hal Sherwood Thomas, born Nov. 27, 1905.
4. Arthur Winstead Thomas, born May 26, 1911.
5. Frances Fay Thomas, born Oct. 11, 1914.

———————x———————

MARY ELIZABETH HART (9th Gen), daughter of Rouanna (Cushman) Hart and Morgan Larue Hart, born in 1875. Married Stamp Woolridge. Children born:
1. Eva Woolridge, deceased.
2. Rufus Woolridge, deceased.

Stamp Woolridge died and Mary Elizabeth (Hart) Woolridge married, secondly, Owen Brown. No issue.

———————x———————

HENRY HART (9th Gen.), son of Rouanna (Cushman) Hart and Morgan Larue Hart, born Aug. 24, 1878. Married Iva Hart, of his own name but not related. Children born:
1. Mamie Gladys Hart, born May 27, 1898.
2. Venice Hart, born Nov., 1900.
3. Collier Hart, born Dec. 6, 1903.
4. Cary Leigh Hart, born May 25, 1905.
5. Nama Izetta Hart, born Feb. 12, 1908.
6. Wesley Hart, born April 19, 1910; died in childhood.
7. Richard Heskel Hart, born Sept. 21, 1912.
8. Geneva Katharine Hart, born July 23, 1915.
9. Russell Frankie Hart, born 1918.
10. Nola Inez Hart, born Dec. 11, 1919.

———————x———————

BLAINE HART (9th Gen.), son of Rouanna (Cushman) Hart and Morgan Larue Hart, born April 2, 1882. Married, first, Maggie Hatfield. Children born:
1. Pauline Hart, born June 21, 1907.
2. Dennis Rupert Hart, born Oct. 3, 1909.
3. Aubrey Edward Hart, born March 21, 1913.

Blaine Hart married, secondly, Mollie Phillips. No issue.

———————x———————

ROY BLANKS HART (10th Gen.), son of James Morgan Hart and Mary (Akers) Hart, born Aug. 24, 1897. Married, first, Ressie Anderson. Roy Blanks Hart married, secondly, Mary

Tate, of Summit, Hardin County, Ky. Children born:
1. Marion Howard Hart, born Aug. 10, 1921.
2. Leatrice Fern Hart, born March 1, 1923.
3. Thelma Joyce Hart, born Aug. 22, 1924.
4. Virginia Anne Hart, born July 11, 1931.
5. James John Hart, born July 15, 1933.

———————x———————

LAWRENCE WESLEY HART (10th Gen.), son of James Morgan Hart and Mary (Akers) Hart, born May 21, 1899. Married, first, Aug. 1, 1918, Roxie Noe. Children born:
1. Blanks Leslie Hart, born June 17, 1919.
2. Carroll Clodus Hart, born Feb. 24, 1921.

Lawrence Wesley Hart married, secondly, Tressie Roff, born July 14, 1912. Children born:
1. Laymon Hart, born Jan. 23, 1929.
2. Thelma Hart, born July 30, 1931.
3. Deloras Hart, born April 10, 1933.
4. Charles Hart, born April 25, 1935.
5. Alice Marie Hart, born May 10, 1936.
6. Zona May Hart, born Dec. 9, 1938.

———————x———————

ETHEL MAY HART (10th Gen.), daughter of James Morgan Hart and Mary (Akers) Hart, born Feb. 23, 1903. Married Feb. 1, 1919, Dewey Noe. Children born:
1. Louis Elmer Noe, born March 14, 1920.

———————x———————

JAMES OSCAR HART (10th Gen.), son of James Morgan Hart and Mary (Akers) Hart, born Jan. 9, 1906. Married Aileen Love, born March 12, 1906. Children born:
1. Helen Hart, born Oct. 16, 1927.
2. William Earl Hart, born May 12, 1930.

———————x———————

WILLIAM HENRY HART (10th Gen.), son of James Morgan Hart and Mary (Akers) Hart, born July 20, 1911. Married Pearl Jeffers, born Sept. 9, 1917. Children born:
1. Irena Pearl Hart, born Aug. 30, 1937.
2. Bobby Eugene Hart, born Jan. 1, 1940.

———————x———————

STELLA ELIZABETH HART (10th Gen.), daughter of James Morgan Hart and Mary (Akers) Hart, born Aug. 4, 1914. Married Harry Sapp.

GENEVA KATHARINE HART (10th Gen.), daughter of Henry Hart and Iva Hart, born July 23, 1915. Married Sear Richardson.

———————x———————

RUSSELL FRANKIE HART (10th Gen.), son of Henry Hart and Iva Hart, born 1918. Married Ella Sinkovic, born Nov. 9, 1919. Children born:
1. Russell Frankie Hart, Jr., born Jan. 10, 1940.

———————x———————

NOLA INEZ HART (10th Gen.), daughter of Henry Hart and Iva Hart, born Dec. 11, 1920. Married John Dill.

———————x———————

PAULINE HART (10th Gen.), daughter of Blaine Hart and Maggie (Hatfield) Hart, born June 21, 1907. Married George A. Stessel. Children born:
1. Dian Stessel, born Dec. 27, 1932.
2. Carmen Stessel, born June 15, 1935.
3. Sally Stessel, born Feb. 1, 1939.

———————x———————

DENNIS RUPERT HART (10th Gen.), son of Blaine Hart and Maggie (Hatfield) Hart, born Oct. 31, 1909. Married Vera Frittz. Children born:
1. Dennis Rupert Hart, Jr., born Jan. 13, 1937.

———————x———————

AUBREY EDWARD HART (10th Gen.), son of Blain Hart and Maggie (Hatfield) Hart, born March 21, 1913. Married Thelma Stone. Children born:
1. Larry Roger Hart, born July 10, 1934.
2. Patricia Hart, born June 7, 1938.

———————x———————

WALTER KLINGER THOMAS (10th Gen.), son of Nancy Katharine or Katie (Hart) Thomas and Walter Thomas, born Oct. 9, 1898. Married Mayme Herr Anderson, born Sept. 4, 1902. Children born:
1. Walter Anderson Thomas, born Oct. 30, 1922.
2. Harold Lee Thomas, born June 9, 1924; died March 30, 1933.
3. Ruth Joan Thomas, born Sept. 30, 1926.
4. Robert Paul Thomas, born Oct. 31, 1932.

The foregoing information, concerning the family of Walter Klinger Thomas, with names and dates, furnished by his mother, Katie Thomas, and his aunt, Carmine Collier.

ROMA THOMAS (10th Gen.), daughter of Nancy Katharine or Katie (Hart) Thomas and Walter Thomas, born Sept. 6, 1901. Married John Edgar Clark, born June 25, 1876; died July 11, 1932. Children born:
1. Laurabell Katharine Clark, born Feb. 27, 1931.

———————x———————

HAL SHERWOOD THOMAS (10th Gen.), son of Nancy Katharine or Katie (Hart) Thomas and Walter Thomas, born Nov. 27, 1905. Married Eleanor Gelhaus, born Nov. 3, 1913. No issue.

———————x———————

ARTHUR WINSTEAD THOMAS (10th Gen.), son of Nancy Katharine or Katie (Hart) Thomas and Walter Thomas, born May 26, 1911. Married Thelma McCutcheon. Children born:
1. Jean Thomas, born Dec. 18, 1929.

———————x———————

FRANCES FAY THOMAS (10th Gen.), daughter of Nancy Katharine or Katie Thomas and Walter Thomas, born Oct. 11, 1914. Married Lamar Mayfield, born Jan. 2, 1907. Children born:
1. Shirley Fay Mayfield, born March 3, 1935.
2. Larry Mayfield, born Nov. 15, 1938.

Mrs. Nancy Katharine, or Katie (Hart) Thomas, and Miss Carmine Collier, of Murfreesboro, Tenn., kindly furnished the foregoing information relating to the families of the children and grandchildren of Nancy Katharine, or Katie (Hart) Thomas, and Walter Thomas.

———————x———————

MAYME GLADYS HART (10th Gen.), daughter of Henry Hart and Iva Hart, born May 27, 1898. Married, Feb. 12, 1921, Arvil Hicks, born April 7, 1897. Children born:
1. Nina Hart Hicks, born April 5, 1922.
2. Lucille Hicks, born Nov. 15, 1924.
3. Roberta Ann Hicks, born June 12, 1929.
4. Arvil Hicks, Jr., born Aug. 14, 1936.

———————x———————

NINA HART HICKS (11th Gen.), daughter of Mayme Gladys (Hart) Hicks and Arvil Hicks, born April 5, 1922. Married Frenchie Boling, born May 22, 1920. Children born:
1. Iva Lillian Boling, born Jan. 1, 1940.

VENICE HART (10th Gen.), daughter of Henry Hart and Iva Hart, born Nov., 1900. Married, Aug. 5, 1915, Frank McGrew. Children born:
1. Frank Edward McGrew, born 1916.
2. Gladys Irene McGrew, born April 21, 1918.
3. Christine McGrew, born April 21, 1920.
4. Thomas McGrew, born 1922.
5. Beatrice McGrew, born 1924.
6. Venice McGrew.
7. Norma Bell McGrew, born 1930.

―――――x―――――

COLLIER HART (10th Gen.), son of Henry Hart and Iva Hart, born Dec. 6, 1903. Married Ethel Bevel. Children born:
1. James Collier Hart, born April 27, 1924.
2. Gladys May Hart, born June 12, 1925.
3. Charles Sherlock Hart, born Aug. 21, 1927.
4. Glen Walter Hart, born Aug. 11, 1929.
5. Anna Bell Hart, born Feb. 29, 1932.
6. Billy Reno Hart, born Sept. 11, 1934.
7. Mabel Christine Hart, born April 21, 1937.
8. Henry Morgan Hart, born May 25, 1939.

―――――x―――――

CARY LEIGH HART (10th Gen.), son of Henry Hart and Iva Hart, born May 25, 1905. Married Hilda Krause, born Aug. 23, 1902.

―――――x―――――

NAMA IZETTA HART (10th Gen.), daughter of Henry Hart and Iva Hart, born Feb. 12, 1908. Married, June 6, 1925, Emmett Brandon Sheroan, born March 9, 1907. Children born:
1. Nellie Izetta Sheroan, born May 23, 1926.
2. Elsie Beatrice Sheroan, born Sept. 10, 1927; deceased.
3. Wm. Russell Sheroan, born Jan. 9, 1930.

―――――x―――――

RICHARD HESKELL HART (11th Gen.), son of Henry Hart and Iva Hart, born Sept. 21, 1912. Married Anna Sucky, born Sept. 9, 1912. Children born:
1. Marion Genet Hart, born Aug. 25, 1932.
2. Elaine Venice Hart, born Sept. 5, 1934.
3. Nancy Fay Hart, born April 26, 1937.

FRANKIE EDWARD MCGREW (11th Gen.), son of Venice (Hart) McGrew and Frank McGrew, born in 1916. Married Pearl Vass, born Nov. 27, 1919. Children born:
1. David William McGrew, born Dec. 23, 1936.

---x---

GLADYS IRENE MCGREW (11th Gen.), daughter of Venice (Hart) McGrew and Frank McGrew, born April 21, 1918. Married Albert Spell, born Sept. 13, 1909. Children born:
1. Barbara Ann Spell, born April 16, 1935.
2. Ronald Albert Spell, born May 23, 1939.

---x---

(FRAZIER) FRAZEE CUSHMAN (7th Gen.), son of Isaac Cushman and Deborah Frazee Cushman, born April 7, 1800; died Nov. 9, 1889. He was born in Fayette County, Pennsylvania; because he had but one given name and an initial, and as some of the Frazee family had changed their name to Frazier, also, because some of the children at school insisted on nicknaming him "Crazee Cushman," he added to his name, "Frazier," and from that time on he became Frazier Frazee Cushman and signed his name, F. F. Cushman.

His mother, Deborah Frazee Cushman, daughter of Ephraim Frazee, by the wife of his third marriage, was born May 12, 1760, and died upon the day of the birth of Frazee Cushman, April 7, 1800.

She was a half sister to Mary Frazee Cushman, daughter of Ephraim Frazee, by the wife of his first marriage; Mary Frazee was born April 3, 1744, and married Thomas Cushman, the elder brother of Frazee Cushman; Thomas Cushman was born Dec. 19, 1739.

After the death of Deborah Frazee Cushman, Isaac Cushman married a second time, and agreeable to grandfather Frazee Cushman's record, left with us, the step-mother made life so onerous and unhappy for him that rather than bear the unpleasant and unfair treatment she insisted was his lot, he decided to try life on his own responsibility. He came down the Ohio River by flat-boat with a family by the name of Vance, in the year of 1817, to Fulton, Hamilton County, Ohio, now Cincinnati, Ohio, where he learned his trade, that of a potter.

Frazier Frazee Cushman married, Dec. 20, 1821, Sarah

FRAZIER FRAZEE CUSHMAN

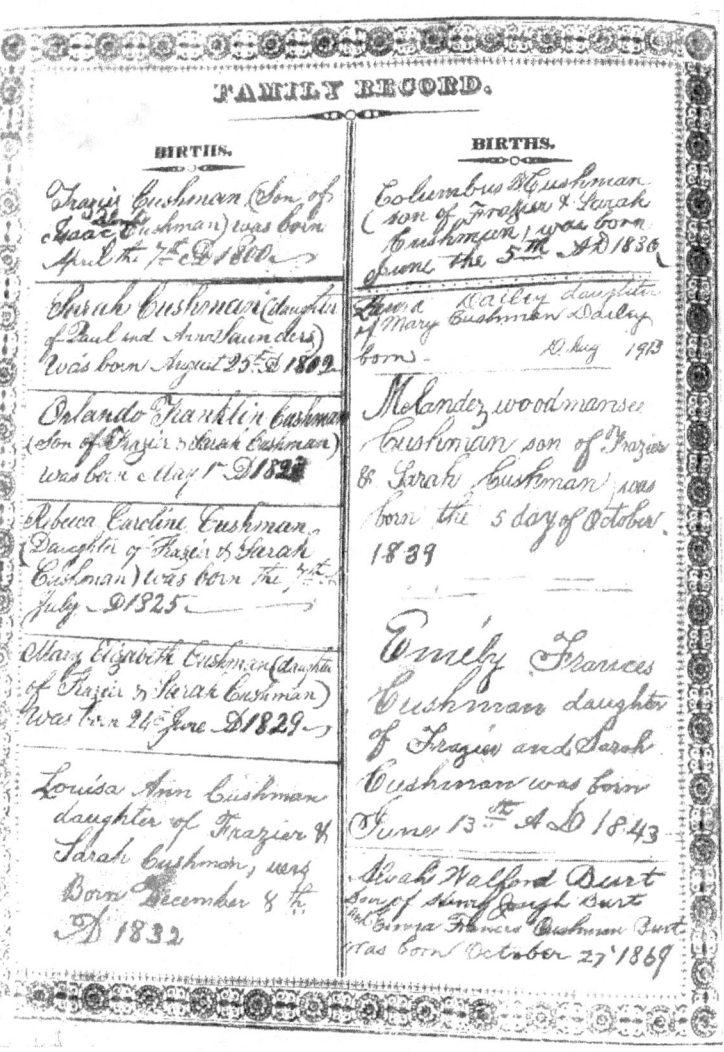

Family Record taken from an Old Bible of the Frazier Frazee Cushman Family
Now in possession of the author, Alvah W. Burt.

FAMILY RECORD.

BIRTHS.

Orrel Morton Burt. Son of Henry Joseph Burt and Emma Frances Cushman Burt was born May 17° 1872

Estella May Burt daughter of Henry Joseph Burt and Emma Frances Cushman Burt was born April 2nd 1875

Enora Maud Burt daughter of Henry Joseph Burt and Emma Frances Cushman Burt was born March 26th 1879

Iva Marie Burt daughter of Henry Joseph Burt and Emma Frances Cushman Burt was born June 19th 1886

Ella May Cushman daughter of William A. Cushman and Rebecca Cordelia Cushman Cushman was born D. June 18th 1927

Charles Cushman Son of Milander W. Cushman was born June 29th 1867
Died Jan 9th 1920

BIRTHS.

Gladys Marie Shroyer daughter of Estella May Burt & James Leslie Shroyer was born July 21st 1900

Robert Cushman Burt son of Ira M. Burt and Florence Acuity Burt Born Feb 2nd 1924

Dorothy Jean Shafer daughter of Gladys Marie Shryers Shafer and Hadley Shafer Born Jan 30th 1930

Frances Joan Shafer daughter of Gladys Marie Shroyer Shafer and Hadley Shafer Born August 25th 1931

Donald Leslie Shafer Son of Gladys Marie Shafer and Hadley Shafer Born Jan 21st 1934
Died Feb 22nd 1936

FAMILY RECORD TAKEN FROM AN OLD BIBLE OF THE FRAZIER FRAZEE CUSHMAN FAMILY
Now in possession of the author, Alvah W. Burt.

Saunders, the fourth child of Paul Saunders and Anna Thorne Saunders. Sarah Saunders Cushman was born Aug. 25, 1802, died May 9, 1855, at Hamilton, Butler County, Ohio, and was buried at Connersville, Fayette County, Indiana. The father and mother, Paul Saunders and Anna Thorne Saunders, came to Ohio from Philadelphia, Pennsylvania; they settled, lived, died and were buried near New Trenton, Butler County, Ohio. Paul Saunders and Anna Thorne Saunders had the following children:

1. Elizabeth Saunders, born Nov. 14, 1795. Married, first, John Pheris, and married, secondly, Isaac Paxton, a Revolutionary soldier.
2. Isaac Saunders, lived and died in Hamilton, Ohio.
3. Joseph Saunders, lived in Rush County, Indiana, and died there in 1847.
4. Sarah Saunders, born Aug. 25, 1802; died at Hamilton, Ohio; buried at Connersville, Indiana. Her children passed on to her grandchildren their memory of her as a good and loving mother, with a gentle, kindly and forgiving disposition.
5. Nancy Saunders, born 1805. Married Michael DeBolt in 1822. Michael was Moderator of the Primitive Baptist Church at Fairfield, Franklin County, Indiana. He died Nov. 23, 1872, and was buried at Blooming Grove, Franklin County, Indiana. His wife, Nancy, died in 1879 and is buried by the side of her husband.
6. Rebecca Saunders, born 1808. Married Caleb Bowers; she died in 1871 and he died in 1873; both lie buried at Blooming Grove, Franklin County, Indiana.
7. Mary Ann Saunders, born 1813. Married David Bowers, brother of Caleb Bowers. David was bitten by his little dog when playing with him. He developed hydrophobia and died in great agony from its effect. Mary Ann Saunders Bowers married, secondly, Harvey Clayton, of Iowa, and both she and Mr. Clayton lie buried at Kesauquah, VanBuren County, Iowa.

The following is the early recollection, of his grandfather, Frazier Frazee Cushman, by the author and compiler:

He was a sturdy, square-shouldered man of about five feet, eight inches, with a pleasant countenance and even temperament. I have no recollection of ever seeing him in anger or mental confusion. He was a Primitive Baptist and, within my recollection, walked to his country church from Fairfield, Franklin County, Indiana, at which place he lived.

As a child of three or four years and entering the age of childish understanding and recollections, I recall his visits to our home, which was on a farm about three and one-half miles east from Fairfield, and especially I have a vivid remembrance of his taking me upon his knee and telling me of the Bible and its meaning, and his teaching me to sing with him, "Jesus, Lover of My Soul," his favorite hymn.

He, later on, as I had grown older, told me that when he first married, money was very scarce and that when he and my grandmother had finished buying the scanty house furnishings their meager fund would purchase, there was but thirty cents left over to go on.

He and grandmother lived the first two years on her father's property, referred to as Paul Saunders Place, and, according to Uncle Melandez Woodmansee Cushman, they then moved to New Richmond, Ohio, where for a time he worked at his trade making pottery. They then moved to Jacksonburg, Butler County, Ohio, where he still worked at pottery making. They then moved to Oxford, Ohio, where he operated a retail grocery store.

He, later on, bought a farm near the Bethlehem Church in the eastern part of Franklin County, Indiana, and there farmed for a period, after which he moved to Goodwin's Corner, Indiana, in Union County, and lived there in the year 1833, when the "Stars Fell." He moved to Rush County, Indiana, in 1835, where he had bought one hundred and sixty acres of land and then later bought the adjoining quarter section on the west. At this point all the family, then living, lived together. After selling his holding at this point the family moved to Connersville, Fayette County, Indiana, in 1851, where he again engaged in the grocery business, on the west side of the Canal near Frybergers Mill. On the 20th of January, 1854, his son, Columbus, died of typhoid fever and was buried at Connersville. He soon sold out and moved from Connersville, Indiana, to Hamilton, Ohio, where he went into the grocery business, but death still stalked him and on May 9, 1855, his beloved wife, and mother of his children, died. She was taken back to Connersville, Indiana, and was buried by the side of her son, Columbus Cushman.

Selling out in Hamilton, Ohio, he bought a farm east of Fairfield, in Franklin County, Indiana, in the old Salt-Well-Neighborhood.

Children born to Frazier Frazee Cushman and Sarah Saunders Cushman:

1. Orlando Franklin Cushman, born May 17, 1823; died Aug. 27, 1824; buried at New Trenton, Butler County, Ohio.
2. Rebecca Caroline Cushman, born July 7, 1825; died Dec. 14, 1893.
3. Mary Elizabeth Cushman, born June 24, 1829; died Dec. 20, 1853.
4. Louisa Ann Cushman, born Dec. 8, 1832; died Oct. 13, 1896.
5. Columbus Bowers Cushman, born June 5, 1836; died Jan. 20, 1854.
6. Melandez Woodmansee Cushman, born Oct. 5, 1839; died April 3, 1902.
7. Emily Frances Cushman, born June 13, 1843; died Aug. 25, 1932.

Frazier Frazee Cushman married, secondly, Margaret Price and family records of her bespeak a noble Christian woman and one beloved by all of the children of Frazier Frazee Cushman. There was no issue and she died April 14, 1869, and lies buried by his side on the hill-top in the old Symmes' Graveyard at Fairfield, Franklin County, Indiana.

In October, 1868, he moved from the old Salt-Well farm to Fairfield, Indiana. After the death of his second wife, April 14, 1869, heavy local pressure was brought, and, with much reasoning that he should again marry. Thus influenced by non-related interests, he married, thirdly, October, 1869, Mrs. Mary Fowler, who died in September, 1891, and lies buried at Fairfield, Franklin County, Indiana, in the Lower Cemetery.

In the falltime, on the 19th day of November, 1889, Frazier Frazee Cushman died, being 89 years, seven months and 12 days old, and so passed a faithful and devoted father. He lies buried in the old Symmes' Graveyard on the hill-top at the north end of Fairfield, Indiana.

---x---

REBECCA CAROLINE CUSHMAN (8th Gen.), daughter of Frazier Frazee Cushman and Sarah Saunders Cushman, born July 7, 1825; died Dec. 14, 1893. Married William A. Conner. She was born in Jacksonboro, Butler County, Ohio. William A. Conner was a successful merchant of Wabash, Indiana. He died October 26, 1871, at Fairfield, Indiana, while on a visit in the home of the father of his wife. He lies buried by the side of his wife in Falls Cemetery, at Wabash, Indiana. Children born:

1. Ella May Conner, died June 18, 1929. She occupied herself by managing the affairs of the estate left by her deceased father and mother; her nature and disposition, one of sunshine and cheer, surrounded her with numerous friends. Charitably inclined she was a contributor to the First Methodist Church of Wabash, Indiana, although not a member; she was a member of the Baptist Church, located at La Fontaine, Wabash County, Indiana.

She entertained, from early childhood, a love and affection for her cousins, the children of her mother's youngest sister, Emily Frances Cushman Burt, and these children returned in full that affection and love for their cousin Ella.

---x---

MARY ELIZABETH CUSHMAN (8th Gen.), daughter of Frazier Frazee Cushman and Sarah Saunders Cushman, born June 24, 1829, near old Bethlehem Church, Franklin County, Indiana, on her father's farm; died Dec. 20, 1853. Married, Dec. 18, 1850, John Dailey. Children born:

1. Laura Dailey, born 1852; died August, 1913.

---x---

LAURA DAILEY (9th Gen.), daughter of Mary Elizabeth Cushman Dailey and John Dailey, born 1852; died Aug., 1913. Married Reuben Conner, of Connersville, Indiana, a lawyer. Children born:

1. Alonzo Conner, born Jan. 22, 1873; died Dec. 7, 1937.

---x---

ALONZO CONNER (10th Gen.), son of Laura Dailey Conner and Reuben Conner, born Jan. 22, 1873, in Union County,

Indiana; died Dec. 7, 1937; buried in Dale Cemetery, at Connersville, Indiana. Married, April 19, 1930, Mrs. Nelle (Murray) Perkins. No issue.

———————x———————

LOUISA ANN CUSHMAN (8th Gen.), daughter of Frazier Frazee Cushman and Sarah Saunders Cushman, born Dec. 8, 1832, at Goodwin's Corner, Union County, Indiana; died Oct. 13, 1896, at the home of her sister, Mrs. Emily Frances Cushman Burt, at Liberty, Union County, Indiana, and lies buried by the side of her father, in the old Symmes' Graveyard, on the hill-top at the north side of Fairfield, Franklin County, Indiana. She was an invalid all the latter years of her life and was cared for by her sister, Mrs. Emily Frances Cushman Burt. She never married.

———————x———————

COLUMBUS BOWERS CUSHMAN (8th Gen.), son of Frazier Frazee Cushman and Sarah Saunders Cushman, born June 5, 1836, in Union Township, Rush County, Indiana; died Jan. 20, 1854, of typhoid fever, at Connersville, Indiana, and lies buried there by the side of his mother.

———————x———————

MELANDEZ WOODMANSEE CUSHMAN (8th Gen.), son of Frazier Frazee Cushman and Sarah Saunders Cushman, born Oct. 5, 1839, in Union Township, Rush County, Indiana; died April 3, 1902, in the State of Florida. Married, Oct. 19, 1864, at Brookville, Indiana, Angie DeYarmon, who died, Jan. 5, 1928. Children born:

1. Charles Cushman, born June 29, 1867; died Jan. 9, 1920. Charles Cushman, at the age of eleven years, began to show signs of a nervous condition, which, from year to year, grew worse, and through the greater part of his life he was an invalid. His beloved mother was faithfully and devotedly at his side until his death. She was a sincere Christian Scientist. The following verses, entitled, "Beyond," were given to our family by her on the occasion of the funeral of her son, Charles, as an expression of the hope she entertained of the future beyond the grave:

    It seemeth such a little way to me,
      Across to that strange country, the Beyond,

And yet not strange, for it has grown to be
    The home of those of whom I am so fond;
They make it seem familiar and most dear,
As journeying friends bring distant countries near.

So close it lies that, when my sight is clear,
    I think I see the gleaming strand;
I know I feel that those who have gone from here
    Come near enough to touch my hand,
I often think, but for our veiled eyes,
We would find Heaven right round about us lies.

I can not make it seem a day to dread,
    When from this dear earth I shall journey out
To that still dearer country of the dead,
    And join the lost ones so long dreamed about;
I love this world, yet shall I love to go
And meet the friends who wait for me, I know.

I never stand about a bier and see
    The seal of death set on some well-loved face;
But that I think, one more to welcome me
    When I shall cross the intervening space
Between this land and the one over there;
One more to make the strange Beyond seem fair.

And so for me there is no sting to death,
    And so the grave has lost its victory;
It is but crossing, with a bated breath,
    And white set face, a little strip of sea,
To find the loved ones waiting on the shore,
More beautiful, more precious than before.

  Melandez Woodmansee Cushman and Angie DeYarmon Cushman after their marriage started family life on their farm in Wabash County, Indiana. This was the only place where they kept house and maintained a home. They left the farm and moved to Richmond, Indiana, and for the balance of his life he was known as Professor Cushman or Doctor Cushman.

  He traveled from state to state with a coachman, Charles Murdock, of Liberty, Indiana, having his family with him, and driving a finely-matched four-horse conveyance. He lectured on wild horse training and breaking, selling his own book entitled, "Ferriers Prescriptions," containing sixty-five receipts in plain language for plain men. It also contained instructions for the care of horses and how to properly break and train them for service.

He traveled in every state in the Union and with the P. T. Barnum Circus as animal surgeon, dentist and trainer, through the British Isles and Continental Europe. He was loved by those who knew him well and, when on a trip through Florida, he died of acute indigestion, aged 62 years, seven months and 28 days.

His remains were brought to the home of his sister, Mrs. Henry Joseph Burt, at Liberty, Indiana, where his funeral was preached by Rev. A. R. Beach, of the Methodist Episcopal Church, who was a friend that knew him well and loved him for his worth. The sermon preached by Rev. Beach follows:

"I would have crossed the continent to say the last words at the grave of Melandez Cushman because he was my friend. Five and one-half years ago I met him for the first time; it was the occasion of his sister's funeral, and since that day I have numbered him as one of my friends, and he has proved his friendship for me in many ways and on many different occasions.

"Mr. Cushman belonged to that class of men who are sometimes partially described by that much hackneyed phrase 'unique character.'

"Certainly he was different from what we call 'the rank and file.' He had points about him which attracted attention wherever he went, and assured for him a certain measure of conspicuousness in every company of which he formed a part. The stalwart form! The patriarchial beard! The kindly beaming eye! The sympathetic nature! The well modulated voice, almost marvelous in its smoothness and quality, together with his wit and friendliness marked him at once, even to the stranger and casual observer, as an uncommon and intensely interesting character.

"It has been my lot to enter strange cities along with him and I never failed to notice many persons turn upon the street to take a second look; their glance never rested upon me but always upon him; young and old seemed to recognize him as the possessor of certain personal qualities not found in the average man.

"His mental make-up was equally as unique and distinctive as his physical; he had a great memory, and could remember more names of persons and places than any man I ever knew. He knew men and knew them at a glance; he either liked or disliked on the instant, and he seldom was deceived or mistaken in his judgment. He had a somewhat strange way of reaching conclusions; he never seemed to reason, but always reached his conclusions at one bound, by that one-step-stairway which the psychologist calls intuition; but anyone closely associated with him would soon learn not only to respect but to admire the ease and accuracy of his estimates.

"He knew the geography of his native country by actual observation, perhaps, as well as any man in America. For forty years he traversed the states from ocean to ocean and from the lakes down to the gulf. He was equally at home in country, village or crowded city and always knew which way to turn and kept his bearings as one whose foot was treading upon familiar ground.

"He was like some wandering wild bird with the migration instinct strong within it; he followed the seasons as they ebbed and flowed across the continent. When the frost line crept down over the Central States he plumed his pinions for the sunny South and made his winter home in the land of the magnolia and the palm.

"Such a man as this could not be other than liberal in spirit, broad in views and philanthropic in his disposition. Such a man must, from very necessity, be largely freed from the spirit of tyranny and bigotry and vindictiveness; indeed, with him, these found no place at all.

"He was true and loyal to his friends and forgiving toward his enemies; his generosity knew no bounds; he had as big a heart as ever beat within any man's breast. Sometimes we hear it said of the very generous 'that they would have shared their last crust of bread with a fellow mortal in distress'; but such was not the case with him, for he would have saved none of the last crust for himself but would have given it all away to those he loved or who loved him.

"He toiled like a Trojan and coined his intense energy and tireless industry into money by the thousands and then gave it away. He might have made millions but he never could have become a millionaire because his generous nature acted as a dispenser of his means in commensurate proportion with his incoming revenues.

"He had his sorrows and his disappointments in life in common with us all, but he bore them with a bravery that was sublime. To see him on the street or hear him talk one might be easily deceived and think that he was without a sorrow or a care, but many a time he has uncovered his heart to me and then I learned that back of all his joyful disposition and bouyancy of spirit, he carried a great burden of sorrow, which at times almost prostrated him to the earth, and no doubt this had much to do in the shortening of his days, for as the years passed by the burden seemed to increase, the great disappointment of his life grew more bitter; the giant that stood up under the blow a decade or more ago now began to stagger under its lingering influence. There are sorrows that can be fairly met and overcome and sometimes routed from the field, but there are others that will not down—they stay with us through the years—they cling to us and gather force like the barnacles on the breast of a ship—every step in life's pathway becomes impeded by their persistency—they hover over us like ravens waiting the death of a wounded victim, until death comes to the rescue at last; such a sorrow was carried by our friend and brother who now lies sleeping the sleep of death.

"He has laid down his lance forever; the great journey of life is over. Others will come and enter the lists and meet strong foes and brave their tilt and joist, and will fight and fall. The great struggle of life will go on; right and wrong will cross swords on a thousand fields, but with him the warfare is over. The ruddy ensign of life has been removed from cheek and lip and death's pale flag has been advanced to where life's crimson banner once flung out their challenge to the great Destroyer; but it is all over now. The last earthly step has been taken, the last sad sigh has been breathed, the last foe has been met and his soul has baffled at last the fetters of mortality and found its legitimate environment in the spirit world.

"The life that began in Rush County, Indiana, October 5, 1839, ended April 3, 1902, at Jacksonville, Florida. This life was full of activity, full of good deed, full of generous overflow for all humanity. As a man he was entirely free from all bad habits! How he traveled so much and mingled with all classes of people and met all kinds of conditions, and yet kept himself so free from all bad habits is an index to his inherent worth and to his indomitable will.

"While not a member of any church, yet we believe he was a child of the Kingdom. We have heard him express his views so often, we know the profound respect he had for Christianity and for all good people, and something of the noble impulses and purposes that entered into his life and character.

"We know also how forgiving he was toward all who ever wronged him, and that he had only words of kindness for those who brought on him the great sorrow of his life. So we believe his heart was right toward God and that he had a conscience void of offense toward God and toward man.

"And now dear old Uncle Meland we part with thee for time, but hope to meet thee in eternity; we lay thy form away to rest in the quiet valley surrounded by the green hills so dear to the memory of other days. We loved thee because thou wast lovable; we honored thee because honor reposed in thy soul; we weep for thee because thou didst come to us as a friend, and now about thy lifeless remains we stand with those who loved thee and say our sad farewell."

This funeral sermon was preached by Rev. A. R. Beach, April 8, 1902, at the home of his sister, Mrs. Henry Joseph Burt, nee Emily Francis Cushman Burt. Rev. A. R. Beach was the Corresponding Secretary for "Preachers Aid and Veterans Home Societies," Indiana Conference, Indianapolis, Indiana.

From Liberty, Indiana, the procession moved toward Fairfield, Indiana, eleven miles south, where he was buried beside his father, in the old Symmes' Graveyard, on the hill-top, north of town.

EMILY FRANCES CUSHMAN BURT AND HENRY JOSEPH BURT
Taken at the time of their marriage.

EMILY FRANCES CUSHMAN (8th Gen.), daughter of Frazier Frazee Cushman and Sarah Saunders Cushman, born June 13, 1843, in Rush County, Indiana; died Aug. 25, 1932, aged 89 years, two months and 13 days.

She married, Nov. 17, 1868, Henry Joseph Burt, born Sept. 11, 1844, in Franklin County, Indiana; died June 17, 1919. They engaged in farming three and one-half miles east of Fairfield, Franklin County, Indiana, and also kept a country general store. After selling out their interest there they moved to Mixerville, Franklin County, Indiana, where they kept a general store and ran two wagons on a country route; one a huckster's wagon of the usual type and the other a large cabinet body, with compartments having doors and locks, each trip loaded with all kinds of farm-home supplies embracing sugar, coffee, tea, spices, extracts, hand soaps, washing soaps, dry goods, notions, and etc.

In 1879 they decided to seek a larger trading field and moved to Liberty, Union County, Indiana, where, after a period of time, he became associated with others in the sale of sewing machines and organs. Later he opened a branch store or salesroom for the D. S. Johnston Company, of Cincinnati, Ohio, who handled the W. W. Kimball organ which was branded D. S. Johnston & Company, Cincinnati, Ohio. They also dealt in the Kimball, the Emerson, the Hardman and Chickering pianos.

Later he branched out, on his own responsibility, adding a line of jewelry and sundry small musical instruments. In 1892 the jewelry and musical business was sold out. They then entered the hotel business, operating the Corington Central Hotel at Liberty, Indiana, following which they decided to try city life and moved to Dayton, Campbell County, Kentucky. Finding this agreeable and satisfactory they bought a home property at 155 Foote Avenue, Bellevue, Campbell County, Kentucky, where, on June 17, 1919, his career ended with death, the victor.

He was a devoted father and generous to his family, even to self-denial to give to his children. He had been an invalid for about two years, and on a fine June morning, as he was dressing himself, with the assistance of his beloved wife, he fell back into her arms and with a beautiful smile on his face, expired.

Frazier Frazee Cushman and family were devout Primitive Baptist Church folk and Emily Frances Cushman grew to young womanhood in this religious influence, while her husband, Henry Joseph Burt, in the United Brethren Church. Upon their moving to Liberty, Union County, Indiana, there being no church of either of the two above named denominations in that town, they attended, from time to time, the different churches there, the Methodist Epsicopal, the Presbyterian and the Campbellite-Christian Church, until in the year 1886 when they became members of the Methodist Episcopal Church, and so continued as Methodists to the end of their lives. They were both Republicans.

Following her death at Chicago, in the home of her daughter, Mrs. R. B. Kinkaid, her remains were brought to Cincinnati, to the W. Mack Johnson Funeral Home, McMillan and Upland Place, where the funeral service was held by the Minister of the Methodist Episcopal Church of Walnut Hills, Cincinnati, Ohio. The Sunday following, the bulletin of the Methodist Episcopal Church of Walnut Hills carried, enclosed in black or mourning border: "Mrs. Emma Burt passed away Thursday morning at the home of her son and daughter, Mr. and Mrs. R. B. Kinkaid, at Chicago, Illinois. Mrs. Burt was a true follower of the Lord. She spent a large part of each day reading and studying her Bible. She was a devoted mother and was greatly beloved by all who knew her. She will long be remembered for her sweet and cheerful disposition. The sympathy of the congregation is extended to Mr. and Mrs. Kinkaid and family in their bereavement."

At the funeral service the following two poems were read as part of the service. The first:

"You are not dead Mother dear, Life has just set you free;
Your years of life were like a lovely song,
The last sweet poignant notes of which held long, passed
Into silence while we listened:
We who loved you listened, still expectantly!
And we about you, whom you moved among,

Would feel that grief for you were surely wrong,
You have but passed beyond where we can not see.

For us who knew you Mother Dear, dread of age is past,
You stood tip-toe to the very last.
Life never lost for you, its lovely look;
You kept your interest in its thrilling book,
To you, death came no conqueror; in the end
You smiled to greet the Savior and your friend.''

At the close of a funeral sermon, of chosen words full of hope for the faithful Christian believer, the following poem was read:

MOTHER

"You gave the best years of your life
With joy for us; and gave of yourself
With loving heart unstintingly;
With willing hands you toiled from day to day,
For us you prayed when headstrong youth would have its way.
Your gentle arms, a cradle once, are folded now;
And time has ceased and set a seal upon your brow;
And tho no other eyes than ours their meaning trace,
We read our history in the lines of your dear face;
And mid His gems who showers gifts as shining sands,
We count your days as pearls that fell from His dear hands.''

Following the close of this service, the procession moved toward Evergreen Cemetery, Southgate, Campbell County, Kentucky, where her body was laid to rest beside that of her beloved husband.

Her last words, spoken to her daughter, Mrs. Estella M. Shroyer, at the home of her daughter, Mrs. Kinkaid, were: "Oh! It is so marvelous—so beautiful"; she then passed into a state of coma from which she did not recover.

Children born:
1. Alvah Walford Burt, born Oct. 27, 1869.
2. Orvel or (Ora) Morton Burt, born May 17, 1872.
3. Estella May Burt, born April 2, 1875.
4. Lenora Maud Burt, born March 26, 1879.
5. Iva Marie Burt, born June 19, 1886.

Emily Frances Cushman Burt, our beloved mother, was a devoted and loving parent; the day was never too arduous, tiresome or too long for her loving hand to come to the relief of aching brow or head, with no exception or for any favorite one, she bearing an even and abundant love for one and all alike.

Her afflicted and invalid sister, Louisa Ann Cushman, living in our home all the latter days of her life, required much attention and this threw a considerable burden and responsibility upon her eldest daughter, Estella May, who accepted it without complaint as a matter of duty, doing her part nobly well. This foregoing fact being apparent to the writer and author prompted him to see to it, that at all times a provision was made that this sister had an escort to and from all social affairs and entertainments. And so we, she and I, were pals through our young lives even to going fishing and field hunting.

Following the death of her husband, our mother, Emily Frances Cushman Burt, finally decided to quit housekeeping and from that time on lived in the home of one or the other of her daughters. Her last days were spent in the home of her baby daughter, Iva Marie Kinkaid, at Chicago, Illinois, where she died August 25, 1932, and lies buried by the side of her beloved husband, in Evergreen Cemetery, Southgate, Campbell County, Kentucky.

The writer feels that no family of children were ever blessed with parents of a more sympathetic and companionable nature than his own.

---x---

ALVAH WALFORD BURT (9th Gen.), son of Emily Frances Cushman Burt and Henry Joseph Burt, born Oct. 27, 1869. Married, Sept. 5, 1906, Ida E. Keaten, born Feb. 13, 1879. No issue.

They are communicants of the Protestant Episcopal Church and active in the affairs of the church.

They are members of the order of the Eastern Star; she was Worthy Matron and he Worthy Patron, serving together for the years 1912 and 1913 for Gertrude Chapter, Number 19,

Newport, Kentucky.

They are both past officers, she president and he associate president of the Society of Past Matrons and Patrons of Northern Kentucky, Third District.

He became a Master Mason May 11, 1901.

A Scottish-Rite, 32nd Degree Mason, March 27, 1902.

A Noble of the Mystic-Shrine, November 25, 1909.

He is an active member of the Cincinnati Chapter, Sons of the American Revolution.

They are both Republicans.

———————x———————

ORVEL (OR ORA) MORTON BURT (9th Gen.), son of Emily Frances Cushman Burt and Henry Joseph Burt, born May 17, 1872; died Aug. 18, 1942. Married, March 26, 1921, Florence Margaret Kountz, of Newport, Kentucky. He lies buried in Falls Cemetery, Wabash, Indiana. Children born:
1. Robert Cushman Burt, born Feb. 2, 1924, at Milan, Ripley County, Indiana.

Orvel Morton, or Ora as he preferred to call himself, was born on a farm three and one-half miles east of Fairfield, Franklin County, Indiana. He started his school life at Mixerville, Indiana, with James Seal as his first teacher. After moving to Liberty, Indiana, and attaining young manhood he associated himself with his father, at that time, in the jewelry and musical instrument business, and upon closing out this business he became the local agent for the United States Express Company at that point. He later became connected with the Fitch-Dust-Down Company of Cincinnati, Ohio, and traveled as commercial representative, for a time, finally settling on his farm at Wabash, devoting himself to the affairs of farm life until death.

———————x———————

ESTELLA MAY BURT (9th Gen.), daughter of Emily Frances Cushman Burt and Henry Joseph Burt, born April 2, 1875, on a farm three and one-half miles east of Fairfield, Franklin County, Indiana. Married, Sept. 20, 1899, at Liberty, Union County, Indiana, at the home of her father and mother, Rev. James Leslie Shroyer, born Aug. 2, 1867, at New Trenton, Indiana. Children born:

1. Gladys Marie Shroyer, born July 31, 1900, at Clarksburg, Decatur County, Indiana.

Reverend Shroyer was a member of the Southern Indiana Conference of the Methodist Episcopal Church. He was a graduate of Moores-Hill College, now Evansville College, located at Evansville, Indiana.

In 1907 they moved to Evanston, Illinois, where both entered Garrett Biblical Institute of the Chicago Northwestern University where he finished his theological course. In 1910 they moved to Pomeroy, Iowa, a part of the Northwest Conference of Iowa, and, in which conference, he served for twenty years. He had served thirty-five years, in all, at the time of his retirement.

Reverend Shroyer died October 10, 1930, by accident; just how the accident happened is not known. It is supposed that a fork that he had picked up had caught on the threshing belt and struck him with such force as to crush a rib into the lung; he was found in an unconscious condition in which condition he remained until his passing on, the following morning at five o'clock.

After active service of thirty-five years, because of ill health, Reverend Shroyer was retired but a few days, when, after locating in Lake Park, Iowa, he and Mrs. Shroyer went out to the farm of his son-in-law and daughter, just a short distance northwest of Lake Park, to see them thresh buckwheat. After the noontime dinner he accompanied his son-in-law across the road to the threshing machine where all were busy working. He was soon after, found lying on the ground unconscious, unable to explain just how the accident really happened, and, remaining unconscious, he passed on at five o'clock the next morning.

He was a Thirty-Second Degree Scottish-Rite Mason and a Republican.

In October, 1910, four months after arriving in Iowa, Estella M. Shroyer was elected Conference Secretary of the Womans' Foreign Missionary Society of the DesMoines branch of the Northwest Iowa Conference, and so served that office for twenty-seven years and three months. She was then elected branch Christian Stewardship Secretary, which office she filled until the uniting of the churches of the North and South, a period of two years and nine months. The Des-Moines Branch included four states and she served this branch for a period of thirty years as an official of the Womans' Foreign Missionary Society. This service she has referred to as having left with her many happy and sweet memories of a worthwhile task, and which she had considered a privilege and a joy to perform; and as the years pass by the ties of friendship created through this service become the more beautiful. She is a Republican.

---x---

GLADYS MARIE SHROYER (10th Gen.), daughter of Estella May (Burt) Shroyer and Rev. James Leslie Shroyer, born July 31, 1900, at Clarksburg, Decatur County, Indiana. Married, Aug. 31, 1927, Hadley G. Shafer, of Lake Park, Dickinson County, Iowa. Children born:
1. Dorothy Jean Shafer, born Jan. 30, 1930.
2. Frances Joan Shafer, born Aug. 25, 1931.
3. Donald Leslie Shafer, born Jan. 21, 1934; died Feb. 22, 1936, aged two years, one month, and one day.

She was graduated from Anthon, Iowa High School in 1919 and entered Morningside College for two years, after which she taught one year at Bronson, Iowa. She re-entered Morningside College and graduated June, 1924, with her major as public school music and with English her minor. Following her graduation she taught as public school music supervisor for three years and since marriage she has devoted her talent to the training of church choir and Sunday, or Church School, chorals, in support of such work.

---x---

LENORA MAUD BURT (9th Gen.), daughter of Emily Frances Cushman Burt and Henry Joseph Burt, born March 26, 1879, at Mixerville, Franklin County, Indiana. Married, July 9, 1912, George Leonard Slaline, of Dayton, Campbell County, Kentucky, at the home of her father and mother in Bellevue, Campbell County, Kentucky. He died Feb. 28, 1933. No issue.

Lenora Maud Burt Slaline spent her young womanhood in Liberty, Indiana, where she was active in Methodist Episcopal Church work, and having been blessed with a beautiful voice, contributed her given genius to the Church's cause. She graduated from the public high school at Liberty, Indiana. Following the death of her husband she moved to Chicago, Illinois, to be near her younger sister, Mrs. Roy B. Kinkaid, and at a later date she moved to 672 West Main Street, Wabash, Indiana, her present home.

George Leonard Slaline was connected with the American Book Company, Cincinnati branch, during the entire of his business life. He was the assistant cashier of the Cincinnati branch at the time of his death and had been for several years past. She is a Republican.

---x---

IVA MARIE BURT (9th Gen.), daughter of Emily Frances Cushman Burt and Henry Joseph Burt, born June 19, 1886, at Liberty, Union County, Indiana. Married, June 26, 1912, Roy Blaine Kinkaid, at the home of her parents. No issue.

Mr. and Mrs. Kinkaid first lived in Indianapolis, Indiana, where he was chief of the Tariff Bureau of the Lake Erie and Western Railroad and Mrs. Kinkaid was active in the Broadway Methodist Episcopal Church and the Woman's Round Table Club.

At a later date when Mr. Kinkaid was made Assistant General Freight Agent of the Baltimore and Ohio Railroad at Cincinnati, Ohio, they moved to that point, where she continued her church activities in the Walnut-Hills Methodist Episcopal Church and with the Riverside Culture Club.

In June, 1932, Mr. Kinkaid was made General Freight Agent of the Baltimore and Ohio Railroad with offices at Chicago, Illinois, to which point they at once removed and where they became affiliated with the Bryn Mawr Community Church. Mrs. Kinkaid became active in the Bryn Mawr Womans' Club and The Daughters of Indiana.

They are members of the South Shore Country Club. Mr. Kinkaid is a Thirty-Second Degree Scottish-Rite Mason and a member of the Mystic Shrine. They are Republicans.

---x---

And here in closing the author clings to the hope that his labors and effort will not have been in vain but that they may prove of benefit to the future Cushman line and descent.

That, as time moves on, the descendants of Robert Cushman,

through his son, Thomas, later Ruling Elder of the First Church of Plymouth, and his wife, Mary Allerton Cushman, and, especially, our own Thomas Cushman (3rd Gen.) and his wife, Ruth Howland, may find comfort and profit in reflecting upon the sturdy, unyielding and unwavering determination of their ancestors, as a family, as believers in individual rights and religious freedom, and that THEY too may lend their personal and material support to all features of, and for, general social uplift and some church organization of the Christian faith, of a denomination of their own choosing.

That their next pride shall be their political contribution to the defense of representative government, a democracy, and by their voice and acts condemning attempts to attain place and preferment at the expense of personal honor, holding their citizenship and devotion to national interests, far above the taint of political corruption.

And lastly ever keeping in mind, foremost, even though worn and outmoded: "THAT IT ALWAYS PAYS TO BE A GENTLEMAN AND THAT IT ALWAYS PAYS TO BE A LADY."

As I have strayed, in my construction, far from the usual numerical and highly abbreviated manner of genealogical compilation, to that of the "Family Type" because of the (might I say) too frequent use of the same given name, so often employed in giving children the same name from generation to generation, I have, therefore, attempted to clear the line of descent, familywise, so that the person not accustomed to family research, could more easily and with greater assurance trace his own lineal descent down to the present.

The following display of my own lineal descent may assist you, my reader, in arranging yours, relating to your own family.

The Lineal Descent of Alvah Walford Burt

1. Isaac Allerton married Mary Norris; their daughter, Mary Allerton (2), married Thomas Cushman (2), later Ruling Elder of the First Church of Plymouth. Isaac Allerton and his wife and daughter, Mary, came over in the Mayflower.

1. John Howland married Elizabeth Tilley, daughter of John Tilley; their daughter, Ruth Howland (2), married Thomas Cushman (3), son of Elder Thomas Cushman and Mary Allerton Cushman. John Howland and his wife, Elizabeth Tilley Howland, and also, John Tilley and his wife, Bridget Van Der Velde Tilley, all came over in the Mayflower.
1. Robert Cushman married Sarah Reder.
2. Elder Thomas Cushman married Mary Allerton.
3. Thomas Cushman married Ruth Howland.
4. Thomas Cushman married Sarah Strong.
5. Thomas Cushman, of Lebanon, Connecticut, and Essex County New Jersey, married Mary ―――――.
6. Isaac Cushman, of Essex County, New Jersey, and Fayette County, Pennsylvania, married Deborah Frazee, daughter of Ephraim Frazee, by his third wife, who was the father of 18 children by three marriages.
7. Frazier Frazee Cushman, born in Fayette County, Pennsylvania, married Sarah Saunders, of New Trenton, Butler County, Ohio.
8. Emily Frances Cushman married Henry Joseph Burt, of Franklin County, Indiana.
9. Alvah Walford Burt married Ida E. Keaten, of Indianapolis, Indiana. No issue.

www.ingramcontent.com/pod-product-compliance
Lightning Source LLC
Chambersburg PA
CBHW050830230426
43667CB00012B/1948